STUDY GUIDE FOR

Essentials of Psychology

NINTH EDITION

Dennis Coon

THOMSON
‐‐‐‐*‐‐‐‐ ™
WADSWORTH

Australia • Canada • Mexico • Singapore • Spain • United Kingdom • United States

Printed in the United States of America

6 7 06 05

0-534-59791-2

Cover image: © David Manje/Serrato, *Spectrum V*. Mixed media monotype, 16 x 16 in. Courtesy of the artist

For more information about our products, contact us at:
Thomson Learning Academic Resource Center
1-800-423-0563

For permission to use material from this text, contact us by:
Phone: 1-800-730-2214
Fax: 1-800-730-2215
Web: www.thomsonrights.com

Asia
Thomson Learning
5 Shenton Way #01-01
UIC Building
Singapore 068808

Australia
Nelson Thomson Learning
102 Dodds Street
South Street
South Melbourne, Victoria 3205
Australia

Canada
Nelson Thomson Learning
1120 Birchmount Road
Toronto, Ontario M1K 5G4
Canada

Europe/Middle East/South Africa
Thomson Learning
High Holborn House
50-51 Bedford Row
London WC1R 4LR
United Kingdom

Latin America
Thomson Learning
Seneca, 53
Colonia Polanco
11560 Mexico D.F.
Mexico

Spain
Paraninfo Thomson Learning
Calle/Magallanes, 25
28015 Madrid, Spain

CONTENTS

Introduction
How to Use this Study Guide

This *Study Guide* for *Essentials of Psychology* is designed to help you learn more, study efficiently, and get better grades. The exercises in this guide are closely coordinated with text chapters so that you can practice and review what you have read.

Each *Study Guide* chapter contains the following sections:

- **Chapter Overview**
- **Learning Objectives**
- **Recite and Review**
- **Connections**
- **Check Your Memory**
- **Final Survey and Review**
- **Mastery Test**
- **Answers**

A brief description of each section follows, along with suggestions for using them.

Chapter Overview

The Chapter Overview is a highly focused summary of major ideas in the text. By boiling chapters down to their essence, the Chapter Overview will give you a framework to build on as you learn additional ideas, concepts, and facts. Before you work on any other sections of this guide, read the Chapter Overview. In fact, it would be a good idea to re-read the Chapter Overview each time you use the *Study Guide*.

Learning Objectives

The Learning Objectives will show you, in detail, if you have mastered a reading assignment. To use them, you may want to write brief responses for each objective after you finish reading a chapter of the text. As an alternative, you may want to just read the Learning Objectives, pausing after each to see if you can respond in your own words. Then, after you have completed all of the other exercises in the *Study Guide* you can return to the Learning Objectives. At that time, you can either respond verbally or in writing. In either case, give special attention to any objectives you can't complete.

Recite and Review

This section will give you a chance to review major terms and concepts. Recite and Review is organized with the same Survey Questions found in the textbook chapters. This exercise will help you actively process information, so that it becomes more meaningful. Recite and Review also gives you a chance to practice recalling ideas from your reading, after you've closed the book.

As you work through Recite and Review, don't worry if you can't fill in all of the blanks. All of the answers are listed at the end of each *Study Guide* chapter. Filling in missing terms with the help of the answer key will focus your attention on gaps in your knowledge. That way, you can add new information to what you *were* able to remember. Page numbers are provided for each section of Recite and Review so you can return to the text to clarify any points that you missed.

Connections

This section contains matching-type items. It will help you build associations between related terms, facts, concepts, and ideas. Where appropriate, art is reproduced from the text so that you can match to images, rather than words. This is a good way to add links to your memory networks. Again, answers are listed at the end of the chapter.

Check Your Memory

The true-false statements in Check Your Memory highlight facts and details that you may have overlooked when you read the text. It's easy to fool yourself about how much you are remembering as you read. If you answered wrong for any of the items in Check Your Memory, you should return to the textbook to find out why. Page numbers listed for each group of items will make it easy for you to locate the relevant information in the textbook.

Final Survey and Review

This exercise might seem like a repeat of the Recite and Review section, but it's not. This time, you must supply a different set of more difficult terms and concepts to complete the review. The Final Survey and Review challenges you to consolidate your earlier learning and to master key concepts from the text. The Final Survey and Review is not a test. Don't be upset if you can't fill in some of the blanks. But do give missing ideas extra practice when you check your answers. Indeed, try to learn more each time you complete a *Study Guide* exercise, check your answers, or return to the text for review and clarification.

Mastery Test

The multiple-choice items of the Mastery Test are at least as difficult as those found on typical in-class tests. If you do well on the Mastery Test, you can be confident that you are prepared for in-class tests. On the other hand, a low score is a clear signal that further study and review are needed. However, don't expect to always get perfect scores on the Mastery Tests. In some cases, the questions cover information that was not reviewed in any of the preceding *Study Guide* sections. The Mastery Tests are designed to continue the learning process, as well as to give you feedback about your progress.

Answers

Answers for all of the preceding exercises are listed at the end of each *Study Guide* chapter. Answers for the Mastery Test include page numbers so you can locate the source of the question in the textbook.

A FIVE-DAY STUDY PLAN

There is no single "best" way to use this guide. Getting the most out of the *Study Guide* depends greatly on your personal learning style and study habits. Nevertheless, as a starting point, you might want to give the following plan a try.

Days 1 and 2   Read the assigned chapter in the textbook. As you do, be sure to make use of the Knowledge Builders and all the steps of the SQ4R method described in the textbook.

Day 3   Review the textbook chapter and any notes you made as you read it. Read the Chapter Overview in the *Study Guide* and read the Learning Objectives. Now do the Recite and Review section.

Day 4   Read the margin definitions in the textbook and the Chapter Overview in the *Study Guide*. Do the Connections and Check Your Memory sections of the *Study Guide*. Return to the textbook and make sure you understand why any items you missed were wrong.

Day 5   Review the textbook chapter and any notes you made as you read it. Read the Chapter Overview in the *Study Guide*. Then do the Final Survey and Review section, and check your answers. Return to the textbook and clarify any items you missed. Now take the Mastery Test. If you miss any questions, review appropriate sections of the textbook again. To really consolidate your learning, say or write responses to all of the Learning Objectives.

Summary

The close ties between *Essentials of Psychology* and the *Study Guide* make it possible for the *Study Guide* to be used in a variety of ways. You may prefer to turn to the *Study Guide* for practice and review after you have completed a reading assignment, as suggested in the Five-Day Plan. Or, you might find it more helpful to treat the *Study Guide* as a reading companion. In that case, you would complete appropriate *Study Guide* sections from each type of exercise as you progress through the text. In any event, it is nearly certain that if you use the *Study Guide* conscientiously, you will retain more, learn more efficiently, and perform better on tests. I hope you enjoy your journey into the fascinating realm of human behavior.

Chapter 1
Psychology: The Search for Understanding

CHAPTER OVERVIEW

Psychology is the scientific study of behavior and mental processes. Psychology's goals are to describe, understand, predict, and control behavior. Psychologists answer questions about behavior by applying the scientific method and gathering empirical evidence.

Psychology grew out of philosophy. The first psychological laboratory was established by Wilhelm Wundt, who studied conscious experience. The first school of thought in psychology was structuralism, a kind of "mental chemistry." Structuralism was followed by the rise of functionalism, behaviorism, Gestalt psychology, psychoanalytic psychology, and humanistic psychology. Five main streams of thought in modern psychology are behaviorism, humanism, the psychodynamic approach, biopsychology, and cognitive psychology.

The training of psychologists differs from that of psychiatrists, psychoanalysts, counselors, and social workers. Clinical and counseling psychologists specialize in doing psychotherapy. Other specialties are industrial-organizational, educational, consumer, school, developmental, engineering, medical, environmental, forensic, psychometric, and experimental psychology.

Scientific investigation involves observing, defining a problem, proposing a hypothesis, gathering evidence/testing the hypothesis, publishing results, and forming a theory.

Many psychological investigations begin with naturalistic observation, which is informative despite its limitations. In the correlational method, the strength of the relationship between two measures is investigated. Correlations allow predictions, but they do not demonstrate cause-and-effect connections.

Experiments show whether an independent variable has an effect on a dependent variable. This allows cause-and-effect connections to be identified.

The clinical method employs detailed case studies of single individuals. In the survey method, people in a representative sample are asked a series of questions. This provides information on the behavior of large groups of people.

A key element of critical thinking is an ability to weigh the evidence bearing on a claim and to evaluate the quality of that evidence.

Belief in various pseudo-psychologies is based in part on uncritical acceptance, the fallacy of positive instances, and the Barnum effect.

Information in the popular media varies greatly in quality and accuracy. It is wise to approach such information with skepticism regarding the source of information, uncontrolled observation, correlation and causation, inferences, over-simplification, single examples, and unrepeatable results.

LEARNING OBJECTIVES

To demonstrate mastery of this chapter, you should be able to:

1. List two reasons for studying psychology.
2. Define *psychology*.
3. Define the term *behavior* and differentiate overt from covert behavior.
4. Explain the term *empirical evidence* and give an example of it.
5. Explain the term *scientific observation*.
6. Give two reasons why the study of some topics in psychology is difficult.
7. Write a brief summary of each of the following areas of specialization in psychology:
   a. developmental
   b. learning
   c. personality
   d. sensation and perception
   e. comparative
   f. biopsychology
   g. psychology of gender
   h. social
   i. cultural
   j. evolutionary
8. Explain why animals are used in research and define the term *animal model* in your discussion.
9. Explain the four goals of psychology.
10. Describe the field known as positive psychology.
11. Explain the sentence "Psychology has a long past but a short history."
12. Describe the school of psychology known as structuralism, including:
    a. where and when it was established
    b. who established it (the "father" of psychology)
    c. the focus of its study
    d. research method and its drawback
    e. goal
    f. who took structuralism to the United States
13. Describe the functionalist school of psychology, including:
    a. its founder
    b. its goal
    c. major interests
    d. impact on modern psychology
14. Describe behaviorism, including:
    a. its founder
    b. why its founder could not accept structuralism or functionalism
    c. its emphasis
    d. Skinner's contribution and his concept of a "designed culture"
    e. its application in therapy
15. Describe the view of cognitive behaviorism.

16. Describe the Gestalt school of psychology, including:
    a. who founded it
    b. its goal
    c. its slogan
    d. areas of interest
17. Describe the contribution of women in the early history of psychology, and contrast the representation of women in psychology then and now. Name the first woman to receive her doctorate in psychology.
18. Describe the psychoanalytic school of psychology, including:
    a. who founded it
    b. its major emphasis
    c. the concept of repression
    d. its method of psychotherapy
19. Describe the humanistic school of psychology, including:
    a. how its approach differs from psychoanalytic and behavioristic thought
    b. who its major representatives are
    c. its position on free will (as contrasted with determinism)
    d. its focus on psychological needs
    e. its stress of subjective factors rather than a scientific approach
    f. the concept of self-actualization
20. Describe the eclectic approach.
21. List and briefly describe the five major perspectives in modern psychology.
22. Briefly describe biopsychology and cognitive psychology.
23. Describe how an appreciation of cultural relativity and human diversity might enrich the understanding of psychology.
24. Characterize the differences in training, emphasis, and/or expertise among psychologists, psychiatrists, psychoanalysts, counselors, and psychiatric social workers. Describe the roles of clinical and counseling psychologists, and define the term *scientist-practitioner model*.
25. List the three points in the professional ethics code for psychologists established by the APA.
26. Identify the largest areas of specialization among psychologists. Name the major sources of employment for psychologists.
27. Differentiate basic from applied research.
28. Explain the problem with using common sense as a source of information.
29. List the six steps of the scientific method.
30. Define the term *hypothesis* and be able to identify one. Explain what an operational definition is.
31. Explain the purpose of theory building and the importance of publication.
32. Describe the technique of naturalistic observation including both the advantages and limitations of this method. Explain what the anthropomorphic fallacy is, and how it can lead to problems in psychological research.
33. Describe what a correlational study is, and list any advantages and disadvantages of this method. Explain what a correlation coefficient is, how it is expressed, what it means, and how it is related to causation.

34. List and describe the three essential variables of the experimental method.

35. Explain the nature and the purpose for the control group and the experimental group in an experiment.

36. Explain the purpose of randomly assigning subjects to either the control or the experimental group.

37. Identify the advantages and disadvantages of the experimental method.

38. Explain what a placebo is, how effective it is, how it probably works, and what its purpose in an experiment is.

39. Explain what single-blind and double-blind experimental arrangements are.

40. Explain the nature of the experimenter effect and how it is related to the self-fulfilling prophecy.

41. List and describe the three areas of ethical concern in psychological experiments, and explain the position of the APA in terms of ethical guidelines.

42. Briefly describe the clinical method of research, including advantages and disadvantages. Give an example of a case in which the clinical method would be used.

43. Briefly describe the survey method of investigation including the importance of a representative sample, and an advantage and a disadvantage of the method. Define the term *courtesy bias*.

44. Define the term *critical thinking*. Describe each of the four principles that form the foundation of critical thinking.

The following objectives are related to the material in the "Exploring Psychology" section of the text.

45. Briefly describe each of the following pseudo-psychologies:
    a. palmistry
    b. phrenology
    c. graphology
    d. astrology

46. List and explain the three reasons why pseudo-psychologies continue to thrive even though they have no scientific basis.

The following objective is related to the material in the "Psychology in Action" section of the text.

47. List eight suggestions that your author gives to help you become a more critical reader of psychological information in the popular press.

RECITE AND REVIEW

● *What is psychology? What are its goals?*

Recite and Review: Pages 12-16

1. Psychology is both a science and a _____.
2. Psychology is defined as the scientific study of behavior and _____ processes.
3. Psychologists study overt and covert _____.

4. Psychologists seek empirical _____ based on scientific observation.
5. Scientific observation is _____ so that it answers questions about the world.
6. Answering psychological questions requires a valid research _____.
7. Developmental psychologists study the course of human _____.
8. Learning theorists study how and why _____ occurs.
9. Personality _____ study personality traits and dynamics.
10. Sensation and perception psychologists study the _____ organs and perception.
11. Comparative psychologists study different species, especially _____.
12. Biopsychologists study the connection between biological processes and _____.
13. Gender psychologists study differences between _____ and _____.
14. Social psychologists study _____ behavior.
15. Cultural psychologists study the ways that culture affects _____.
16. Evolutionary psychologists are interested in patterns of behavior that were shaped by

_____.
17. Other species are used as _____ models in psychological research to discover principles that apply to human behavior.
18. Psychology's goals are to describe, _____, predict, and control behavior.
19. Positive psychology focuses on topics that relate to _____ human functioning.

● *How did psychology emerge as a field of knowledge?*

Recite and Review: Pages 17-22

20. Historically, psychology is an outgrowth of philosophy, the study of _____, reality, and human nature.
21. The first psychological _____ was established in Germany by Wilhelm Wundt.
22. Wundt tried to apply scientific methods to the study of conscious _____.
23. Functionalism was concerned with how the mind helps us _____ to our environments.
24. Behaviorism was launched by John B. _____.
25. Behaviorists objectively study the relationship between stimuli and _____.
26. The modern behaviorist B. F. Skinner believed that most behavior is controlled by _____ reinforcers.
27. Cognitive behaviorism combines _____, reinforcement, and environmental influences to explain behavior.
28. Gestalt psychology emphasizes the study of _____ units, not pieces.
29. According to the Gestalt view, in psychology the whole is often _____ than the sum of its parts.
30. The psychoanalytic approach emphasized the _____ origins of behavior.
31. Psychoanalytic psychology, developed by Austrian physician Sigmund _____, is an early psychodynamic approach.
32. Humanistic psychology emphasizes free will, subjective experience, human potentials, and personal

_____.
33. Psychologically, humanists believe that self-_____ and self-evaluation are important elements of personal adjustment.
34. Humanists also emphasize a capacity for self-actualization—the full development of personal

_____.

● *What are the major trends and specialties in psychology?*

Recite and Review: Pages 22-24

35. Five main streams of thought in modern psychology are behaviorism, _____, the psychodynamic approach, biopsychology, and cognitive psychology.
36. Much of contemporary psychology is an eclectic _____ of the best features of various viewpoints.
37. To fully understand behavior, psychologists must be aware of human _____ as well as human universals.
38. Our behavior is greatly affected by cultural _____ and by social norms (_____ that define acceptable behavior).
39. Psychologists who treat emotional problems specialize in _____ or counseling psychology.
40. Psychiatrists typically use both _____ and psychotherapy to treat emotional problems.
41. Freudian psychoanlysis is a specific type of _____.
42. Both counselors and psychiatric social workers have _____ degrees.
43. Some major _____ in psychology are clinical, counseling, industrial-organizational, educational, consumer, school, developmental, engineering, medical, environmental, forensic, psychometric, and experimental psychology.
44. Scientific research in psychology may be either _____ or applied.

● *Why is the scientific method important to psychologists?*

Recite and Review: Pages 28-30

45. Scientific investigation in psychology is based on reliable evidence, accurate description and _____, precise definition, controlled observation, and repeatable results.
46. The scientific method involves observing, defining a _____, proposing a hypothesis, gathering evidence/testing the hypothesis, publishing _____, and forming a theory.
47. To be scientifically _____ a hypothesis must be testable.
48. Psychological concepts are given operational _____ so that they can be observed.
49. A _____ is a system of ideas that interrelates facts and concepts.
50. Published research reports usually include the following sections: an _____, an introduction, a methods section, a _____ section, and a final discussion.

● *How do psychologists collect information?*

Recite and Review: Pages 30-33

51. The tools of psychological research include naturalistic observation, the correlational method, the experimental method, the _____ method, and the survey method.
52. Naturalistic observation refers to actively observing behavior in _____ settings.
53. Two problems with naturalistic studies are the effects of the observer on the observed (the observer _____) and _____ bias.
54. The anthropomorphic fallacy is the error of attributing human qualities to _____.
55. Problems with naturalistic studies can be minimized by keeping careful observational

_____.

56. In the correlational method, the _____ between two traits, responses, or events is measured.

57. Correlation coefficients range from +1.00 to –1.00. A correlation of _____ indicates that there is no relationship between two measures.

58. Correlations of +1.00 and –1.00 reveal that _____ relationships exist between two measures.

59. The closer a correlation coefficient is to plus or _____ 1, the stronger the measured relationship is.

60. A positive correlation shows that _____ in one measure correspond to increases in a second measure.

61. In a negative correlation, _____ in one measure correspond to decreases in a second measure.

62. Correlations allow us to make _____, but correlation does not demonstrate causation.

63. _____-and-effect relationships in psychology are best identified by doing a controlled experiment.

● *How is an experiment performed?*

Recite and Review: Pages 34-37

64. In an experiment, conditions that might affect behavior are intentionally _____. Then, changes in behavior are observed and recorded.

65. In an experiment, a variable is any condition that can _____, and that might affect the outcome of the experiment (the behavior of subjects).

66. Experimental conditions that are intentionally varied are called _____ variables.

67. _____ variables measure the results of the experiment.

68. Extraneous variables are conditions that a researcher wishes to _____ from affecting the outcome of the experiment.

69. Extraneous variables are controlled by making sure that they are the same for all _____ in an experiment.

70. Subjects exposed to the independent variable are in the experimental _____. Those not exposed to the independent variable form the control _____.

71. Extraneous variables that involve personal _____, such as age or intelligence, can be controlled by randomly assigning subjects to the experimental and control groups.

72. If all extraneous variables are _____ for the experimental group and the control group, any differences in behavior must be caused by differences in the independent variable.

73. Experiments involving drugs must control for the placebo _____.

74. In a single-_____ study, subjects don't know if they are getting a drug or a placebo. In a double-_____ study, neither experimenters nor subjects know who is receiving a real drug.

75. Researchers must minimize the experimenter effect (the tendency for people to do what is _____ of them).

76. In many situations, the experimenter effect leads to self-fulfilling _____.

● *What other research methods do psychologists use?*

Recite and Review: Pages 38-40

77. Clinical psychologists frequently gain information from _____ studies.

78. Case studies may be thought of as _____ clinical tests.
79. In the survey method, information about large populations is gained by asking people in a representative _____ a series of carefully worded questions.
80. The value of surveys is lowered when the sample is biased and when replies to questions are _____.

● *What is critical thinking?*

Recite and Review: Pages 40-41

81. Critical thinking is the ability to _____, compare, analyze, critique, and synthesize information.
82. In psychology, _____ thinking skills help evaluate claims about human behavior.
83. Critical thinking involves a willingness to _____ evaluate _____.
84. Scientific observations usually provide the highest quality _____ about various claims.

● *How does psychology differ from false explanations of behavior?*

Recite and Review: Pages 42-44

85. Palmistry, phrenology, graphology, and astrology are _____ systems or pseudo-psychologies.
86. Belief in pseudo-psychologies is encouraged by uncritical acceptance, the fallacy of positive instances, and the _____ effect, named after a famous showman who had "something for everyone."

● *How good is psychological information found in the popular media?*

Recite and Review: PSYCHOLOGY IN ACTION

87. _____ and critical thinking are called for when evaluating claims in the popular media.
88. You should be on guard for _____ or biased sources of information in the media.
89. Many claims in the media are based on unscientific observations that lack control _____.
90. In the popular media, a failure to distinguish between correlation and _____ is common.
91. Inferences and opinions may be reported as if they were _____ observations.
92. Single cases, unusual _____, and testimonials are frequently reported as if they were valid generalizations.

CONNECTIONS

1. _____ biopsychology
2. _____ psychology
3. _____ personality theorist
4. _____ empirical evidence
5. _____ covert behavior
6. _____ scientific observation
7. _____ EEG
8. _____ comparative psychology
9. _____ description
10. _____ understanding

a. hidden from view
b. brain waves
c. systematic observation
d. animal behavior
e. detailed record
f. human and animal behavior
g. "why" questions
h. brain and behavior
i. direct observation
j. traits, dynamics, individual differences

11. _____ psychometrics
12. _____ control
13. _____ Wundt
14. _____ Titchener
15. _____ James
16. _____ Darwin
17. _____ Skinner
18. _____ Pavlov
19. _____ Wertheimer
20. _____ Ladd-Franklin

a. father of psychology
b. natural selection
c. behaviorism
d. mental measurement
e. functionalism
f. conditioned responses
g. Gestalt
h. color vision
i. introspection
j. influencing behavior

21. _____ Freud
22. _____ Maslow
23. _____ psychodynamic view
24. _____ behavioristic view
25. _____ humanistic view
26. _____ biopsychology
27. _____ cognitive view
28. _____ psychologist
29. _____ psychiatrist
30. _____ scientific method

a. self-actualization
b. self-image
c. psychoanalysis
d. information processing
e. Ph.D., Psy.D., Ed.D.
f. M.D.
g. internal forces
h. physiological processes
i. controlled observation
j. environmental forces

31. _____ common sense
32. _____ hypothesis
33. _____ operational definition
34. _____ Clever Hans
35. _____ observational record
36. _____ correlational study
37. _____ correlation of +3.5
38. _____ identify causes of behavior
39. _____ independent variable
40. _____ dependent variable

a. tentative explanation
b. formal log
c. specific procedures
d. related traits, behaviors
e. math error
f. head signals
g. effect on behavior
h. experimental method
i. unscientific information
j. varied by experimenter

41. _____	extraneous variables	a. Phineas Gage
42. _____	control group	b. done by using chance
43. _____	random assignment to groups	c. participation is voluntary
44. _____	lobotomy	d. excluded by experimenter
45. _____	placebos	e. clinical method
46. _____	endorphins	f. representative of population
47. _____	case studies	g. inaccurate answers
48. _____	valid sample	h. opiate-like
49. _____	courtesy bias	i. reference for comparison
50. _____	ethical research	j. sugar pills

CHECK YOUR MEMORY

Check Your Memory: Pages 12-16

1. Psychology can best be described as a profession, not a science. T or F?
2. Psychology is defined as the scientific study of human behavior. T or F?
3. Although it is a covert activity, dreaming is a behavior. T or F?
4. The term *empirical evidence* refers to the opinion of an acknowledged authority. T or F?
5. The term *data* refers to a systematic procedure for answering scientific questions. T or F?
6. Naming and classifying are the heart of psychology's second goal, understanding behavior. T or F?

Check Your Memory: Pages 17-22

7. In 1879, Wundt established a lab to study the philosophy of behavior. T or F?
8. Wundt used introspection to study conscious experiences. T or F?
9. Edward Titchener is best known for promoting functionalism in America. T or F?
10. The functionalists were influenced by the ideas of Charles Darwin. T or F?
11. Behaviorists define psychology as the study of conscious experience. T or F?
12. Watson used Pavlov's concept of conditioned responses to explain most behavior. T or F?
13. The "Skinner Box" is used primarily to study learning in animals. T or F?
14. Cognitive behaviorism combines thinking and Gestalt principles to explain human behavior. T or F?
15. Margaret Washburn was the first woman in America to be awarded a Ph.D. in psychology. T or F?
16. Mary Calkins did early research on memory. T or F?
17. According to Freud, repressed thoughts are held out of awareness, in the unconscious. T or F?
18. Humanists generally reject the determinism of the behavioristic and psychodynamic approaches. T or F?

Check Your Memory: Pages 22-24

19. The five major perspectives in psychology today are behaviorism, humanism, functionalism, biopsychology, and cognitive psychology. T of F?
20. Humanism offers a positive, philosophical view of human nature. T or F?
21. The cognitive view explains behavior in terms of information processing. T or F?
22. To understand behavior, psychologists must be aware of the cultural relativity of standards for evaluating behavior. T or F?

23. Most psychologists work in private practice. T or F?
24. The differences between clinical and counseling psychology are beginning to fade. T or F?
25. To enter the profession of psychology today you would need to earn a doctorate degree. T or F?
26. The Psy.D. degree emphasizes scientific research skills. T or F?
27. More than half of all psychologists specialize in clinical or counseling psychology. T or F?
28. Clinical psychologists must be licensed to practice legally. T or F?
29. Over 40 percent of all psychologists are employed by the military. T or F?
30. Studying ways to improve the memories of eyewitnesses to crimes would be an example of applied research. T or F?

Check Your Memory: Pages 28-30

31. The scientific method involves testing a proposition by systematic observation. T or F?
32. An operational definition states the exact hypothesis used to represent a concept. T or F?
33. Clever Hans couldn't do math problems when his owner left the room. T or F?
34. Operational definitions link concepts with concrete observations. T or F?
35. Most research reports begin with an abstract. T or F?

Check Your Memory: Pages 30-33

36. Jane Goodall's study of chimpanzees made use of the clinical method. T or F?
37. Concealing the observer helps reduce the observer effect. T or F?
38. A correlation coefficient of +.100 indicates a perfect positive relationship. T or F?
39. Strong relationships produce positive correlation coefficients; weak relationships produce negative correlations. T or F?
40. Perfect correlations demonstrate that a causal relationship exists. T or F?
41. The best way to identify cause-and-effect relationships is to perform a case study. T or F?

Check Your Memory: Pages 34-37

42. Extraneous variables are those that are varied by the experimenter. T or F?
43. Independent variables are suspected causes for differences in behavior. T or F?
44. In an experiment to test whether hunger affects memory, hunger is the dependent variable. T or F?
45. Independent variables are randomly assigned to the experimental and control groups. T or F?
46. A person who takes a drug may be influenced by his or her expectations about the drug's effects. T or F?
47. Placebos appear to reduce pain because they cause a release of endogenous dexedrine. T or F?
48. In a single-blind experiment, the experimenter remains blind as to whether she or he is administering a drug. T or F?
49. Subjects in psychology experiments can be very sensitive to hints about what is expected of them. T or F?

Check Your Memory: Pages 38-40

50. Phineas Gage is remembered as the first psychologist to do a case study. T or F?
51. Case studies may be inconclusive because they lack formal control groups. T or F?
52. Representative samples are often obtained by randomly selecting people to study. T or F?
53. A tendency to give socially desirable answers to questions can lower the accuracy of surveys. T or F?

Check Your Memory: Pages 40-41

54. Critical thinking is the ability to make good use of intuition and mental imagery. T or F?
55. Critical thinkers actively evaluate claims, ideas, and propositions. T or F?
56. A key element of critical thinking is evaluating the quality of evidence related to a claim. T or F?
57. Critical thinkers recognize that the opinions of experts and authorities should be respected without question. T or F?

Check Your Memory: Pages 42-44

58. Pseudo-scientists test their concepts by gathering data. T or F?
59. Phrenologists believe that lines on the hands reveal personality traits. T or F?
60. Graphology is only valid if a large enough sample of handwriting is analyzed. T or F?
61. Astrological charts consisting of positive traits tend to be perceived as "accurate" or true, even if they are not. T or F?
62. The Barnum effect refers to our tendency to remember things that confirm our expectations. T or F?

Check Your Memory: PSYCHOLOGY IN ACTION

63. The existence of dermo-optical perception was confirmed by recent experiments. T or F?
64. Psychological courses and services offered for profit may be misrepresented, just as some other products are. T or F?
65. At least some psychic ability is necessary to perform as a stage mentalist. T or F?
66. Successful firewalking requires neurolinguistic programming. T or F?
67. Violent crime rises and falls with lunar cycles. T or F?
68. If you see a person crying, you must infer that he or she is sad. T or F?
69. Individual cases and specific examples tell us nothing about what is true in general. T or F?

FINAL SURVEY AND REVIEW

● *What is psychology? What are its goals?*

1. Psychology is both a _____ and a _____.
2. Psychology is defined as the scientific study of _____ and _____
_____.
3. Psychologists study both overt and _____ behavior.
4. Psychologists seek _____ evidence based on scientific observation. They settle disputes by collecting _____.
5. _____ observation is structured and systematic.
6. Answering psychological questions requires a valid _____ _____.
7. _____ psychologists study the course of human development.
8. Learning _____ study how and why learning occurs.
9. _____ theorists study personality traits and dynamics.
10. _____ and perception psychologists study the sense organs and perception.

11. _____ psychologists study different species, especially animals.
12. _____ study biological processes and behavior.
13. _____ psychologists study differences between males and females.
14. Social psychologists study _____ _____.
15. _____ psychologists study the ways that culture affects behavior.
16. _____ psychologists are interested in patterns of behavior that were shaped by natural selection.
17. Other species are used as _____ _____ in psychological research to discover principles that apply to human behavior.
18. Psychology's goals are to describe, understand, _____ and _____ behavior.
19. _____ psychology focuses on topics that relate to optimal human functioning.

● How did psychology emerge as a field of knowledge?

20. Historically, psychology is an outgrowth of _____.
21. The first psychological laboratory was established in Germany by _____ _____.
22. His goal was to apply scientific methods to the study of _____ _____.
23. The first school of thought in psychology was _____, a kind of "mental chemistry."
24. _____ was concerned with how the mind helps us adapt to our environments. William _____ was one of its proponents.
25. _____ was launched by John B. Watson, who wanted to study the relationship between _____ and responses.
26. The modern behaviorist B. F. _____ believed that most behavior is controlled by positive _____.
27. _____ behaviorism combines thinking and environmental influences to explain behavior.
28. _____ psychology emphasizes the study of whole experiences, not elements or pieces.
29. According to Max _____ and other _____ psychologists, the whole is often greater than the _____ of its parts.
30. The _____ approach emphasizes the unconscious origins of behavior.
31. The Austrian physician, Sigmund _____, developed a psychodynamic system called _____.
32. _____ psychology emphasizes free will, subjective experience, human _____, and personal growth.
33. Psychologically, humanists believe that _____, self-evaluation, and one's _____ of reference are important elements of personal adjustment.
34. Humanists also emphasize a capacity for _____—the full development of personal potential.

● *What are the major trends and specialties in psychology?*

35. Five main streams of thought in modern psychology are _____,
_____, the psychodynamic approach, _____, and cognitive
psychology.

36. Much of contemporary psychology is an _____ blend of the best features of various
viewpoints.

37. To fully understand behavior, psychologists must be aware of human _____, as reflected
in personal and _____ differences.

38. Our behavior is greatly affected by _____ values and by social _____ (rules that
define acceptable behavior).

39. Psychologists who treat emotional problems specialize in _____ or _____
psychology.

40. _____ are medical doctors who typically use both drugs and
_____ to treat emotional problems.

41. Freudian _____ is a specific type of psychotherapy.

42. Both counselors and _____ _____ workers have Master's degrees.

43. _____ psychologists specialize in the growth of children;
_____ psychologists help design machinery; _____ psychologists
study classroom dynamics.

44. Scientific research in psychology may be either basic or _____.

● *Why is the scientific method important to psychologists?*

45. Scientific investigation in psychology is based on reliable _____, accurate description and
_____, precise definition, controlled observation, and repeatable results.

46. The scientific method involves observing, defining a problem, proposing a _____,
gathering evidence/testing the hypothesis, publishing results, and forming a _____.

47. To be _____ valid a hypothesis must be _____.

48. Psychological concepts are given _____ definitions so that they can be observed. Such
definitions state the exact _____ used to represent a concept.

49. A _____ is a system of ideas that interrelates facts and concepts. In general, good
_____ summarize existing _____ explain them, and guide further research.

50. The results of scientific studies are _____ in professional _____ so they will
be publicly available.

● *How do psychologists collect information?*

51. The tools of psychological research include naturalistic observation, the correlational method, the
_____ method, the clinical method, and the _____ method.

52. Naturalistic observation refers to actively observing behavior in _____
_____, which are the typical _____ in which people and animals live.

53. Two problems with naturalistic observation are the effects of the observer on the _____ and observer _____.

54. The _____ fallacy is the error of attributing human qualities to animals.

55. Problems with naturalistic observation can be minimized by keeping careful _____ _____.

56. In the _____ method, the strength of the relationship between two traits, responses, or events is measured.

57. Correlation _____ range from +1.00 to –1.00.

58. A correlation of _____ indicates that there is no relationship between two measures. Correlations of +1.00 and –1.00 reveal that _____ relationships exist between two measures.

59. The _____ a correlation coefficient is to plus or minus 1.00, the stronger the measured relationship is.

60. A _____ correlation or relationship shows that increases in one measure correspond to increases in a second measure.

61. In a negative correlation, _____ in one measure correspond to _____ in a second measure.

62. Correlations allow prediction, but correlation does not demonstrate _____.

63. Cause-and-effect relationships in psychology are best identified by doing a _____ _____.

● How is an experiment performed?

64. In an experiment, conditions that might affect behavior are intentionally varied. Then, changes in behavior are _____ and _____.

65. In an experiment a _____ is any condition that can change, and that might affect the outcome of the experiment.

66. Experimental conditions that are intentionally varied are called _____ variables; they are potential _____ of changes in behavior.

67. _____ variables measure the results of the experiment; they reveal any _____ on behavior.

68. _____ variables are conditions that a researcher wishes to prevent from affecting the _____ of the experiment.

69. Extraneous variables are _____ by making sure that they are the same for all subjects in an experiment.

70. Subjects exposed to the independent variable are in the _____ group. Those not exposed to the independent variable form the _____ group.

71. Extraneous variables that involve _____ characteristics, such as age or intelligence, can be controlled by _____ assigning subjects to the experimental and control groups.

72. If all extraneous variables are identical for the experimental group and the control group, any differences in behavior must be caused by differences in the _____ variable

73. Experiments involving drugs must control for the _____ effect.

74. In a _____ study, subjects don't know if they are getting a drug or a placebo. In a _____ study, neither experimenters nor subjects know who is receiving a real drug.

75. Researchers must also minimize the _____ _____ (the tendency for people to do what is expected of them).
76. In many situations, the experimenter effect leads to _____ prophecies.

● *What other research methods do psychologists use?*

77. Clinical psychologists frequently gain information from _____ _____, which focus on all aspects of a single _____.
78. Case studies may be thought of as natural _____ _____ of the effects of brain tumors, accidental poisonings, and other unusual conditions.
79. In the survey method, information about large _____ is gained by asking people in a _____ sample a series of carefully worded questions.
80. The value of surveys is lowered when the sample is _____ and when replies to _____ are inaccurate or untruthful.

● *What is critical thinking?*

81. Critical thinking is the ability to evaluate, compare, analyze, _____, and _____ information.
82. In psychology, critical thinking skills help _____ claims about human behavior.
83. Critical thinking involves evaluating the quality of the _____ used to support various claims.
84. _____ observations usually provide the highest quality evidence about various claims.

● *How does psychology differ from false explanations of behavior?*

85. Palmistry, _____, graphology, and astrology are _____-psychologies.
86. Belief in false psychologies is encouraged by _____ acceptance, the fallacy of _____ instances, and the _____ effect.

● *How good is psychological information found in the popular media?*

87. _____ and _____ thinking are called for when evaluating claims in the popular media.
88. You should be on guard for unreliable or _____ sources of information in the media.
89. Many claims in the media are based on unscientific observations that lack _____ groups.
90. _____ does not demonstrate causation. In the popular media, a failure to distinguish between _____ and causation is common.
91. Inferences and opinions may be reported as if they were objective _____.
92. Single _____, unusual examples, and testimonials are frequently reported as if they were valid _____.

MASTERY TEST

1. Data in psychology are typically gathered to answer questions about
   a. clinical problems   b. human groups   c. human cognition   d. overt or covert behavior

2. Who among the following would most likely study the behavior of gorillas?
   a. developmental psychologist   b. comparative psychologist   c. environmental psychologist
   d. forensic psychologist

3. An engineering psychologist helps redesign an airplane to make it safer to fly. The psychologist's work
   reflects which of psychology's goals?
   a. understanding   b. control   c. prediction   d. description

4. Who among the following placed the greatest emphasis on introspection?
   a. Watson   b. Wertheimer   c. Washburn   d. Wundt

5. Which pair of persons had the most similar ideas?
   a. Titchener—Skinner   b. James—Darwin   c. Watson—Rogers   d. Wertheimer—Maslow

6. The behaviorist definition of psychology clearly places great emphasis on
   a. overt behavior   b. conscious experience   c. psychodynamic responses   d. introspective analysis

7. As a profession, psychology is fully open to men and women, a fact that began with the success of
   a. O'Sullivan-Calkins   b. Tyler-James   c. Ladd-Franklin   d. Neal-Collins

8. The idea that threatening thoughts are sometimes repressed would be of most interest to a
   a. structuralist   b. psychoanalyst   c. humanist   d. Gestaltist

9. "A neutral, reductionistic, mechanistic view of human nature." This best describes which viewpoint?
   a. psychodynamic   b. cognitive   c. psychoanalytic   d. biopsychological

10. Which of the following professional titles usually requires a doctorate degree?
    a. psychologist   b. psychiatric social worker   c. counselor   d. all of the preceding

11. Who among the following is most likely to treat the physical causes of psychological problems?
    a. scientist-practitioner   b. psychoanalyst   c. forensic psychologist   d. psychiatrist

12. More than half of all psychologists specialize in what branches of psychology?
    a. counseling and comparative   b. applied and counseling   c. psychodynamic and clinical
    d. counseling and clinical

13. When critically evaluating claims about behavior it is important to also evaluate
    a. the source of anecdotal evidence   b. the credentials of an authority   c. the quality of the evidence
    d. the strength of one's intuition

14. Which of the following pairs is most different?
    a. pseudo-psychology—critical thinking   b. graphology—pseudo-psychology
    c. palmistry—phrenology   d. psychology—empirical evidence

15. The German anatomy teacher Franz Gall popularized
    a. palmistry b. phrenology c. graphology d. astrology

16. A tendency to believe flattering descriptions of oneself is called
    a. the Barnum effect b. the astrologer's dilemma c. the fallacy of positive instances
    d. uncritical acceptance

17. Descriptions of personality that contain both sides of several personal dimensions tend to create
    a. an illusion of accuracy b. disbelief and rejection c. the astrologer's dilemma
    d. a system similar to phrenology

18. If an entire population is surveyed, it becomes unnecessary to obtain a
    a. control group b. random comparison c. random sample d. control variable

19. Control groups are most often used in
    a. naturalistic observation b. the clinical method c. parascience d. experiments

20. Concealing the observer can be used to minimize the
    a. observer bias effect b. double-blind effect c. observer effect d. effects of extraneous correlations

21. A psychologist studying lowland gorillas should be careful to avoid the
    a. anthropomorphic error b. Gestalt fallacy c. psychodynamic fallacy
    d. fallacy of positive instances

22. Testing the hypothesis that frustration encourages aggression would require
    a. a field study b. operational definitions c. adult subjects d. perfect correlations

23. In experiments involving drugs, experimenters remain unaware of who received placebos in a
    _____ arrangement
    a. zero-blind b. single-blind c. double-blind d. control-blind

24. The idea that Clever Hans's owner might be signaling him was an informal
    a. research hypothesis b. self-fulfilling prophecy c. operational definition d. dependent variable

25. In psychology, the _____ variable is a suspected cause of differences in

    _____.

    a. independent, the control group b. dependent, the experimenter effect c. independent, behavior
    d. dependent, correlations

26. A person who is observed crying may not be sad. This suggests that it is important to distinguish
    between
    a. individual cases and generalizations b. correlation and causation c. control groups and
    experimental groups d. observation and inference

27. In an experiment on the effects of hunger on the reading scores of elementary school children, reading scores are the
    a. control variable   b. independent variable   c. dependent variable   d. reference variable

28. Which of the following correlation coefficients indicates a perfect relationship?
    a. 1.00   b. 100.0   c. –1   d. both a and c

29. Jane Goodall's studies of chimpanzees in Tanzania are good examples of
    a. field experiments   b. experimental control   c. correlational studies   d. naturalistic observation

30. To equalize the intelligence of members of the experimental group and the control group in an experiment, you could use
    a. extraneous control   b. random assignment   c. independent control   d. subject replication

31. Which method would most likely be used to study the effects of tumors in the frontal lobes of the brain?
    a. sampling method   b. correlational method   c. clinical method   d. experimental method

32. The release of endorphins by the pituitary gland helps explain the
    a. experimenter effect   b. placebo effect   c. multiple-personality effect   d. gender-bias effect

33. Cause is to effect as _____ variable is to _____ variable.
    a. extraneous, dependent   b. dependent, independent   c. independent, extraneous
    d. independent, dependent

34. The specific procedures used to gather data are described in which section of a research report?
    a. introduction   b. abstract   c. method   d. discussion

35. Which of the following correlations demonstrates a cause-effect relationship?
    a. .980   b. 1.00   c. .50   d. none of the preceding

ANSWERS

Recite and Review

1. profession
2. mental
3. behavior
4. evidence
5. planned or structured
6. method
7. development
8. learning
9. theorists
10. sense (or sensory)
11. animals
12. behavior
13. males, females
14. social
15. behavior
16. evolution
17. animal
18. understand
19. optimal
20. knowledge
21. laboratory
22. experience
23. adapt
24. Watson
25. responses
26. positive
27. thinking
28. whole
29. greater
30. unconscious
31. Freud

32. growth
33. image
34. potentials
35. humanism
36. blend
37. diversity (or differences)
38. values, rules
39. clinical
40. drugs
41. psychotherapy
42. Master's
43. specialties
44. basic
45. measurement
46. problem, results
47. valid (or useful)
48. definitions
49. theory
50. abstract, results
51. clinical
52. natural
53. effect, observer
54. animals
55. records
56. correlation (or relationship)
57. zero
58. perfect
59. minus
60. increases
61. increases
62. predictions
63. Cause
64. varied
65. change
66. independent
67. Dependent
68. prevent
69. subjects
70. group, group
71. characteristics
72. identical
73. effect
74. blind, blind
75. expected
76. prophecies
77. case
78. natural
79. sample
80. untruthful (or inaccurate)

81. evaluate
82. critical
83. actively, ideas
84. evidence
85. false
86. Barnum
87. Skepticism
88. unreliable (or inaccurate)
89. groups
90. causation
91. valid (or scientific)
92. examples

Connections

1. h
2. f
3. j
4. i
5. a
6. c
7. b
8. d
9. e
10. g
11. d
12. j
13. a
14. i
15. e
16. b
17. c
18. f
19. g
20. h
21. c
22. a
23. g
24. j
25. b
26. h
27. d
28. e
29. f
30. i
31. i
32. a
33. c

34. f
35. b
36. d
37. e
38. h
39. j
40. g
41. d
42. i
43. b
44. a
45. j
46. h
47. e
48. f
49. g
50. c

Check Your Memory

1. F
2. F
3. T
4. F
5. F
6. F
7. F
8. T
9. F
10. T
11. F
12. T
13. T
14. F
15. T
16. T
17. T
18. T
19. F
20. T
21. T
22. T
23. F
24. T
25. F
26. F
27. T
28. T

29. F
30. T
31. T
32. F
33. F
34. T
35. T
36. F
37. T
38. F
39. F
40. F
41. F
42. F
43. T
44. F
45. F
46. T
47. F
48. F
49. T
50. F
51. T
52. T
53. T
54. F
55. T
56. T
57. F
58. F
59. F
60. F
61. T
62. F
63. F
64. T
65. F
66. F
67. F
68. F
69. T

Final Survey and Review

1. science, profession
2. behavior, mental, processes
3. covert
4. empirical, data
5. scientific
6. research method
7. Developmental
8. theorists
9. Personality
10. Sensation
11. Comparative
12. Biopsychologists
13. Gender
14. social behavior
15. Cultural
16. Evolutionary
17. animal models
18. predict, control
19. Positive
20. philosophy
21. Wilhelm Wundt
22. conscious experience
23. structuralism
24. Functionalism, James
25. Behaviorism, stimuli
26. Skinner, reinforcers
27. Cognitive
28. Gestalt
29. Wertheimer, Gestalt, sum
30. Psychoanalytic (or psychodynamic)
31. Freud, psychoanalysis
32. Humanistic, potentials
33. self-image, frame
34. self-actualization
35. behaviorism, humanism, biopsychology
36. eclectic
37. diversity, cultural
38. cultural, norms
39. clinical, counseling
40. Psychiatrists, psychotherapy
41. psychoanalysis
42. psychiatric social
43. Developmental, engineering, educational
44. applied
45. evidence, measurement
46. hypothesis, theory
47. scientifically, testable
48. operational, procedures
49. theory, theories, observations
50. published, journals
51. experimental, survey
52. natural settings, environments
53. observed, bias
54. anthropomorphic
55. observational records
56. correlational
57. coefficients
58. zero, perfect
59. closer
60. positive
61. increases, decreases
62. causation
63. controlled experiment
64. observed, recorded
65. variable
66. independent, causes
67. Dependent, effects
68. Extraneous, outcome
69. controlled
70. experimental, control
71. personal, randomly
72. independent
73. placebo
74. single-blind, double-blind
75. experimenter effect
76. self-fulfilling
77. case studies, subject
78. clinical tests
79. populations, representative
80. biased, questions
81. critique, synthesize
82. evaluate
83. evidence
84. Scientific
85. phrenology, pseudo
86. uncritical, positive, Barnum
87. Skepticism, critical
88. biased
89. control
90. Correlation, correlation
91. observations
92. cases, generalizations

Mastery Test

1. d (p. 13)
2. b (p. 14)

 3. b (p. 16)
 4. d (p. 17)
 5. b (p. 18)
 6. a (p. 18)
 7. c (p. 20)
 8. b (p. 21)
 9. d (p. 23)
10. a (p. 25)
11. d (p. 25)
12. d (p. 25)
13. c (p. 40)
14. a (p. 42)
15. b (p. 42)
16. d (p. 43)
17. a (p. 43)
18. c (p. 39)
19. d (p. 34)
20. c (p. 31)
21. a (p. 31)
22. b (p. 29)
23. c (p. 37)
24. a (p. 29)
25. c (p. 35)
26. d (p. 46)
27. c (p. 34)
28. d (p. 32)
29. d (p. 31)
30. b (p. 35)
31. c (p. 38)
32. b (p. 36)
33. d (p. 34-35)
34. c (p. 30)
35. d (p. 33)

Chapter 2
Brain and Behavior

CHAPTER OVERVIEW

The brain and nervous system are made up of networks of neurons. Nerve impulses are basically electrical. Communication between neurons is chemical in that neurons release neurotransmitters which affect other neurons. Rather than merely carrying messages, neuropeptides regulate the activity of neurons in the brain.

The nervous system includes the central nervous system (CNS), consisting of the brain and spinal cord, and the peripheral nervous system (PNS). The PNS includes the somatic system and the autonomic system, with its sympathetic and parasympathetic branches.

Conventional brain research relies on dissection, staining, ablation, deep lesioning, electrical recording, electrical stimulation, micro-electrode recording, EEG recording, and clinical studies. Newer methods make use of computer-enhanced images of the brain and its activities.

The basic functions of the lobes of the brain are as follows: occipital lobes—vision; parietal lobes—bodily sensation; temporal lobes—hearing and language; frontal lobes—motor control, speech, and abstract thought. Association areas of the cortex are related to complex abilities such as language, memory, and problem solving. The left and right cerebral hemispheres have different specialized abilities.

The brain is subdivided into the forebrain, midbrain, and hindbrain. The subcortex includes important brain structures at all three levels. These are: the medulla ("vegetative" functions), the cerebellum (coordination), the reticular formation (sensory and motor messages and arousal), the thalamus (sensory information), and the hypothalamus (basic motives). The limbic system is related to emotion.

The endocrine system provides chemical communication in the body through the release of hormones into the bloodstream.

Hand dominance ranges from strongly left- to strongly right-handed, with mixed handedness and ambidexterity in between. In general, the left-handed are less strongly lateralized in brain function than are right-handed persons.

LEARNING OBJECTIVES

To demonstrate mastery of this chapter, you should be able to:

1. Name the basic unit of the nervous system, state what it is specifically designed to do, and list and describe its four parts.

2. Explain how a nerve impulse (action potential) occurs, how it is an all-or-nothing event, and how the cell returns to its resting state after the nerve impulse passes.

3. Describe the difference between the nature of a nerve impulse and the nature of the communication between neurons.

4. Explain how nerve impulses are carried from one neuron to another at the synapse.

5. Explain what determines whether a neuron will have an action potential triggered.

6. Explain the function of neuropeptides.

7. Differentiate a nerve from a neuron.

8. Describe the process of neurogenesis and its connection to brain repair.

9. Describe the effect of myelin on the speed of the nerve impulse.

10. Explain what determines whether or not a neuron or a nerve will regenerate. Briefly describe the progress in generating regrowth of brain and spinal cord neurons.

11. Chart the various subparts of the human nervous system and generally explain their functions.

12. Differentiate between the two branches of the autonomic nervous system.

13. Explain the mechanism of the reflex arc.

The following objectives are related to the material in the "Exploring Psychology" section of the text.

14. List and describe five techniques for studying the brain.

15. Briefly describe how an EEG works.

16. Describe each of the four scanning techniques for studying the entire brain as it functions.

17. Describe the main difference between the brains of lower and higher animals. Name what appears to be the foundation of human intellectual superiority.

18. Describe the main difference between the brains of people who score high versus low on mental tests.

19. Define the term *hemispheres* and explain the function of the corpus callosum. Describe the problem known as spatial neglect.

20. Explain how and why a brain is "split" and describe what the resulting effects are.

21. Differentiate the abilities of the two hemispheres of the cerebral cortex. Describe what is known about their working together as well as how they process information.

22. Describe the function(s) of each of the following:
    a. occipital lobes
    b. parietal lobes (include the somatosensory areas)
    c. temporal lobes
    d. frontal lobes (include the motor cortex)
    e. associative areas (include Broca's and Wernicke's areas)
    f. Explain the relationship between the size of the various parts of the somatosensory and motor areas of the cortex and the degree of sensitivity or importance of the corresponding body parts.

23. Describe the cause and effect of aphasia. Explain why there may be gender differences in aphasia.

24. List and be able to recognize the three areas of the subcortex.

25. Explain the function of each of the following parts of two of the three areas of the subcortex:
    a. hindbrain (brainstem)
        i) pons
        ii) medulla
        iii) cerebellum

iv) reticular formation
   b. forebrain
      i) thalamus
      ii) hypothalamus

26. Name the structures that comprise the limbic system and explain its function (include a description of the function of the amygdala and the hippocampus).

27. Briefly describe the significance of "pleasure" and "aversive" areas in the limbic system.

28. List six basic functions of the brain.

29. Briefly describe the research of Bakay and Kennedy with cortical stimulation in paralyzed persons.

30. Briefly explain the purpose of the endocrine system. Describe the action of hormones in the body.

31. Describe the effect that the following glands have on the body and behavior:
   a. pituitary (include a description of giantism, hypopituitary dwarfism, and acromegaly)
   b. pineal
   c. thyroid (include a description of hyperthyroidism and hypothyroidism)
   d. adrenal medulla
   e. adrenal cortex (include a description of virilism, premature puberty, and the problems of anabolic steroids)

The following objectives are related to the material in the "Psychology in Action" section of the text.

32. Describe the relationship among handedness, brain dominance, and speech. Describe the element of handedness that appears to be inherited.

33. Explain how a person can determine which hemisphere is dominant.

34. State the incidence of left-handedness and discuss the relative advantages and/or disadvantages of being right-handed versus left-handed.

RECITE AND REVIEW

● *How do nerve cells operate and communicate?*

Recite and Review: Pages 50-54

1. The _____ and nervous system are made up of linked nerve cells called _____, which pass information from one to another through synapses.

2. The basic conducting fibers of neurons are _____, but dendrites (a receiving area), the soma (the cell body and also a receiving area), and _____ terminals (the branching ends of a neuron) are also involved in communication.

3. The firing of an action potential (_____ _____) is basically electrical, whereas communication between neurons is chemical.

4. An action potential occurs when the _____ potential is altered enough to reach the threshold for firing. At that point, sodium _____ flow into the axon, through _____ channels.

5. After each action potential, the neuron has a brief _____ after-potential. Next, potassium ions flow out of the _____, restoring the resting potential.

6. The _____ potential is an all-or-nothing event.

7. Neurons release neurotransmitters at the synapse. These cross to _____ sites on the receiving cell, causing it to be excited or inhibited. For example, the transmitter chemical acetylcholine activates _____.

8. Chemicals called neuropeptides do not carry messages directly. Instead, they _____ the activity of other neurons.

9. Opiate-like neural regulators called enkephalins and endorphins are released in the brain to relieve _____ and stress.

● *What are the functions of major parts of the nervous system?*

Recite and Review: Pages 54-57

10. Nerves are made of large bundles of _____ and dendrites. Neurons and nerves in the peripheral nervous system can often regenerate; damage in the central nervous system is usually _____, unless a repair is attempted by grafting or implanting healthy tissue.

11. The nervous system can be divided into the _____ nervous system (the _____ and spinal cord) and the peripheral nervous system.

12. The CNS includes the somatic (_____) and autonomic (_____) nervous systems.

13. The autonomic system has two divisions: the sympathetic (emergency, activating) _____ and the parasympathetic (sustaining, conserving) _____.

14. Thirty one pairs of spinal _____ leave the spinal cord. Twelve pairs of cranial _____ leave the brain directly. Together, they carry sensory and motor messages between the brain and the body.

15. The simplest _____ is a reflex arc, which involves a sensory neuron, a connector neuron, and a _____ neuron.

● *How do we know how the brain works?*

Recite and Review: Pages 57-59

16. Conventional brain research relies on dissection, staining, ablation, deep lesioning, electrical recording, _____ stimulation, micro-electrode recording, EEG recording, and _____ studies.

17. Computer-enhanced techniques are providing three-dimensional _____ of the living human brain and its _____. Examples of such techniques are CT scans, MRI scans, and PET scans.

● *How is the brain organized and what do its higher structures do?*

Recite and Review: Pages 60-65

18. The human _____ is marked by advanced corticalization, or enlargement of the cerebral _____, which covers the outside surface of the cerebrum.

19. The _____ cerebral hemisphere contains speech or language "centers" in most people. It also specializes in _____, calculating, judging time and rhythm, and ordering complex movements.

20. The _____ hemisphere is largely non-verbal. It excels at spatial and perceptual skills, visualization, and recognition of _____, faces, and melodies.

21. "Split brains" have been created by _____ the corpus callosum. The split-brain individual shows a remarkable degree of independence between the right and left _____.

22. Another way to summarize specialization in the brain is to say that the _____ hemisphere is good at analysis and processing information sequentially; the _____ hemisphere processes information simultaneously and holistically.

23. The most basic functions of the lobes of the cerebral cortex are as follows: occipital lobes— _____; parietal lobes—bodily sensation; temporal lobes—_____and language; frontal lobes—motor control, speech, and abstract thought.

● *Why are the brain's association areas important? What happens when they are injured?*

Recite and Review: Pages 65-66

24. Association areas on the cortex are neither _____ nor _____ in function. They are related to more complex skills such as language, memory, recognition, and problem solving.

25. Damage to either Broca's area or Wernicke's area causes _____ and language problems known as aphasias.

26. Damage to Broca's area causes problems with _____ and pronunciation. Damage to Wernicke's area causes problems with the _____ of words.

● *What kinds of behaviors are controlled by the subcortex?*

Recite and Review: Pages 68-71

27. All of the brain areas below the _____ are called the subcortex.

28. The medulla contains centers essential for reflex control of _____ _____, breathing, and other "vegetative" functions.

29. The cerebellum maintains _____, posture, and muscle tone.

30. The reticular formation directs sensory and motor messages, and part of it, known as the RAS, acts as an _____ system for the cerebral cortex.

31. The thalamus carries _____ information to the cortex. The hypothalamus exerts powerful control over eating, drinking, sleep cycles, body temperature, and other basic _____ and behaviors.

32. The limbic system is strongly related to _____ and motivated behavior. It also contains distinct reward and punishment areas.

33. A part of the limbic system called the amygdala is related to _____. An area known as the hippocampus is important for forming _____.

● *Does the glandular system affect behavior?*

Recite and Review: Pages 71-74

34. The endocrine system provides _____ communication in the body through the release of _____ into the bloodstream. Endocrine glands influence moods, behavior, and even personality.

35. Many of the endocrine glands are influenced by the pituitary (the "_____ gland"), which is in turn influenced by the hypothalamus.

36. The pituitary supplies _____ hormone. Too little GH causes _____; too much causes giantism or acromegaly.

37. Body rhythms and _____ cycles are influenced by melatonin, secreted by the pineal gland.

38. The thyroid gland regulates _____. Hyperthyroidism refers to an overactive thyroid gland; hypothyroidism to an underactive thyroid.

39. The adrenal glands supply _____ and norepinephrine to activate the body. They also regulate salt balance, responses to stress, and they are a secondary source of _____ hormones.

● *In what ways do right- and left-handed individuals differ?*

Recite and Review: PSYCHOLOGY IN ACTION

40. Hand dominance ranges from strongly left- to strongly right-handed, with _____ handedness and ambidexterity in between.

41. Ninety percent of the population is basically _____, 10 percent _____.

42. The vast majority of people are right-handed and therefore _____ brain dominant for motor skills. Ninety-seven percent of right-handed persons and 68 percent of the left-handed also produce _____ from the left hemisphere.

43. In general, the _____ are less strongly lateralized in brain function than are _____ persons.

CONNECTIONS

1. _____   soma
2. _____   neurilemma
3. _____   axon collateral
4. _____   myelin
5. _____   dendrites
6. _____   axon terminals
7. _____   axon

8. _____ spinal cord
9. _____ autonomic system
10. _____ parasympathetic branch
11. _____ peripheral nervous system
12. _____ sympathetic branch
13. _____ brain
14. _____ somatic system

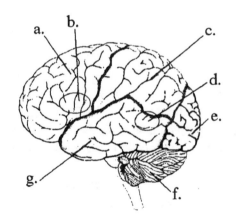

15. _____ Wernicke's area
16. _____ temporal lobe
17. _____ cerebellum
18. _____ Broca's area
19. _____ parietal lobe
20. _____ frontal lobe
21. _____ occipital lobe

22. _____ midbrain
23. _____ reticular formation
24. _____ cerebrum
25. _____ medulla
26. _____ hypothalamus
27. _____ corpus callosum
28. _____ pituitary
29. _____ spinal cord
30. _____ thalamus

31.	_____	pituitary	a. brain waves
32.	_____	pineal gland	b. radioactive glucose
33.	_____	thyroid gland	c. testosterone
34.	_____	adrenal glands	d. surgery
35.	_____	testes	e. metabolism
36.	_____	CT scan	f. electrode
37.	_____	EEG	g. growth hormone
38.	_____	ablation	h. epinephrine
39.	_____	deep lesioning	i. computerized X-rays
40.	_____	PET scan	j. melatonin

CHECK YOUR MEMORY

Check Your Memory: Pages 50-54

1. The dendrites receive incoming information from the neurilemma. T or F?
2. Human axons may be up to a meter long. T or F?
3. The resting potential is about plus 70 millivolts. T or F?
4. The interior of the axon becomes positive during an action potential. T or F?
5. The action potential is an all-or-nothing event. T or F?
6. The negative after-potential is due to an inward flow of potassium ions. T or F?
7. Nerve impulses travel faster in axons surrounded by myelin. T or F?
8. Neurotransmitters activate other neurons, neuropeptides activate muscles and glands. T or F?
9. Enkephalins are neuropeptides. T or F?
10. Neuropeptides regulate the activity of other neurons. T or F?

Check Your Memory: Pages 54-57

11. The neurilemma helps damaged nerve cell fibers regenerate after an injury. T or F?
12. Neurons in the brain and spinal cord can sometimes be repaired by neurogenesis. T or F?
13. The word *autonomic* means "self-limiting." T or F?
14. The parsympathetic branch quiets the body and returns it to a lower level of arousal. T or F?
15. The sympathetic system generally controls voluntary behavior. T or F?
16. Thirty-one cranial nerves leave the brain directly. T or F?
17. "Fight-or-flight" emergency reactions are produced by the autonomic nervous system. T or F?
18. Activity in the parasympathetic system increases heart rate and respiration. T or F?
19. In a reflex arc, motor neurons carry messages to effector cells. T or F?

Check Your Memory: Pages 57-59

20. Deep lesioning in the brain is usually done surgically. T or F?
21. Micro-electrodes are needed in order to record from single neurons. T or F?
22. CT scans form "maps" of brain activity. T or F?

23. Electroencephalography records waves of electrical activity produced by the brain. T or F?
24. Radioactive glucose is used to make PET scans. T or F?

Check Your Memory: Pages 60-65

25. Elephants have brain-body ratios similar to those of humans. T or F?
26. The corpus callosum connects the right and left brain hemispheres. T or F?
27. The cerebellum makes up a large part of the cerebral cortex. T or F?
28. Much of the cerebral cortex is made up of gray matter. T or F?
29. Damage to the left cerebral hemisphere usually causes spatial neglect. T or F?
30. In general, smart brains tend to be the hardest working brains. T or F?
31. The right half of the brain mainly controls left body areas. T or F?
32. Roger Sperry won a Nobel prize for his work on corticalization. T or F?
33. Cutting the reticular formation produces a "split brain." T or F?
34. Information from the right side of vision is sent directly to the right cerebral hemisphere. T or F?
35. The right hemisphere tends to be good at speaking, writing, and math. T or F?
36. The left hemisphere is mainly involved with analysis. T or F?
37. Both brain hemispheres are normally active at all times. T or F?
38. The motor cortex is found on the occipital lobes. T or F?
39. The somatosensory area is located on the parietal lobes. T or F?
40. Electrically stimulating the motor cortex causes movement in various parts of the body. T or F?

Check Your Memory: Pages 65-66

41. Large parts of the lobes of the brain are made up of association cortex. T or F?
42. Damage to either brain hemisphere usually causes an aphasia. T or F?
43. A person with Broca's aphasia might say "pear" when shown an apple. T or F?
44. Damage to Wernicke's area causes the condition known as spatial neglect. T or F?
45. Women are much more likely than men to use both cerebral hemispheres for language processing. T or F?

Check Your Memory: Pages 68-71

46. The cerebrum makes up much of the medulla. T or F?
47. Injury to the medulla may affect breathing. T or F?
48. Injury to the cerebellum affects attention and wakefulness. T or F?
49. Smell is the only major sense that does not pass through the thalamus. T or F?
50. Stimulating various parts of the limbic system can produce rage, fear, pleasure, or arousal. T or F?
51. The hippocampus is associated with hunger and eating. T or F?

Check Your Memory: Pages 71-74

52. Androgens ("male" hormones) are related to the sex drive in both men and women. T or F?
53. "Normal short" children grow faster when given synthetic growth hormone, but their final height is not taller. T or F?
54. Activity of the pituitary is influenced by the hypothalamus. T or F?
55. A person who is slow, sleepy, and overweight could be suffering from hypothyroidism. T or F?

56. Virilism and premature puberty may be caused by problems with the adrenal glands. T or F?
57. Steroid drugs may cause sexual impotence and breast enlargement in males. T or F?

Check Your Memory: PSYCHOLOGY IN ACTION

58. Left-handers have an advantage in fencing, boxing, and baseball. T or F?
59. Most left-handed persons produce speech from their right hemispheres. T or F?
60. Left- or right-handedness is inherited from one's parents. T or F?
61. On average, left-handed persons die at younger ages than right-handed persons do. T or F?

FINAL SURVEY AND REVIEW

● *How do nerve cells operate and communicate?*

1. The brain and nervous system are made up of linked nerve cells called _____, which pass information from one to another through _____.
2. The basic conducting fibers of neurons are axons, but _____ (a receiving area), the _____ (the cell body and also a receiving area), and axon terminals (the branching ends of an axon) are also involved in communication.
3. The firing of an _____ _____ (nerve impulse) is basically electrical, whereas communication between neurons is chemical.
4. An action potential occurs when the resting potential is altered enough to reach the _____ for firing. At that point, _____ ions flow into the axon, through ion channels.
5. After each action potential, the neuron has a brief negative _____. Next, _____ ions flow out of the axon, restoring the resting potential.
6. The action potential is an _____ event.
7. In chemical synapses, neurons release _____. These cross to receptor sites on the receiving cell, causing it to be excited or inhibited. For example, the transmitter chemical _____ activates muscles.
8. Chemicals called _____ do not carry messages directly. Instead, they regulate the activity of other neurons.
9. Opiate-like neural regulators called enkephalins and _____ are released in the brain to relieve pain and stress.

● *What are the functions of major parts of the nervous system?*

10. _____ are made of axons and associated tissues. Neurons and nerves in the _____ nervous system can often regenerate; damage in the _____ nervous system is usually permanent.
11. The nervous system can be divided into the _____ nervous system (the brain and _____ _____) and the peripheral nervous system.

12. The CNS includes the _____ (bodily) and _____ (involuntary) nervous systems.

13. The autonomic system has two divisions: the _____ (emergency, activating) branch and the _____ (sustaining, conserving) branch.

14. Thirty-one pairs of _____ nerves leave the spinal cord. Twelve pairs of _____ nerves leave the brain directly. Together, these nerves carry sensory and _____ messages between the brain and the body.

15. The simplest behavior is a _____ _____, which involves a sensory neuron, an _____ neuron, and a _____ neuron.

● How do we know how the brain works?

16. Conventional brain research relies on _____ (separation into parts), staining, ablation, deep lesioning, electrical recording, electrical _____, micro-electrode recording, EEG recording, and clinical studies.

17. Computer-enhanced techniques are providing three-dimensional images of the living human brain and its activities. Examples of such techniques are CT scans, _____ scans, and _____ scans, which record brain activity.

● How is the brain organized and what do its higher structures do?

18. The human brain is marked by advanced _____, or enlargement of the cerebral cortex, which covers the outside surface of the _____.

19. The right cerebral _____ contains speech or language "centers" in most people. It also specializes in writing, calculating, judging time and rhythm, and ordering complex _____.

20. The left hemisphere is largely non-verbal. It excels at _____ and perceptual skills, visualization, and recognition of patterns, _____, and melodies.

21. "Split brains" have been created by cutting the _____ _____. The split-brain individual shows a remarkable degree of independence between the right and left _____.

22. Another way to summarize specialization in the brain is to say that the left hemisphere is good at _____ and processing information sequentially; the right hemisphere processes information _____ and holistically.

23. The most basic functions of the lobes of the cerebral _____ are as follows: occipital lobes—vision; parietal lobes—bodily _____; temporal lobes—hearing and language; frontal lobes—motor control, _____, and abstract thought.

● Why are the brain's association areas important? What happens when they are injured?

24. Association areas on the cortex are neither _____ nor _____ in function. They are related to more complex skills such as _____, memory, recognition, and problem solving.

25. Damage to either Broca's area or Wernicke's area causes speech and language problems known as _____.

26. Damage to _____ area causes problems with speech and pronunciation. Damage to _____ area causes problems with the meaning of words.

● *What kinds of behaviors are controlled by the subcortex?*

27. All of the brain areas below the cortex are called the _____.
28. The _____ contains centers essential for reflex control of heart rate, breathing, and other "vegetative" functions.
29. The _____ maintains coordination, posture, and muscle tone.
30. The _____ formation directs sensory and motor messages, and part of it, known as the RAS, acts as an activating system for the _____ _____.
31. The _____ carries sensory information to the cortex. The _____ exerts powerful control over eating, drinking, sleep cycles, body temperature, and other basic motives and behaviors.
32. The _____ system is strongly related to emotion and motivation. It also contains distinct _____ and punishment areas.
33. A part of the limbic system called the _____ is related to fear. An area known as the _____ is important for forming lasting memories.

● *Does the glandular system affect behavior?*

34. The _____ system provides chemical communication in the body through the release of hormones into the _____.
35. Many of the endocrine glands are influenced by the _____ (the "master gland"), which is in turn influenced by the _____.
36. The _____ supplies growth hormone. Too little GH causes dwarfism; too much causes giantism or _____.
37. Body rhythms and sleep cycles are influenced by _____, secreted by the _____ gland.
38. The thyroid gland regulates metabolism. Hyperthyroidism refers to an _____ thyroid gland; hypothyroidism to an _____ thyroid.
39. The _____ glands supply epinephrine and norepinephrine to activate the body. They also regulate salt balance, responses to _____, and they are a secondary source of sex hormones.

● *In what ways do right- and left-handed individuals differ?*

40. _____ _____ ranges from strongly left- to strongly right-handed, with mixed handedness and _____ in between.
41. _____ percent of the population is basically right-handed, _____ percent left-handed.
42. The vast majority of people are _____ and therefore _____ brain dominant for motor skills. Ninety-seven percent of right-handed persons and 68 percent of the left-handed produce speech from the _____ hemisphere.

43. In general, the left-handed are less strongly _____ in brain function than are right-handed persons.

MASTERY TEST

1. At times of emergency, anger, or fear, what part of the nervous system becomes more active?
   a. corpus callosum of the forebrain   b. sympathetic branch of the ANS
   c. parasympathetic branch of the PNS   d. Broca's area

2. The highest and largest brain area in humans is the
   a. cerebrum   b. cerebellum   c. frontal lobes   d. gray matter of the callosum

3. A tumor in which brain area would most likely cause blind spots in vision?
   a. occipital lobe   b. temporal lobe   c. somatosensory area   d. association cortex

4. Neurotransmitters are found primarily in
   a. the spinal cord   b. the neurilemma   c. synapses   d. motor neurons

5. Enkephalins are an example of
   a. acetylcholine blockers   b. neuropeptides   c. receptor sites   d. adrenal hormones

6. Electrically stimulating a portion of which brain area would produce movements in the body?
   a. occipital lobe   b. frontal lobe   c. parietal lobe   d. temporal lobe

7. When a neuron reaches its threshold, a/an _____ occurs.
   a. volume potential   b. ion potential   c. action potential   d. dendrite potential

8. A person's ability to work as a commercial artist would be most impaired by damage to the
   a. left temporal lobe   b. right cerebral hemisphere   c. left cerebral hemisphere
   d. frontal association cortex

9. ESB will most likely produce anger if it is applied somewhere in the
   a. association cortex   b. limbic system   c. parasympathetic branch   d. reticular activating system

10. Information in neurons usually flows in what order?
    a. soma, dendrites, axon   b. dendrites, soma, axon   c. dendrites, myelin, axon terminals
    d. axon, soma, axon terminals

11. Regulating the activity of other neurons is most characteristic of
    a. neuropeptides   b. acetylcholine   c. reflex arcs   d. resting potentials

12. Nerve impulses occur when _____ rush into the axon.
    a. sodium ions   b. potassium ions   c. negative charges   d. neurotransmitters

13. Attempts to repair brain injuries by injecting immature neurons into the damaged area make use of the recently discovered existence of
    a. myelin   b. neurogenesis   c. neuropeptides   d. corticalization

14. Negative after-potentials are caused by the outward flow of _____ from the axon.
    a. negative charges   b. potassium ions   c. neurotransmitters   d. sodium ions

15. A person who says "bife" for bike and "seep" for sleep probably suffers from
    a. Broca's aphasia   b. Wernicke's aphasia   c. spatial neglect
    d. the condition known as "mindblindness"

16. Damage to which part of the limbic system would most likely impair memory?
    a. thalamus   b. hypothalamus   c. amygdala   d. hippocampus

17. Changes in heart rate, blood pressure, digestion, and sweating are controlled by the
    a. thoracic nerves   b. parietal lobes   c. somatic system   d. autonomic system

18. In which of the following pairs are both structures part of the forebrain?
    a. medulla, hypothalamus   b. cerebrum, cerebellum   c. medulla, thalamus   d. cerebrum, thalamus

19. Which of the following is a specialized type of X-ray?
    a. PET scan   b. CT scan   c. MRI scan   d. EEG scan

20. Which two problems are associated with the pituitary gland?
    a. dwarfism, acromegaly   b. virilism, acromegaly   c. mental retardation, dwarfism
    d. giantism, premature puberty

21. The cerebral hemispheres are interconnected by the
    a. reticular system   b. cerebellum   c. cerebrum   d. corpus callosum

22. Damage to which of the following would most likely make it difficult for a person to play catch with a ball?
    a. reticular formation   b. limbic system   c. cerebellum   d. association cortex

23. Speech, language, calculation, and analysis are special skills of the
    a. right cerebral hemisphere   b. limbic system   c. left cerebral hemisphere
    d. right somatosensory area

24. The usual flow of information in a reflex arc is
    a. cranial nerve, connector neuron, spinal nerve   b. sensory neuron, connector neuron, motor neuron
    c. effector cell, interneuron, connector neuron   d. sensory neuron, connector neuron, reflex neuron

25. A person will "hear" a series of sounds when which area of the cortex is electrically stimulated?
    a. frontal lobe   b. parietal lobe   c. occipital lobe   d. temporal lobe

26. Which of the following pairs contains the "master gland" and its master?
    a. pineal—thalamus   b. thyroid—RAS   c. pituitary—hypothalamus   d. adrenal—cortex

27. Many basic motives and emotions are influenced by the
    a. thalamus   b. hypothalamus   c. corpus callosum   d. cerebellum

28. Both surgical ablation and _____ remove brain tissue.
    a. the MEG technique   b. tomography   c. micro-electrode sampling   d. deep lesioning

29. Which of the following techniques requires access to the interior of the brain?
    a. micro-electrode recording   b. EEG recordings   c. PET scanning   d. functional MRI

30. Which of the following statements about handedness is FALSE?
    a. Handedness is directly inherited from one's parents.   b. A majority of left-handers produce speech from the left hemisphere.   c. The left-handed are less lateralized than the right-handed.   d. Left-handedness is an advantage in boxing and fencing.

ANSWERS

Recite and Review

1. brain, neurons
2. axons, axon
3. nerve impulse
4. resting, ions, ion
5. negative, axon
6. action
7. receptor, muscles
8. regulate
9. pain
10. axons, permanent
11. central, brain
12. bodily, involuntary
13. branch, branch
14. nerves, nerves
15. behavior, motor
16. electrical, clinical
17. images, activity
18. brain, cortex
19. left, writing
20. right, patterns
21. cutting, hemispheres
22. left, right
23. vision, hearing
24. sensory, motor
25. speech
26. grammar, meaning
27. cortex
28. heart rate
29. coordination
30. activating
31. sensory, motives
32. emotion
33. fear, memories
34. chemical, hormones
35. master
36. growth, dwarfism
37. sleep
38. metabolism
39. epinephrine, sex
40. mixed
41. right-handed, left-handed
42. left, speech
43. left-handed, right-handed

Connections

1. g
2. d
3. e
4. c
5. a
6. f
7. b
8. c or b
9. e
10. f or g
11. a
12. f or g
13. c or b
14. d

15. d
16. g
17. f
18. b
19. c
20. a
21. e
22. d
23. e
24. a
25. g
26. i
27. b
28. h
29. f
30. c
31. g
32. j
33. e
34. h
35. c
36. i
37. a
38. d
39. f
40. b

Check Your Memory

1. F
2. T
3. F
4. T
5. T
6. F
7. T
8. F
9. T
10. T
11. T
12. T
13. F
14. T
15. F
16. F
17. T
18. F
19. T

20. F
21. T
22. F
23. T
24. T
25. F
26. T
27. F
28. T
29. F
30. F
31. T
32. F
33. F
34. F
35. F
36. T
37. T
38. F
39. T
40. T
41. T
42. F
43. F
44. F
45. T
46. F
47. T
48. F
49. T
50. T
51. F
52. T
53. T
54. T
55. T
56. T
57. T
58. F
59. F
60. F
61. F

Final Survey and Review

1. neurons, synapses
2. dendrites, soma
3. action potential

4. threshold, sodium
5. after-potential, potassium
6. all-or-nothing
7. neurotransmitters, acetylcholine
8. neuropeptides
9. endorphins
10. Nerves, peripheral, central
11. central, spinal cord
12. somatic, autonomic
13. sympathetic, parasympathetic
14. spinal, cranial, motor
15. reflex arc, connector, motor
16. dissection, stimulation
17. MRI, PET
18. corticalization, cerebrum
19. hemisphere, movements
20. spatial, faces
21. corpus callosum, hemispheres
22. analysis, simultaneously
23. cortex, sensation, speech
24. sensory, motor, language
25. aphasias
26. Broca's, Wernicke's
27. subcortex
28. medulla
29. cerebellum
30. reticular, cerebral cortex
31. thalamus, hypothalamus
32. limbic, reward
33. amygdala, hippocampus
34. endocrine, bloodstream
35. pituitary, hypothalamus
36. pituitary, acromegaly
37. melatonin, pineal
38. overactive, underactive
39. adrenal, stress
40. Hand dominance, ambidexterity
41. Ninety, 10
42. right-handed, left, left
43. lateralized

Mastery Test

1. b (p. 56)
2. a (p. 60)
3. a (p. 64)
4. c (p. 53)
5. b (p. 53)
6. b (p. 65)
7. c (p. 51)
8. b (p. 63)
9. b (p. 69)

10. b (p. 50)
11. a (p. 53)
12. a (p. 51)
13. b (p. 54)
14. b (p. 52)
15. a (p. 66)
16. d (p. 70)
17. d (p. 54)
18. d (p. 69)
19. b (p. 58)
20. a (p. 72)

21. d (p. 61)
22. c (p. 68)
23. c (p. 62-63)
24. b (p. 56)
25. d (p. 65)
26. c (p. 72)
27. b (p. 68)
28. d (p. 57)
29. a (p. 58)
30. a (p. 76)

Chapter 3

Child Development

CHAPTER OVERVIEW

Heredity affects personal characteristics, including temperament, and it organizes the human growth sequence. Environmental influences can have especially lasting effects during sensitive periods in development. Prenatal development is affected by diseases, drugs, radiation, or the mother's diet and health. Early perceptual, intellectual, and emotional deprivation seriously retards development. Deliberate enrichment of the environment has a beneficial effect on early development.

Most psychologists accept that heredity and environment are inseparable and interacting forces. A child's developmental level reflects heredity, environment, and the effects of the child's own behavior.

Human newborns have adaptive reflexes, are capable of learning, and have visual preferences, especially for familiar faces. Maturation underlies the orderly sequence of motor, cognitive, language, and emotional development.

Emotional attachment of infants to their caregivers is a critical event in social development.

Caregiving styles affect social, emotional, and intellectual development. Optimal caregiving includes proactive involvement, a good fit between the temperaments of parent and child, and responsiveness to a child's needs and signals. Three major parenting styles are authoritarian, permissive, and authoritative (effective). Effective parental discipline tends to emphasize child management techniques, rather than power assertion or withdrawal of love.

Language development is based on a biological predisposition, which is augmented by learning. Language acquisition begins with prelanguage communication between parent and child.

Jean Piaget theorized that children go through a series of cognitive stages as they develop intellectually. Learning principles provide an alternate explanation which does not assume that cognitive development occurs in stages. Lev Vygotsky's sociocultural theory says that cognitive gains occur primarily in a child's zone of proximal development. Adults who engage in the scaffolding of a child's intellectual growth also impart cultural values and beliefs to the child.

Responsibility, mutual respect, consistency, love, encouragement, and clear communication are features of effective parenting.

LEARNING OBJECTIVES

To demonstrate mastery of this chapter, you should be able to:

1. Define *developmental psychology* and name its principal focus.
2. Define the terms *nature* and *nurture* as they relate to human development. Define the terms *heredity* and *conception.*
3. Define or describe each of the following terms:
   a. chromosome   b. gene   c. polygenic   d. dominant gene   e. recessive gene
4. Describe genetic counseling and genetic screening. Differentiate amniocentesis from chorionic villus sampling.
5. Characterize the three types of children according to temperament and explain how these temperamental differences influence development.
6. Discuss the concept of sensitive periods.
7. Distinguish between congenital and genetic disorders.
8. Describe the relationship between the blood supplies of the mother and her developing child. Discuss the effect of teratogens on the unborn child, including the effects of drugs, alcohol (include a description of fetal alcohol syndrome), and tobacco.
9. Briefly differentiate conventional deliveries from prepared childbirth in terms of methods and effects.
10. Briefly describe the two most important differences in the brain of a newborn and brain of an adult.
11. Briefly discuss the impact of poverty on children's IQ and behavior.
12. Review the research demonstrating the benefits of enriched environments.
13. Briefly discuss the "Mozart effect" and the problems surrounding the original research.
14. Describe the apparent outcome of the nature-nurture debate. List the three factors that combine to determine a person's developmental level.
15. Name and describe four adaptive reflexes of a neonate.
16. Describe the intellectual capabilities and the sensory preferences of a neonate.
17. Discuss the concept of maturation and define the terms *cephalocaudal* and *proximodistal.*
18. Discuss the concept of readiness. Include in your answer the outcome of forcing a child to learn skills too early.
19. With respect to maturation, describe the course of emotional development.
20. Explain how there is an interplay between the emotions of infants and adults. Include the concept of the social smile.
21. Explain the concepts of self-awareness and social referencing.
22. Discuss the importance of emotional attachment, including the concept of separation anxiety. Include in your answer a differentiation of Ainsworth's attachment types as well as the key to secure attachments.
23. Define *contact comfort,* and explain the importance of breastfeeding and meeting a child's affectional needs.
24. Discuss the effects of daycare on attachment.
25. Discuss the importance of children's play, including the concepts of solitary play and cooperative play.

26. Describe the extremes of the maternal caregiving styles and their results.
27. Discuss the importance of paternal influences in child development. Compare these influences to maternal ones.
28. Compare and contrast the following three parenting styles and their effects on children:
    a. authoritarian   b. overly permissive   c. authoritative

The following objective is related to the material in the "Exploring Psychology" section of the text.
29. Briefly describe some of the differences in child-rearing practices of the four ethnic groups listed in this section, and the conclusion that can be drawn from these differences.

30. Give a brief description of each of the following childrearing techniques and describe their effects on children:
    a. power assertion   b. withdrawal of love   c. management techniques (include the concept of self-esteem)
31. List and briefly describe the five stages of language acquisition.
32. Briefly discuss the concept of the "terrible twos."
33. Describe what the "language dance" is and explain why children probably do it.
34. Define the term *psycholinguist*. Describe the role of learning in the acquisition of language.
35. Explain how parents communicate with infants before infants can talk. Include the ideas of signals, turn taking, and parentese.
36. Explain how a child's intelligence and thinking differ from an adult's. Explain the concept of transformations.
37. List (in order) and briefly describe Piaget's four stages of cognitive development. Include an explanation of assimilation and accommodation.
38. Briefly describe the research concerning a child's theory of mind.
39. Describe the methods of encouraging intellectual development in children in each of Piaget's cognitive stages.
40. Briefly describe the dangers of forced teaching.
41. Describe the research that indicates that Piaget may have underestimated infant cognitive abilities.
42. Describe the sociocultural theory of Lev Vygotsky, including a comparison to Piaget and the terms *zone of proximal development* and *scaffolding*.

The following objectives are related to the material in the "Psychology in Action" section of the text.
43. Name the two most important areas of effective parent-child relationships.
44. Discuss the importance of using consistent discipline in childrearing.
45. List seven guidelines that should be followed if physical punishment is used in disciplining children.
46. List the four basic ingredients (Dinkmeyer & McKay) of a positive parent-child relationship.
47. Describe four important aspects of communication between parents and children, including what Dr. Thomas Gordon calls an "I" message.
48. Describe the use of natural and logical consequences to correct children's misbehavior.

RECITE AND REVIEW

● *How do heredity and environment affect development?*

Recite and Review: Pages 81-88

1. Developmental psychology is the study of progressive changes in _____ and abilities, from _____ to _____.

2. The nature-nurture debate concerns the relative contributions to development of heredity (_____) and environment (_____).

3. Hereditary instructions are carried by _____ (deoxyribonucleic acid) in the form of chromosomes and _____ in each cell of the body.

4. Most characteristics are polygenic (influenced by a combination of _____) and reflect the combined effects of dominant and recessive _____.

5. Heredity organizes the general human growth sequence—the general pattern of _____ _____ from birth to death.

6. Heredity also influences differences in temperament (the physical core of _____). Most infants fall into one of three temperament categories: easy children, _____ children, and slow-to-warm-up children.

7. During pregnancy, _____ testing of the fetus can be done by amniocentesis or chorionic villlus _____.

8. Environment refers to all _____ conditions that affect development.

9. A variety of sensitive periods (times of increased _____ to environmental influences) exist in development.

10. Prenatal development is subject to _____ influences in the form of diseases, drugs, radiation, or the mother's diet and health.

11. Prenatal damage to the fetus may cause congenital problems, or _____ _____. In contrast, genetic problems are inherited from one's parents.

12. Prepared childbirth tends to reduce pain and shorten _____.

13. Early perceptual, intellectual, and emotional deprivation seriously retards _____.

14. Poverty greatly increases the likelihood that children will experience various forms of _____.

15. Deliberate enrichment of the _____ in infancy and early childhood has a beneficial effect on development.

16. Ultimately, most psychologists accept that _____ and environment are inseparable and interacting forces.

17. A child's developmental level (current state of development) reflects heredity, environment, and the effects of the child's _____ _____.

● *What can newborn babies do?*

Recite and Review: Pages 89-91

18. The human _____ (newborn) has a number of _____ reflexes, including the grasping, rooting, sucking, and Moro reflexes.

19. Newborns begin to _____ immediately and they imitate adults.

20. Tests in a looking chamber reveal a number of _____ preferences in the newborn. The neonate is drawn to complex, _____, curved, and brightly-lighted designs.

21. Infants prefer human face patterns, especially _____ _____. In later infancy, interest in the unfamiliar emerges.

● *What influence does maturation have on early development?*

Recite and Review: Pages 91-94

22. Maturation of the body and nervous system underlies the orderly _____ of motor, cognitive, language, and emotional development.

23. While the rate of maturation varies from child to child, the _____ is nearly universal.

24. The development of _____ control (motor development) is cephalocaudal (from head to toe) and proximodistal (from the _____ of the body to the extremities).

25. Many early _____ are subject to the principle of readiness.

26. Emotional development begins with a capacity for _____ excitement. After that the first pleasant and unpleasant emotions develop.

27. Some psychologists believe that basic emotional expressions are _____ and that some appear as early as 2.5 months of age.

28. By age 10 months, babies display a social smile when other _____ are nearby.

● *Of what significance is a child's emotional bond with parents?*

Recite and Review: Pages 94-97

29. _____ development refers to the emergence of self-awareness and forming relationships with parents and others.

30. Self-awareness (consciousness of oneself as a person) and _____ referencing (obtaining guidance from others) are elements of early _____ development.

31. Emotional attachment of human infants to their _____ is a critical early event.

32. Infant attachment is reflected by _____ anxiety (distress when infants are away from parents).

33. The quality of attachment can be classified as _____, insecure-avoidant, or insecure-ambivalent.

34. High-quality day care does not _____ children; high-quality care can, in fact, accelerate some areas of development.

35. Babies need contact comfort, a reassuring feeling they get from _____ their mother.

36. A child's _____ development is also affected by playing with other children. For example, cooperative _____ is a major step toward participation in social life outside the family.

37. An infant's affectional _____ are every bit as important as more obvious needs for physical care.

● *How important are parenting styles?*

Recite and Review: Pages 98-101

38. Caregiving styles (patterns of parental care) have a substantial impact on emotional and intellectual

_____.

39. Maternal influences (the effects _____ have on their children) tend to center on caregiving.

40. Optimal caregiving includes proactive maternal _____, a good fit between the temperaments of parent and child, and responsiveness to a child's needs and _____.

41. Paternal influences differ in their impact because _____ tend to function as a playmate for the infant.

42. Authoritarian parents enforce rigid _____ and demand strict obedience to

_____.

43. Overly permissive parents give little _____ and don't hold children accountable for their actions.

44. Authoritative (_____) parents supply firm and consistent guidance, combined with love and affection.

45. Effective child _____ is based on a consistent framework of guidelines for acceptable behavior.

46. Good discipline tends to emphasize child management techniques (especially communication), rather than _____ assertion or withdrawal of _____.

47. _____ techniques tend to produce the highest levels of self-esteem in children.

● *How do children acquire language?*

Recite and Review: Pages 102-105

48. Language development proceeds from control of _____, to cooing, then babbling, the use of single words, and then to telegraphic _____.

49. The patterns of early speech suggest a _____ predisposition to acquire language.

50. Psycholinguists (psychologists who study _____) believe that innate language predispositions are augmented by _____.

51. Prelanguage communication between parent and child involves shared rhythms, non-verbal _____, and turn-taking.

52. Parents help children learn language by using distinctive caretaker _____ or parentese.

● *How do children learn to think?*

Recite and Review: Pages 105-111

53. The intellects of children are _____ abstract than those of adults. Jean Piaget theorized that _____ growth occurs through a combination of assimilation and accommodation.

54. Piaget also held that children go through a fixed series of cognitive _____.

55. These are: sensorimotor (0-2), preoperational (2-7), _____ operational (7-11), and formal _____ (11-adult).

56. Learning theorists dispute the idea that cognitive development occurs in _____. Recent studies suggest infants are capable of levels of thinking beyond that observed by _____.

57. Young children don't seem to understand that the _____ of other people contain different information, beliefs, and thoughts than theirs do. In other words, they have a very simplified theory of _____.

58. A one-step-ahead strategy that takes into account the child's level of _____ development helps adapt instruction to a child's needs.

59. According to the sociocultural theory of Russian scholar Lev Vygotsky, a child's interactions with others are most likely to aid _____ development if they they take place within the child's _____ of proximal _____.

60. Adults help children learn how to think by scaffolding, or _____, their attempts to solve problems or discover principles.

61. During their collaborations with adults, children learn important cultural _____ and values.

● *How do effective parents discipline their children?*

Recite and Review: PSYCHOLOGY IN ACTION

62. Responsibility, mutual _____, consistency, love, encouragement, and clear _____ are features of effective parenting.

63. Much misbehavior can be managed by use of I-_____ and by applying _____ and logical consequences to children's behavior.

CONNECTIONS

1. _____	grasping reflex	a.	rapid motor learning
2. _____	rooting reflex	b.	DNA area
3. _____	Moro reflex	c.	old age
4. _____	readiness	d.	nature
5. _____	gene	e.	palm grip
6. _____	chromosome	f.	nurture
7. _____	senescence	g.	startled embrace
8. _____	heredity	h.	conception to birth
9. _____	environment	i.	colored body
10. _____	prenatal period	j.	food search

11. _____ FAS   a. control of muscles and movement

12. _____ Vygotsky   b. caregiving style

13. _____ motor development   c. love and attention

14. _____ super mother   d. vowel sounds

15. _____ sensitive period   e. prenatal alcohol

16. _____ attachment   f. sociocultural theory

17. _____ affectional needs   g. vowels and consonants

18. _____ cooing   h. emotional bond

19. _____ babbling   i. caretaker speech

20. _____ parentese   j. magnified environmental impact

21. _____ assimilation   a. changing existing mental patterns

22. _____ accommodation   b. egocentricism

23. _____ sensorimotor stage   c. applying mental patterns

24. _____ preoperational stage   d. abstract principles

25. _____ concrete operations   e. social development

26. _____ formal operations   f. stage theory of cognitive development

27. _____ cooperative play   h. conservation

28. _____ Piaget   i. object permanence

29. _____ hothousing   j. skilled support for learning

30. _____ scaffolding   k. forced teaching

CHECK YOUR MEMORY

Check Your Memory: Pages 81-88

1. Developmental psychology is the study of progressive changes in behavior and abilities during childhood. T or F?

2. Each cell in the human body (except sperm cells and ova) contains 23 chromosomes. T or F?

3. The order of organic bases in DNA acts as a genetic code. T or F?

4. Two brown-eyed parents cannot have a blue-eyed child. T or F?

5. Identical twins have identical genes. T or F?

6. More children have a slow-to-warm-up temperament than a difficult temperament. T or F?

7. The sensitive period during which German measles can damage the fetus occurs near the end of pregnancy. T or F?

8. Teratogens are substances capable of causing birth defects. T or F?

9. An infant damaged by exposure to X-rays during the prenatal period suffers from a genetic problem. T or F?

10. Many drugs can reach the fetus within the intrauterine environment. T or F?

11. To prevent FAS, the best advice to pregnant women is to get plenty of rest, vitamins, and good nutrition. T or F?

12. Prepared childbirth tends to reduce the need for pain medications during birth. T or F?

13. Poverty is associated with retarded emotional and intellectual development. T or F?

14. In animals, enriched environments can actually increase brain size and weight. T or F?

15. There is evidence that the "Mozart effect" might just be based on the fact that college students were more alert or in a better mood after listening to music. T or F?

Check Your Memory: Pages 89-91

16. The Moro reflex helps infants hold onto objects placed in their hands. T or F?

17. As early as 9 weeks of age, infants can imitate actions a full day after seeing them. T or F?

18. Three-day-old infants prefer to look at simple colored backgrounds, rather than more complex patterns. T or F?

19. After age 2, familiar faces begin to hold great interest for infants. T or F?

Check Your Memory: Pages 91-94

20. Most infants learn to stand alone before they begin crawling. T or F?

21. Motor development follows a top-down, center-outward pattern. T or F?

22. Toilet training should begin soon after a child is 1 year old. T or F?

23. Anger and fear are the first two emotions to emerge in infancy. T or F?

24. An infant's social smile appears within one month after birth. T or F?

Check Your Memory: Pages 94-97

25. Most infants have to be 15 weeks old before they can recognize themselves on videotape. T or F?

26. Securely attached infants turn away from mother when she returns after a period of separation. T or F?

27. A small number of children per caregiver is desirable in day care settings. T or F?

28. Children who spend too much time in poor quality day care tend to be insecure and aggressive. T or F?

29. The question of when secure attachment occurs is less important than the question of whether it occurs at all. T or F?

30. Children typically first begin to engage in cooperative play around age 4 or 5. T or F?

Check Your Memory: Pages 98-101

31. Early patterns of competence are well established by the time a child reaches age 3. T or F?

32. The "zoo-keeper" mother provides poor physical, emotional, and intellectual care for her child. T or F?

33. The goodness of fit between parents and children refers mainly to how compatible their temperaments are. T or F?

34. Responsive parents are sensitive to a child's feelings, need, rhythms, and signals. T or F?

35. Fathers typically spend about half their time in caregiving and half playing with the baby. T or F?
36. Paternal play tends to be more physically arousing for infants than maternal play is. T or F?
37. Authoritarian parents view children as having adult-like responsibilities. T or F?
38. Permissive parents basically give their children the message "Do it because I say so." T or F?
39. The children of authoritarian parents tend to be independent, assertive, and inquiring. T or F?
40. Asian cultures tend to be group-oriented and they emphasize interdependence among individuals. T or F?
41. As a means of child discipline, power assertion refers to rejecting a child. T or F?
42. Severely punished children tend to be defiant and aggressive. T or F?
43. Punishment is most effective when it is given immediately after a disapproved act. T or F?

Check Your Memory: Pages 102-105

44. The single-word stage begins at about 6 months of age. T or F?
45. "That red ball mine," is an example of telegraphic speech. T or F?
46. Noam Chomsky believes that basic language patterns are innate. T or F?
47. The "terrible twos" refers to the two-word stage of language development. T or F?
48. The "I'm going to get you" game is an example of prelanguage communication. T or F?
49. Parentese is spoken in higher pitched tones with a musical inflection. T or F?

Check Your Memory: Pages 105-111

50. According to Piaget, children first learn to make transformations at about age 3. T or F?
51. Assimilation refers to modifying existing ideas to fit new situations or demands. T or F?
52. Cognitive development during the sensorimotor stage is mostly non-verbal. T or F?
53. Reversibility of thoughts and the concept of conservation both appear during the concrete operational stage. T or F?
54. Three-year-old children are surprisingly good at understanding what other people are thinking. T or F?
55. An understanding of hypothetical possibilities develops during the preoperational stage. T or F?
56. Playing peekaboo is a good way to establish the permanence of objects for children in the sensorimotor stage. T or F?
57. Contrary to what Piaget observed, infants as young as 3 months of age show signs of object permanence. T or F?
58. Vygotsky's key insight was that children's thinking develops through dialogues with more capable persons. T or F?
59. Learning experiences are most helpful when they take place outside of a child's zone of proximal development. T or F?
60. Scaffolding is like setting up temporary bridges to help children move into new mental territory. T or F?
61. Vygotsky empasized that children use adults to learn about their culture and society. T or F?

Check Your Memory: PSYCHOLOGY IN ACTION

62. Consistency of child discipline is more important than whether limits on children's behavior are strict or lenient. T or F?
63. Encouragement means giving recognition for effort and improvement. T or F?
64. Logical consequences should be stated as you-messages. T or F?

FINAL SURVEY AND REVIEW

● *How do heredity and environment affect development?*

1. _____ psychology is the study of _____ changes in behavior and abilities, from birth to death.

2. The nature-nurture debate concerns the relative contributions to development of _____ (nature) and _____ (nurture).

3. Hereditary instructions are carried by DNA (_____ acid) in the form of _____ ("colored bodies") and genes in every cell.

4. Most characteristics are _____ (influenced by a combination of genes) and reflect the combined effects of dominant and _____ genes.

5. Heredity organizes the general human _____ _____—the general pattern of physical development from birth to death.

6. Heredity also influences differences in _____ (the physical foundations of personality). Most infants fall into one of three categories: _____ children, difficult children, and _____ children.

7. During pregnancy, genetic testing of the fetus can be done by _____ of the amniotic fluid or _____ villlus sampling.

8. _____ refers to all external conditions that affect development.

9. A variety of _____ _____ (times of increased sensitivity to environmental influences) exist in development.

10. During pregnancy, _____ development is subject to environmental influences in the form of diseases, _____, _____, or the mother's diet and health.

11. Prenatal damage to the fetus may cause _____ problems, or birth defects. In contrast, _____ problems are inherited from one's parents.

12. _____ childbirth tends to reduce _____ and shorten labor.

13. Early perceptual and intellectual _____ seriously retards development.

14. _____ greatly increases the likelihood that children will experience various forms of deprivation.

15. Deliberate _____ of the environment in infancy and early childhood has a beneficial effect on development.

16. Ultimately, most psychologists accept that heredity and environment are inseparable and _____ forces.

17. A child's _____ _____ (current state of development) reflects heredity, environment, and the effects of the child's own behavior.

● *What can newborn babies do?*

18. The human neonate (newborn) has a number of adaptive reflexes, including the _____, rooting, _____, and _____ reflexes.

19. Newborns begin to learn immediately and they _____ (mimic) adults.

20. Tests in a _____ _____ reveal a number of visual preferences in the newborn. The neonate is drawn to _____, circular, curved, and brightly-lighted designs.

21. Infants prefer _____ _____ patterns, especially familiar faces. In later infancy, interest in the _____ emerges.

● *What influence does maturation have on early development?*

22. _____ of the body and _____ _____ underlies the orderly sequence of motor, cognitive, language, and emotional development.

23. While the _____ of maturation varies from child to child, the order is nearly _____.

24. The development of muscular control (_____ development) is _____ (from head to toe) and _____ (from the center of the body to the extremities.

25. Many early skills are subject to the principle of _____.

26. Emotional development begins with a capacity for general _____. After that the first _____ and _____ emotions develop.

27. Some psychologists believe that basic _____ expressions are innate and that some appear as early as 2.5 _____ of age.

28. By age 10 months, babies display a _____ smile when other people are nearby.

● *Of what significance is a child's emotional bond with parents?*

29. Social development refers to the emergence of self-_____ and forming _____ with parents and others.

30. _____ (consciousness of oneself as a person) and social _____ (obtaining guidance from others) are elements of early social development.

31. Emotional _____ of human infants to their caregivers is a critical early event.

32. Infant attachment is reflected by separation _____ (distress when infants are away from parents).

33. The quality of attachment can be classified as secure, insecure-_____, or insecure- _____.

34. _____ day care does not harm children; excellent care can, in fact, _____ some areas of development.

35. Babies need _____ comfort, a reassuring feeling they get from touching their mother.

36. A child's social development is also affected by playing with other children. For example, _____ play is a major step toward participation in social life outside the family.

37. An infant's _____ needs are every bit as important as more obvious needs for physical care.

How important are parenting styles?

38. _____ _____ (patterns of parental care) have a substantial impact on emotional and intellectual development.
39. _____ influences (the effects mothers have on their children) tend to center on _____.
40. Optimal caregiving includes _____ maternal involvement, a good fit between the _____ of parent and child, and responsiveness to a child's needs and signals.
41. _____ influences differ in their impact because fathers tend to function as a _____ for the infant.
42. _____ parents enforce rigid rules and demand strict obedience to authority.
43. Overly _____ parents give little guidance and don't hold children accountable for their actions.
44. _____ (effective) parents supply firm and consistent guidance, combined with love and affection.
45. Effective child discipline is based on consistent parental _____ concerning acceptable behavior.
46. Good discipline tends to emphasize child _____ techniques (especially communication), rather than power _____ or withdrawal of love.
47. Management techniques tend to produce the highest levels of _____ in children.

How do children acquire language?

48. Language development proceeds from control of crying, to _____, then _____, the use of single words, and then to _____ speech (two-word sentences).
49. The patterns of early speech suggest a biological _____ to acquire language.
50. _____ (psychologists who study language) believe that innate language predispositions are augmented by learning.
51. _____ communication between parent and child involves shared rhythms, non-verbal signals, and _____-taking.
52. Parents help children learn language by using distinctive caretaker speech or _____.

How do children learn to think?

53. The intellects of children are less _____ than those of adults. Jean Piaget theorized that cognitive growth occurs through a combination of _____ and accommodation.
54. Piaget also held that children go through a fixed series of _____ stages.
55. The stages are: _____ (0-2), _____ (2-7), concrete operational (7-11), and formal operations (11-adult).
56. _____ theorists dispute the idea that cognitive development occurs in stages. Recent studies suggest infants are capable of levels of _____ beyond that observed by Piaget.

57. Young children don't seem to understand that the _____ of other people contain different information, beliefs, and thoughts than theirs do. In other words, they have a very simplified _____ of _____.

58. A _____ strategy that takes into account the child's level of cognitive development helps adapt instruction to a child's needs.

59. According to the _____ theory of Russian scholar Lev _____, a child's interactions with others are most likely to aid cognitive development if they they take place within the child's zone of _____ development.

60. Adults help children learn how to think by _____, or supporting, their attempts to solve problems or discover principles.

61. During their collaborations with others, children learn important _____ beliefs and values.

● *How do effective parents discipline their children?*

62. Responsibility, mutual respect, _____, love, _____, and clear communication are features of effective parenting.

63. Much misbehavior can be managed by use of I-messages and by applying natural and _____ _____ to children's behavior.

MASTERY TEST

1. The universal patterns of the human growth sequence can be attributed to
   a. recessive genes   b. environment   c. polygenic imprinting   d. heredity

2. Exaggerated or musical voice inflections are characteristic of
   a. prelanguage turn-taking   b. parentese   c. telegraphic speech   d. prompting and expansion

3. The emotion most clearly expressed by newborn infants is
   a. joy   b. fear   c. anger   d. excitement

4. Explaining things abstractly or symbolically to a child becomes most effective during which stage of cognitive development?
   a. postconventional   b. formal operations   c. preoperational   d. post-intuitive

5. An infant startled by a loud noise will typically display
   a. a Moro reflex   b. a rooting reflex   c. a Meltzoff reflex   d. an imprinting reflex

6. If one identical twin has a *Y* chromosome, the other must have a
   a. recessive chromosome   b. sex-linked trait   c. dominant chromosome   d. *Y* chromosome

7. Ideas about Piaget's stages and the cognitive abilities of infants are challenged by infants' reactions to
   a. hypothetical possibilities   b. impossible events   c. turn-taking   d. separation anxiety

8. The type of play that is observed first in most children is called
   a. selective play   b. secure play   c. solitary play   d. social play

9. The largest percentage of children display what type of temperament?
   a. easy   b. difficult   c. slow-to-warm-up   d. generic

10. Which of the following is a congenital problem?
    a. FAS   b. sickle-cell anemia   c. hemophilia   d. muscular dystrophy

11. A child might begin to question the idea that Santa Claus's sack could carry millions of toys when the child has grasped the concept of
    a. assimilation   b. egocentricism   c. conservation   d. reversibility of permanence

12. In most areas of development, heredity and environment are
    a. independent   b. interacting   c. conflicting   d. responsible for temperament

13. Children who grow up in poverty run a high risk of
    a. insecure scaffolding   b. hospitalism   c. deprivation   d. colostrum

14. By definition, a trait that is controlled by a dominant gene cannot be
    a. eugenic   b. hereditary   c. carried by DNA   d. polygenic

15. _____ development proceeds head-down and center-outward.
    a. Cognitive   b. Motor   c. Prelanguage   d. Preoperational

16. You could test for _____ by videotaping a child and then letting the child see the video on television.
    a. social referencing   b. self-awareness   c. the quality of attachment   d. the degree of readiness

17. After age 2, infants become much more interested in
    a. bonding   b. non-verbal communication   c. familiar voices   d. unfamiliar faces

18. According to Piaget, one of the major developments during the sensorimotor stage is emergence of the concept of
    a. assimilation   b. accommodation   c. object permanence   d. transformation

19. Poverty is to deprivation as early childhood stimulation is to
    a. imprinting   b. enrichment   c. responsiveness   d. assimilation

20. Which principle is most relevant to the timing of toilet training?
    a. readiness   b. sensitive periods   c. non-verbal signals   d. assimilation

21. High self-esteem is most often a product of what style of child discipline?
    a. power assertion   b. child management   c. withdrawal of love   d. the natural consequences method

22. Consonants first enter a child's language when the child begins
    a. babbling b. cooing c. the single word stage d. turn-taking

23. Physically arousing play is typically an element of
    a. the zoo-keeper mother's caregiving style b. paternal influences c. proactive maternal involvement
    d. secure attachment

24. Insecure attachment is revealed by
    a. separation anxiety b. seeking to be near the mother after separation
    c. turning away from the mother after separation d. social referencing

25. A healthy balance between the rights of parents and their children is characteristic of
    a. authoritarian parenting b. permissive parenting c. authoritative parenting d. consistent parenting

26. Studies of infant imitation
    a. are conducted in a looking chamber b. confirm that infants mimic adult facial gestures
    c. show that self-awareness precedes imitation d. are used to assess the quality of infant attachment

27. Threatening, accusing, bossing, and lecturing children is most characteristic of
    a. PET b. you-messages c. applying natural consequences d. management techniques

28. Three-year-old Sheila is unable to fully understand what other people think and feel, because at
    her age she has a very limited
    a. attachment to others b. theory of mind c. sensorimotor capacity
    d. zone of proximal development

29. According to Vygotsky, children learn important cultural beliefs and values when adults provide
    _____ to help them gain new ideas and skills.
    a. scaffolding b. proactive nurturance c. imprinting stimuli d. parentese

30. One thing that all forms of effective child discipline have in common is that they
    a. are consistent b. make use of punishment c. involve temporary withdrawal of love
    d. emphasize you-messages

31. A *major* problem with using the "Mozart effect" as a basis for promoting intellectual
    development in babies is that the original research was done on
    a. laboratory animals b. mentally retarded infants c. children in the concrete operations stage
    d. college students

ANSWERS

Recite and Review

1. behavior, birth, death
2. nature, nurture
3. DNA, genes
4. genes, genes
5. physical development
6. personality, difficult
7. genetic, sampling
8. external
9. sensitivity
10. environmental
11. birth defects
12. labor
13. development
14. deprivation
15. environment
16. heredity
17. own behavior
18. neonate, adaptive
19. learn
20. visual, circular
21. familiar faces
22. sequence
23. order
24. muscular, center
25. skills
26. general
27. innate
28. people
29. Social
30. social, social
31. caregivers
32. separation
33. secure
34. harm
35. touching
36. social, play
37. needs
38. development
39. mothers
40. involvement, preferences
41. fathers
42. rules, authority
43. guidance
44. effective
45. discipline
46. power, love
47. Management
48. crying, speech
49. biological
50. language, learning
51. signals
52. speech
53. less, intellectual
54. stages
55. concrete, operations
56. stages, Piaget
57. minds, mind
58. cognitive
59. cognitive, zone, development
60. supporting
61. beliefs
62. respect, communication
63. messages, natural

Connections

1. e
2. j
3. g
4. a
5. b
6. i
7. c
8. d
9. f
10. h
11. e
12. f
13. a
14. b
15. j
16. h
17. c
18. d
19. g
20. i
21. c
22. a
23. j
24. b
25. h
26. d
27. e
28. f
29. k
30. j

Check Your Memory

1. F
2. F
3. T
4. F
5. T
6. T
7. F
8. T
9. F
10. T
11. F
12. T
13. T
14. T
15. T
16. F
17. F
18. F
19. F

20. F
21. T
22. F
23. F
24. F
25. F
26. F
27. T
28. T
29. T
30. T
31. T
32. F
33. T
34. T
35. F
36. T
37. T
38. F
39. F
40. T
41. F
42. T
43. T
44. F
45. F
46. T
47. F
48. T
49. T
50. F
51. F
52. T
53. T
54. F
55. F
56. T
57. T
58. T
59. F
60. T
61. T
62. T
63. T
64. F

Final Survey and Review

1. Developmental, progressive
2. heredity, environment
3. deoxyribonucleic, chromosomes
4. polygenic, recessive
5. growth sequence
6. temperament, easy, slow-to-warm-up
7. amniocentesis, chorionic
8. Environment
9. sensitive periods
10. prenatal, drugs, radiation
11. congenital, genetic
12. Prepared, pain
13. deprivation
14. Poverty
15. enrichment
16. interacting
17. developmental level
18. grasping, sucking, Moro
19. imitate
20. looking chamber, complex
21. human face, unfamiliar
22. Maturation, nervous system
23. rate, universal
24. motor, cephalocaudal, proximodistal
25. readiness
26. excitement, pleasant, unpleasant
27. emotional, months
28. social
29. awareness, relationships
30. Self-awareness, referencing
31. attachment
32. anxiety
33. avoidant, ambivalent
34. High-quality, accelerate
35. contact
36. cooperative
37. affectional
38. Caregiving styles
39. Maternal, caregiving
40. proactive, temperaments
41. Paternal, playmate
42. Authoritarian
43. permissive
44. Authoritative
45. guidance
46. management, assertion
47. self-esteem
48. cooing, babbling, telegraphic
49. predisposition
50. Psycholinguists
51. Prelanguage, turn
52. parentese
53. abstract, assimilation
54. cognitive
55. sensorimotor, preoperational
56. Learning, thinking
57. minds, theory, mind
58. one-step-ahead
59. sociocultural, Vygotsky, proximal
60. scaffolding
61. cultural
62. consistency, encouragement
63. logical consequences

Mastery Test

1. d (p. 82)
2. b (p. 104)
3. e (p. 93)
4. b (p. 109)
5. a (p. 90)
6. d (p. 83)
7. b (p. 110)
8. c (p. 97)
9. a (p. 84)
10. a (p. 85)
11. c (p. 108)

12. b (p. 88)	**19.** b (p. 87)	**26.** b (p. 90)
13. c (p. 87)	**20.** a (p. 92)	**27.** b (p. 113)
14. d (p. 82)	**21.** b (p. 101)	**28.** b (p. 108)
15. b (p. 92)	**22.** a (p. 102)	**29.** a (p. 111)
16. b (p. 94)	**23.** b (p. 99)	**30.** a (p. 112)
17. d (p. 90)	**24.** c (p. 95)	**31.** d (p. 88)
18. c (p. 107)	**25.** c (p. 100)	

Chapter 4
From Birth to Death:
Life-Span Development

CHAPTER OVERVIEW

Life-span psychologists study continuity and change in behavior, as well as tasks, challenges, milestones, and problems throughout life. According to Erikson, each life stage provokes a different psychosocial dilemma.

Some major problems in childhood are toilet training, feeding disturbances, speech disturbances, learning disorders, and attention-deficit hyperactivity disorder. Childhood autism and child abuse are examples of the more severe problems that can occur.

Adolescence is culturally defined; puberty is a biological event. Early maturation is beneficial mostly for boys; its effects are mixed for girls. Adolescent identity formation is accelerated by cognitive development and influenced by parents and peer groups.

Moral development bridges childhood, adolescence, and early adulthood. Lawrence Kohlberg believed that moral development occurs in stages. Some psychologists question whether moral development is based only on a sense of justice. Caring for others also appears to be important.

Adult development is marked by events that range from escaping parental dominance in the late teens to a noticeable acceptance of one's lot in life during the 50s. Some people experience a mid-life crisis, but this is not universal. Adjustment to later middle age is sometimes complicated by menopause and the climacteric. Biological aging begins between 25 and 30, but peak performance in specific pursuits may come at any point in life. Intellectual declines due to aging are limited. Two major theories of successful aging are disengagement and activity. Activity theory appears to apply to more people. Ageism is especially damaging to older people.

Impending death and bereavement both produce a series of typical emotional reactions. New approaches to death include the hospice movement and living wills.

Subjective well-being (happiness) is a combination of general life satisfaction and positive emotions. People with extraverted and optimistic personalities tend to be happy. Making progress toward your goals is associated with happiness, especially if the goals express your personal interests and values.

LEARNING OBJECTIVES

To demonstrate mastery of this chapter, you should be able to:

1. Define the terms *developmental milestones* and *life-span perspective*.

2. Describe the term *psychosocial dilemma* and explain, according to Erikson, how the resolution of the psychosocial dilemmas affects a person's adjustment to life.

3. State the nature of the psychosocial crisis and the nature of an adequate or inadequate outcome for each of Erikson's eight life stages. Match each crisis with the corresponding age.

4. Discuss the positive and negative aspects of stress on a developing child.

5. List and describe (where applicable) nine "normal" childhood problems.

6. Give a brief description of the following childhood disorders and their possible causes:

    a. enuresis   e. pica

    b. encopresis   f. delayed speech

    c. overeating   g. stuttering

    d. anorexia nervosa

7. Describe what the label "learning disorder" includes. Briefly describe dyslexia, including its possible cause.

8. Describe the following disorders in terms of symptoms, causes, and treatments:

    a. ADHD (also explain what relationship sugar has to ADHD and the controversy surrounding the use of Ritalin for treatment of ADHD)

    b. autism (include a definition of echolalia)

The following objectives are related to the material in the "Exploring Psychology" section of the text.

9. Describe the characteristics of abusive parents and the conditions likely to foster abusive behavior.

10. Describe what can be done to prevent child abuse.

11. Define and differentiate the terms *adolescence* and *puberty,* and list the three most widely accepted criteria for adult status in North America.

12. Discuss the advantages and disadvantages of early and late puberty for males and females.

13. Explain why Elkind believes that our society is rushing adolescents and what he feels the net effect will be.

14. Briefly discuss the impact of ethnic heritage on identity formation. Describe the interactions between an adolescent and his/her parents as identity formation occurs.

15. Discuss the importance of imaginary audiences to adolescents.

16. Describe the importance of the peer group in identity formation, including the danger of foreclosure.

17. Briefly describe each of Kohlberg's three levels or moral development as well as their respective stages.

18. Describe how Kohlberg's moral development levels are distributed among the population.

19. Explain Gilligan's argument against Kohlberg's system of moral development. Describe the current status of the argument.

20. Generally describe the pattern of adult life stages proposed by Roger Gould.

21. Describe what a midlife crisis is and how it can be both a danger and an opportunity. Explain how the midlife transition is different for women as opposed to men.

22. Distinguish menopause from the male climacteric and describe the typical reactions to each.

23. Briefly discuss the empty nest syndrome and the different effects of this syndrome on mothers who work at home versus mothers who work outside the home.

24. List six elements of well-being during adulthood.

25. Describe what is meant by the term "biological aging." Include the concepts of fluid and crystallized abilities in your answer.

26. Differentiate the concepts maximum life span and life expectancy. List seven suggestions for increasing life expectancy.

27. Describe the disengagement theory and the activity theory of aging.

28. Describe Baltes's view of selective optimization with compensation.

29. Outline the characteristics of ageism. List four significant myths of aging, and relate them to the concept of ageism.

30. Explain how fears about death might be expressed as a denial of death.

31. Explain the purpose or intent of a living will.

32. List and briefly characterize the five emotional reactions typically experienced by people facing death.

33. Explain how knowledge of the reactions to coping with death is important.

34. Describe what generally happens during a near-death experience (NDE), how it can be explained in two different ways, and how an NDE can change a person's life.

35. Describe the purpose of a hospice.

36. Discuss the general characteristics of the process of bereavement. Explain how suppression of the grieving process is related to later problems.

The following objectives are related to the material in the "Psychology in Action" section of the text.

37. Define the term *subjective well-being*.

38. List five characteristics of a satisfied life.

39. Briefly discuss the relationship of positive and negative emotional experiences to happiness.

40. Briefly discuss the way in which perception, interpretation, and management of events is related to happiness.

41. List and briefly discuss eight personal factors related to overall happiness.

42. Discuss the connection between one's goals in life and happiness. Include a discussion of the findings of McGregor and Little.

RECITE AND REVIEW

● *What are the typical tasks and dilemmas through the life span?*

Recite and Review: Pages 118-121

1. Life-span psychologists study continuity and _____ over the life span.

2. They are also interested in _____ milestones, or prominent landmarks in personal development.

3. According to Erik Erikson, each life stage provokes a specific psychosocial _____.

4. During childhood these are: trust versus mistrust, autonomy versus _____ and doubt, initiative versus _____, and industry versus _____.

5. In _____, identity versus role confusion is the principal dilemma.

6. In young adulthood we face the dilemma of intimacy versus _____. Later, generativity versus _____ becomes prominent.

7. Old age is a time when the dilemma of integrity versus _____ must be faced.

8. In addition, each life stage requires successful mastery of certain _____ tasks (personal changes required for optimal development).

● *What are some of the more serious childhood problems?*

Recite and Review: Pages 122-127

9. Few children grow up without experiencing some of the normal problems of childhood, including negativism, clinging, specific fears, sleep _____, general dissatisfaction, regression, sibling _____, and rebellion.

10. Major areas of difficulty in childhood are _____ _____ (including enuresis and encopresis) and _____ disturbances, such as overeating, anorexia nervosa (self-starvation), and pica (eating non-food substances).

11. Other problems include _____ disturbances (delayed speech, stuttering); _____ disorders, including dyslexia (an inability to read with understanding); and attention-deficit hyperactivity _____ (ADHD).

12. Childhood _____ is a severe problem involving mutism, sensory disturbances, tantrums, and a lack of responsiveness to other people.

13. Some cases of autism are being treated successfully with _____ modification.

14. Child abuse (physically or emotionally _____ a child) is a major problem. Roughly _____ percent of all abused children become abusive adults. Emotional support and therapy can help break the cycle of abuse.

● *Why is adolescent development especially challenging?*

Recite and Review: Pages 128-131

15. Adolescence is a culturally defined _____ status. Puberty is a _____ event.

16. On average, the peak growth spurt during puberty occurs earlier for _____ than for _____.

17. Early maturation is beneficial mostly for _____; its effects are mixed for _____.

18. Establishing a clear sense of personal identity is a major task of _____. One danger of _____ maturation is premature identity formation.

19. Many adolescents become self-conscious and preoccupied with imaginary _____ (imagined viewers).

20. Adolescent identity formation is accelerated by cognitive development and influenced by _____ and peer groups (age mates).

● *How do we develop morals and values?*

Recite and Review: Pages 131-133

21. Lawrence Kohlberg theorized that _____ development passes through a series of stages revealed by _____ reasoning about _____ dilemmas.

22. Kohlberg identified preconventional, conventional, and postconventional levels of moral _____.

23. Some psychologists have questioned whether measures of moral development should be based only on a morality of _____. Adults appear to base moral choices on either _____ or caring, depending on the situation.

● *What happens psychologically during adulthood?*

Recite and Review: Pages 134-136

24. Certain relatively consistent events mark _____ _____ in our society.

25. In order these are: _____ from parental dominance, leaving the _____, building a workable life, a crisis of questions, a crisis of urgency, attaining stability, and mellowing.

26. A midlife crisis affects many people in the 37-41 age range, but this is by no means _____.

27. Adjustment to later middle age is sometimes complicated for _____ by menopause and for _____ by a climacteric.

28. When the last child leaves home, women who define themselves as traditional _____ may become _____ (the empty nest syndrome).

29. Well-being at midlife is related to self-acceptance, positive relationships, autonomy, mastery, a _____ in life, and continued personal _____.

● *What are some of the psychological challenges of aging?*

Recite and Review: Pages 137-141

30. The elderly are the _____ growing segment of society in North America.

31. Biological _____ begins between 25 and 30, but peak performance in specific pursuits may come at various points throughout life.

32. The length of human lives is limited by the _____ life span. _____ expectancy (the average number of years people live) is much shorter.

33. Intellectual declines associated with aging are limited, at least through one's _____. This is especially true of individuals who remain mentally _____.

34. The greatest losses occur for fluid abilities (which require _____ or rapid learning); crystallized abilities (stored up _____ and skills) show much less decline and may actually improve.

35. Gerontologists (those who study _____) have proposed the disengagement theory of successful _____. It holds that withdrawal from society is necessary and desirable in old age.

36. The activity theory states that optimal adjustment to aging is tied to continuing _____ and involvement. The activity theory applies to more people than disengagement does.

37. Ageism refers to prejudice, discrimination, and stereotyping on the basis of _____. It affects people of all ages, but is especially damaging to _____ people.

● *How do people typically react to death and bereavement?*

Recite and Review: Pages 141-146

38. Older people fear the circumstances of _____ more than the fact that it will occur.
39. Typical emotional reactions to impending death are denial, _____, bargaining, _____, and acceptance.
40. A living will may help a person ensure that his or her life will not be artificially prolonged during a _____ illness.
41. Near-death _____ (NDEs) frequently result in significant changes in personality, _____, and life goals.
42. One approach to death is the hospice movement, which is devoted to providing humane care to persons who are _____.
43. Bereavement also brings forth a typical series of _____ reactions.
44. Initial shock is followed by pangs of _____. Later, apathy, dejection, and depression may occur. Eventually, grief moves toward _____, an acceptance of the loss.
45. Grief _____ helps people adapt to their loss and integrate changes into their lives.

● *What factors contribute most to a happy and fulfilling life?*

Recite and Review: PSYCHOLOGY IN ACTION

46. Subjective well-being (_____) occurs when _____ emotions outnumber _____ emotions and a person is satisfied with his or her life.
47. Happiness is only mildly related to _____, education, marriage, religion, age, sex, and work. However, people who have an extraverted, optimistic _____ do tend to be happier.
48. People who are making progress toward their long-term _____ tend to be happier. This is especially true if the _____ have integrity and personal meaning.

CONNECTIONS

1. _____	Erik Erikson	a.	"smother love"
2. _____	overprotection	b.	"soiling"
3. _____	regression	c.	reading disorder
4. _____	enuresis	d.	autism symptom
5. _____	encopresis	e.	psychosocial dilemmas
6. _____	pica	f.	hyperactive
7. _____	dyslexia	g.	bed wetting
8. _____	echolalia	h.	clinical death
9. _____	NDE	i.	eating disorder
10. _____	ADHD	j.	infantile behavior

11. _____	child abuse	a. sexual maturation
12. _____	adolescence	b. reaction to impending death
13. _____	puberty	c. social-contract/individual principles
14. _____	social marker	d. good boy or girl/respect for authority
15. _____	preconventional	e. avoiding punishment or seeking pleasure
16. _____	conventional	f. children leave
17. _____	postconventional	g. life change
18. _____	bargaining	h. cultural status
19. _____	"empty nest"	i. status or role clue
20. _____	transition period	j. shaken baby

21. _____	menopause	a. successful aging
22. _____	climacteric	b. expert on death
23. _____	Roger Gould	c. happiness and meaningful goals
24. _____	Elizabeth Kübler-Ross	d. care for dying
25. _____	ageism	e. expert on aging
26. _____	gerontologist	f. common prejudice
27. _____	thanatologist	g. end of menstruation
28. _____	compensation and optimization	h. reactions to dying
29. _____	good life	i. significant physical change
30. _____	hospice	j. adult development

CHECK YOUR MEMORY

Check Your Memory: Pages 118-121

1. Learning to read in childhood and establishing a vocation as an adult are typical life stages. T or F?
2. Psychosocial dilemmas occur when a person is in conflict with his or her social world. T or F?
3. Initiative versus guilt is the first psychosocial dilemma a child faces. T or F?
4. Answering the question "Who am I?" is a primary task during adolescence. T or F?
5. Generativity is expressed through taking an interest in the next generation. T or F?

Check Your Memory: Pages 122-127

6. It is best for parents to protect children from all stressful stimulation, as much as possible. T or F?
7. Clinging is one of the more serious problems of childhood. T or F?
8. Supportive and affectionate fathers tend to minimize sibling rivalry. T or F?
9. Toilet training is typically completed by age 3 or earlier. T or F?
10. A child who eats mud, buttons, or rubber bands suffers from enuresis nervosa. T or F?

11. Stuttering is more common among girls than boys. T or F?
12. Autism can be described as "word blindness." T or F?
13. ADHD affects 5 times as many boys as girls and may be partly hereditary. T or F?
14. Eating too much sugar is one of the main causes of hyperactivity in children. T or F?
15. The first signs of autism often appear in infancy, when autistic children may be extremely aloof and withdrawn. T or F?
16. Ritalin is used primarily to treat delayed speech. T or F?
17. The risk of committing child abuse is highest for young parents. T or F?
18. Abusive mothers tend to believe that their children are intentionally annoying them. T or F?
19. One third of abused children become abusive adults. T or F?
20. Parents Anonymous is an organization for parents who have autistic children. T or F?

Check Your Memory: Pages 128-131

21. The length of adolescence varies in different cultures. T or F?
22. The average onset of puberty is age 12 for boys and age 14 for girls. T or F?
23. Early maturation tends to enhance self-image for boys. T or F?
24. Early-maturing girls tend to date sooner and are more likely to get into trouble. T or F?
25. David Elkind believes that today's adolescents should be "hurried into adulthood" to maximize their potentials. T or F?
26. The term *imaginary audience* refers to adolescent peer groups and the influence they have on personal identity. T or F?
27. Being able to think about hypothetical possibilities helps adolescents in their search for identity. T or F?
28. Increased conflict with parents tends to occur early in adolescence. T or F?
29. Early maturation can contribute to adopting a foreclosed identity. T or F?

Check Your Memory: Pages 131-133

30. Lawrence Kohlberg used moral dilemmas to assess children's levels of moral development. T or F?
31. At the preconventional level, moral decisions are guided by the consequences of actions, such as punishment or pleasure. T or F?
32. The traditional morality of authority defines moral behavior in the preconventional stage. T or F?
33. Most adults function at the conventional level of moral reasoning. T or F?
34. Both men and women may use justice or caring as a basis for making moral judgments. T or F?

Check Your Memory: Pages 134-136

35. According to Gould, building a workable life is the predominant activity between ages 16 to 18. T or F?
36. A crisis of urgency tends to hit people around the age of 30. T or F?
37. Maintaining good health is a prominent goal among the elderly. T or F?
38. Levinson places the midlife transition in the 40-55 age range. T or F?
39. Only a small minority of the men studied by Levinson experienced any instability or urgency at midlife. T or F?
40. During the mid-life transition, women are less likely than men to define success in terms of a key event. T or F?
41. Wealth is one of the primary sources of happiness in adulthood. T or F?

42. Over half of all women have serious emotional problems during menopause. T or F?
43. After the climacteric has occurred, men become infertile. T or F?
44. Having a sense of purpose in life is one element of well-being during adulthood. T or F

Check Your Memory: Pages 137-141

45. By the year 2020, 1 out of every 5 North Americans will be over age 65. T or F?
46. Peak functioning in most physical capacities occurs between ages 25 and 30. T or F?
47. The maximum human life span is around 120 years. T or F?
48. Life expectancy has increased dramatically in the last 200 years. T or F?
49. Crystallized abilities are the first to decline as a person ages. T or F?
50. Perceptual speed declines steadily after age 25. T or F?
51. For many people, successful aging requires a combination of activity and disengagement. T or F?
52. Ageism refers to prejudice and discrimination toward the elderly. T or F?
53. Few elderly persons become senile or suffer from mental decay. T or F?

Check Your Memory: Pages 141-146

54. Most of the deaths portrayed on television are homicides. T or F?
55. A living will is not legally binding in most states in the U.S. T or F?
56. The "Why me" reaction to impending death is an expression of anger. T or F?
57. Trying to be "good" in order to live longer is characteristic of the denial reaction to impending death. T or F?
58. It is best to go through all the stages of dying described by Kübler-Ross in the correct order. T or F?
59. Medical explanations of NDEs attribute them to brain activities caused by oxygen starvation. T or F?
60. Hospice care can be provided at home, as well as in medical centers. T or F?
61. Hospice programs are designed to avoid the use of painkilling drugs. T or F?
62. Bereaved persons should work through their grief as quickly as possible. T or F?

Check Your Memory: PSYCHOLOGY IN ACTION

63. Subjective well-being is primarily a matter of having relatively few negative emotions. T or F?
64. A person who agrees that "The conditions of my life are excellent" would probably score high in life satisfaction. T or F?
65. Wealthier people are generally happier people. T or F?
66. Life satisfaction and happiness generally decline with increasing age. T or F?
67. You are likely to be happy if you are making progress on smaller goals that relate to long-term, life goals. T or F?
68. Usually, a good life is one that is happy and meaningful. T or F?

FINAL SURVEY AND REVIEW

● *What are the typical tasks and dilemmas through the life span?*

1. _____ psychologists study _____ and change from birth to death.
2. They are also interested in developmental _____, or prominent landmarks in personal development.
3. According to Erik _____, each life stage provokes a specific _____ dilemma.
4. During childhood these are: _____ versus mistrust, _____ versus shame and doubt, initiative versus guilt, and _____ versus inferiority.
5. In adolescence, _____ versus _____ confusion is the principal dilemma.
6. In young adulthood we face the dilemma of _____ versus isolation. Later, _____ versus stagnation becomes prominent.
7. Old age is a time when the dilemma of _____ versus despair must be faced.
8. In addition, each life stage requires successful mastery of certain developmental _____ (personal changes required for optimal development).

● *What are some of the more serious childhood problems?*

9. Few children grow up without experiencing some of the normal problems of childhood, including _____, _____, specific _____, sleep disturbances, general dissatisfaction, regression, sibling rivalry, and rebellion.
10. Major areas of difficulty in childhood are toilet training (including _____ and _____) and feeding disturbances, such as overeating, anorexia nervosa (self-starvation), and _____ (eating non-food substances).
11. Other problems include speech disturbances (delayed speech, _____); learning disorders, including _____ (an inability to read with understanding); and attention-deficit _____ disorder (ADHD).
12. Childhood autism is a severe problem involving _____ (failure to speak), sensory disturbances, tantrums, and a lack of responsiveness to _____ _____.
13. Some cases of autism are being treated successfully with behavior _____.
14. _____ _____ (physically or emotionally harming a child) is a major problem. Roughly 30 percent of all abused children become abusive _____. Emotional support and therapy can help break the cycle of abuse.

● *Why is adolescent development especially challenging?*

15. _____ is a culturally defined social status. _____ is a biological event.
16. On average, the peak _____ spurt during _____ occurs earlier for girls than for boys.

17. Early _____ is beneficial mostly for boys; its effects are mixed for girls.

18. Establishing a clear sense of personal _____ is a major task of adolescence. One danger of early maturation is premature _____ formation.

19. Many adolescents become self-conscious and preoccupied with _____ audiences.

20. Adolescent identity formation is accelerated by _____ development and influenced by parents and _____ groups (age mates).

● *How do we develop morals and values?*

21. Lawrence Kohlberg theorized that moral development passes through a series of stages revealed by moral _____ about moral _____.

22. Kohlberg identified _____, conventional, and postconventional levels of moral reasoning.

23. Some psychologists have questioned whether measures of moral development should be based only on a morality of justice. Adults appear to base moral choices on either justice or _____, depending on the _____.

● *What happens psychologically during adulthood?*

24. Certain relatively _____ events mark adult development in our society.

25. In order these are: escape from parental _____, leaving the family, building a workable life, a crisis of _____, a crisis of _____, attaining stability, and mellowing.

26. A _____ _____ affects many people in the 37-41 age range, but this is by no means universal.

27. Adjustment to later middle age is sometimes complicated for women by menopause and for men by a _____.

28. When the last child leaves home, women who define themselves as traditional mothers may become depressed (the _____ _____ _____).

29. Well-being at midlife is related to self-_____, positive relationships, _____, mastery, a purpose in life, and continued personal growth.

● *What are some of the psychological challenges of aging?*

30. The _____ are the fastest growing segment of society in North America.

31. Biological aging begins between 25 and 30, but _____ _____ in specific pursuits may come at various points throughout life.

32. The length of human lives is limited by the maximum _____ _____. Life _____ (the average number of years people live) is much shorter.

33. _____ declines associated with aging are limited, at least through one's 70s. This is especially true of individuals who remain mentally active.

34. The greatest losses occur for _____ abilities (which require speed or rapid learning); _____ abilities (stored up knowledge and skills) show much less decline and may actually improve.

35. _____ (those who study aging) have proposed the _____ theory of successful aging. It holds that withdrawal from society is necessary and desirable in old age.

36. The _____ theory states that optimal adjustment to aging is tied to continuing action and involvement. This theory applies to more people than withdrawal from society does.

37. _____ refers to prejudice, discrimination, and stereotyping on the basis of age. It affects people of all ages, but is especially damaging to older people.

● *How do people typically react to death and bereavement?*

38. Older people fear the _____ of death more than the fact that it will occur.

39. Typical emotional reactions to impending death are _____, anger, _____, depression, and acceptance.

40. A _____ _____ may help a person ensure that his or her life will not be artificially prolonged during a terminal illness.

41. _____ experiences (NDEs) frequently result in significant changes in personality, values, and life goals.

42. One approach to death is the _____ movement, which is devoted to providing humane care to persons who are dying.

43. _____ also brings forth a typical series of grief reactions.

44. Initial _____ is followed by _____ of grief. Later, apathy, dejection, and _____ may occur. Eventually, grief moves toward resolution, an acceptance of the loss.

45. _____ work helps people adapt to their loss and _____ changes into their lives.

● *What factors contribute most to a happy and fulfilling life?*

46. _____ _____ _____ (happiness) occurs when positive emotions outnumber negative emotions and a person is satisfied with his or her life.

47. Happiness is only mildly related to wealth, education, marriage, religion, age, sex, and work. However, people with _____, optimistic personalities do tend to be happier.

48. People who are making progress toward their long-term goals tend to be happier. This is especially true if the goals have _____ and personal _____.

MASTERY TEST

1. According to Erikson, a conflict between trust and mistrust is characteristic of
   a. infancy b. adolescence c. marriage d. old age

2. Identity formation during adolescence is aided by
   a. cognitive development b. attaining the preoperational stage c. emotional bargaining
   d. you-messages from parents

3. Which of the following is not a normal, relatively mild childhood problem?
   a. negativism   b. clinging   c. sibling rivalry   d. delayed speech

4. Infancy, childhood, adolescence, and young adulthood are
   a. developmental tasks   b. life stages   c. psychosocial dilemmas   d. biologically defined social statuses

5. Premature identity formation is one of the risks of early
   a. generativity   b. preoccupation with imaginary audiences   c. trust-mistrust resolution   d. puberty

6. The thought, "It's all a mistake" would most likely occur as part of which reaction to impending death?
   a. anger   b. freezing up   c. denial   d. bargaining

7. The choice of whether to use justice or caring to make moral decisions depends on the
   _____ a person faces.
   a. situation   b. punishment   c. level of authority   d. exchange

8. Which of the following is a correct match?
   a. enuresis—eating disorder   b. anorexia—speech disturbance   c. dyslexia—learning disorder
   d. pica—autism

9. According to Erikson, the first dilemma a newborn infant must resolve is
   a. independence versus dependence   b. initiative versus guilt   c. trust versus mistrust
   d. attachment versus confusion

10. Seeking approval and upholding law, order, and authority are characteristics of what stage of moral development?
    a. preconventional   b. conventional   c. postconventional   d. postformal

11. An inability to read with understanding defines the problem formally known as
    a. ADHD   b. dyslexia   c. NDE   d. echolalia

12. For both boys and girls, a growth spurt corresponds with _____.
    a. adolescence   b. puberty   c. cognitive maturation   d. less prestige with peers

13. Autonomy, environmental mastery, a purpose in life, and continued personal growth help maintain well-being in old age. This observation supports the _____ theory of successful aging.
    a. disengagement   b. re-engagement   c. activity   d. re-activation

14. Research on well-being suggests that a good life is one that combines happiness and
    a. financial success   b. educational achievement   c. an introverted personality
    d. achieving meaningful goals

15. According to Erikson, developing a sense of integrity is a special challenge in
    a. adolescence   b. young adulthood   c. middle adulthood   d. late adulthood

16. The event for males that is most comparable to menopause in women is the
    a. climacteric   b. midlife crisis   c. generativity transition   d. genophase

17. Grief following bereavement typically begins with _____ and ends with _____.
    a. anger, disengagement b. dejection, disengagement c. isolation, depression d. shock, resolution

18. Physicians typically use the stimulant drug Ritalin to control
    a. encopresis b. ADHD c. echolalia d. anorexia nervosa

19. The smallest number of Levinson's subjects experienced midlife as a(an)
    a. last chance b. period of serious decline c. time to start over d. escape from dominance

20. According to Erikson, a dilemma concerning _____ usually follows one that focuses on identity.
    a. trust b. industry c. initiative d. intimacy

21. Which combination would lead to the highest risk of child abuse?
    a. young parent, high income, child over 3 years b. young parent, low income, abused as a child
    c. older parent, low income, child over 3 years d. older parent, high income, abused as a child

22. Foreclosed identity formation is a special risk for
    a. late maturing boys b. adolescents c. the elementary school years d. the preoperational stage

23. Oxygen deprivation in the brain best accounts for which element of a NDE?
    a. the tunnel of light b. the pangs of grief c. the period of depression d. the life review and personality changes

24. People who have many positive emotional experiences and relatively few negative experiences usually rate high in
    a. generativity b. moral reasoning c. subjective well-being d. crystallized abilities

25. Overprotective parenting ignores the fact that _____ is a normal part of life.
    a. rebellion b. punishment c. rejection d. stress

26. Ivar Lovaas has successfully used _____ to treat _____.
    a. Ritalin, echolalia b. operant shaping, dyslexia c. restricted sugar diets, ADHD
    d. behavior modification, autism

27. Skills that rely on fluid abilities could be expected to show declines beginning in
    a. adolescence b. young adulthood c. middle adulthood d. late adulthood

28. Which of the following is a common myth about old age?
    a. Most elderly persons are isolated and neglected.
    b. A large percentage of the elderly suffer from senility.
    c. A majority of the elderly are dissastified with their lives.
    d. All of the preceding are myths.

29. Gould's study of adult development found that a crisis of _____ is common between the ages of 35 and 43.
   a. urgency b. questions c. dominance d. stability

30. With respect to aging, it is least possible to modify which of the following?
   a. life expectancy b. crystallized abilities c. mental abilities d. maximum life span

ANSWERS

Recite and Review

1. change
2. developmental
3. dilemma
4. shame, guilt, inferiority
5. adolescence
6. isolation, stagnation
7. despair
8. developmental
9. disturbances, rivalry
10. toilet training, feeding
11. speech, learning, disorder
12. autism
13. behavior
14. harming, 30
15. social, biological
16. girls, boys
17. boys, girls
18. adolescence, early
19. audiences
20. parents
21. moral, moral, moral
22. reasoning
23. justice, justice
24. adult development
25. escape, family
26. universal
27. women, men
28. mothers, depressed

29. purpose, growth
30. fastest
31. aging
32. maximum, Life
33. 70s, active
34. speed, knowledge
35. aging, aging
36. activity
37. age, older
38. death
39. anger, depression
40. terminal
41. experiences, values
42. dying
43. grief
44. grief, resolution
45. work
46. happiness, positive, negative
47. wealth, personality
48. goals, goals

Connections

1. e
2. a
3. j
4. g
5. b
6. i
7. c
8. d
9. h
10. f
11. j
12. h
13. a
14. i

15. e
16. d
17. c
18. b
19. f
20. g
21. g
22. i
23. j
24. h
25. f
26. e
27. b
28. a
29. c
30. d

Check Your Memory

1. F
2. T
3. F
4. T
5. T
6 F
7. F
8. T
9. T
10. F
11. F
12. F
13. T
14. F
15. T
16. F
17. T
18. T

19. T
20. F
21. T
22. F
23. T
24. T
25. F
26. F
27. T
28. T
29. T
30. T
31. T
32. F
33. T
34. T
35. F
36. F
37. T
38. F
39. F
40. T
41. F
42. F
43. F
44. T
45. T
46. T
47. T
48. T
49. F
50. T
51. T
52. F
53. T
54. T
55. T
56. T
57. F
58. F
59. T
60. T
61. F
62. F
63. F
64. T

65. F
66. F
67. T
68. T

Final Survey and Review

1. Life-span, continuity
2. milestones
3. Erikson, psychosocial
4. trust, autonomy, industry
5. identity, role
6. intimacy, generativity
7. integrity
8. tasks
9. negativism, clinging, fears
10. enuresis, encopresis, pica
11. stuttering, dyslexia, hyperactivity
12. mutism, other people
13. modification
14. Child abuse, adults
15. Adolescence, Puberty
16. growth, puberty
17. maturation
18. identity, identity
19. imaginary
20. cognitive, peer
21. reasoning, dilemmas
22. preconventional
23. caring, situation
24. consistent
25. dominance, questions, urgency
26. midlife crisis
27. climacteric
28. empty nest syndrome
29. acceptance, autonomy
30. elderly
31. peak performance
32. life span, expectancy
33. Intellectual
34. fluid, crystallized
35. Gerontologists, disengagement
36. activity
37. Ageism
38. circumstances
39. denial, bargaining
40. living will
41. Near-death
42. hospice
43. Bereavement
44. shock, pangs, depression
45. Grief, integrate
46. Subjective, well, being
47. extraverted
48. integrity, meaning

Mastery Test

1. a (p. 119)
2. a (p. 130)
3. d (p. 122)
4. b (p. 118)
5. d (p. 129)
6. c (p. 143)
7. a (p. 133)
8. c (p. 124)
9. c (p. 119)
10. b (p. 132)
11. b (p. 124)
12. b (p. 128)
13. c (p. 139)
14. d (p. 148)
15. d (p. 120)
16. a (p. 136)
17. d (p. 145)
18. b (p. 124)
19. c (p. 135)
20. d (p. 120)
21. b (p. 126)
22. b (p. 131)
23. a (p. 144)
24. c (p. 147)
25. d (p. 122)
26. d (p. 125)
27. b (p. 138)
28. d (p. 141)
29. a (p. 134)
30. d (p. 138)

Chapter 5

Sensation and Perception

CHAPTER OVERVIEW

Sensory systems collect, select, transduce, analyze, and code information from the environment and send it to the brain.

Vision and visual problems can be partly understood by viewing the eyes as optical systems. However, the visual system also analyzes light stimuli to identify patterns and basic visual features. Color sensations are explained by the trichromatic theory (in the retina) and the opponent-process theory (for the rest of the visual system).

The inner ear is a sensory mechanism for transducing sound waves in the air into nerve impulses. The frequency and place theories of hearing explain how sound information is coded.

Olfaction is based on receptors that respond to gaseous molecules in the air. The lock-and-key theory and the locations of olfactory receptors activated by different scents explain how various odors are coded. Taste is another chemical sense. A lock-and-key match between dissolved molecules and taste receptors also explains many taste sensations.

The somesthetic, or bodily, senses include the skin senses, the kinesthetic senses, and the vestibular senses.

Our awareness of sensory information is altered by sensory adaptation, selective attention, and sensory gating.

Perception involves organizing sensations into meaningful patterns. Visual perceptions are stabilized by size, shape, and brightness constancies. The most basic perceptual pattern (in vision) is figure-ground organization. Sensations tend to be organized on the basis of nearness, similarity, continuity, closure, contiguity, and common region.

Depth perception depends on accommodation, convergence, retinal disparity, and various pictorial cues. The pictorial cues include linear perspective, relative size, light and shadow, overlap, texture gradients, aerial haze, and relative motion.

Learning, in the form of perceptual habits, influences perceptions. Perceptions are also greatly affected by attention, motives, values, and expectations (perceptual sets).

Parapsychology is the study of purported psi phenomena, including clairvoyance, telepathy, precognition, and psychokinesis. The bulk of the evidence to date is against the existence of extrasensory perception. Stage ESP is based on deception and tricks.

Because perceptions are reconstructions of events, eyewitness testimony can be unreliable. Perceptual accuracy can be improved by reality testing, dishabituation, actively paying attention, breaking perceptual habits, using broad frames of reference, and being aware of perceptual sets.

LEARNING OBJECTIVES

To demonstrate mastery of this chapter, you should be able to:

1. Explain how our senses act as a data reduction system by selecting, analyzing, and condensing incoming information.

2. Explain how sensory receptors act as biological transducers. Define *sensory coding*.

3. Explain the concept of sensory localization including the idea behind the statement "Seeing does not take place in the eyes."

4. Define *sensation* and *perception*.

5. Describe hue, saturation, and brightness in terms of their representation in the visual spectrum. Briefly compare the structure of the eye to a camera and explain the process of accommodation.

6. Describe the following four conditions:

    a. hyperopia b. myopia c. astigmatism d. presbyopia

7. Describe the location and explain the functions of the following parts of the eye:

    a. lens   b. retina c. cornea d. rods (including sensitivity to light)

    e. cones f. blind spot g. fovea

8. Discuss peripheral vision. Include the structures responsible for it and how this type of vision affects night vision.

9. Discuss the following theories of color vision:

    a. trichromatic theory

    b. opponent-process theory (include a description of afterimage)

10. Describe color blindness and color weakness.

11. Explain the purpose of the Ishihara test.

12. Briefly describe the process of dark adaptation including the function of rhodopsin in night vision and night blindness.

13. Explain how dark adaptation can be speeded up.

14. Describe the process by which sound travels and what psychological dimensions correspond to the physical ones.

15. Describe the location and explain the function(s) of the following parts of the ear:

    a. pinna b. tympanic membrane (eardrum) c. auditory ossicles

    d. cochlea e. oval window f. hair cells g. organ of Corti

    h. stereocilia

16. Briefly explain how the sense of hearing works by tracing an incoming stimulus from the time it strikes the tympanic membrane until it is sent to the brain.

17. Describe the frequency and the place theories of hearing.

18. List and describe the three general types of deafness.

19. Describe how cochlear implants can help overcome deafness.

20. Describe the factors that determine whether hearing loss will occur from stimulation deafness.

21. Describe the sense of olfaction (smell) including:
    a. its nature   b. how it works   c. a description of the condition anosmia
    d. a description of the lock and key theory
22. Describe the sense of gustation (taste) including:
    a. its nature   b. the four basic taste sensations
    c. the tastes to which humans are most and least sensitive
    d. how the vast number of flavors is explained
    e. how it works
23. List the three somesthetic senses and be able to describe the function of each.
24. List and be able to recognize the five different sensations produced by the skin receptors.
25. Explain why certain areas of the body are more sensitive to touch than other areas.
26. List the numbers of nerve endings for each of the following: temperature, touch and pressure, and pain.
27. Name and describe the two different pain systems in the body.
28. List and describe three ways to reduce pain.
29. Name and describe the functions of the structures responsible for the vestibular sense.
30. Explain how the sensory conflict theory explains motion sickness.
31. List and discuss the three reasons many sensory events never reach conscious awareness.
32. Describe sensory adaptation, selective attention, and the gate control theory of pain.
33. List and describe three characteristics of a stimulus that can make it attention-getting.
34. Explain the "boiled frog syndrome" and how it may affect the ultimate survival of humans.
35. Discuss how acupuncture may work in controlling pain.
36. Describe the visual abilities of a person who has just had his or her sight restored.
37. Describe the following constancies:
    a. size   b. shape   c. brightness
38. Give examples of the following as they relate to the organization of perception:
    a. figure-ground (include the concept of reversible figures)
    b. nearness   c. similarity   d. continuation   e. closure (include the concept of illusory figures)
    f. contiguity   g. common region
39. Explain the meaning of the term *perceptual hypothesis*.
40. Define and give an example of an *ambiguous stimulus*.
41. Define *depth perception*.
42. Describe two techniques for investigating depth perception, and describe the end results of studies with each technique.
43. Describe the following cues for depth perception and indicate in each case whether the due is monocular or binocular:
    a. accommodation   b. convergence   c. retinal disparity
44. Describe the following two-dimensional, monocular, pictorial depth cues:
    a. linear perspective   b. relative size   c. height in the picture plane
    d. light and shadow   e. overlap (interposition)   f. texture gradients
    g. aerial perspective   h. relative motion (motion parallax)

45. Describe the phenomenon of the moon illusion. Include in your explanation the apparent distance hypothesis.
46. Define *perceptual habit* and explain how it allows learning to affect perception.
47. Explain how the Ames room poses problems for organization and for a person's perceptual habits.
48. Describe the research that demonstrates the brain's sensitivity to perceptual features in the environment.
49. Differentiate between an illusion and a hallucination.
50. Describe the Müller-Lyer illusion and explain how perceptual habits may account for this illusion.
51. Explain and give experimental evidence of how motives may alter attention and perception.
52. Explain what bottom-up and top-down processing are.
53. Explain how perceptual expectancies may influence perception.

The following objectives are related to the material in the "Exploring Psychology" section of the text.
54. Define the terms *extrasensory perception* and *parapsychology*.
55. Describe the following purported psychic abilities:
     a. clairvoyance   b. telepathy   c. precognition   d. psychokinesis
56. Describe the research with Zener cards, and explain why most psychologists remain skeptical about psi abilities.
57. Describe the best conclusion to make about psi events.

The following objective is related to the material in the "Psychology in Action" section of the text.
58. Explain why most eyewitness testimony is inaccurate, including the concept of weapon focus.
59. Explain what the term *reality testing* means.
60. Explain Maslow's concept of perceptual awareness and discuss how attention affects perception.
61. List seven ways to become a better "eyewitness" to life.

RECITE AND REVIEW

● *In general, how do sensory systems function?*

Recite and Review: Pages 152-154

1. Sensory organs transduce physical energies into _____ impulses.
2. The senses act as _____ reduction systems that select, _____, and filter sensory information.
3. A good example of sensory analysis is the identification of basic _____ features in a stimulus pattern.
4. In fact, many sensory systems act as feature _____.
5. Phosphenes and visual pop-out are examples of feature detection and _____ coding in action.

6. Sensory response can be partially understood in terms of _____ localization in the brain. That is, the area of the brain _____ ultimately determines which type of sensory experience we have.

● *How is vision accomplished?*

Recite and Review: Pages 154-160

7. The _____ spectrum consists of electromagnetic radiation in a narrow range.

8. The electromagnetic spectrum ranges from violet, with a _____ of 400 nanometers, to red with a _____ of 700 nanometers.

9. Hue refers to a color's name, which corresponds to its _____. Saturated or "pure" colors come from a _____ band of wavelengths. Brightness corresponds to the amplitude of light waves.

10. The eye is in some ways like a camera. At its back lies an array of photoreceptors, called _____ and _____, that make up a light-sensitive layer called the retina.

11. Vision is focused by the _____ of the cornea and lens and by changes in the _____ of the lens, called accommodation.

12. Four common visual defects, correctable with glasses, are myopia (_____), hyperopia (farsightedness), presbyopia (loss of _____), and astigmatism (in which portions of vision are out of focus).

13. In the retina, the _____ specialize in night vision, black and white reception, and motion detection.

14. The _____, found exclusively in the fovea and otherwise toward the middle of the eye, specialize in _____ vision, acuity (perception of fine detail), and daylight vision.

15. The _____ supply much of our peripheral vision. Loss of peripheral vision is called tunnel vision.

16. The rods and cones differ in color _____. Yellow-green is brightest for cones; blue-green for the rods (although they will see it as colorless).

17. In the _____, color vision is explained by the trichromatic theory. The theory says that three types of _____ exist, each most sensitive to either red, green, or blue.

18. Three types of light-sensitive visual pigments are found in the _____, each pigment is most sensitive to either red, green, or blue light.

19. Beyond the retina, the visual system analyzes colors into _____ messages. According to the opponent-process theory, color information can be coded as either red or green, yellow or blue, and _____ _____ _____ messages.

20. _____ color blindness is rare, but 8 percent of males and 1 percent of females are red-green color blind or color weak.

21. The Ishihara test is used to detect _____ _____.

22. Dark adaptation, an _____ in sensitivity to light, is caused by increased concentrations of visual pigments in the _____ and the _____.

23. Most dark adaptation is the result of increased rhodopsin concentrations in the _____. Vitamin A deficiencies may cause _____ blindness by impairing the production of rhodopsin.

● *What are the mechanisms of hearing?*

Recite and Review: Pages 161-164

24. Sound waves are the stimulus for hearing. Sound travels as waves of compression (_____) and rarefaction (_____) in the air.

25. The _____ of a sound corresponds to the frequency of sound waves. Loudness corresponds to the amplitude (_____) of sound waves.

26. Sound waves are transduced by the _____, auditory ossicles, oval window, cochlea, and ultimately, the _____ cells in the organ of Corti.

27. The frequency theory says that the _____ of nerve impulses in the auditory nerves matches the _____ of incoming sounds (up to 4000 hertz).

28. Place theory says that _____ tones register near the base of the cochlea and _____ tones near its tip.

29. Three basic types of deafness are _____ deafness, conduction deafness, and stimulation deafness.

30. Conduction deafness can often be overcome with a hearing aid. _____ deafness can sometimes be alleviated by cochlear implants.

31. Stimulation deafness can be prevented by avoiding excessive exposure to _____ sounds. Sounds above 120 decibels pose an immediate danger to hearing. Two warning signs of stimulation deafness are temporary threshold _____ and tinnitus.

● *How do the chemical senses operate?*

Recite and Review: Pages 164-165

32. Olfaction (_____) and gustation (_____) are chemical senses responsive to airborne or liquefied molecules.

33. The lock and key theory partially explains smell. In addition, the _____ of the olfactory receptors in the nose helps identify various scents.

34. The top outside edges of the tongue are responsive to sweet, salty, sour, and _____ tastes. It is suspected that a fifth taste quality called *umami* also exists.

35. Taste also appears to be based in part on lock-and-key _____ of molecule shapes.

● *What are the somesthetic senses and why are they important?*

Recite and Review: Pages 166-168

36. The somesthetic senses include the _____ senses, vestibular senses, and kinesthetic senses (receptors that detect muscle and joint positioning).

37. The skin senses include touch, _____, pain, cold, and warmth. Sensitivity to each is related to the _____ of receptors found in an area of skin.

38. Distinctions can be made between warning system pain, and _____ system pain.

39. Pain can be reduced by _____ anxiety and redirecting attention to stimuli other than the pain stimulus.

40. Feeling that you have control over a stimulus tends to _____ the amount of pain you experience.

41. Various forms of motion sickness are related to messages received from the vestibular system, which senses gravity and _____ movement.

42. The otolith organs detect the pull of _____ and rapid head movements.

43. The movement of _____ within the semicircular canals, and the movement of the _____ within each ampulla, detects head movement and positioning.

44. According to sensory conflict theory, motion sickness is caused by a _____ of visual, kinesthetic, and vestibular sensations. Motion sickness can be avoided by minimizing sensory conflict.

● *Why are we more aware of some sensations than others?*

Recite and Review: Pages 169-171

45. Incoming sensations are affected by sensory adaptation (a _____ in the number of nerve impulses sent).

46. Selective attention (selection and diversion of messages in the brain) and sensory _____ (blocking or alteration of messages flowing toward the brain) also alter sensations.

47. Selective gating of pain messages apparently takes place in the _____ _____. Gate control theory proposes an explanation for many pain phenomena.

● *How do perceptual constancies affect our perceptions?*

Recite and Review: Pages 172-173

48. Perception is the process of assembling sensations into _____ that provide a usable mental _____ of the world.

49. In vision, the retinal _____ changes from moment to moment, but the external world appears stable and undistorted because of _____ constancies.

50. In size and shape _____, the perceived sizes and shapes of objects remain the same even though their retinal images change size and shape. The apparent brightness of objects remains stable (a property called brightness constancy) because each reflects a _____ proportion of light.

51. Perceptual constancies are partly native (_____) and partly empirical (_____).

● *What basic principles do we use to group sensations into meaningful patterns?*

Recite and Review: Pages 173-176

52. The most basic organization of sensations is a division into figure and ground (_____ and _____). Reversible figures, however, allow figure-ground organization to be reversed.

53. A number of factors, identified by the Gestalt psychologists, contribute to the _____ of sensations. These are nearness, _____, continuity, closure, contiguity, _____ region, and combinations of the preceding.

54. Stimuli near one another tend to be perceptually _____ together. So, too, do stimuli that are similar in _____. Continuity refers to the fact that perceptions tend to be organized as simple, uninterrupted patterns.

55. Closure is the tendency to _____ a broken or incomplete pattern. Contiguity refers to nearness in _____ and space. Stimuli that fall in a defined area, or common region, also tend to be grouped together.

56. A perceptual organization may be thought of as an _____ held until evidence contradicts it. Camouflage patterns disrupt perceptual _____, especially figure-ground perceptions.

57. Perceptual organization shifts for ambiguous _____, which may have more than one interpretation. An example is Necker's _____. Impossible figures resist stable organization altogether.

● *How is it possible to see depth and judge distance?*

Recite and Review: Pages 176-182

58. _____ perception is the ability to perceive three-dimensional space and judge distances.

59. Depth perception is present in basic form soon after _____ as shown by testing with the visual cliff and other methods. As soon as infants become active _____ they refuse to cross the visual cliff.

60. Depth perception depends on the muscular cues of accommodation (bending of the _____) and convergence (inward movement of the _____).

61. A number of pictorial _____, which will work in _____ paintings, drawings, and photographs, also underlie normal depth perception.

62. Some pictorial cues are: linear perspective (the apparent convergence of _____ _____), relative size (more distant objects appear _____), height in the _____ plane, light and shadow (shadings of light), and overlap or interposition (one object overlaps another).

63. Additional pictorial cues include: texture gradients (textures become _____ in the distance), aerial haze (loss of color and detail at large distances), and relative _____ or _____ parallax (differences in the apparent movement of objects when a viewer is moving).

64. All the pictorial cues are monocular depth cues (only _____ _____ is needed to make use of them).

65. The moon illusion refers to the fact that the moon appears _____ near the horizon than it does when overhead.

66. The moon illusion appears to be explained by the apparent _____ _____ hypothesis, which emphasizes the greater number of depth cues present when the moon is on the _____.

● *How is perception altered by learning, expectations, and motives?*

Recite and Review: Pages 182-187

67. Organizing and interpreting sensations is greatly influenced by learned perceptual _____. An example is the Ames room, which looks rectangular but is actually distorted so that objects in the room appear to change _____.

68. Sensitivity to perceptual _____ is also partly learned. Studies of inverted vision show that even the most basic organization is subject to a degree of change. Active _____ speeds adaptation to new perceptual environments.

69. Illusions are often related to perceptual _____. One of the most familiar of all illusions, the Müller-Lyer illusion, seems to be related to perceptual learning based on experience with box-shaped _____ and rooms.

70. Linear perspective, _____ invariance relationships, and mislocating the end-points of the _____ also contribute to the Müller-Lyer illusion.

71. Personal motives and _____ often alter perceptions by changing the evaluation of what is seen or by altering attention to specific details.

72. Perceptions may be based on _____ or bottom-up processing of information.

73. In bottom-up processing, perceptions begin with the organization of low-level _____. In top-down processing, previous knowledge is used to rapidly _____ sensory information.

74. Attention, prior experience, suggestion, and motives combine in various ways to create perceptual sets, or _____. A perceptual set is a readiness to perceive in a particular way, induced by strong expectations.

● *Is extrasensory perception possible?*

Recite and Review: Pages 188-190

75. Parapsychology is the study of purported _____ phenomena, including clairvoyance (perceiving events at a distance), _____ ("mind reading"), precognition (perceiving future events), and psychokinesis (mentally influencing inanimate objects).

76. Clairvoyance, telepathy, and precognition are purported types of extrasensory _____.

77. Research in parapsychology remains controversial owing to a variety of problems. _____ and after-the-fact reinterpretation are problems with "natural" ESP episodes.

78. Many studies of ESP overlook the impact of statistically unusual outcomes that are no more than runs of _____.

79. The bulk of the evidence to date is _____ the existence of ESP. Very few positive results in ESP research have been replicated (_____) by independent scientists.

80. Stage ESP is based on _____ and tricks.

● *What can be done to enhance perceptual accuracy?*

Recite and Review: PSYCHOLOGY IN ACTION

81. Perceptions are a reconstruction of events. This is one reason why eyewitness testimony is surprisingly _____.

82. In many crimes, eyewitness accuracy is further damaged by weapon _____. Similar factors, such as observer stress, brief exposure times, cross-racial inaccuracies, and the wording of questions can _____ eyewitness accuracy.

83. Perceptual accuracy is enhanced by reality _____, dishabituation, and conscious efforts to pay _____.

84. It is also valuable to break perceptual habits, to _____ frames of reference, to beware of perceptual sets, and to be aware of the ways in which motives and emotions influence perceptions.

CONNECTIONS

1. _____   ciliary muscle

2. _____   iris

3. _____   cornea

4. _____   blind spot

5. _____   lens

6. _____   fovea

7. _____   retinal veins

8. _____   optic nerve

9. _____   aqueous humor

10. _____   pupil

11. _____   retina

12. _____ vestibular system

13. _____ cochlea

14. _____ round window

15. _____ auditory canal

16. _____ stapes

17. _____ auditory nerve

18. _____ incus

19. _____ oval window

20. _____ tympanic membrane

21. _____ malleus

22. _____ texture gradients

23. _____ stereoscopic vision

24. _____ convergence

25. _____ continuity

26. _____ light and shadow

27. _____ common region

28. _____ relative size

29. _____ closure

30. _____ overlap

31. _____ retinal disparity

32. _____ linear perspective

33. _____ nearness

34. _____ similarity

35. _____	reversible figure	a. convergence
36. _____	visual cliff	b. stereoscopic vision
37. _____	binocular muscle cue	c. run of luck
38. _____	mismatch	d. moon illusion
39. _____	Ponzo illusion	e. clairvoyance test
40. _____	Zulus	f. diminished Müller-Lyer illusion
41. _____	top-down	g. infant depth perception
42. _____	perceptual awareness	h. figure-ground
43. _____	Zener cards	i. surrender to experience
44. _____	decline effect	j. perceptual expectancy

CHECK YOUR MEMORY

Check Your Memory: Pages 152-154

1. The electromagnetic spectrum includes ultraviolet light and radio waves. T or F?
2. Each sensory organ is sensitive to a select range of physical energies. T or F?
3. The artificial vision system described in the text is based on electrodes implanted in the retina. T or F?
4. The retina responds to pressure, as well as light. T or F?

Check Your Memory: Pages 154-160

5. A nanometer is one-millionth of a meter. T or F?
6. The lens of the eye is about the size and thickness of a postage stamp. T or F?
7. Farsightedness is corrected with a convex lens. T or F?
8. The myopic eye is longer than normal. T or F?
9. There are more rods than cones in the eyes. T or F?
10. The blind spot is the point where the optic nerve leaves the eye. T or F?
11. Vision rated at 20/200 is better than average. T or F?
12. Blue emergency lights and taxiway lights are used because at night they are more visible to the cones. T or F?
13. The trichromatic theory of color vision says that black and white are produced by the rods. T or F?
14. According to the opponent-process theory it is impossible to have a reddish green or yellowish blue. T or F?
15. Yellow-blue color weakness is very rare. T or F?
16. In the U.S. and Canada, stoplights are always on the bottom of traffic signals. T or F?
17. Complete dark adaptation takes about 12 minutes. T or F?
18. Dark adaptation can be preserved by working in an area lit with red light. T or F?

Check Your Memory: Pages 161-164

19. Sound cannot travel in a vacuum. T or F?

20. The visible, external portion of the ear is the malleus. T or F?
21. The hair cells are part of the organ of Corti. T or F?
22. Hunter's notch occurs when the auditory ossicles are damaged by the sound of gunfire. T or F?
23. Cochlear implants stimulate the auditory nerve directly. T or F?
24. A 40 decibel sound could be described as quiet. T or F?
25. A 100 decibel sound can damage hearing in less than 8 hours. T or F?
26. Every 20 decibels increases sound energy by a factor of 10. T or F?

Check Your Memory: Pages 164-165

27. At least 1,000 different types of olfactory receptors exist. T or F?
28. Etherish odors smell like garlic. T or F?
29. Human pheromones (if they exist) are sensed as a subtle, perfume-like odor. T or F?
30. Flavors are greatly influenced by odor, as well as taste. T or F?
31. Taste buds are found throughout the mouth, not just on the tongue. T or F?
32. *Umami* is a pleasant "brothy" taste. T or F?

Check Your Memory: Pages 166-168

33. Vibration is one of the five basic skin sensations. T or F?
34. Areas of the skin that have high concentrations of pain receptors are no more sensitive to pain than other areas of the body. T or F?
35. Small nerve fibers generally carry warning-system pain messages. T or F?
36. High levels of anxiety tend to amplify the amount of pain a person experiences. T or F?
37. As a means of reducing pain, hot-water bottles are an example of counterirritation. T or F?
38. The semicircular canals are especially sensitive to the pull of gravity. T or F?
39. Motion sickness is believed to be related to the body's reactions to being poisoned. T or F?

Check Your Memory: Pages 169-171

40. If you wear a ring, you are rarely aware of it because of sensory gating. T or F?
41. The "seat-of-your pants" phenomenon is related to selective attention. T or F?
42. Attention is related to contrast or changes in stimulation. T or F?
43. Mild electrical stimulation of the skin can block reminding system pain. T or F?
44. Mild electrical stimulation of the skin causes a release of endorphins in free nerve endings. T or F?

Check Your Memory: Pages 172-173

45. Perception involves selecting, organizing, and integrating sensory information. T or F?
46. Some perceptual abilities must be learned after sight is restored to the previously blind. T or F?
47. Newborn babies show some evidence of size constancy. T or F?
48. Houses and cars look like toys from a low-flying airplane because of shape constancy. T or F?
49. Brightness constancy does not apply to objects illuminated by different amounts of light. T or F?

Check Your Memory: Pages 173-176

50. Basic figure-ground organization is learned at about age 2. T or F?
51. Contiguity refers to our tendency to see lines as continuous. T or F?

52. Necker's cube and the "three-pronged widget" are impossible figures. T or F?

Check Your Memory: Pages 176-182

53. Depth perception is partly learned and partly innate. T or F?
54. Human depth perception typically emerges at about 4 months of age. T or F?
55. Accommodation and convergence are muscular depth cues. T or F?
56. Accommodation acts as a depth cue primarily for distances greater than 4 feet from the eyes. T or F?
57. Convergence acts as a depth cue primarily for distances less than 4 feet from the eyes. T or F?
58. With one eye closed, the pictorial depth cues no longer provide information about depth and distance. T or F?
59. Changing the image size of an object implies that its distance from the viewer has changed, too. T or F?
60. In a drawing, the closer an object is to the horizon line, the nearer it appears to be to the viewer. T or F?
61. Aerial perspective is most powerful when the air is exceptionally clear. T or F?
62. When an observer is moving forward, objects beyond the observer's point of fixation appear to move forward too. T or F?
63. The moon's image is magnified by the dense atmosphere near the horizon. T or F?
64. More depth cues are present when the moon is viewed near the horizon. T or F?

Check Your Memory: Pages 182-187

65. The Ames room is primarily used to test the effects of inverted vision. T or F?
66. Cats who grow up surrounded by horizontal stripes are unusually sensitive to vertical stripes when they reach maturity. T or F?
67. Hearing voices when no one is speaking is an example of a perceptual illusion. T or F?
68. According to Richard Gregory, the arrowhead-tipped line in the Müller-Lyer illusion looks like the outside corner of a building. T or F?
69. Zulus rarely see round shapes and therefore fail to experience the Müller-Lyer illusion. T or F?
70. Analyzing information into small features and then building a recognizable pattern is called top-up processing. T or F?
71. Perceptual sets are frequently created by suggestion. T or F?
72. Labels and categories have been shown to have little real effect on perceptions. T or F?

Check Your Memory: Pages 188-190

73. Uri Geller was one of the first researchers in parapsychology to use the Zener cards. T or F?
74. Psychokinesis is classified as a psi event, but not a form of ESP. T or F?
75. Prophetic dreams are regarded as a form of precognition. T or F?
76. Strange coincidences are strong evidence for the existence of ESP. T or F?
77. The Zener cards eliminated the possibility of fraud and "leakage" of information in ESP experiments. T or F?
78. "Psi missing" is perhaps the best current evidence for ESP. T or F?
79. Belief in psi events has declined among parapsychologists in recent years. T or F?

Check Your Memory: PSYCHOLOGY IN ACTION

80. In many ways we see what we believe, as well as believe what we see. T or F?

81. The more confident an eyewitness is about the accuracy of his or her testimony, the more likely it is to be accurate. T or F?

82. The testimony of crime victims is generally more accurate than the testimony of bystanders. T or F?

83. Police officers and other trained observers are more accurate eyewitnesses than the average person. T or F?

84. Reality testing is the process Abraham Maslow described as a "surrender" to experience. T or F?

85. Perceptually, Zen masters have been shown to habituate more rapidly than the average person. T or F?

FINAL SURVEY AND REVIEW

● *In general, how do sensory systems function?*

1. Sensory organs _____ physical energies into nerve impulses.

2. The senses act as data _____ systems that select, analyze, and _____ sensory information.

3. A good example of _____ _____ is the identification of basic perceptual features in a stimulus pattern.

4. In fact, many sensory systems act as _____ detectors.

5. _____ and visual pop-out are examples of feature detection and sensory _____ in action.

6. Sensory response can be partially understood in terms of sensory _____ in the brain. That is, the _____ of the brain activated ultimately determines which type of sensory experience we have.

● *How is vision accomplished?*

7. The visible spectrum consists of _____ radiation in a narrow range.

8. The visible spectrum ranges from violet, with a wavelength of _____ _____, to red with a wavelength of _____ _____.

9. _____ refers to a color's name, which corresponds to its wavelength. Saturated or "pure" colors come from a narrow band of wavelengths. Brightness corresponds to the _____ of light waves.

10. The eye is in some ways like a camera. At its back lies an array of _____, called rods and cones, that make up a light-sensitive layer called the _____.

11. Vision is focused by the shape of the _____ and lens and by changes in the shape of the lens, called _____.

12. Four common visual defects, correctable with glasses, are _____ (nearsightedness), hyperopia (farsightedness), presbyopia (loss of accommodation), and _____ (in which portions of vision are out of focus).

13. In the retina, the rods specialize in night vision, black and white reception, and _____ detection.

14. The cones, found exclusively in the _____ and otherwise toward the middle of the eye, specialize in color vision, _____ (perception of fine detail), and daylight vision.

15. The rods supply much of our _____ vision. Loss of _____ vision is called tunnel vision.

16. The rods and cones differ in color sensitivity. _____-green is brightest for cones; _____-green for the rods (although they will see it as colorless).

17. In the retina, color vision is explained by the _____ theory. The theory says that three types of cones exist, each most sensitive to either red, green, or blue.

18. Three types of light-sensitive visual _____ are found in the cones, each is most sensitive to either red, green, or blue light.

19. Beyond the retina, the visual system analyzes colors into either-or messages. According to the _____ theory, color information can be coded as either _____ _____ _____, yellow or blue, and black or white messages.

20. Total color blindness is rare, but 8 percent of males and 1 percent of females are _____ color blind or color weak.

21. The _____ test is used to detect color blindness.

22. Dark adaptation, an increase in sensitivity to light, is caused by increased concentrations of _____ _____ in the rods and the cones.

23. Most dark adaptation is the result of increased _____ concentrations in the rods. Vitamin ____ deficiencies may cause night blindness.

● *What are the mechanisms of hearing?*

24. Sound waves are the stimulus for hearing. Sound travels as waves of _____ (peaks) and _____ (valleys) in the air.

25. The pitch of a sound corresponds to the _____ of sound waves. Loudness corresponds to the _____ (height) of sound waves.

26. Sound waves are transduced by the eardrum, auditory _____, oval window, cochlea, and ultimately, the hair cells in the organ of _____.

27. The frequency theory says that the frequency of nerve impulses in the _____ _____ matches the frequency of incoming sounds (up to 4000 hertz).

28. Place theory says that high tones register near the _____ of the cochlea and low tones near its _____.

29. Three basic types of deafness are nerve deafness, conduction deafness, and _____ deafness.

30. Conduction deafness can often be overcome with a hearing aid. Nerve deafness can sometimes be alleviated by _____ implants.

31. Stimulation deafness can be prevented by avoiding excessive exposure to loud sounds. Sounds above _____ _____ pose an immediate danger to hearing. Two warning signs of stimulation deafness are temporary threshold shift and a ringing in the ears, called _____.

● *How do the chemical senses operate?*

32. _____ (smell) and _____ (taste) are chemical senses responsive to airborne or liquefied molecules.

33. The _____ _____ _____ theory partially explains smell. In addition, the location of the olfactory receptors in the nose helps identify various scents.

34. The top outside edges of the tongue are responsive to _____, _____, _____, and bitter tastes. It is suspected that a fifth taste quality called _____ also exists.

35. Taste also appears to be based in part on lock-and-key coding of _____ shapes.

● *What are the somesthetic senses and why are they important?*

36. The somesthetic senses include the skin senses, vestibular senses, and _____ senses (receptors that detect muscle and joint positioning).

37. The skin senses include touch, pressure, _____, cold, and warmth. Sensitivity to each is related to the number of _____ found in an area of skin.

38. Distinctions can be made between _____ system pain, and _____ system pain.

39. Pain can be reduced by lowering anxiety and redirecting _____ to stimuli other than the pain stimulus.

40. Feeling that you have _____ over a stimulus tends to reduce the amount of pain you experience.

41. Various forms of motion sickness are related to messages received from the _____ system, which senses gravity and head movement.

42. The _____ organs detect the pull of gravity and rapid head movements.

43. The movement of fluid within the _____ canals, and the movement of the crista within each _____, detects head movement and positioning.

44. According to _____ _____ theory, motion sickness is caused by a mismatch of visual, kinesthetic, and vestibular sensations. Motion sickness can be avoided by minimizing sensory conflict.

● *Why are we more aware of some sensations than others?*

45. Incoming sensations are affected by sensory _____ (a decrease in the number of nerve impulses sent).

46. Selective _____ (selection and diversion of messages in the brain) and sensory gating (blocking or alteration of messages flowing toward the brain) also alter sensations.

47. Selective gating of pain messages apparently takes place in the spinal cord. _____ _____ theory proposes an explanation for many pain phenomena.

● *How do perceptual constancies affect our perceptions?*

48. Perception is the process of assembling _____ into patterns that provide a usable _____ _____ of the world.

49. In vision, the _____ image changes from moment to moment, but the external world appears stable and undistorted because of perceptual _____.

50. In size and shape constancy, the perceived sizes and shapes of objects remain the same even though their retinal images change size and shape. The apparent _____ of objects remains stable (a property called brightness constancy) because each reflects a constant _____ of _____.

51. Perceptual constancies are partly _____ (inborn) and partly _____ (learned).

● *What basic principles do we use to group sensations into meaningful patterns?*

52. The most basic organization of sensations is a division into _____ and _____ ? (object and background).

53. A number of factors, identified by the _____ psychologists, contribute to the organization of sensations. These are _____, similarity, continuity, _____, contiguity, common region, and combinations of the preceding.

54. Stimuli near one another tend to be perceptually grouped together. So, too, do stimuli that are similar in appearance. _____ refers to the fact that perceptions tend to be organized as simple, uninterrupted patterns.

55. _____ refers to nearness in time and space. Stimuli that fall in a defined area, or common region, also tend to be grouped together.

56. A perceptual organization may be thought of as an hypothesis held until evidence contradicts it. _____ patterns disrupt perceptual organization, especially figure-ground perceptions.

57. Perceptual organization shifts for _____ stimuli, which may have more than one interpretation. An example is _____ cube. Impossible _____ resist stable organization altogether.

● *How is it possible to see depth and judge distance?*

58. Depth perception is the ability to perceive _____ space and judge distances.

59. Depth perception is present in basic form soon after birth as shown by testing with the _____ _____ and other methods. As soon as infants become active crawlers they refuse to cross the deep side of the _____ _____.

60. Depth perception depends on the muscular cues of _____ (bending of the lens) and _____ (inward movement of the eyes).

61. A number of _____ cues, which will work in flat paintings, drawings, and photographs, also underlie normal depth perception.

62. Some of these cues are: _____ _____ (the apparent convergence of parallel lines), relative size (more distant objects appear smaller), height in the picture plane, light and shadow (shadings of light), and overlap or _____ (one object overlaps another).

63. Additional pictorial cues include: texture _____ (textures become finer in the distance), aerial haze (loss of color and detail at large distances), and relative motion or motion _____ (differences in the apparent movement of objects when a viewer is moving).

64. All the pictorial cues are _____ depth cues (only one eye is needed to make use of them).

65. The moon illusion refers to the fact that the moon appears larger near the _____.

66. The moon illusion appears to be explained by the _____ _____ hypothesis, which emphasizes the greater number of _____ _____ present when the moon is on the horizon.

● *How is perception altered by learning, expectations, and motives?*

67. Organizing and interpreting sensations is greatly influenced by learned _____ _____. An example is the _____ room, which looks rectangular but is actually distorted so that objects in the room appear to change size.

68. Sensitivity to perceptual features is also partly learned. Studies of _____ vision show that even the most basic organization is subject to a degree of change. Active movement speeds _____ to new perceptual environments.

69. Illusions are often related to perceptual habits. One of the most familiar of all illusions, the _____ illusion, involves two equal-length lines tipped with arrowheads and V's. This illusion seems to be related to perceptual learning based on experience with box-shaped buildings and rooms.

70. Linear perspective, size-distance _____ relationships, and mislocating the _____ of the lines also contribute to the Müller-Lyer illusion.

71. Personal _____ and values often alter perceptions by changing the evaluation of what is seen or by altering attention to specific details.

72. Perceptions may be based on top-down or bottom-up _____ of information.

73. _____ perceptions begin with the organization of low-level features. In _____ processing, previous knowledge is used to rapidly organize sensory information.

74. Attention, prior experience, suggestion, and motives combine in various ways to create _____ _____, or expectancies. A _____ _____ is a readiness to perceive in a particular way, induced by strong expectations.

● *Is extrasensory perception possible?*

75. _____ is the study of purported psi phenomena, including clairvoyance (perceiving events at a distance), telepathy ("mind reading"), _____ (perceiving future events), and psychokinesis (mentally influencing inanimate objects).

76. Clairvoyance, telepathy, and precognition are purported types of _____ perception.

77. Research in parapsychology remains controversial owing to a variety of problems. Coincidence and after-the-fact _____ are problems with "natural" ESP episodes.
78. Many studies of ESP overlook the impact of _____ unusual outcomes that are no more than runs of luck.
79. The bulk of the evidence to date is against the existence of ESP. Very few positive results in ESP research have been _____ (repeated) by independent scientists.
80. _____ ESP is based on deception and tricks.

● *What can be done to enhance perceptual accuracy?*

81. Perception is an active _____ of events. This is one reason why eyewitness testimony is surprisingly inaccurate.
82. In many crimes, eyewitness accuracy is further damaged by _____ focus. Similar factors, such as observer _____, brief exposure times, cross-racial inaccuracies, and the wording of questions can lower eyewitness accuracy.
83. Perceptual accuracy is enhanced by reality testing, _____, and conscious efforts to pay attention.
84. It is also valuable to break _____ _____, to broaden frames of reference, to beware of perceptual sets, and to be aware of the ways in which motives and emotions influence perceptions.

MASTERY TEST

1. Sensory conflict theory attributes motion sickness to mismatches between what three systems?
   a. olfaction, kinesthesis, and audition   b. vision, kinesthesis, and the vestibular system
   c. kinesthesis, audition, and the somesthetic system   d. vision, gustation, and the skin senses

2. Which of the following types of color blindness is most common?
   a. yellow-blue, male   b. yellow-blue, female   c. red-green, female   d. red-green, male

3. Which of the following does not belong with the others?
   a. Pacinian corpuscle   b. Merkle's disk   c. organ of Corti   d. free nerve endings

4. Which theory of color vision best explains the fact that we do not see yellowish blue?
   a. trichromatic   b. chromatic gating   c. Ishihara hypothesis   d. opponent process

5. Dark adaptation is closely related to concentrations of _____ in the _____.
   a. retinal, aqueous humor   b. photopsin, cones   c. rhodopsin, rods   d. photons, optic nerve

6. Sensory analysis tends to extract perceptual _____ from stimulus patterns.
   a. thresholds   b. features   c. transducers   d. amplitudes

7. Which pair of terms is most closely related?
   a. hyperopia—color blindness b. astigmatism—presbyopia c. myopia—astigmatism
   d. hyperopia—presbyopia

8. The painkilling effects of acupuncture are partly explained by _____ theory.
   a. lock-and-key b. gate control c. opponent-process d. frequency

9. According to the _____ theory of hearing, low tones cause the greatest movement near
   the _____ of the cochlea.
   a. place, outer tip b. frequency, outer tip c. place, base d. frequency, base

10. Which of the following best represents the concept of a transducer?
    a. Translating English into Spanish. b. Copying a computer file from one floppy disk to another.
    c. Speaking into a telephone receiver. d. Turning water into ice.

11. Rods and cones are to vision as _____ are to hearing.
    a. auditory ossicles b. vibrations c. pinnas d. hair cells

12. You lose the ability to smell floral odors. This is called _____ and it is compatible with
    the _____ theory of olfaction.
    a. anosmia, lock-and-key b. anhedonia, place c. tinnitus, gate-control
    d. sensory adaptation, molecular

13. The main problem with current artificial vision systems is
    a. the retina's lack of an absolute threshold b. the danger of damaging the eyes while
    producing phosphenes c. their inability to transduce letters d. the rejection of implanted electrodes

14. Which two dimensions of color are related to the wavelength of electromagnetic energy?
    a. hue and saturation b. saturation and brightness c. brightness and hue
    d. brightness and amplitude

15. The existence of the blind spot is explained by a lack of
    a. rhodopsin b. peripheral vision c. photoreceptors d. activity in the fovea

16. In vision, a loss of accommodation is most associated with aging of the
    a. iris b. fovea c. lens d. cornea

17. Visual acuity and color vision are provided by the _____ found in large numbers in the _____
    of the eye.
    a. cones, fovea b. cones, periphery c. rods, fovea d. rods, periphery

18. The Ames room creates a conflict between
    a. horizontal features and vertical features b. attention and habituation c. top-down and bottom-up
    processing d. shape constancy and size constancy

19. Weapon focus tends to lower eyewitness accuracy because it affects
    a. selective attention   b. the adaptation level   c. perceptions of contiguity   d. dishabituation

20. The fact that American tourists in London tend to look in the wrong direction before stepping into crosswalks is based on
    a. sensory localization   b. perceptual habits   c. sensory gating   d. unconscious transference

21. Size constancy
    a. emerges at about 4 months of age   b. is affected by experience with seeing objects of various sizes
    c. requires that objects be illuminated by light of the same intensity   d. all of the preceding

22. Which of the following cues would be of greatest help to a person trying to thread a needle?
    a. light and shadow   b. texture gradients   c. linear perspective   d. overlap

23. Size-distance invariances contribute to which of the following?
    a. Müller-Lyer illusion   b. the stroboscopic illusion   c. perceptual hallucinations
    d. changes in perceptual sets

24. The visual cliff is used primarily to test infant
    a. size constancy   b. figure-ground perception   c. depth perception
    d. adaptation to spatial distortions

25. Which of the following organizational principles is based on nearness in time and space?
    a. continuity   b. closure   c. contiguity   d. size constancy

26. Which of the following is both a muscular and a monocular depth cue?
    a. convergence   b. relative motion   c. aerial perspective   d. accommodation

27. A previously blind person has just had her sight restored. Which of the following perceptual experiences is she most likely to have?
    a. perceptual set   b. size constancy   c. linear perspective   d. figure-ground

28. An artist manages to portray a face with just a few unconnected lines. Apparently the artist has capitalized on
    a. closure   b. contiguity   c. the reversible figure effect   d. the principle of camouflage

29. The most basic source of stereoscopic vision is
    a. accommodation   b. retinal disparity   c. convergence   d. stroboscopic motion

30. Necker's cube is a good example of
    a. an ambiguous stimulus   b. an impossible figure   c. camouflage   d. a binocular depth cue

31. Skeptics regard the decline effect as evidence that _____ occurred in an ESP test.
    a. replication   b. cheating   c. a run of luck   d. leakage

32. Which of the following is a binocular depth cue?
    a. accommodation   b. convergence   c. linear perspective   d. motion parallax

33. Ambiguous stimuli allow us to hold more than one perceptual
    a. gradient   b. parallax   c. constancy   d. hypothesis

34. Increased perceptual awareness is especially associated with
    a. dishabituation   b. unconscious transference   c. high levels of stress
    d. stimulus repetition without variation

ANSWERS

Recite and Review

1. nerve
2. data, analyze
3. perceptual
4. detectors
5. sensory
6. sensory, activated
7. visible
8. wavelength, wavelength
9. wavelength, narrow
10. rods, cones
11. shape, shape
12. nearsightedness, accommodation
13. rods
14. cones, color
15. rods
16. sensitivity
17. retina, cones
18. cones
19. either-or, black or white
20. Total
21. color blindness
22. increase, rods, cones
23. rods, night
24. peaks, valleys
25. pitch, height
26. eardrum, hair
27. frequency, frequency
28. high, low

29. nerve
30. Nerve
31. loud, shifts
32. smell, taste
33. location
34. bitter
35. coding
36. skin
37. pressure, number
38. reminding
39. lowering
40. reduce
41. head
42. gravity
43. fluid, crista
44. mismatch
45. reduction (or decrease)
46. gating
47. spinal cord
48. patterns, model
49. image, perceptual
50. constancy, constant
51. inborn, learned
52. object, background
53. organization, similarity, common
54. grouped, appearance
55. complete, time
56. hypothesis, organization
57. stimuli, cube
58. Depth

59. birth, crawlers
60. lens, eyes
61. cues, flat
62. parallel lines, smaller, picture
63. finer, motion, motion
64. one eye
65. larger
66. distance, horizon
67. habits, size
68. features, movement
69. habits, buildings
70. size-distance, lines
71. values
72. top-down
73. features, organize
74. expectancies
75. psi, telepathy
76. perception
77. Coincidence
78. luck
79. against, repeated
80. deception
81. inaccurate
82. focus, lower
83. testing, attention
84. broaden

Connections

1. d
2. f
3. h
4. b
5. i
6. c
7. k
8. a
9. e
10. g
11. j
12. e
13. g
14. h
15. a
16. d
17. f
18. c
19. i
20. j
21. b
22. m
23. g
24. f
25. c
26. l
27. e
28. j
29. d
30. k
31. h
32. i
33. a
34. b
35. h
36. g
37. a
38. b
39. d
40. f
41. j
42. i
43. e
44. c

Check Your Memory

1. T
2. T
3. F
4. T
5. F
6. F
7. T
8. T
9. T
10. T
11. F
12. F
13. T
14. T
15. T
16. F
17. F
18. T
19. T
20. F
21. T
22. F
23. T
24. T
25. T
26. T
27. T
28. F
29. F
30. T
31. T
32. T
33. F
34. F
35. F
36. T
37. T
38. F
39. T
40. F
41. T
42. T
43. T
44. F
45. T
46. T
47. T
48. F
49. T
50. F
51. F
52. F
53. T
54. T
55. T
56. F
57. F
58. F
59. T
60. F
61. F
62. T
63. F
64. T
65. F
66. F
67. F
68. T
69. F
70. F
71. T
72. F
73. F
74. T
75. T
76. F
77. F
78. F
79. T
80. T
81. F
82 F
83. F
84. F
85. F

Final Survey and Review

1. transduce
2. reduction, filter
3. sensory analysis
4. feature
5. Phosphenes, coding
6. localization, area
7. electromagnetic

8. 400 nanometers, 700 nanometers
9. Hue, amplitude
10. photoreceptors, retina
11. cornea, accommodation
12. myopia, astigmatism
13. motion
14. fovea, acuity
15. peripheral, peripheral
16. Yellow, blue
17. trichromatic
18. pigments
19. opponent-process, red or green
20. red-green
21. Ishihara
22. visual pigments
23. rhodopsin, A
24. compression, rarefaction
25. frequency, amplitude
26. ossicles, Corti
27. auditory nerves
28. base, tip
29. stimulation
30. cochlear
31. 120 decibels, tinnitus
32. Olfaction, gustation
33. lock and key
34. sweet, salty, sour, umami
35. molecule
36. kinesthetic
37. pain, receptors
38. warning, reminding
39. attention
40. control
41. vestibular
42. otolith
43. semicircular, ampulla
44. sensory conflict
45. adaptation
46. attention
47. Gate control

48. sensations, mental model
49. retinal, constancies
50. brightness, proportion, light
51. native, empirical
52. figure, ground
53. Gestalt, nearness, closure
54. Closure
55. Contiguity
56. Camouflage
57. ambiguous, Necker's, figures
58. three-dimensional
59. visual cliff, visual cliff
60. accommodation, convergence
61. pictorial
62. linear perspective, interposition
63. gradients, parallax
64. monocular
65. horizon
66. apparent distance, depth cues
67. perceptual habits, Ames
68. inverted, adaptation
69. Müller-Lyer
70. invariance, end-points habituation
71. motives
72. processing
73. Bottom-up, top-down
74. perceptual sets, perceptual set
75. Parapsychology, precognition
76. extrasensory
77. reinterpretation
78. statistically
79. replicated
80. Stage
81. reconstruction

82. weapon, stress
83. dishabituation
84. perceptual habits

Mastery Test

1. b (p. 168)
2. d (p. 158)
3. c (p. 167)
4. d (p. 157)
5. c (p. 160)
6. b (p. 152)
7. d (p. 155)
8. b (p. 170)
9. a (p. 162)
10. c (p. 152)
11. d (p. 161)
12. a (p. 164)
13. d (p. 153)
14. a (p. 154)
15. c (p. 156)
16. c (p. 155)
17. a (p. 156)
18. d (p. 183)
19. a (p. 191)
20. b (p. 183)
21. b (p. 172)
22. d (p. 179)
23. a (p. 185)
24. c (p. 177)
25. c (p. 175)
26. d (p. 177)
27. d (p. 173)
28. a (p. 175)
29. b (p. 177)
30. a (p. 175)
31. c (p. 189)
32. b (p. 177)
33. d (p. 175)
34. a (p. 193)

Chapter 6
States of Consciousness

CHAPTER OVERVIEW

Consciousness consists of everything you are aware of at a given instant. Altered states of consciousness (ASCs) differ significantly from normal waking consciousness. Many conditions produce ASCs, which frequently have culturally defined meanings.

Sleep is an innate biological rhythm characterized by changes in consciousness and brain activity. Brain-wave patterns and sleep behaviors define four stages of sleep. The two most basic forms of sleep are rapid eye movement (REM) sleep and non-rapid eye movement (NREM) sleep. Dreams and nightmares occur primarily in REM sleep. Sleepwalking, sleeptalking, and night terrors are NREM events. Insomnia and other sleep disturbances are common, but generally treatable. Dreaming is emotionally restorative and it may help form adaptive memories. The psychodynamic view portrays dreams as a form of wish fulfillment; the activation-synthesis hypothesis says that dreaming is a physiological process with little meaning.

Hypnosis is characterized by narrowed attention and increased openness to suggestion. People vary in hypnotic susceptibility. Most hypnotic phenomena are related to the basic suggestion effect. Hypnosis can relieve pain and it has other useful effects, but it is not magic. Stage hypnotists simulate hypnosis in order to entertain.

Meditation can be used to alter consciousness, promote relaxation, and reduce stress. Two particular benefits of meditation are its ability to interrupt anxious thoughts and its ability to elicit the relaxation response. Sensory deprivation refers to any major reduction in external stimulation. Sensory deprivation also produces deep relaxation and a variety of perceptual effects. It can be used to help people enhance creative thinking and to change bad habits.

Psychoactive drugs are substances that alter consciousness. Most can be placed on a scale ranging from stimulation to depression, although some drugs are better classified as hallucinogens. The potential for abuse is high for drugs that lead to physical dependence, but psychological dependence can also be a serious problem. Drug abuse is often a symptom, rather than a cause, of personal maladjustment. It is supported by the immediate pleasure but delayed consequences associated with many psychoactive drugs and by cultural values that encourage drug abuse.

Various strategies, ranging from literal to highly symbolic, can be used to reveal the meanings of dreams. Dreaming—especially lucid dreaming—can be a source of creativity and it may be used for problem solving and personal growth.

LEARNING OBJECTIVES

To demonstrate mastery of this chapter, you should be able to:

1. Define *consciousness* and explain what waking consciousness is.
2. Define and describe an *altered state of consciousness.* Include a description of the meaning and uses of altered states of consciousness in other cultures.
3. Describe the limitations of sleep learning.
4. Define the term *biological rhythm* and explain its relationship to sleep.
5. Define and describe the term *microsleep.*
6. Describe the general effects of 2 to 3 days of sleep deprivation. Name and describe the condition that occurs when a person is deprived of sleep for a longer period of time.
7. State how long the average sleep-waking cycle is. Explain how we tie our sleep rhythms to a 24 hour day.
8. Describe the normal range of sleep needs. Describe how the aging process affects sleep.
9. State the average ratio of time awake to time asleep.
10. Explain how and why shift work and jet lag may adversely affect a person. Explain how the direction of travel (or of rotating shifts) affects rhythms and how to minimize the effects of shifting one's rhythms.
11. Describe how the brain's systems and chemistry promote sleep.
12. Briefly describe each of the four stages of sleep. Include a description of the brain waves associated with each and those associated with wakefulness.
13. Describe the cyclical nature of the sleep stages.
14. Name and differentiate the two basic states of sleep. Explain how the relative amounts of each these two sleep states can be influenced by events of the day.
15. State how long dreams usually last.
16. List the physiological changes that occur during REM sleep, including a description of REM behavior disorder.
17. Describe the probable functions of REM sleep.
18. List and briefly describe the twelve sleep disorders that are found in DSM-IV. (See Table 6.1.)
19. Define *insomnia*. Describe the effects of nonprescription and prescription drugs on insomnia.
20. List and describe the characteristics and treatment of the three types of insomnia.
21. List and briefly describe six behavioral remedies which can be used to combat insomnia.
22. Characterize the following major sleep disturbances of NREM sleep.
    a. somnambulism
    b. sleeptalking
    c. night terrors (include a differentiation between night terrors and nightmares)

The following objectives are related to the material in the "Exploring Psychology" section of the text.
23. Explain Calvin Hall's view of dreams.
24. Explain how Freud viewed dreams, and present the evidence against his view.
25. Describe the activation-synthesis hypothesis concerning dreaming.

26. Give the general definition of hypnosis and then describe how it is that the general definition is not accepted by all psychologists.

27. Briefly trace the history of hypnosis from Mesmer through its use today.
28. State the proportion of people who can be hypnotized.
29. Explain how a person's hypnotic susceptibility can be determined. Include a brief description of the dimensions of the Stanford Hypnotic Susceptibility Scale.
30. List the four common factors in all hypnotic techniques. Explain why all hypnosis may really be self-hypnosis.
31. Explain what the basic suggestion effect is.
32. Explain how hypnosis can affect:

    a. strength   b. memory   c. amnesia   d. pain relief   e. age regression   f. sensory changes

33. List three areas in which hypnosis appears to have its greatest value, and then state a general conclusion concerning the effectiveness of hypnosis.
34. Using the five characteristics of the stage setting outlined in the chapter, explain how a stage hypnotist gets people to perform the way they do in front of an audience.
35. Name and describe the two major forms of meditation.
36. Describe the relaxation response.
37. Describe what is known about the effects of meditation.
38. Explain what sensory deprivation is. Include a discussion of the positive and negative effects of this procedure.
39. Define the term *psychoactive drug.*
40. Differentiate physical dependence from psychological dependence.
41. Describe the following frequently abused drugs in terms of their effects, possible medical uses, side effects or long term symptoms, organic damage potential, and potential for physical and/or psychological dependence.

    a. amphetamines (include the term amphetamine psychosis)
    b. cocaine (include the three signs of abuse)
    c. MDMA ("Ecstasy")
    d. caffeine (include the term *caffeinism*)
    e. nicotine
    f. barbiturates
    g. GHB
    h. tranquilizers (including the concept of drug interaction)
    i. alcohol (include the concept of binge drinking)
    j. hallucinogens (including marijuana)

42. Compare the efficacy of quitting smoking "cold turkey" versus cutting down or smoking low-tar cigarettes. (Also see the Highlight.)
43. List and explain the three steps in the development of a drinking problem.
44. Generally describe the treatment process for alcoholism. Name the form of therapy that has probably been the most successful.
45. Explain why drug abuse is such a common problem.

The following objectives are related to the material in the "Psychology in Action" section of the text.
46. List and describe the four processes identified by Freud which disguise the hidden meaning of dreams.
47. Contrast Hall's and Cartwright's views of dream interpretation.
48. List the eight steps for remembering dreams.
49. Explain how Perls viewed dreams and how he suggested that people interpret them.

50. Describe how one could use dreams to aid in problem solving. Include a description of lucid dreams and how they have been used in the problem solving process.

RECITE AND REVIEW

● *What is an altered state of consciousness?*

Recite and Review: Page 198

  1. States of _____ that differ from normal, alert, _____ consciousness are called altered states of consciousness (ASCs).

  2. ASCs involve distinct shifts in the quality and _____ of mental activity.

  3. Altered states are especially associated with _____ and _____, hypnosis, meditation, _____ deprivation, and psychoactive drugs.

  4. Cultural conditioning greatly affects what altered states a person recognizes, seeks, considers _____, and attains.

● *What are the effects of sleep loss or changes in sleep patterns?*

Recite and Review: Pages 198-202

  5. Sleep is an innate biological _____ essential for _____.

  6. Higher animals and people deprived of sleep experience _____ microsleeps.

  7. Moderate sleep loss mainly affects alertness and self-motivated performance on _____ or boring tasks.

  8. Extended sleep _____ can (somewhat rarely) produce a _____ sleep-deprivation psychosis, marked by confusion, delusions, and possibly hallucinations.

  9. Circadian _____ within the body are closely tied to sleep, activity levels, and energy cycles.

10. Sleep patterns show some flexibility, but 7 to 8 hours remains average. The unscheduled human sleep-waking cycle averages _____ hours and _____ minutes, but cycles of _____ and _____ tailor it to 24-hour days.

11. The amount of daily sleep _____ steadily from birth to old age and switches from multiple sleep-wake cycles to once-a-day sleep periods.

12. Adapting to _____ or _____ sleep cycles is difficult and inefficient for most people.

13. Time zone travel and _____ work can cause jet lag, a serious disruption of _____ and bodily rhythms.

14. If you are flying east, it is best to _____ early in the day. If you are flying west, it is better to _____ late in the day. If you anticipate a major change in _____ rhythms, it helps to preadapt to the new _____.

● *Are there different stages of sleep?*

Recite and Review: Pages 202-205

15. Sleepiness is associated with the accumulation of a sleep hormone in the _____ and spinal cord.

16. Sleep depends on which of _____ opposed sleep and waking systems in the _____ is dominant at any given moment.

17. Sleep occurs in _____ stages defined by changes in behavior and brain _____ recorded with an electroencephalograph (EEG).

18. Stage 1, _____ sleep, has small irregular brain waves. In stage 2, _____ spindles appear. _____ waves appear in stage 3. Stage 4, or deep sleep, is marked by almost pure delta waves.

19. Sleepers _____ between stages 1 and 4 (passing through stages 2 and 3) several times each night.

20. There are two basic sleep states, rapid eye _____ (REM) sleep and non-REM (NREM) sleep.

21. REM sleep is much more strongly associated with _____ than non-REM sleep is.

22. _____ and REMs occur mainly during stage 1 sleep, but usually not during the first stage 1 period.

23. Dreaming is accompanied by sexual and _____ arousal but relaxation of the skeletal _____. People who move about violently while asleep may suffer from _____ behavior disorder.˙

24. People deprived of REM sleep showed an urgent need to _____ and mental disturbances the next day. However, total sleep loss seems to be more important than loss of a single sleep _____.

25. One of the more important functions of REM sleep appears to be the processing of adaptive _____.

● *What are the causes of sleep disorders and unusual sleep events?*

Recite and Review: Pages 206-209

26. Insomnia, which is difficulty in getting to sleep or staying asleep, may be _____ or chronic.

27. When insomnia is treated with drugs, sleep quality is often _____ and drug-dependency _____ may develop.

28. The amino acid tryptophan, found in bread, pasta, and other foods, helps promote _____.

29. Behavioral approaches to managing insomnia, such as relaxation, sleep restriction, _____ control, and paradoxical _____ are quite effective.

30. _____ (somnambulism) and sleeptalking occur during NREM sleep in stages 3 and 4.

31. Night terrors occur in _____ sleep, whereas nightmares occur in _____ sleep.

32. Nightmares can be eliminated by the method called imagery _____.

33. During sleep apnea, people repeatedly stop _____. Apnea is suspected as one cause of _____ infant death syndrome (SIDS).

● *Do dreams have meaning?*

Recite and Review: Pages 209-210

34. Calvin Hall found that most dream content is about _____ settings, people, and actions. Dreams more often involve negative _____ than positive _____.

35. The Freudian, or psychodynamic, view is that dreams express unconscious _____, frequently hidden by dream symbols.

36. Allan Hobson and Robert McCarley's _____-synthesis model portrays dreaming as a physiological process. The brain, they say, creates dreams to explain _____ and motor messages that occur during REM sleep.

● *How is hypnosis done, and what are its limitations?*

Recite and Review: Pages 211-214

37. Hypnosis is an altered state characterized by narrowed attention and _____ suggestibility.

38. In the 1700s, Franz Mesmer (whose name is the basis for the term mesmerize) practiced "_____ magnetism," which was actually a demonstration of the power of

_____.

39. The term _____ was first used by James Braid, an English doctor.

40. People vary in hypnotic susceptibility; _____ out of 10 can be hypnotized, as revealed by scores on the Stanford Hypnotic Susceptibility _____.

41. The core of hypnosis is the _____ suggestion effect—a tendency to carry out suggested actions as if they were involuntary.

42. Hypnosis appears capable of producing relaxation, controlling _____, and altering perceptions.

43. Stage hypnotism takes advantage of typical stage behavior, _____ suggestibility, responsive subjects, disinhibition, and _____ to simulate hypnosis.

● *What is meditation? Does it have any benefits?*

Recite and Review: Pages 214-215

44. Meditation refers to mental exercises that are used to alter _____.

45. In receptive meditation, attention is _____ to include an awareness of one's entire moment-by-moment experience.

46. In concentrative meditation, attention is focused on a _____ object or thought.

47. Two major benefits of meditation are its ability to interrupt anxious thoughts and its ability to elicit the relaxation response (the pattern of changes that occur in the body at times of deep _____).

48. Sensory deprivation takes place when there is a major reduction in the amount or variety of sensory _____ available to a person.

49. Prolonged sensory deprivation is stressful and disruptive, leading to _____ distortions.

50. Brief or mild sensory deprivation can enhance sensory sensitivity and induce deep

_____.

51. Sensory deprivation also appears to aid the breaking of long-standing _____ and promotes creative thinking. This effect is the basis for Restricted Environmental Stimulation Therapy (REST).

● *What are the effects of the more commonly used psychoactive drugs?*

Recite and Review: Pages 216-230

52. A psychoactive drug is a substance that affects the brain in ways that _____ consciousness.

53. Most psychoactive drugs can be placed on a scale ranging from stimulation to _____. Some, however, are best described as hallucinogens (drugs that alter _____ impressions).

54. Drugs may cause a physical dependence (_____) or a psychological dependence, or both.

55. The physically addicting drugs are alcohol, amphetamines, barbiturates, cocaine, codeine, GHB, heroin, methadone, morphine, tobacco, and tranquilizers. All psychoactive drugs can lead to _____ dependence.

56. Stimulant drugs are readily abused because of the period of _____ that often follows stimulation. The greatest risks are associated with amphetamines, cocaine, MDMA, and nicotine, but even _____ can be a problem.

57. MDMA or "_____," which is similar to amphetamine, has been linked with numerous deaths and with mental impairment.

58. _____ includes the added risk of lung cancer, heart disease, and other health problems.

59. Barbiturates are _____ drugs whose overdose level is close to the intoxication dosage, making them dangerous drugs. Mixing barbiturates and alcohol may result in a fatal _____ interaction (in which the joint effect of two drugs exceeds the effects of adding one drug's effects to the other's).

60. The depressant drug _____ (gamma-hydroxybuyrate) can cause coma, breathing failure, and death in relatively low doses.

61. Benzodiazepine tranquilizers, such as _____, are used to lower anxiety. When abused, they have a strong _____ potential.

62. Alcohol is the most heavily abused drug in common use today. The development of a drinking problem is usually marked by an _____ phase of increasing consumption, a crucial phase, in which a _____ drink can set off a chain reaction, and a chronic phase, in which a person lives to drink and drinks to live.

63. Marijuana is a hallucinogen subject to an _____ pattern similar to alcohol. Studies have linked chronic marijuana use with memory impairment, lung cancer, reproductive problems, immune system disorders, and other health problems.

64. Drug abuse is related to personal and social maladjustment, attempts to cope, and the _____ reinforcing qualities of psychoactive drugs.

● *How are dreams used to promote personal understanding?*

Recite and Review: PSYCHOLOGY IN ACTION

65. Freud held that the meaning of dreams is _____ by four dream _____ he called condensation, displacement, symbolization, and secondary elaboration.

66. Calvin Hall emphasizes the setting, cast, _____, and emotions of a dream.

67. Rosalind Cartwright's view of dreams as feeling statements and Fritz Perls's technique of _____ for dream elements are also helpful.

68. Dreams may be used for _____ problem solving, especially when dream control is achieved through lucid dreaming (a dream in which the dreamer feels capable of normal thought and action).

CONNECTIONS

1. _____	REST	a.	over 9 hours
2. _____	Randy Gardner	b.	infancy
3. _____	long sleepers	c.	reflex muscle contraction
4. _____	sleep patterns	d.	awake, alert
5. _____	short sleep cycles	e.	sensory deprivation
6. _____	beta waves	f.	interrupted breathing
7. _____	alpha waves	g.	relaxed
8. _____	hypnic jerk	h.	sleep deprivation
9. _____	apnea	i.	sexual arousal
10. _____	REM sleep	j.	2 to 1 ratio

11. _____	sleep drunkenness	a.	violent actions
12. _____	hypersomnia	b.	fatal to infants
13. _____	REM behavior disorder	c.	unconscious meanings
14. _____	narcolepsy	d.	slow awakening
15. _____	SIDS	e.	dangerous stimulant
16. _____	tryptophan	f.	sudden daytime REM sleep
17. _____	dream symbols	g.	sensory deprivation
18. _____	autosuggestion	h.	self-hypnosis
19. _____	MDMA	i.	sleep inducing foods
20. _____	flotation tank	j.	excessive sleepiness

21. _____	drug tolerance	a. cocaine rush
22. _____	amphetamine	b. cancer agent
23. _____	dopamine	c. addiction
24. _____	nicotine	d. sedative
25. _____	carcinogen	e. hallucinogen
26. _____	barbiturate	f. detoxification
27. _____	AAA	g. loss of pleasure
28. _____	alcohol treatment	h. stimulant
29. _____	THC	i. self-help group
30. _____	anhedonia	j. insecticide

CHECK YOUR MEMORY

Check Your Memory: Page 198

1. The quality and pattern of mental activity changes during an ASC. T or F?
2. All people experience at least some ASCs. T or F?
3. Both sensory overload and monotonous stimulation can produce ASCs. T or F?
4. Almost every known religion has accepted some ASCs as desirable. T or F?

Check Your Memory: Pages 198-202

5. Through sleep learning it is possible to master a foreign language. T or F?
6. A total inability to sleep results in death. T or F?
7. Even after extended sleep loss, most symptoms are removed by a single night's sleep. T or F?
8. Hallucinations and delusions are the most common reaction to extended sleep deprivation. T or F?
9. Without scheduled light and dark periods, human sleep rhythms would drift into unusual patterns. T or F?
10. The average human sleep-wake cycle lasts 23 hours and 10 minutes. T or F?
11. Short sleepers are defined as those who average less than 5 hours of sleep per night. T or F?
12. Shortened sleep cycles, such as 3 hours of sleep to 6 hours awake, are more efficient that sleeping once a day. T or F?

Check Your Memory: Pages 202-205

13. Sleep is promoted by a chemical that accumulates in the bloodstream. T or F?
14. Body temperature drops as a person falls asleep. T or F?
15. A hypnic jerk is a sign of serious problems. T or F?
16. Delta waves typically first appear in stage 2 sleep. T or F?
17. About 45 percent of awakenings during REM periods produce reports of dreams. T or F?
18. REM sleep occurs mainly in stages 3 and 4. T or F?
19. REM sleep increases when a person is subjected to daytime stress. T or F?

20. The average dream only lasts 3 to 4 minutes. T or F?
21. Most people change positions in bed during REM sleep. T or F?
22. REM behavior disorder causes people to briefly fall asleep and become paralyzed during the day. T or F?

Check Your Memory: Pages 206-209

23. Bread, pasta, pretzels, cookies, and cereals all contain melatonin. T or F?
24. Caffeine, alcohol, and tobacco can all contribute to insomnia. T or F?
25. The two most effective behavioral treatments for insomnia are sleep restriction and stimulus control. T or F?
26. Sleepwalking occurs during NREM periods, sleeptalking during REM periods. T or F?
27. People who have NREM night terrors usually can remember very little afterward. T or F?
28. Imagery rehearsal is an effective way to treat recurrent nightmares. T or F?
29. REM sleep appears to help the brain process memories formed during the day. T or F?
30. People who take barbiturate sleeping pills may develop drug-dependency insomnia. T or F?
31. Newborn babies spend 8 or 9 hours a day in REM sleep. T or F?

Check Your Memory: Pages 209-210

32. The favorite dream setting is outdoors. T or F?
33. Pleasant emotions are more common in dreams than unpleasant emotions. T or F?
34. According to Freud, dreams represent thoughts and wishes expressed as images. T or F?
35. The activation-synthesis hypothesis emphasizes the unconscious meanings of dream symbols. T or F?

Check Your Memory: Pages 211-214

36. The Greek word hypnos means "magnetism." T or F?
37. Only about 4 people out of 10 can be hypnotized. T or F?
38. The "finger-lock" is an example of animal magnetism. T or F?
39. Physical strength cannot be increased with hypnosis. T or F?
40. Hypnosis is better at changing subjective experiences than behaviors. T or F?
41. Stage hypnotists look for responsive volunteers who will cooperate and not spoil the show. T or F?

Check Your Memory: Pages 214-215

42. Receptive meditation is typically harder to do than concentrative meditation. T or F?
43. A mantra is used as a focus for attention during receptive meditation. T or F?
44. Herbert Benson states that the physical benefits of meditation are based on evoking the body's relaxation response. T or F?
45. The harder you try to meditate the more likely you are to succeed. T or F?
46. Sensory deprivation is almost always unpleasant, and it usually causes distorted perceptions. T or F?
47. Prolonged sensory deprivation produces deep relaxation. T or F?
48. REST is a form of brainwashing used during the Vietnam war. T or F?

Check Your Memory: Pages 216-230

49. Abuse of any psychoactive drug can produce physical dependence. T or F?

50. Amphetamines are used to treat narcolepsy and hyperactivity. T or F?
51. Amphetamine is more rapidly metabolized by the body than cocaine is. T or F?
52. MDMA is chemically similar to amphetamine. T or F?
53. Disregarding consequences is a sign of cocaine abuse. T or F?
54. Caffeine can increase the risk of miscarriage during pregnancy. T or F?
55. Twenty-five cigarettes could be fatal for a non-smoker. T or F?
56. Regular use of nicotine leads to drug tolerance, and often to physical addiction. T or F?
57. Every cigarette reduces a smoker's life expectancy by 7 minutes. T or F?
58. In order to stop smoking, tapering off is generally more successful than quitting abruptly. T or F?
59. One of the most effective ways to stop smoking is to schedule the number of cigarettes smoked each day. T or F?
60. There have been no known deaths caused by barbiturate overdoses. T or F?
61. It is legal and safe to drive as long as blood alcohol level does not exceed .8. T or F?
62. Drinking alone is a serious sign of alcohol abuse. T or F?
63. To pace alcohol intake, you should limit drinking primarily to the first hour of a social event or party. T or F?
64. Over 80 percent of fraternity and sorority members in the U.S. have engaged in binge drinking. T or F?
65. Hallucinogens generally affect brain transmitter systems. T or F?
66. THC receptors are found in large numbers in the cerebellum of the brain. T or F?
67. Drug abuse is frequently part of general pattern of personal maladjustment. T or F?
68. The negative consequences of drug use typically follow long after the drug has been taken. T or F?

Check Your Memory: PSYCHOLOGY IN ACTION

69. Displacement refers to representing two or more people with a single dream image. T or F?
70. Secondary elaboration is the tendency to make a dream more logical when remembering it. T or F?
71. According to Calvin Hall, the overall emotional tone of a dream is the key to its meaning. T or F?
72. Alcohol decreases REM sleep. T or F?
73. It is basically impossible to solve daytime problems in dreams. T or F?
74. Lucid dreams either occur or they don't; there is no way to increase their frequency. T or F?

FINAL SURVEY AND REVIEW

● *What is an altered state of consciousness?*

1. States of awareness that differ from normal, alert, waking _____ are called altered states of _____ (ASCs).
2. ASCs involve distinct shifts in the quality and pattern of _____ _____.
3. Altered states are especially associated with sleep and dreaming, _____, meditation, sensory _____, and psychoactive drugs.
4. _____ conditioning greatly affects what altered states a person recognizes, seeks, considers normal, and attains.

● *What are the effects of sleep loss or changes in sleep patterns?*

5. Sleep is an _____ _____ rhythm essential for survival.

6. Higher animals and people deprived of sleep experience involuntary _____ (a brief shift to sleep patterns in the brain).

7. Moderate sleep loss mainly affects _____ and self-motivated performance on routine or boring tasks.

8. Extended sleep loss can (somewhat rarely) produce a temporary sleep-deprivation _____, marked by confusion, _____, and possibly hallucinations.

9. _____ rhythms within the body are closely tied to sleep, activity levels, and energy cycles.

10. Sleep patterns show some flexibility, but 7 to 8 hours remains average. The unscheduled human _____ _____ averages 24 hours and 10 minutes, but cycles of light and dark tailor it to 24-hour days.

11. The amount of daily sleep decreases steadily from birth to _____ _____ and switches from _____ sleep-wake cycles to once-a-day sleep periods.

12. Adapting to shorter or longer _____ _____ is difficult and inefficient for most people.

13. Time zone travel and shift work can cause _____ _____, a serious disruption of sleep and _____ _____.

14. If you are flying east, it is best to travel _____ in the day. If you are flying west, it is better to travel _____ in the day. If you anticipate a major change in sleep rhythms, it helps to _____ to the new schedule.

● *Are there different stages of sleep?*

15. Sleepiness is associated with the accumulation of a sleep _____ in the brain and _____ _____.

16. Sleep depends on which of two _____ sleep and waking _____ in the brain is dominant at any given moment.

17. Sleep occurs in 4 stages defined by changes in behavior and brain waves recorded with an _____ (EEG).

18. Stage 1, light sleep, has small irregular brain waves. In stage 2, sleep _____ appear. Delta waves appear in stage 3. Stage 4, or deep sleep, is marked by almost pure _____ _____.

19. Sleepers alternate between stages _____ and _____ (passing through stages _____ and _____) several times each night.

20. There are two basic sleep states, _____ _____ movement (REM) sleep and non-REM (NREM) sleep.

21. _____ sleep is much more strongly associated with dreaming than _____ sleep is.

22. Dreams and REMs occur mainly during _____ _____ sleep, but usually not during the first _____ _____ period.

23. Dreaming is accompanied by sexual and emotional _____ but _____ of the skeletal muscles. People who move about violently while asleep may suffer from REM behavior _____.

24. People deprived of _____ sleep showed an urgent need to dream and _____ disturbances the next day. However, the _____ amount of sleep loss seems to be more important than loss of a single sleep stage.

25. One of the more important functions of _____ _____ appears to be the processing of adaptive memories.

● *What are the causes of sleep disorders and unusual sleep events?*

26. Insomnia, which is difficulty in getting to sleep or staying asleep, may be temporary or _____.

27. When insomnia is treated with drugs, sleep quality is often lowered and drug-_____ insomnia may develop.

28. The amino acid _____, found in bread, pasta, and other foods, helps promote sleep.

29. Behavioral approaches to managing insomnia, such as relaxation, sleep _____, stimulus control, and _____ intention are quite effective.

30. Sleepwalking (_____) and sleeptalking occur during _____ sleep in stages 3 and 4.

31. Night terrors occur in _____ sleep, whereas nightmares occur in _____ sleep.

32. Nightmares can be eliminated by the method called _____ _____.

33. During sleep _____, people repeatedly stop breathing. _____ is suspected as one cause of sudden _____ _____ syndrome.

● *Do dreams have meaning?*

34. Calvin _____ found that most dream content is about familiar settings, people, and actions. Dreams more often involve _____ emotions than _____ emotions.

35. The Freudian, or _____, view is that dreams express unconscious wishes, frequently hidden by dream _____.

36. Allan Hobson and Robert McCarley's activation-_____ model portrays dreaming as a physiological process. The brain, they say, creates dreams to explain sensory and _____ messages that occur during REM sleep.

● *How is hypnosis done, and what are its limitations?*

37. Hypnosis is an altered state characterized by narrowed attention and increased _____.

38. In the 1700s, Franz _____ (whose name is the basis for the term _____) practiced "animal magnetism," which was actually a demonstration of the power of suggestion.

39. The term hypnosis was first used by James _____, an English doctor.

40. People vary in hypnotic susceptibility; 8 out of 10 can be hypnotized, as revealed by scores on the _____ Hypnotic Susceptibility Scale.

41. The core of hypnosis is the basic _____ effect—a tendency to carry out suggested actions as if they were _____.

42. Hypnosis appears capable of producing _____, controlling pain, and altering perceptions.

43. _____ _____ takes advantage of typical stage behavior, waking suggestibility, responsive subjects, disinhibition, and deception to _____ hypnosis.

● *What is meditation? Does it have any benefits?*

44. _____ refers to mental exercises that are used to alter consciousness.

45. In _____ meditation, attention is broadened to include an awareness of one's entire moment-by-moment experience.

46. In _____ meditation, attention is focused on a single object or thought.

47. Two major benefits of meditation are its ability to interrupt anxious thoughts and its ability to elicit the _____ _____ (the pattern of changes that occur in the body at times of deep relaxation).

48. Sensory deprivation takes place when there is a major reduction in the amount or variety of _____ _____ available to a person.

49. _____ sensory deprivation is stressful and disruptive, leading to perceptual distortions.

50. Brief or mild sensory _____ can induce deep _____.

51. Sensory deprivation also appears to aid the breaking of long-standing habits and promotes creative thinking. This effect is the basis for _____ _____ Stimulation Therapy (REST).

● *What are the effects of the more commonly used psychoactive drugs?*

52. A psychoactive drug is a substance that affects the brain in ways that alter _____.

53. Most psychoactive drugs can be placed on a scale ranging from _____ to _____. Some, however, are best described as _____ (drugs that alter sensory impressions).

54. Drugs may cause a physical _____ (addiction) or a psychological _____, or both.

55. The _____ _____ drugs are alcohol, amphetamines, barbiturates, cocaine, codeine, GHB, heroin, methadone, morphine, tobacco, and tranquilizers. All psychoactive drugs can lead to psychological dependence.

56. Stimulant drugs are readily abused because of the period of depression that often follows stimulation. The greatest risks are associated with amphetamines, _____, MDMA, and nicotine, but even caffeine can be a problem.

57. MDMA or "Ecstsay," which is similar to _____, has been linked with numerous deaths and with _____ impairment.

58. Nicotine (smoking) includes the added risk of _____ _____, heart disease, and other health problems.

59. Barbiturates are depressant drugs whose overdose level is close to the intoxication dosage, making them dangerous drugs. Mixing barbiturates and _____ may result in a fatal drug

_____ (in which the joint effect of two drugs exceeds the effects of adding one drug's effects to the other's).

60. The _____ drug GHB (_____) can cause coma, breathing failure, and death in relatively low doses.

61. _____ tranquilizers, such as Valium, are used to lower anxiety. When abused, they have a strong addictive potential.

62. _____ is the most heavily abused drug in common use today. The development of a drinking problem is usually marked by an initial phase of increasing consumption, a _____
phase, in which a single drink can set off a chain reaction, and a chronic phase, in which a person lives to drink and drinks to live.

63. Marijuana is a _____ subject to an abuse pattern similar to alcohol. Studies have linked chronic marijuana use with memory impairment, _____ cancer, reproductive problems, immune system disorders, and other health problems.

64. Drug abuse is related to personal and social _____, attempts to cope, and the immediate reinforcing qualities of psychoactive drugs.

● *How are dreams used to promote personal understanding?*

65. Freud held that the meaning of dreams is hidden by the dream processes he called _____, displacement, symbolization, and _____ elaboration.

66. Calvin Hall emphasizes the _____, _____, plot, and emotions of a dream.

67. Rosalind Cartwright's view of dreams as _____ statements and Fritz _____ technique of speaking for dream elements are also helpful.

68. Dreams may be used for creative problem solving, especially when dream control is achieved through _____ dreaming (a dream in which the dreamer feels capable of normal thought and action).

MASTERY TEST

1. Delirium, ecstasy, and daydreaming all have in common the fact that they are
   a. forms of normal waking consciousness   b. caused by sensory deprivation
   c. perceived as subjectively real   d. ASCs

2. The street drug GHB is
   a. chemically similar to morphine   b. a depressant   c. capable of raising body temperature to dangerous levels   d. a common cause of sleep-deprivation psychosis

3. Which of the following does not belong with the others?
   a. nicotine   b. caffeine   c. cocaine   d. codeine

4. Sleep spindles usually first appear in stage _____, whereas delta waves first appear in stage _____.
   a. 1, 2   b. 2, 3   c. 3, 4   d. 1, 4

5. Which of the following is NOT one of the dream processes described by Freud?
   a. condensation b. illumination c. displacement d. symbolization

6. Which of the following most clearly occurs under hypnosis?
   a. unusual strength b. memory enhancement c. pain relief d. age regression

7. Alcohol, amphetamines, cocaine, and marijuana have in common the fact that they are all
   a. physically addicting b. psychoactive c. stimulants d. hallucinogens

8. Emotional arousal, blood pressure changes, and sexual arousal all primarily occur during
   a. REM sleep b. NREM sleep c. Delta sleep d. stage 4 sleep

9. The REST technique makes use of
   a. sensory deprivation b. hypodynamic imagery c. hallucinogens d. a CPAP mask

10. Mesmerism, hypnosis, hypnotic susceptibility scales, and stage hypnotism all rely in part on
    a. disinhibition b. rapid eye movements c. suggestibility d. imagery rehearsal

11. Shortened sleep-waking cycles overlook the fact that sleep
    a. must match a 3 to 1 ratio of time awake and time asleep b. is an innate biological rhythm
    c. is caused by a sleep-promoting substance in the blood d. cycles cannot be altered by external factors

12. Morning drinking appears during the _____ phase in the development of a drinking problem.
    a. initial b. crucial c. chronic d. rebound

13. Which of the following statements about sleep is true?
    a. Learning math or a foreign language can be accomplished during sleep. b. Some people can learn to do without sleep. c. Calvin Hall had hallucinations during a sleep deprivation experiment. d. Randy Gardner slept for 14 hours after ending his sleep deprivation.

14. Amphetamine is very similar in effects to
    a. narcotics and tranquilizers b. methaqualone c. codeine d. cocaine

15. Microsleeps would most likely occur
    a. in stage 4 sleep b. in a 3 to 1 ratio to microawakenings c. in conjunction with delusions and hallucinations d. during sleep deprivation

16. Adolescents who abuse drugs tend to be
    a. suffering from brain dysfunctions b. high in self-esteem but unrealistic about consequences
    c. maladjusted and impulsive d. similar in most respects to non-abusers

17. Sleepwalking, sleeptalking, and severe nightmares all have in common the fact that they
    a. are REM events b. are NREM events c. are sleep disorders d. can be controlled with imagery rehearsal

18. In its milder forms, sensory deprivation sometimes produces
    a. cataplectic images b. deep relaxation c. tryptophanic images d. REM symbolizations

19. The basic suggestion effect is closely related to
a. hypnosis   b. sensory enhancement after sensory deprivation   c. hypersomnia   d. the frequency of dreaming during REM sleep

20. A person who feels awake and capable of normal action while sleeping has experienced
a. lucid dreaming   b. the basic suggestion effect   c. sleep drunkeness   d. REM rebound

21. Which of the following is a hallucinogen?
a. LSD   b. THC   c. hashish   d. all of the preceding

22. The two most basic states of sleep are
a. stage 1 sleep and stage 4 sleep   b. REM sleep and NREM sleep   c. Alpha sleep and Delta sleep
d. Alpha sleep and hypnic sleep

23. A mantra would most commonly be used in
a. Perls's method of dream interpretation   b. sensory deprivation research   c. inducing hypnosis
d. concentrative meditation

24. Learning to use a computer would most likely be slowed if you were _____ each night.
a. deprived of a half hour of NREM sleep   b. allowed to engage in extra REM sleep
c. prevented from dreaming   d. awakened three times at random

25. By definition, compulsive drug use involves
a. dependence   b. experimentation   c. repeated overdoses   d. anhedonia

26. A particularly dangerous drug interaction occurs when _____ and _____ are combined.
a. alcohol, amphetamine   b. barbiturates, nicotine   c. alcohol, barbiturates   d. amphetamine, codeine

27. Narcolepsy is an example of
a. a night terror   b. a sleep disorder   c. a tranquilizer   d. an addictive drug

28. Sleep restriction and stimulus control techniques would most likely be used to treat
a. insomnia   b. narcolepsy   c. sleepwalking   d. REM behavior disorder

29. In addition to the nicotine they contain, cigarettes release
a. dopamine   b. tryptophan   c. noradrenaline   d. carcinogens

30. Disguised dream symbols are to psychodynamic dream theory as sensory and motor messages are to
a. the Freudian theory of dreams   b. the activation-synthesis hypothesis   c. Fritz Perls' methods of dream interpretation   d. paradoxical intention

ANSWERS

Recite and Review

1. awareness, waking
2. pattern
3. sleep, dreaming, sensory
4. normal
5. rhythm, survival
6. involuntary
7. routine
8. loss, temporary
9. rhythms
10. 24, 10, light, dark
11. decreases
12. shorter, longer
13. shift, sleep
14. travel, travel, sleep, schedule
15. brain
16. two, brain
17. 4, waves
18. light, sleep, Delta
19. alternate
20. movement
21. dreaming
22. Dreaming
23. emotional, muscles, REM
24. dream, stage
25. memories
26. temporary
27. lowered, insomnia
28. sleep
29. stimulus, intention
30. Sleepwalking
31. NREM, REM
32. rehearsal
33. breathing, sudden
34. familiar, emotions, emotions
35. wishes
36. activation, sensory
37. increased
38. animal, suggestion
39. hypnosis
40. 8, Scale
41. basic
42. pain
43. waking, deception
44. consciousness
45. widened
46. single
47. relaxation
48. stimulation
49. perceptual
50. relaxation
51. habits
52. alter (affect or change)
53. depression, sensory
54. addiction
55. psychological
56. depression, caffeine
57. Ecstasy
58. Nicotine (or Smoking)
59. depressant, drug
60. GHB
61. Valium, addictive
62. initial, single
63. abuse
64. immediate
65. hidden, processes
66. plot
67. speaking
68. creative

Connections

1. e
2. h
3. a
4. j
5. b
6. d
7. g
8. c
9. f
10. i
11. d
12. j
13. a
14. f
15. b
16. i
17. c
18. h
19. e
20. g
21. c
22. h
23. a
24. j
25. b
26. d
27. i
28. f
29. e
30. g

Check Your Memory

1. T
2. T
3. T
4. T
5. F
6. T
7. T
8. F
9. T
10. F
11. T
12. F
13. F
14. T
15. F
16. F
17. F
18. F
19. T
20. F
21. F
22. F
23. F
24. T
25. T
26. F
27. T
28. T

29. T
30. T
31. T
32. F
33. F
34. T
35. F
36. F
37. F
38. F
39. T
40. T
41. T
42. T
43. F
44. T
45. F
46. F
47. F
48. F
49. F
50. T
51. F
52. T
53. T
54. T
55. T
56. T
57. T
58. T
59. T
60. F
61. F
62. T
63. T
64. T
65. T
66. F
67. T
68. T
69. F
70. T
71. F
72. T
73. F
74. F

Final Survey and Review

1. consciousness, consciousness
2. mental activity
3. hypnosis, deprivation
4. Cultural
5. innate biological
6. microsleeps
7. alertness
8. psychosis, delusions
9. Circadian
10. sleep-waking cycle
11. old age, multiple
12. sleep cycles
13. jet lag, bodily rhythms
14. early, late, preadapt
15. hormone, spinal cord
16. opposed, systems
17. electroencephalograph
18. spindles, delta waves
19. 1, 4, 2, 3
20. rapid eye
21. REM, non-REM
22. stage 1, stage 1
23. arousal, relaxation, disorder
24. chronic
25. dependency
26. tryptophan
27. restriction, paradoxical
28. somnambulism, NREM
29. NREM, REM
30. imagery rehearsal
31. apnea, Apnea, infant death
32. REM, mental, total
33. REM sleep
34. Hall, negative, positive
35. psychodynamic, symbols
36. synthesis, motor
37. suggestibility
38. Mesmer, mesmerize
39. Braid
40. Stanford
41 suggestion, involuntary
42. relaxation
43. Stage hypnotism, simulate
44. Meditation
45. receptive
46. concentrative

47. relaxation response
48. sensory stimulation
49. Prolonged
50. deprivation, relaxation
51. Restricted Environmental
52. consciousness
53. stimulation, depression, hallucinogens
54. dependence, dependence
55. physically addicting
56. cocaine
57. amphetamine, mental
58. lung cancer
59. alcohol, interaction
60. depressant, gamma-hydroxybuyrate
61. Benzodiazepine
62. Alcohol, crucial
63. hallucinogen, lung
64. maladjustment
65. condensation, secondary
66. setting, cast
67. feeling, Perls's
68. lucid

Mastery Test

1. d (p. 198)
2. b (p. 224)
3. d (p. 217-222)
4. b (p. 204)
5. b (p. 230)
6. c (p. 212-213)
7. b (p. 216)
8. a (p. 205)
9. a (p. 215)
10. c (p. 211-212)
11. b (p. 202)
12. a (p. 226)
13. d (p. 200)
14. d (p. 217, 220)
15. d (p. 199)
16. c (p. 229)
17. c (p. 207-208)
18. b (p. 215)
19. a (p. 212)
20. a (p. 232)
21. d (p. 228)
22. b (p. 204)

23. d (p. 214)   **26.** c (p. 224)   **29.** d (p. 222)
24. c (p. 205)   **27.** b (p. 207)   **30.** b (p. 210)
25. a (p. 217)   **28.** a (p. 208)

Chapter 7
Conditioning and Learning

CHAPTER OVERVIEW

Learning is a relatively permanent change in behavior due to experience. Two basic forms of learning are classical conditioning and operant conditioning.

Classical conditioning is also called respondent or Pavlovian conditioning. Classical conditioning occurs when a neutral stimulus is associated with an unconditioned stimulus (which reliably elicits an unconditioned response). After many pairings of the NS and the US, the NS becomes a conditioned stimulus that elicits a conditioned response. Learning is reinforced during acquisition of a response. Withdrawing reinforcement leads to extinction (although some spontaneous recovery of conditioning may occur). It is apparent that stimulus generalization has occurred when a stimulus similar to the CS also elicits a learned response. In stimulus discrimination, people or animals learn to respond differently to two similar stimuli. Conditioning often involves simple reflex responses, but emotional conditioning is also possible.

In operant conditioning (or instrumental learning), the consequences that follow a response alter the probability that it will be made again. Positive and negative reinforcers increase responding; punishment suppresses responding; non-reinforcement leads to extinction. Various types of reinforcers and different patterns of giving reinforcers greatly affect operant learning. Informational feedback (knowledge of results) also facilitates learning and performance. Antecedent stimuli (those that precede a response) influence operant learning, through stimulus generalization, discrimination, and stimulus control.

Learning, even simple conditioning, is based on acquiring information. Higher level cognitive learning involves memory, thinking, problem solving, and language. At a simpler level, cognitive maps, latent learning, and discovery learning show that learning is based on acquiring information. Learning also occurs through observation and imitating models. Observational learning imparts large amounts of information that would be hard to acquire in other ways.

Operant principles can be applied to manage one's own behavior and to break bad habits. A mixture of operant principles and cognitive learning underlies self-regulated learning—a collection of techniques to improve learning in school.

LEARNING OBJECTIVES

To demonstrate mastery of this chapter, you should be able to:

1. Define *learning*.
2. Define *reinforcement* and explain its role in conditioning. (See also Table 7.1.)
3. Differentiate between antecedents and consequences and explain how they are related to classical and operant conditioning. (See also Table 7.1.)
4. Give a brief history of classical conditioning.
5. Describe the following terms as they apply to classical conditioning:
    a. neutral stimulus (NS)
    b. conditioned stimulus (CS)
    c. unconditioned stimulus (US)
    d. unconditioned response (UR)
    e. conditioned response (CR)
6. Describe and give an example of classical conditioning using the abbreviations US, UR, CS, and CR.
7. Explain how reinforcement occurs during the acquisition of a classically conditioned response. Include an explanation of higher order conditioning.
8. Explain classical conditioning in terms of the informational view.
9. Describe and give examples of the following concepts as they relate to classical conditioning:
    a. extinction
    b. spontaneous recovery
    c. stimulus generalization
    d. stimulus discrimination
10. Describe the relationship between classical conditioning and reflex responses.
11. Explain what a conditioned emotional response (CER) is and how it is acquired. Include definitions of the terms *phobia* and *desensitization*.
12. Explain the concept and the importance of vicarious classical conditioning.
13. State the basic principle of operant conditioning.
14. Contrast operant conditioning with classical conditioning. Include a brief comparison of the differences between what is meant by the terms *reward* and *reinforcement*. (See also Table 7.2.)
15. Explain operant conditioning in terms of the informational view. Explain what response-contingent reinforcement is.
16. Describe how the delay of reinforcement can influence the effectiveness of the reinforcement.
17. Describe response chaining and explain how it can counteract the effects of delaying reinforcement.
18. Explain why superstitious behavior develops and why it persists.
19. Explain how shaping occurs. Include a definition of the term *successive approximations*.
20. Explain how extinction and spontaneous recovery occur in operant conditioning.
21. Describe how negative attention seeking demonstrates reinforcement and extinction in operant conditioning. (See also Table 7.3.)
22. Compare and contrast positive reinforcement, negative reinforcement, punishment, and response cost punishment and give an example of each.
23. Differentiate primary reinforcers from secondary reinforcers and list four examples of each kind.
24. Discuss two ways in which a secondary reinforcer becomes reinforcing.
25. Discuss the major advantages and disadvantages of primary reinforcers and secondary reinforcers (tokens, for instance), and describe how tokens have been used to help "special" groups of people.
26. Define *social reinforcers*. Name two key elements that underlie learning and explain how they function together in learning situations.

27. Define *feedback,* indicate three factors which increase its effectiveness, and explain its importance in learning.

28. Briefly describe some ways in which conditioning techniques can be used to help people learn to conserve our energy resources.

29. Describe the following kinds of instruction and discuss their application in learning and teaching: programmed, computer-assisted, and interactive videodisc.

30. Compare and contrast the effects of continuous and partial reinforcement.

31. Describe, give and example of, and explain the effects of the following schedules of partial reinforcement:
    a. fixed ratio (FR)   b. variable ratio (VR)   c. fixed interval (FI)   d. variable interval (VI)

32. Explain the concept of stimulus control.

33. Describe the processes of generalization and discrimination as they relate to operant conditioning.

34. Explain how punishers can be defined by their effects on behavior.

35. List and discuss three factors which influence the effectiveness of punishment.

36. Differentiate the effects of severe punishment from mild punishment.

37. List the three basic tools available to control simple learning.

38. Discuss how and why reinforcement should be used with punishment in order to change an undesirable behavior.

39. List six guidelines which should be followed when using punishment.

40. List and discuss three problems associated with punishment.

41. Explain how using punishment can be habit forming and describe the behavior of children who are frequently punished.

42. Define *cognitive learning.*

43. Describe the concepts of a cognitive map and latent learning.

44. Explain the difference between discovery learning and rote learning. Describe the behavior of the students who used each approach in the Wertheimer study.

45. Discuss the factors which determine whether observational learning (modeling) will occur.

46. Describe the experiment with children and the Bo-Bo doll that demonstrates the powerful effect of modeling on behavior.

47. Explain why what a parent does is more important than what a parent says.

The following objectives are related to the material in the "Exploring Psychology" section of the text.

48. Briefly describe the general conclusion that can be drawn from studies on the effects of TV violence on children. Explain why it would be an exaggeration to say that TV violence *causes* aggression.

49. Describe the procedures and results of Williams's natural experiment with TV.

The following objectives are related to the material in the "Psychology in Action " section of the text.

50. List and briefly describe the seven steps in a behavioral self-management program. Explain how the Premack principle may apply.

51. Describe how self-recording can aid a self-management program.

52. List four strategies for changing bad habits.

53. Briefly describe eight strategies of self-regulated learning.

RECITE AND REVIEW

● *What is learning?*

Recite and Review: Pages 237-238

1. Learning is a relatively permanent change in _____ due to experience. To understand learning we must study antecedents (events that _____ responses) and consequences (events that _____ responses).

2. Classical, or respondent, _____ and instrumental, or operant, _____ are two basic types of learning.

3. In classical conditioning, a previously neutral _____ is associated with a stimulus that elicits a response. In operant conditioning, the pattern of voluntary _____ is altered by consequences.

4. Both types of conditioning depend on reinforcement. In classical conditioning, learning is _____ when a US follows the NS or CS. _____ reinforcement is based on the consequences that follow a response.

● *How does classical conditioning occur?*

Recite and Review: Pages 238-241

5. Classical conditioning, studied by Ivan Pavlov, occurs when a _____ stimulus (NS) is associated with an unconditioned stimulus (US). The US triggers a reflex called the unconditioned _____ (UR).

6. If the NS is consistently paired with the US, it becomes a conditioned _____ (CS) capable of producing a response by itself. This response is a conditioned (_____) response (CR).

7. During acquisition of classical conditioning, the conditioned stimulus must be consistently followed by the unconditioned _____.

8. Higher-order conditioning occurs when a well-learned conditioned stimulus is used as if it were an unconditioned _____, bringing about further learning.

9. When the CS is repeatedly presented alone, extinction takes place. That is, _____ is weakened or inhibited.

10. After extinction seems to be complete, a rest period may lead to the temporary reappearance of a conditioned _____. This is called spontaneous recovery.

11. Through stimulus generalization, stimuli _____ to the conditioned stimulus will also produce a response.

12. Generalization gives way to _____ discrimination when an organism learns to respond to one stimulus, but not to similar stimuli.

13. From an informational view, conditioning creates expectancies (or expectations about events), which alter _____ patterns.

14. In classical conditioning, the CS creates an expectancy that the US will _____ it.

● *Does conditioning affect emotions?*

Recite and Review: Pages 241-243

15. Conditioning applies to visceral or emotional responses as well as simple _____. As a result, _____ emotional responses (CERs) also occur.

16. Irrational fears called phobias may be CERs that are extended to a variety of situations by _____ generalization.

17. The conditioning of emotional responses can occur vicariously (_____) as well as directly. Vicarious classical conditioning occurs when we _____ another person's emotional responses to a stimulus.

● *How does operant conditioning occur?*

Recite and Review: Pages 243-248

18. Operant conditioning (or instrumental _____) occurs when a voluntary action is followed by a reinforcer.

19. Reinforcement in operant conditioning _____ the frequency or probability of a response. This result is based on what Edward L. Thorndike called the law of _____.

20. An operant reinforcer is any event that follows a _____ and _____ its probability.

21. Learning in operant conditioning is based on the expectation that a response will have a specific _____.

22. To be effective, operant _____ must be _____ contingent.

23. Delay of reinforcement reduces its effectiveness, but long _____ of responses may be built up so that a _____ reinforcer maintains many responses.

24. Superstitious behaviors (unnecessary responses) often become part of _____ chains because they appear to be associated with reinforcement.

25. In a process called shaping, complex _____ responses can be taught by reinforcing successive approximations (ever closer matches) to a final desired response.

26. If an operant response is not reinforced, it may extinguish (disappear). But after extinction seems complete, it may temporarily reappear (spontaneous _____).

27. In positive reinforcement, _____ or a pleasant event follows a response. In negative reinforcement, a response that _____ discomfort becomes more likely to occur again.

28. Punishment _____ responding. Punishment occurs when a response is followed by the onset of an aversive event or by the removal of a positive event (response _____).

● *Are there different kinds of operant reinforcement?*

Recite and Review: Pages 248-252

29. Primary reinforcers are "natural," physiologically-based rewards. Intra-cranial stimulation of "_____ centers" in the _____ can also serve as a primary reinforcer.

30. Secondary reinforcers are _____. They typically gain their reinforcing value by association with primary reinforcers or because they can be _____ for primary reinforcers. Tokens and money gain their reinforcing value in this way.

31. Human behavior is often influenced by social reinforcers, which are based on learned desires for attention and _____ from others.

32. Feedback, or knowledge of _____, aids learning and improves performance.

33. Programmed instruction breaks learning into a series of small steps and provides immediate _____.

34. Computer-assisted _____ (CAI) does the same, but has the added advantage of providing alternate exercises and information when needed.

35. Four variations of CAI are drill and _____, instructional games, educational simulations, and interactive videodisc instruction.

● *How are we influenced by patterns of reward?*

Recite and Review: Pages 253-256

36. Reward or reinforcement may be given continuously (after every _____), or on a schedule of _____ reinforcement. The study of schedules of reinforcement was begun by B. F. Skinner.

37. Partial reinforcement produces greater resistance to extinction. This is the partial reinforcement _____.

38. The four most basic schedules of reinforcement are _____ ratio (FR), variable ratio (VR), _____ interval (FI), and variable interval (VI).

39. FR and VR schedules produce _____ rates of responding. An FI schedule produces moderate rates of responding with alternating periods of activity and inactivity. VI schedules produce _____, steady rates of responding and strong resistance to extinction.

40. Stimuli that _____ a reinforced response tend to control the response on future occasions (stimulus control).

41. Two aspects of stimulus control are generalization and _____.

42. In generalization, an operant response tends to occur when stimuli _____ to those preceding reinforcement are present.

43. In discrimination, responses are given in the presence of discriminative stimuli associated with reinforcement (_____) and withheld in the presence of stimuli associated with non-reinforcement (_____).

● *What does punishment do to behavior?*

Recite and Review: Pages 257-260

44. A punisher is any consequence that _____ the frequency of a target behavior.

45. Punishment is most effective when it is _____, consistent, and intense.

46. Mild punishment tends only to temporarily _____ responses that are also reinforced or were acquired by reinforcement.

47. The undesirable side effects of punishment include the conditioning of fear; the learning of _____ and avoidance responses; and the encouragement of aggression.

48. Reinforcement and non-reinforcement are a better way to change behavior than punishment. When punishment is used, it should be _____ and combined with reinforcement of alternate _____.

● *What is cognitive learning?*

Recite and Review: Pages 260-262

49. Cognitive learning involves higher mental processes, such as understanding, knowing, or anticipating. Evidence of cognitive learning is provided by cognitive _____ (internal representations of spatial relationships) and latent (hidden) _____.
50. Discovery learning emphasizes insight and _____, in contrast to rote learning.

● *Does learning occur by imitation?*

Recite and Review: Pages 262-265

51. Much human learning is achieved through _____, or modeling. Observational learning is influenced by the personal characteristics of the _____ and the success or failure of the _____ behavior.
52. Television characters can act as powerful _____ for observational learning. Televised violence increases the likelihood of aggression by viewers.

● *How does conditioning apply to practical problems?*

Recite and Review: PSYCHOLOGY IN ACTION

53. Operant principles can be readily applied to manage behavior in everyday settings. Self-management of behavior is based on self-reinforcement, self-recording, _____, and behavioral contracting.
54. Prepotent, or frequent, high-probability _____, can be used to reinforce low-frequency responses. This is known as the Premack _____.
55. Attempts to break bad habits are aided by reinforcing alternate _____, by extinction, breaking _____ chains, and _____ cues or antecedents.
56. In school, self-regulated _____ typically involves all of the following: setting learning _____, planning learning strategies, using self-instruction, monitoring progress, evaluating yourself, reinforcing _____, and taking corrective action when required.

CONNECTIONS

1. _____ respondent conditioning
2. _____ instrumental learning
3. _____ antecedents
4. _____ meat powder
5. _____ bell
6. _____ salivation
7. _____ consequences
8. _____ CS used as US
9. _____ extinction
10. _____ acquisition

a. before responses
b. Pavlov's CS
c. after responses
d. higher-order conditioning
e. Pavlovian conditioning
f. US missing
g. reinforcement period
h. UR
i. Pavlov's US
j. operant conditioning

11. _____ phobia
12. _____ desensitization
13. _____ Skinner
14. _____ shaping
15. _____ negative reinforcement
16. _____ punishment
17. _____ tokens
18. _____ approval
19. _____ partial reinforcement
20. _____ stimulus control

a. CER
b. conditioning chamber
c. increased responding
d. decreased responding
e. social reinforcer
f. Chimp-O-Mat
g. approximations
h. resistance to extinction
i. antecedent stimuli
j. extinction of fear

21. _____ punishment
22. _____ expectancies
23. _____ KR
24. _____ CAI
25. _____ discovery learning
26. _____ modeling
27. _____ self-instruction
28. _____ fixed ratio
29. _____ spontaneous recovery
30. _____ fixed interval

a. number of responses per reinforcer
b. reinforcement schedule
c. incomplete extinction
d. escape and avoidance
e. informational view
f. educational simulations
g. feedback
h. insight
i. self-regulated learning
j. imitation

CHECK YOUR MEMORY

Check Your Memory: Pages 237-238

1. Learning to press the buttons on a vending machine is based on operant conditioning. T or F?
2. In classical conditioning, the consequences that follow responses become associated with one another. T or F?
3. Getting compliments from friends could serve as reinforcement for operant learning. T or F?

Check Your Memory: Pages 238-241

4. Ivan Pavlov studied digestion and operant conditioning in dogs. T or F?
5. Pavlov used meat powder to reinforce conditioned salivation to the sound of a bell. T or F?
6. During successful conditioning, the NS becomes a CS. T or F?
7. During acquisition, the CS is presented repeatedly without the US. T or F?
8. The optimal delay between the CS and the US is 5 to 15 seconds. T or F?
9. Spontaneous recovery occurs when a CS becomes strong enough to be used like a US. T or F?
10. Discriminations are learned when generalized responses to stimuli similar to the CS are extinguished. T or F?

Check Your Memory: Pages 241-243

11. Narrowing of the pupils in response to bright lights is learned in early infancy. T or F?
12. Emotional conditioning involves autonomic nervous system responses. T or F?
13. Stimulus generalization helps convert some CERs into phobias. T or F?
14. Pleasant music can be used as a UR to create a CER. T or F?
15. To learn a CER vicariously, you would observe the actions of another person and try to imitate them. T or F?

Check Your Memory: Pages 243-248

16. In operant conditioning, learners actively emit responses. T or F?
17. Rewards are the same as reinforcers. T or F?
18. The Skinner box is primarily used to study classical conditioning. T or F?
19. Reinforcement in operant conditioning alters how frequently involuntary responses are elicited. T or F?
20. Operant reinforcers are most effective when they are response-contingent. T or F?
21. Operant learning is most effective if you wait a minute or two after the response is over before reinforcing it. T or F?
22. Response chains allow delayed reinforcers to support learning. T or F?
23. Superstitious responses appear to be associated with reinforcement, but they are not. T or F?
24. Teaching a pigeon to play Ping-Pong would most likely make use of the principle of response cost. T or F?

25. Children who misbehave may be reinforced by attention from parents. T or F?
26. Negative reinforcement is a type of punishment that is used to strengthen learning. T or F?
27. Both response cost and negative reinforcement decrease responding. T or F?

Check Your Memory: Pages 248-252

28. Food, water, grades, and sex are primary reinforcers. T or F?
29. ICS is a good example of a secondary reinforcer. T or F?
30. Social reinforcers are secondary reinforcers. T or F?
31. Attention and approval can be used to shape another person's behavior. T or F?
32. The effects of primary reinforcers may quickly decline as the person becomes satiated. T or F?
33. The Chimp-O-Mat accepted primary reinforcers and dispensed secondary reinforcers. T or F?
34. People are more likely to recycle used materials if they receive weekly feedback about how much they have recycled. T or F?
35. CAI is another term for informational feedback. T or F?
36. In sports, feedback is most effective when a skilled coach directs attention to important details. T or F?
37. The final level of skill and knowledge is almost always higher following CAI than it is with conventional methods. T or F?

Check Your Memory: Pages 253-256

38. Continuous reinforcement means that reinforcers are given continuously, regardless of whether or not responses are made. T or F?
39. A FR-3 schedule means that each correct response produces 3 reinforcers. T or F?
40. The time interval in FI schedules is measured from the last reinforced response. T or F?
41. In business, commissions and profit sharing are examples of FI reinforcement. T or F?
42. Antecedent stimuli tend to control when and where previously rewarded responses will occur. T or F?
43. Stimulus generalization is the primary method used to train dogs to detect contraband. T or F?

Check Your Memory: 257-260

44. Like reinforcement, punishment should be response-contingent. T or F?
45. Punishment is most effective if it is unpredictable. T or F?
46. Speeding tickets are an example of response cost. T or F?
47. Mild punishment causes reinforced responses to extinguish more rapidly. T or F?
48. Generally, punishment should be the last resort for altering behavior. T or F?
49. An apparatus known as a shuttle box is used to study escape and avoidance learning. T or F?
50. For humans, avoidance learning is reinforced by a sense of relief. T or F?
51. Punishment frequently leads to increases in aggression by the person who is punished. T or F?

Check Your Memory: Pages 260-262

52. Cognitive learning involves thinking, memory, and problem solving. T or F?

53. Animals learning their way through a maze memorize the correct order of right and left turns to make. T or F?

54. Typically, reinforcement must be provided in order to make latent learning visible. T or F?

55. In many situations, discovery learning produces better understanding of problems. T or F?

Check Your Memory: Pages 262-265

56. Modeling is another term for discovery learning. T or F?

57. After a new response is acquired through modeling, normal reinforcement determines if it will be repeated. T or F?

58. Children imitate aggressive acts performed by other people, but they are not likely to imitate cartoon characters. T or F?

59. Violence on television causes children to be more violent. T or F?

Check Your Memory: PSYCHOLOGY IN ACTION

60. Choosing reinforcers is the first step in behavioral self-management. T or F?

61. Self-recording can be an effective way to change behavior, even without using specific reinforcers. T or F?

62. A prepotent response is one that occurs frequently. T or F?

63. To use extinction to break a bad habit, you should remove, avoid, or delay the reinforcement that is supporting the habit. T or F?

64. In a behavioral contract, you spell out what response chains you are going to extinguish. T or F?

65. Self-regulated learners actively seek feedback in both formal and informal ways. T or F?

FINAL SURVEY AND REVIEW

● *What is learning?*

1. Learning is a relatively permanent change in behavior due to experience. To understand learning we must study _____ (events that precede responses) and _____ (events that follow responses).

2. Classical, or _____, conditioning and instrumental, or _____, conditioning are two basic types of learning.

3. In classical conditioning, a previously _____ stimulus is associated with another stimulus that elicits a response. In operant conditioning, the pattern of voluntary responses is altered by _____.

4. Both types of conditioning depend on _____. In classical conditioning, learning is reinforced when a _____ follows the NS or CS. Operant reinforcement is based on the consequences that follow a response.

● *How does classical conditioning occur?*

5. Classical conditioning, studied by _____ _____, occurs when a neutral stimulus (NS) is associated with an _____ stimulus (US). The US triggers a _____ called the unconditioned response (UR).

6. If the NS is consistently paired with the US, it becomes a _____ stimulus (CS) capable of producing a response by itself. This response is a _____ (learned) response (CR).

7. During acquisition of classical conditioning, the conditioned stimulus must be consistently followed by the _____ _____.

8. _____ conditioning occurs when a well-learned conditioned stimulus is used as if it were an unconditioned stimulus, bringing about further learning.

9. When the CS is repeatedly presented alone, _____ takes place (learning is weakened or inhibited).

10. After extinction seems to be complete, a rest period may lead to the temporary reappearance of a conditioned response. This is called _____ _____.

11. Through stimulus _____, stimuli similar to the conditioned stimulus will also produce a response.

12. Generalization gives way to stimulus _____ when an organism learns to respond to one stimulus, but not to similar stimuli.

13. From an _____ view, conditioning creates expectancies (or expectations about events), which alter response patterns.

14. In classical conditioning, the _____ creates an expectancy that the _____ will follow it.

● *Does conditioning affect emotions?*

15. Conditioning applies to visceral or emotional responses as well as simple reflexes. As a result, conditioned _____ _____ (CERs) also occur.

16. Irrational fears called _____ may be CERs that are extended to a variety of situations by stimulus _____.

17. The conditioning of emotional responses can occur secondhand as well as directly. _____ classical conditioning occurs when we observe another person's emotional responses to a stimulus.

● *How does operant conditioning occur?*

18. Operant conditioning (or _____ learning) occurs when a voluntary action is followed by a reinforcer.

19. Reinforcement in operant conditioning increases the frequency or _____ of a response. This result is based on what Edward L. _____ called the law of effect.

20. An operant reinforcer is any event that follows a _____ and _____ its probability.

21. Learning in operant conditioning is based on the _____ that a response will have a specific effect.

22. To be effective, operant reinforcers must be response _____.

23. Delay of reinforcement _____ its effectiveness, but long chains of responses may be built up so that a single _____ maintains many responses.

24. _____ behaviors (unnecessary responses) often become part of response chains because they appear to be associated with reinforcement.

25. In a process called _____, complex operant responses can be taught by reinforcing successive _____ (ever closer matches) to a final desired response.

26. If an operant response is not reinforced, it may _____ (disappear). But after extinction seems complete, it may temporarily reappear (_____ recovery).

27. In _____ reinforcement, reward or a pleasant event follows a response. In _____ reinforcement, a response that ends discomfort becomes more likely to occur again.

28. Punishment decreases responding. Punishment occurs when a response is followed by the onset of an _____ event or by the removal of a _____ event (response cost).

● *Are there different kinds of operant reinforcement?*

29. _____ reinforcers are "natural," physiologically-based rewards. Intra-cranial _____ of "pleasure centers" in the brain can also serve as a reinforcers of this type.

30. _____ reinforcers are learned. They typically gain their reinforcing value by association with _____ reinforcers or because they can be exchanged for _____ reinforcers. Tokens and money gain their reinforcing value in this way.

31. Human behavior is often influenced by _____ reinforcers, which are based on learned desires for attention and approval from others.

32. Feedback, or _____ of results, aids learning and improves performance.

33. Programmed _____ breaks learning into a series of small steps and provides immediate feedback.

34. _____ _____ (CAI) does the same, but has the added advantage of providing alternate exercises and information when needed.

35. Four variations of _____ are drill and practice, instructional games, educational simulations, and interactive videodisc instruction.

● *How are we influenced by patterns of reward?*

36. Reward or reinforcement may be given continuously (after every response), or on a _____ of partial reinforcement like those studied by B. F. _____.

37. Partial reinforcement produces greater resistance to _____. This is the _____ reinforcement effect.

38. The four most basic schedules of reinforcement are fixed and variable _____ (FR and VR) and fixed and variable _____ (FI and VI).

39. _____ and _____ schedules produce high rates of responding. An _____ schedule produces moderate rates of responding with alternating periods of activity and inactivity. VI schedules produce slow, steady rates of responding and strong resistance to _____.

40. Stimuli that precede a reinforced response tend to control the response on future occasions. This is called _____ _____.

41. Two aspects of stimulus control are _____ and discrimination.

42. In _____, an operant response tends to occur when stimuli similar to those preceding reinforcement are present.

43. In _____, responses are given in the presence of stimuli associated with reinforcement (S+) and withheld in the presence of stimuli associated with non-reinforcement (S⁻).

● *What does punishment do to behavior?*

44. A _____ is any consequence that lowers the frequency of a target behavior.

45. Punishment is most effective when it is immediate, _____, and intense.

46. Mild punishment tends only to temporarily suppress responses that are also _____ in some way.

47. The undesirable side effects of punishment include the conditioning of fear; the learning of escape and _____ responses; and the encouragement of _____ against others.

48. _____ and _____ are a better way to change behavior than punishment.

● *What is cognitive learning?*

49. Cognitive learning involves higher mental processes, such as understanding, knowing, or anticipating. Evidence of cognitive learning is provided by _____ _____ (internal representations of spatial relationships) and _____ (hidden) learning.

50. Discovery learning emphasizes insight and understanding, in contrast to _____ learning.

● *Does learning occur by imitation?*

51. Much human learning is achieved through observation, or _____. _____ learning is influenced by the personal characteristics of the model and the success or failure of the model's behavior.

52. Television characters can act as powerful models for _____ learning. Televised violence increases the likelihood of aggression by viewers.

● *How does conditioning apply to practical problems?*

53. Operant principles can be readily applied to manage behavior in everyday settings. Self-management of behavior is based on self-reinforcement, self-recording, feedback, and behavioral _____.

54. Prepotent, or frequent, high-probability responses, can be used to _____ low-frequency responses. This is known as the _____ principle.

55. Attempts to break bad habits are aided by reinforcing _____ responses, by extinction, breaking response _____, and removing cues or _____.

56. In school, self-regulated learning typically involves all of the following: setting learning goals, planning learning _____, using self-instruction, monitoring progress, evaluating yourself, _____ successes, and taking corrective action when required.

MASTERY TEST

1. Tokens are a good example of
   a. secondary reinforcers   b. the effects of ICS on behavior   c. non-contingent reinforcers
   d. generalized reinforcers

2. The principle of feedback is of particular importance to
   a. CERs   b. ICS   c. CAI   d. higher-order conditioning

3. As a coffee lover, you have become very efficient at carrying out the steps necessary to make a cup of espresso. Your learning is an example of
   a. response chaining   b. spontaneous recovery   c. vicarious reinforcement
   d. secondary reinforcement

4. To teach a pet dog to use a new dog door, it would be helpful to use
   a. the Premack principle   b. shaping   c. respondent conditioning   d. delayed reinforcement

5. To test for the presence of classical conditioning you would omit the
   a. CS   b. US   c. CR   d. S+

6. Which of the following does not belong with the others?
   a. Thorndike   b. Skinner   c. Pavlov   d. instrumental learning

7. To teach a child to say "Please" when she asks for things, you should make getting the requested item
   a. the CS   b. a token   c. a negative reinforcer   d. response-contingent

8. Money is to secondary reinforcer as food is to
   a. ICS   b. prepotent responses   c. primary reinforcer   d. negative reinforcer

9. Whether a model is reinforced has a great impact on
   a. discovery learning   b. latent learning   c. observational learning   d. self-regulated learning

10. One thing that classical and operant conditioning have in common is that both
    a. were discovered by Pavlov   b. depend on reinforcement   c. are affected by the consequences of making a response   d. permanently change behavior

11. To shape the behavior of a teacher in one of your classes you would probably have to rely on
    a. tokens   b. primary reinforcers   c. negative attention seeking   d. social reinforcers

12. The concept that best explains persistence at gambling is
    a. partial reinforcement   b. continuous reinforcement   c. fixed interval reinforcement
    d. fixed ratio reinforcement

13. Which of the following is NOT a common side effect of mild punishment?
    a. escape learning   b. avoidance learning   c. aggression   d. accelerated extinction

14. With respect to televised violence it can be said that TV violence
    a. causes viewers to be more aggressive   b. makes aggression more likely   c. has no effect on the majority of viewers   d. vicariously lowers aggressive urges

15. Which of the following types of learning is most related to the consequences of making a response?
    a. Pavlovian conditioning   b. classical conditioning   c. operant conditioning
    d. respondent conditioning

16. Which combination would most likely make a CER into a phobia?
    a. CER-discrimination   b. CER-desensitization   c. CER-response cost   d. CER-generalization

17. Active, goal-oriented learning in school is called _____ learning.
    a. two-factor   b. respondent   c. vicarious   d. self-regulated

18. A loud, unexpected sound causes a startle reflex; thus, a loud sound could be used as a _____ in conditioning.
    a. NS   b. CR   c. UR   d. US

19. Antecedents are to _____ as consequences are to _____.
    a. discriminative stimuli, reinforcers   b. shaping, response chaining   c. conditioned stimuli, cognitive maps   d. punishment, negative reinforcement

20. The use of self-recording to change personal behavior is closely related to the principle of
    a. response chaining   b. feedback   c. two-factor reinforcement   d. stimulus control

21. _____ typically only temporarily suppresses reinforced responses.
    a. Negative reinforcement   b. Extinction   c. Mild punishment   d. Stimulus generalization

22. In general, the highest rates of responding are associated with
    a. delayed reinforcement   b. variable reinforcement   c. interval reinforcement
    d. fixed ratio reinforcement

23. A child who has learned, through classical conditioning, to fear sitting in a dentist's chair becomes
    frightened when he is placed in a barber's chair. This illustrates the concept of
    a. stimulus generalization   b. spontaneous recovery   c. higher-order discrimination
    d. vicarious conditioning

24. The informational view of learning places emphasis on the creation of mental
    a. expectancies   b. reinforcement schedules   c. contracts   d. antecedents

25. For some adults, blushing when embarrassed or ashamed is probably a _____ first formed in childhood.
    a. conditioned stimulus   b. CAI   c. discriminative stimulus   d. CER

26. Learning to obey traffic signals is related to the phenomenon called
    a. stimulus control   b. spontaneous recovery   c. avoidance learning   d. modeling

27. To be most effective, punishment should be combined with
    a. response costs   b. aversive stimuli   c. delayed feedback   d. reinforcement

28. Involuntary responses are to _____ conditioning as voluntary responses are to
    _____ conditioning.
    a. classical, respondent   b. classical, operant   c. operant, classical   d. operant, instrumental

29. Negative attention seeking by children demonstrates the impact of _____ on behavior.
    a. operant extinction   b. social reinforcers   c. response costs   d. prepotent responses

30. Which consequence increases the probability that a response will be repeated?
    a. punishment   b. response cost   c. non-reinforcement   d. negative reinforcement

ANSWERS

Recite and Review

1. behavior, precede, follow
2. conditioning, conditioning
3. stimulus, responses
4. reinforced, Operant
5. neutral, response
6. stimulus, learned
7. stimulus
8. stimulus
9. conditioning
10. response
11. similar
12. stimulus
13. response
14. follow
15. reflexes, conditioned
16. stimulus
17. secondhand, observe
18. learning
19. increases, effect
20. response, increases
21. effect
22. reinforcement, response

23. chains, single
24. response
25. operant
26. recovery
27. reward, ends
28. decreases, cost
29. pleasure, brain
30. learned, exchanged
31. approval
32. results
33. feedback
34. instruction
35. practice
36. response, partial
37. effect
38. fixed, fixed
39. high, slow
40. precede
41. discrimination
42. similar
43. S+, S−
44. decreases
45. immediate
46. suppress
47. escape
48. mild, responses
49. maps, learning
50. understanding
51. imitation, model, model's
52. models
53. feedback
54. responses, principle
55. responses, response, removing
56. learning, goals, successes

Connections

1. e
2. j
3. a
4. i
5. b
6. h
7. c
8. d
9. f
10. g
11. a
12. j
13. b
14. g
15. c
16. d
17. f
18. e
19. h
20. i
21. d
22. e
23. g
24. f
25. h
26. j
27. i
28. a
29. c
30. b

Check Your Memory

1. T
2. F
3. T
4. F
5. T
6. T
7. F
8. F
9. F
10. T
11. F
12. T
13. T
14. F
15. F
16. T
17. F
18. F
19. F
20. T
21. F
22. T
23. T
24. F
25. T
26. F
27. F
28. F
29. F
30. T
31. T
32. T
33. F
34. T
35. F
36. T
37. F
38. F
39. F
40. T
41. F
42. T
43. F
44. T
45. F
46. T
47. F
48. T
49. T
50. T
51. T
52. T
53. F
54. T
55. T
56. F
57. T
58. F
59. F
60. F
61. T
62. T
63. T
64. F
65. T

Final Survey and Review

1. antecedents, consequences
2. respondent, operant
3. neutral, consequences
4. reinforcement, US

5. Ivan Pavlov, unconditioned, reflex
6. conditioned, conditioned
7. unconditioned stimulus
8. Higher-order
9. extinction
10. spontaneous recovery
11. generalization
12. discrimination
13. informational
14. CS, US
15. emotional responses
16. phobias, generalization
17. Vicarious
18. instrumental
19. probability, Thorndike
20. response, increases
21. expectation
22. contingent
23. decreases, reinforcer
24. Superstitious
25. shaping, approximations
26. extinguish, spontaneous
27. positive, negative
28. aversive, positive
29. Primary, stimulation
30. Secondary, primary, primary
31. social
32. knowledge
33. instruction
34. Computer-assisted
35. CAI
36. schedule, Skinner
37. extinction, partial
38. ratio, interval
39. FR, VR, FI, extinction
40. stimulus control
41. generalization
42. generalization
43. discrimination
44. punisher
45. consistent
46. reinforced
47. avoidance, aggression
48. Reinforcement, non-reinforcement
49. cognitive maps, latent
50. rote
51. modeling, Observational
52. observational
53. contracting
54. reinforce, Premack
55. alternate, chains, antecedents
56. strategies, reinforcing

Mastery Test

1. a (p. 249)
2. c (p. 250)
3. a (p. 245)
4. b (p. 246)
5. b (p. 239)
6. c (p. 243-244)
7. d (p. 245)
8. c (p. 248-249)
9. c (p. 262)
10. b (p. 237)
11. d (p. 249)
12. a (p. 253)
13. d (p. 258)
14. b (p. 264)
15. c (p. 237-238)
16. d (p. 242)
17. d (p. 267)
18. d (p. 237)
19. a (p. 237, 255)
20. b (p. 266)
21. c (p. 258)
22. d (p. 254)
23. a (p. 241)
24. a (p. 240)
25. d (p. 242)
26. a (p. 255)
27. d (p. 258)
28. b (p. 244)
29. b (p. 247)
30. d (p. 247)

Chapter 8
Memory

CHAPTER OVERVIEW

Memory systems encode and store information for later retrieval. A popular model divides memory into three systems: sensory memory, short-term memory (STM), and long-term memory (LTM). Sensory memory stores exact copies of sensory information for very brief periods. STM is limited to about 7 bits of information, but chunking and recoding allow more information to be stored. LTM has nearly unlimited storage. Short-term memories last only a short time; long-term memories are relatively permanent. Long-term memories can be further divided into declarative memories (which may be semantic or episodic) and procedural memories.

Explicit memories are revealed by recall, recognition, and relearning tasks. Implicit memories are revealed by priming. Eidetic imagery (photographic memory) is fairly common in children, but rare among adults. Many people have internal memory images and some have exceptional memory based on internal imagery. Exceptional memory capacity is based on both learned strategies and natural abilities.

Forgetting is most rapid immediately after learning. Some "forgetting" is based on a failure to encode information. Short-term forgetting is partly explained by the decay (weakening) of memory traces. Some long-term forgetting may also occur this way. Some forgetting is related to a lack of memory cues. Much forgetting is related to interference among memories. Clinical psychologists believe that memories are sometimes repressed (unconsciously held out of awareness). Some also believe that repressed childhood memories of abuse can be "recovered." However, there is often no way to separate true memories from fantasies.

In the brain, memory traces (engrams) must be consolidated before they become relatively permanent. The hippocampus is a structure involved in memory consolidation. Information appears to be stored in the brain through changes in nerve cells.

Memory can be improved by the use of mnemonic systems and by attention to factors that affect memory, such as overlearning, serial position, organization, and the like.

LEARNING OBJECTIVES

To demonstrate mastery of this chapter, you should be able to:

1. Explain how memory functions like a computer. Include definitions of encoding, storage, and retrieval.
2. Describe sensory memory. Explain how icons and echoes function in this memory system.

3. Explain the function of selective attention in short-term memory. Describe this memory system in terms of capacity, permanence, and how information is stored.

4. Explain what dual memory is.

5. Explain what is meant by "the magic number seven (plus or minus two)."

6. Describe chunking (recoding) and rehearsal, and explain how they help memory. Describe the difference between maintenance and elaborative rehearsal.

7. Discuss the permanence of memory, including the work of Penfield.

8. Explain how memories are constructed. Include the concepts of constructive processing and pseudo-memories.

9. Discuss the effects of hypnosis on memory.

10. Briefly describe how long-term memories are organized, including the network model and redintegrative memories.

11. Differentiate procedural (skill) memory from declarative (fact) memory. Differentiate the two kinds of declarative memory—semantic memory and episodic memory.

12. Explain the tip-of-the-tongue phenomenon.

13. Describe and give an example of each of the following ways of measuring memory:
   a. recall (include the serial position effect)
   b. recognition (compare to recall and include the idea of distractors)
   c. relearning (include the concept of savings)

14. Distinguish between explicit and implicit memory. Describe how the concept of priming can demonstrate the existence of memories outside the realm of awareness.

The following objectives are related to the material in the "Exploring Psychology" section of the text.

15. Describe the concept of internal imagery and explain how it differs from eidetic imagery.

16. Describe eidetic imagery and its effects on long-term memory. Describe some examples of people with exceptional memories and the role of learned strategies in memory retrieval.

18. Characterize memory loss as demonstrated by Ebbinghaus's curve of forgetting. Discuss his findings as they relate to cramming *versus* spaced review.

19. Discuss the following explanations of forgetting:
   a. encoding failure
   b. decay of memory traces
   c. disuse (give three reasons to question this explanation)
   d. cue-dependent forgetting
   e. state-dependent learning
   f. interference (list and explain the two types of interference and how they are investigated in the laboratory)
   g. repression (and differentiate it from suppression)

20. Describe the false memory syndrome.

21. Describe flashbulb memories and explain how they may be formed.

22. Define *anterograde* and *retrograde* amnesia. Describe the role of consolidation in memory, and explain how electroconvulsive shock (ECS) can affect it.

23. Name the structure in the brain that is responsible for switching information from STM to LTM.

24. Discuss how memories are recorded in the brain by describing how learning is related to engrams, transmitter chemicals, and brain circuits.

25. Describe each of the following in terms of how it can improve memory:

    a. memory strategies

    b. knowledge of results

    c. recitation

    d. rehearsal

    e. selection

    f. organization

    g. whole versus part learning

    h. serial position effect

    i. cues

    j. overlearning

    k. spaced practice

    l. sleep

    m. hunger

    n. extending how long you remember

    o. review

    p. using a strategy for recall

26. List and describe the four strategies of a cognitive interview.

The following objectives are related to the material in the "Psychology in Action" section of the text.

27. Define *mnemonics* and explain the four basic principles of using mnemonics.

28. List and describe three techniques for using mnemonics to remember things in order.

RECITE AND REVIEW

● *Is there more than one type of memory?*

Recite and Review: Pages 272-274

1. Memory is an active _____. _____ is first encoded (changed into the form in which it will be retained).

2. Next it is _____ in memory. Later it must be retrieved to be put to use.

3. Humans appear to have _____ interrelated memory systems. These are sensory memory, _____ memory (STM), and _____ memory (LTM).

4. Sensory memory holds an _____ copy of what is seen or heard, in the form of an icon (_____) or echo (sound sensation).

5. Short-term memories tend to be stored as _____. Long-term memories are stored on the basis of _____, or importance.

6. STM acts as a _____ storehouse for small amounts of information. It provides a working memory where thinking, mental arithmetic, and the like take place. LTM acts as a _____ storehouse for meaningful information.

● *What are the features of each type of memory?*

Recite and Review: Pages 274-278

7. Sensory memory is exact, but very brief, lasting only a few _____ or less. Through selective attention, some information is transferred to _____.

8. The digit-span test reveals that STM has an average upper limit of about 7 _____ of information. However, this can be extended by chunking, or recoding information into _____ units or groups.

9. Short-term memories are brief and very sensitive to _____, or interference; however, they can be prolonged by maintenance rehearsal (silent _____).

10. Elaborative rehearsal, which emphasizes meaning, helps transfer information from _____ to LTM. Elaborative rehearsal links new information with existing _____.

11. LTM seems to have an almost unlimited storage capacity. However, LTM is subject to constructive processing, or ongoing revision and _____. As a result, people often have pseudo-memories (_____ memories) that they believe are true.

12. LTM is highly _____ to allow retrieval of needed information. The pattern, or structure, of memory networks is the subject of current memory research. Network _____ portray LTM as a system of linked ideas.

13. Redintegrative memories unfold as each added memory provides a cue for retrieving the next _____. Seemingly forgotten memories may be reconstructed in this way.

● *Is there more than one type of long-term memory?*

Recite and Review: Pages 278-280

14. Within long-term memory, declarative memories for _____ seem to differ from procedural memories for _____.

15. _____ memories may be further categorized as semantic memories or episodic memories.

16. Semantic memories consist of basic factual knowledge that is almost immune to _____.

17. Episodic memories record _____ experiences that are associated with specific times and places.

● *How is memory measured?*

Recite and Review: Pages 280-283

18. The tip-of-the-tongue _____ shows that memory is not an all-or-nothing event. Memories may be revealed by _____, recognition, or relearning.

19. In recall, memory proceeds without specific cues, as in an _____ exam. Recall of listed information often reveals a serial position effect (_____ items on the list are most subject to errors).

20. A common test of _____ is the multiple-choice question. _____ is very sensitive to the kinds of distractors (wrong choices) used.

21. In relearning, "forgotten" material is learned again, and memory is indicated by a _____ score.

22. Recall, recognition, and relearning mainly measure explicit _____ that we are aware of having. Other techniques, such as priming, are necessary to reveal implicit _____, which are unconscious.

● *What are "photographic" memories?*

Recite and Review: Pages 283-285

23. Eidetic imagery (photographic memory) occurs when a person is able to project an _____ onto an external surface. Such images allow brief, nearly complete recall by some children.

24. Eidetic imagery is rarely found in _____. However, many adults have internal images, which can be very vivid and a basis for remembering.

25. Exceptional memory can be learned by finding ways to directly store information in _____. Learning has no effect on the limits of _____. Some people may have naturally superior memory abilities that exceed what can be achieved through learning.

● *What causes forgetting?*

Recite and Review: Pages 286-290

26. Forgetting and memory were extensively studied by Herman Ebbinghaus, whose _____ of forgetting shows that forgetting is typically most rapid immediately _____ learning.

27. Ebbinghaus used nonsense syllables to study memory. The forgetting of _____ material is much _____ than shown by his curve of forgetting.

28. Failure to encode _____ is a common cause of "forgetting."

29. Forgetting in sensory memory and STM probably reflects decay of memory _____ in the nervous system. Decay or _____ of memories may also account for some LTM loss, but most forgetting cannot be explained this way.

30. Often, forgetting is cue dependent. The power of cues to trigger memories is revealed by state-dependent _____, in which bodily _____ at the time of learning and of retrieval affect memory.

31. Much _____ in both STM and LTM can be attributed to interference of memories with one another.

32. When recent learning _____ with retrieval of prior learning, retroactive interference has occurred. If old memories _____ with new memories, proactive interference has occurred.

● *How accurate are everyday memories?*

Recite and Review: Pages 290-292

33. Repression is the _____ of painful, embarrassing, or traumatic memories.
34. Repression is thought to be unconscious, in contrast to suppression, which is a _____ attempt to avoid thinking about something.
35. Experts are currently debating the validity of childhood memories of _____ that reappear after apparently being repressed for decades.
36. Independent evidence has verified that some recovered memories are _____. However, others have been shown to be _____.
37. In the absence of confirming or disconfirming _____, there is currently no way to separate true memories from fantasies. Caution is advised for all concerned with attempts to retrieve supposedly hidden memories.
38. Flashbulb memories, which seem especially vivid, are created at emotionally significant times. While such memories may not be accurate, we tend to place great _____ in them.

● *What happens in the brain when memories are formed?*

Recite and Review: Pages 292-294

39. Retrograde _____ and the effects of electroconvulsive _____ (ECS) may be explained by the concept of consolidation.
40. Consolidation theory holds that engrams (permanent _____ _____) are formed during a critical period after learning. Until they are consolidated, long-term memories are easily destroyed.
41. The hippocampus is a _____ structure associated with the consolidation of memories.
42. The search within the brain for engrams has now settled on changes in individual _____ cells.
43. The best-documented changes are alterations in the amounts of transmitter _____ released by nerve cells.

● *How can memory be improved?*

Recite and Review: Pages 294-297 & PSYCHOLOGY IN ACTION

44. Memory can be improved by using feedback, recitation, and rehearsal, by selecting and _____ information, and by using the progressive _____ method, spaced practice, overlearning, and active search strategies.
45. The effects of serial _____, sleep, review, cues, and elaboration should also be kept in mind when studying or memorizing.
46. Mnemonic systems, such as the _____ method, use mental images and unusual associations to link new information with familiar memories already stored in _____. Such strategies give information personal meaning and make it easier to recall.

CONNECTIONS

1. _____ echos and icons a. STM
2. _____ working memory b. constructive processing
3. _____ 7 information bits c. network model
4. _____ chunking d. sensory memory
5. _____ revised memories e. procedures
6. _____ memory structure f. recoding
7. _____ skill memory g. memory test
8. _____ relearning h. magic number

9. _____ selective attention
10. _____ long-term memory
11. _____ incoming information
12. _____ encoding for LTM
13. _____ sensory memory
14. _____ short-term memory
15. _____ rehearsal buffer

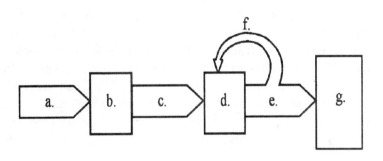

16. _____ semantic memory
17. _____ long-term memory
18. _____ procedural memory
19. _____ sensory memory
20. _____ episodic memory
21. _____ short-term memory
22. _____ declarative memory

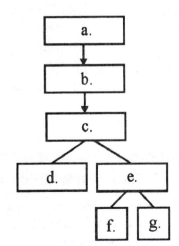

CHECK YOUR MEMORY

Check Your Memory: Pages 272-274

1. Incoming information must be encoded before it is stored in memory. T or F?
2. Sensory memories last for a few minutes or less. T or F?
3. A memory that cannot be retrieved has little value. T or F?
4. Selective attention influences what information enters STM. T or F?
5. Working memory is another name for sensory memory. T or F?
6. Errors in long-term memory tend to focus on the sounds of words. T or F?
7. Generally, the more you know, the more new information you can store in long-term memory. T or F?

Check Your Memory: Pages 274-278

8. For many kinds of information, STM can store an average of 5 bits of information. T or F?
9. Chunking recodes information into smaller units that are easier to fit into STM. T or F?
10. The more times a short-term memory is rehearsed, the better its chance of being stored in LTM. T or F?
11. On average, short-term memories last only about 18 minutes, unless they are rehearsed. T or F?
12. Maintenance rehearsal keeps memories active in sensory memory. T or F?
13. The surface of the brain records the past like a movie, complete with sound track. T or F?
14. Being confident about a memory tells little about the true accuracy of the memory. T or F?
15. Hypnosis increases false memories more than it does true ones. T or F?
16. Long-term memories appear to be organized alphabetically for speedy access. T or F?

Check Your Memory: Pages 278-280

17. Knowing how to swing a golf club is a type of declarative memory. T or F?
18. A person lacking declarative memory might still remember how to solve a mechanical puzzle. T or F?
19. Semantic memories are almost immune to forgetting. T or F?
20. Semantic memories are a type of declarative memory. T or F?
21. Episodic memories have no connection to particular times and places. T or F?

Check Your Memory: Pages 280-283

22. Remembering the first sound of a name you are trying to recall is an example of the tip-of-the-tongue state. T or F?
23. Tests of recognition require verbatim memory. T or F?
24. The serial position effect measures the strength of the feeling of knowing. T or F?
25. Recognition tends to be a more sensitive test of memory than recall. T or F?
26. False positives and distractors greatly affect the accuracy of relearning tests. T or F?
27. Recall, recognition, and relearning are used to measure explicit memories. T or F?
28. Priming is used to activate explicit (hidden) memories. T or F?

Check Your Memory: Pages 283-285

29. Eidetic images last for 30 seconds or more. T or F?
30. About 8 percent of all children have eidetic images. T or F?

31. Eidetic imagery becomes rare by adulthood. T or F?

32. Mr. S (the mnemonist) had virtually unlimited eidetic imagery. T or F?

33. Practice in remembering one type of information increases the capacity of STM to store other types of information, too. T or F?

34. All contestants in the World Memory Championship performed poorly on tasks that prevented the use of learned strategies. T or F?

Check Your Memory: Pages 286-290

35. Ebbinghaus chose to learn nonsense syllables so that they would all be the same length. T or F?

36. Ebbinghaus's curve of forgetting levels off after 2 days, showing little further memory loss after that. T or F?

37. Decay of memory traces clearly applies to information in STM. T or F?

38. Disuse theories of forgetting answer the question: Have I been storing the information in the first place? T or F?

39. The presence of memory cues almost always improves memory. T or F?

40. Information learned under the influence of a drug may be best remembered when the drugged state occurs again. T or F?

41. If you are in a bad mood, you are more likely to remember unpleasant events. T or F?

42. Categorizing a person as a member of a group tends to limit the accuracy of memories about the person's appearance. T or F?

43. Sleeping tends to interfere with retaining new memories. T or F?

44. You learn information A and then information B. If your memory of B is lowered by having first learned A, you have experienced retroactive interference. T or F?

Check Your Memory: Pages 290-292

45. Unconsciously forgetting painful memories is called negative transfer. T or F?

46. A conscious attempt to put a memory out of mind is called repression. T or F?

47. Suggestion and fantasy are elements of many techniques used in attempts to recover repressed memories. T or F?

48. Unless a memory can be independently confirmed, there is no way to tell if it is real or not. T or F?

49. Flashbulb memories tend to be formed when an event is surprising or emotional. T or F?

50. The confidence we have in flashbulb memories is well placed—they are much more accurate than most other memories. T or F?

Check Your Memory: 292-294

51. Retrograde amnesia is a gap in memories of events preceding a head injury. T or F?

52. Stimulant drugs may speed up consolidation, but at high doses they disrupt memory. T or F?

53. People with damage to the hippocampus typically cannot remember events that occurred before the damage. T or F?

54. In the early 1920s, Karl Lashley found the location of engrams in the brain. T or F?

55. Storing memories alters the activity, structure, and chemistry of the brain. T or F?

Check Your Memory: Pages 294-297 & PSYCHOLOGY IN ACTION

56. Recitation is a good way to generate feedback while studying. T or F?
57. Elaborative rehearsal involving "why" questions improves memory. T or F?
58. Overlearning is inefficient; you should stop studying at the point of initial mastery of new information. T or F?
59. Massed practice is almost always superior to spaced practice. T or F?
60. When learning, it helps to gradually extend how long you remember new information before reviewing it again. T or F?
61. Recalling events from different viewpoints is part of doing a cognitive interview. T or F?
62. *Roy G. Biv* is a mnemonic for the notes on a musical staff. T or F?
63. Many mnemonics make use of mental images or pictures. T or F?
64. Mnemonics often link new information to familiar memories. T or F?
65. The keyword method is superior to rote learning for memorizing vocabulary words in another language. T or F?

FINAL SURVEY AND REVIEW

● *Is there more than one type of memory?*

1. Memory is an active system. Information is first _____ (changed into the form in which it will be retained).
2. Next it is stored in memory. Later it must be _____ to be put to use.
3. Humans appear to have 3 interrelated memory systems. These are _____ memory, _____ memory (STM), and long-term memory (LTM).
4. Sensory memory holds an exact copy of what is seen or heard, in the form of an _____ (image) or _____ (sound sensation).
5. _____ memories tend to be stored as sounds. _____ memories are stored on the basis of meaning, or importance.
6. _____ acts as a temporary storehouse for small amounts of information. It provides a _____ memory where thinking, mental arithmetic, and the like take place. LTM acts as a permanent storehouse for _____ information.

● *What are the features of each type of memory?*

7. _____ memory is exact, but very brief, lasting only a few seconds or less. Through _____ _____, some information is transferred to STM.
8. The _____ test reveals that STM has an average upper limit of about 7 bits of information. However, this can be extended by chunking, or _____ information into larger units or groups.
9. Short-term memories are brief and very sensitive to interruption , or _____; however, they can be prolonged by _____ rehearsal (silent repetition).

10. _____ rehearsal, which emphasizes meaning, helps transfer information from STM to LTM.

11. LTM seems to have an almost unlimited storage capacity. However, LTM is subject to _____ processing, or ongoing revision and updating. As a result, people often have _____ (false memories) that they believe are true.

12. LTM is highly organized to allow retrieval of needed information. The pattern, or structure, of memory _____ is the subject of current memory research. _____ models portray LTM as a system of linked ideas.

13. _____ memories unfold as each added memory provides a cue for retrieving the next memory. Seemingly forgotten memories may be reconstructed in this way.

● *Is there more than one type of long-term memory?*

14. Within long-term memory, _____ memories for facts seem to differ from _____ memories for skills.

15. Declarative memories may be further categorized as _____ memories or _____ memories.

16. _____ memories consist of basic factual knowledge that is almost immune to forgetting.

17. _____ memories record personal experiences that are associated with specific times and places.

● *How is memory measured?*

18. The _____-of-the-_____ state shows that memory is not an all-or-nothing event. Memories may be revealed by recall, _____, or relearning.

19. In _____, memory proceeds without specific cues, as in an essay exam. Remembering a list of information often reveals a _____ _____ effect (middle items on the list are most subject to errors).

20. A common test of recognition is the _____-choice question. Recognition is very sensitive to the kinds of _____ (wrong choices) used.

21. In _____, "forgotten" material is learned again, and memory is indicated by a savings score.

22. Recall, recognition, and relearning mainly measure _____ memories that we are aware of having. Other techniques, such as priming, are necessary to reveal _____ memories, which are unconscious.

● *What are "photographic" memories?*

23. _____ _____ (photographic memory) occurs when a person is able to project an image onto an external surface. Such images allow brief, nearly complete recall by some children.

24. _____ _____ is rarely found in adults. However, many adults have internal images, which can be very vivid and a basis for remembering.

25. _____ memory can be learned by finding ways to directly store information in LTM. Learning has no effect on the _____ of STM. Some people may have naturally superior memory abilities that exceed what can be achieved through learning.

● *What causes forgetting?*

26. Forgetting and memory were extensively studied by Herman _____, whose curve of forgetting shows that forgetting is typically most rapid immediately after learning.

27. He used _____ syllables to study memory. The forgetting of meaningful material is much slower than shown by his curve of forgetting.

28. Failure to _____ information is a common cause of "forgetting."

29. Forgetting in _____ memory and _____ probably reflects decay of memory traces in the nervous system. Decay or disuse of memories may also account for some _____ loss, but most forgetting cannot be explained this way.

30. Often, forgetting is _____ dependent. The power of _____ to trigger memories is revealed by _____ learning, in which bodily states at the time of learning and of retrieval affect memory.

31. Much forgetting in both STM and LTM can be attributed to _____ of memories with one another.

32. When recent learning interferes with retrieval of prior learning, _____ interference has occurred. If old memories interfere with new memories, _____ interference has occurred.

● *How accurate are everyday memories?*

33. _____ is the motivated forgetting of painful, embarrassing, or traumatic memories.

34. _____ is thought to be unconscious, in contrast to _____, which is a conscious attempt to avoid thinking about something.

35. Experts are currently debating the validity of childhood memories of abuse that reappear after apparently being _____ for decades.

36. Independent evidence has verified that some _____ memories are true. However, others have been shown to be false.

37. In the absence of confirming or disconfirming evidence, there is currently no way to separate true memories from _____. Caution is advised for all concerned with attempts to retrieve supposedly hidden memories.

38. _____ memories, which seem especially vivid, are created at emotionally significant times. While such memories may not be _____, we tend to place great confidence in them.

● *What happens in the brain when memories are formed?*

39. _____ amnesia and the effects of _____ shock (ECS) may be explained by the concept of consolidation.

40. Consolidation theory holds that _____ (permanent memory traces) are formed during a critical period after learning. Until they are _____, long-term memories are easily destroyed.

41. The _____ is a brain structure associated with the consolidation of memories.

42. The search within the brain for engrams has now settled on changes in individual _____ _____.

43. The best-documented changes are alterations in the amounts of _____ chemicals released by nerve cells.

● *How can memory be improved?*

44. Memory can be improved by using _____ (knowledge of results), recitation, and rehearsal, by _____ and organizing information, and by using the progressive part method, spaced practice, overlearning, and active _____ strategies.

45. The effects of _____ position, sleep, review, cues, and _____ (connecting new information to existing knowledge) should also be kept in mind when studying or memorizing.

46. _____ systems, such as the keyword method, use mental images and unusual associations to link new information with familiar memories already stored in LTM. Such strategies give information personal meaning and make it easier to recall.

MASTERY TEST

1. The meaning and importance of information has a strong impact on
   a. sensory memory   b. eidetic memory   c. long-term memory   d. procedural memory

2. Pseudo-memories are closely related to the effects of
   a. repression   b. suppression   c. semantic forgetting   d. constructive processing

3. The occurrence of _____ implies that consolidation has been prevented.
   a. retrograde amnesia   b. hippocampal transfer   c. suppression   d. changes in the activities of individual nerve cells

4. Most of the techniques used to recover supposedly repressed memories involve
   a. redintegration and hypnosis   b. suggestion and fantasy   c. reconstruction and priming
   d. coercion and fabrication

5. Most daily memory chores are handled by
   a. sensory memory and LTM b. STM and working memory c. STM and LTM
   d. STM and declarative memory

6. Three key processes in memory systems are
   a. storage, organization, recovery b. encoding, attention, reprocessing c. storage, retrieval, encoding
   d. retrieval, reprocessing, reorganization

7. Procedural memories are to skills as _____ memories are to facts.
   a. declarative b. short-term c. redintegrative d. eidetic

8. An ability to answer questions about distances on a map you have seen only once implies that some memories are based on
   a. constructive processing b. redintegration c. internal images d. episodic processing

9. The first potential cause of forgetting that may occur is
   a. engram decay b. disuse c. cue-dependent forgetting d. encoding failure

10. The persistence of icons and echoes is the basis for
    a. sensory memory b. short-term memory c. long-term memory d. working memory

11. Priming is most often used to reveal
    a. semantic memories b. episodic memories c. implicit memories d. eidetic memories

12. "Projection" onto an external surface is most characteristic of
    a. sensory memories b. eidetic images c. flashbulb memories d. mnemonic images

13. Chunking helps especially to extend the capacity of
    a. sensory memory b. STM c. LTM d. declarative memory

14. There is presently no way to tell if a "recovered" memory is true or false unless independent _____ exists.
    a. evidence b. amnesia c. elaboration d. consolidation

15. Taking an essay test inevitably requires a person to use
    a. recall b. recognition c. relearning d. priming

16. A savings score is used in what memory task?
    a. recall b. recognition c. relearning d. priming

17. _____ rehearsal helps link new information to existing memories by concentrating on meaning.
    a. Redintegrative b. Constructive c. Maintenance d. Elaborative

18. Middle items are neither held in STM nor moved to LTM. This statement explains the
    a. feeling of knowing b. serial position effect c. tip-of-the-tongue state d. semantic forgetting curve

19. According to the curve of forgetting, the greatest decline in the amount recalled occurs during the
    _____ after learning.
    a. first hour b. second day c. third to sixth days d. retroactive period

20. Work with brain stimulation, truth serums, and hypnosis suggests that long-term memories are
    a. stored in the hippocampus b. relatively permanent c. unaffected by later input
    d. always redintegrative

21. Which of the following is most likely to improve the accuracy of memory?
    a. hypnosis b. constructive processing c. the serial position effect d. memory cues

22. To qualify as repression, forgetting must be
    a. retroactive b. proactive c. unconscious d. explicit

23. Which of the following typically is NOT a good way to improve memory?
    a. massed practice b. overlearning c. rehearsal d. recall strategies

24. A witness to a crime is questioned in ways that re-create the context of the crime and that provide many
    memory cues. It appears that she is undergoing
    a. retroactive priming b. the progressive part method c. retroactive consolidation
    d. a cognitive interview

25. One thing that is clearly true about flashbulb memories is that
    a. they are unusually accurate b. we place great confidence in them c. they apply primarily to public
    tragedies d. they are recovered by using visualization and hypnosis

26. One common mnemonic strategy is the
    a. serial position technique b. feeling of knowing tactic c. network procedure d. keyword method

27. A perspective that helps explain redintegrative memories is
    a. the feeling of knowing model b. recoding and chunking c. the network model
    d. mnemonic models

28. Which of the following is NOT considered a part of long-term memory?
    a. echoic memory b. semantic memory c. episodic memory d. declarative memory

29. You are very thirsty. Suddenly you remember a time years ago when you became very thirsty while
    hiking. This suggests that your memory is
    a. proactive b. state dependent c. still not consolidated d. eidetic

30. After memorizing 5 lists of words you recall less of the last list than a person who only memorized list number five. This observation is explained by
a. reactive processing   b. reconstructive processing   c. proactive interference
d. retroactive interference

ANSWERS

Recite and Review

1. system, Information
2. stored
3. 3, short-term, long-term
4. exact, image
5. sounds, meaning
6. temporary, permanent
7. seconds, STM
8. bits, larger
9. interruption, repetition
10. STM, memories
11. updating, false
12. organized, models
13. memory
14. facts, skills
15. Declarative
16. forgetting
17. personal
18. state, recall
19. essay, middle
20. recognition, Recognition
21. savings
22. memories, memories
23. image
24. adults
25. LTM, STM
26. curve, after
27. meaningful, slower
28. information
29. traces, disuse
30. learning, states
31. forgetting
32. interferes, interfere
33. forgetting
34. conscious
35. abuse
36. true, false
37. evidence
38. confidence
39. amnesia, shock
40. memory traces
41. brain
42. nerve
43. chemicals
44. organizing, part
45. position
46. keyword, LTM

Connections

1. d
2. a
3. h
4. f
5. b
6. c
7. e
8. g
9. c
10. g
11. a
12. e
13. b
14. d
15. f
16. f or g
17. c
18. d
19. a
20. f or g
21. b
22. e

Check Your Memory

1. T
2. F
3. T
4. T
5. F
6. F
7. T
8. T
9. F
10. T
11. F
12. F
13. F
14. T
15. T
16. F
17. F
18. T
19. T
20. T
21. F
22. T
23. F
24. F
25. T
26. F
27. T
28. F
29. T
30. T
31. T
32. F
33. F
34. F
35. F

36. T
37. T
38. F
39. T
40. T
41. T
42. T
43. F
44. F
45. F
46. F
47. T
48. T
49. T
50. F
51. T
52. T
53. F
54. F
55. T
56. T
57. T
58. F
59. F
60. T
61. T
62. F
63. T
64. T
65. T

Final Survey and Review

1. encoded
2. retrieved
3. sensory, short-term
4. icon, echo

5. Short-term, Long-term
6. STM, working, meaningful
7. Sensory, selective attention
8. digit-span, recoding
9. interference, maintenance
10. Elaborative
11. constructive, pseudo-memories
12. networks, Network
13. Redintegrative
14. declarative, procedural
15. semantic, episodic
16. Semantic
17. Episodic
18. tip, tongue, recognition
19. recall, serial position
20. multiple, distractors
21. relearning
22. explicit, implicit
23. Eidetic imagery
24. Eidetic imagery
25. Exceptional, limits
26. Ebbinghaus
27. nonsense
28. encode
29. sensory, STM, LTM
30. cue, cues, state-dependent
31. interference
32. retroactive, proactive
33. Repression
34. Repression, suppression
35. repressed
36. recovered
37. fantasies
38. Flashbulb, accurate
39. Retrograde, electroconvulsive
40. engrams, consolidated
41. hippocampus

42. nerve cells
43. transmitter
44. feedback, selecting, search
45. serial, elaboration
46. Mnemonic

Mastery Test

1. c (p. 274)
2. d (p. 276-277)
3. a (p. 292)
4. b (p. 291)
5. c (p. 274)
6. c (p. 272)
7. a (p. 278-279)
8. c (p. 283)
9. d (p. 286)
10. a (p. 272)
11. c (p. 282)
12. b (p. 283)
13. b (p. 275)
14. a (p. 291)
15. a (p. 281)
16. c (p. 282)
17. d (p. 276)
18. b (p. 281)
19. a (p. 286)
20. b (p. 276)
21. d (p. 297)
22. c (p. 290)
23. a (p. 296)
24. d (p. 297)
25. b (p. 291)
26. d (p. 299)
27. c (p. 278)
28. a (p. 279)
29. b (p. 288)
30. c (p. 288-289)

Chapter 9
Cognition, Intelligence, and Creativity

CHAPTER OVERVIEW

Thinking is the mental manipulation of images, concepts, and language (or symbols). Most people use internal images (including kinesthetic images) for thinking. A concept is a generalized idea of a class of objects or events. We learn concepts from positive and negative instances and from rules. Prototypes are often used to identify concepts. Language translates events into symbols, which are combined using the rules of grammar and syntax. True languages are productive. Studies suggest that, with training, primates are capable of some language use.

The solution to a problem may be arrived at mechanically (by trial and error or by rote). Solutions by understanding usually begin with discovering the general properties of an answer. Next, functional solutions are proposed. Problem solving is frequently aided by heuristics, which narrow the search for solutions. When understanding leads to a rapid solution, insight has occurred. Insight can be blocked by fixations. Work on artificial intelligence has focused on computer simulations and expert systems. Human expertise is based on organized knowledge and acquired strategies.

Intelligence refers to a general capacity to act purposefully, think rationally, and deal effectively with the environment. In practice, intelligence is operationally defined by creating tests. The first practical individual intelligence test was assembled by Alfred Binet. A modern version is the Stanford-Binet Intelligence Scale. A second major intelligence test is the Wechsler Adult Intelligence Scale. Culture-fair and group intelligence tests are also available. Intelligence is expressed as an intelligence quotient (IQ) or as a deviation IQ. The distribution of IQ scores approximates a normal curve. Intelligence reflects the combined effects of heredity and environment.

People with IQs in the gifted or "genius" range tend to be superior in many respects. In addition, many children are gifted or talented in other ways. The terms mentally retarded and developmentally disabled apply to persons who have an IQ below 70 or who lack various adaptive behaviors. About 50 percent of the cases of mental retardation are organic; the remaining cases are of undetermined cause (many are thought to be familial).

Creative solutions are practical, sensible, and original. Creative thinking requires divergent thought, characterized by fluency, flexibility, and originality. Tests of creativity measure these qualities. Five stages often seen in creative problem solving are orientation, preparation, incubation, illumination, and verification. There is only a small positive correlation between IQ and creativity.

Intuitive thinking often leads to errors. Wrong conclusions may be drawn when an answer seems highly representative of what we already believe is true. A second problem is ignoring the base rate of an event. Clear thinking is usually aided by stating or framing a problem in broad terms. Major sources of thinking errors include rigid mental sets, faulty logic, and over-simplifications. Various strategies, including brainstorming, tend to enhance creative problem solving.

LEARNING OBJECTIVES

To demonstrate mastery of this chapter, you should be able to:

1. Define the terms *cognition* and *cognitive psychology.*
2. List the three basic units of thought.
3. Describe mental imagery (including the concept of mental rotation and a description of what happens in the brain during visual imaging). Explain how both stored and created images may be used to solve problems.
4. Explain how the size of a mental image is important.
5. Explain how kinesthetic imagery aids thinking.
6. Define the terms *concept* and *concept formation*, explain how they aid thought processes, and describe how they are learned. Define the term *conceptual rule.*
7. Define the terms *conjunctive concept, relational concept,* and *disjunctive concept.*
8. Explain the importance of prototypes.
9. Explain the difference between the denotative and the connotative meaning of a word or concept, and describe how the connotative meaning of a word is measured.
10. Define the term *semantic differential* and briefly discuss how using inaccurate concepts may lead to thinking errors.
11. Define *semantics* and explain how semantic problems may arise.
12. Briefly describe the following three requirements of a language and their related concepts:
    1) symbols
        a) phonemes
        b) morphemes
    2) grammar
        a) syntax
        b) transformation rules
    3) productivity

The following objectives are related to the material in the "Exploring Psychology" section of the text.
13. Describe the research involving attempts to teach primates (especially Washoe, Sarah, and Kanzi) to use language. Describe the criticisms and practical value of such attempts.

14. Compare and contrast mechanical solutions with solutions through understanding.

15. Define the term *heuristic* and contrast it with random search strategies.
16. Describe the process of insight as a problem solving technique.
17. List and describe the three abilities involved in insight.
18. Explain how fixation and functional fixedness block problem solving, and give an example of each.
19. List and explain four common barriers to creative thinking.
20. Define the term *artificial intelligence* and state upon what fact it is based.
21. Explain how computer simulations and expert systems are used.
22. Explain the differences between experts and novices.
23. Describe Binet's role in intelligence testing.
24. Define *intelligence*.
25. Explain what an operational definition of intelligence is.
26. Generally describe the construction of the Stanford-Binet Intelligence Scale.
27. Define *intelligence quotient*, and use an example to show how it was computed. Explain the purpose of deviation IQ scores.
28. Distinguish the Wechsler tests from the Stanford-Binet tests.
29. Define the term *culture-fair test*, and explain how IQ tests may be unfair to certain groups.
30. Distinguish between group and individual intelligence tests.
31. Describe the pattern of distribution of IQ scores observed in the general population.
32. Discuss the relationship between IQ and achievement.
33. Briefly describe Terman's study of gifted children. State how successful subjects differed from the less successful ones.
34. List seven early signs of giftedness.
35. Describe Gardner's broader view of intelligence and list the eight different kinds of intelligence he discusses.
36. State the dividing line between normal intelligence and retardation (or developmental disability) and list the degrees of retardation.
37. Differentiate between organic and familial retardation.
38. Explain how the twin (identical and fraternal) studies can be used to support either side of the heredity/environment controversy.
39. Describe the evidence that strongly supports the environmental view of intelligence.
40. Describe the studies that indicate how much the environment can alter intelligence.
41. Discuss how the heredity/environment debate is currently viewed.
42. Describe the following four kinds of thought:
    a. inductive b. deductive c. logical d. illogical
43. Describe the following characteristics of creative thinking:
    a. fluency b. flexibility c. originality
44. Explain the relationship of creativity to divergent and convergent thinking. Describe how the ability to think divergently can be measured.
45. List and describe the five stages of creative thinking, and relate them to a problem that you have solved.
46. List five conclusions about creative people.

47. Define *intuition.*

48. Explain the following errors made when using intuition:

a. representativeness b. underlying odds (base rate) c. framing

The following objectives are related to the material in the "Psychology in Action" section of the text.

49. Briefly describe the relationship between intelligence and wisdom.

50. Describe eight practical steps for encouraging creativity.

51. Describe the process of brainstorming, and explain how it can be used to solve problems.

RECITE AND REVIEW

● *What is the nature of thought?*

Recite and Review: Pages 304-305

1. Cognitive psychology is the study of human _____ processing (thinking, language, and problem solving).

2. Thinking is the manipulation of _____ representations of external problems or situations.

3. Three basic units of thought are images, concepts, and _____ or symbols.

● *In what ways are images related to thinking?*

Recite and Review: Pages 305-307

4. Most people have internal images of one kind or another. Images may be based on information stored in memory or they may be _____.

5. The size of images used in problem solving may _____. Images may be three-dimensional and they may be rotated in _____ to answer questions.

6. Many of the systems in the brain that are involved in processing _____ images work in reverse to create mental images.

7. Kinesthetic images are created from produced, remembered, or imagined _____ sensations. _____ sensations and micromovements seem to help structure thinking for many people.

● *How are concepts learned?*

Recite and Review: Pages 307-309

8. A concept is a generalized idea of a _____ of objects or events.

9. Forming concepts may be based on experiences with _____ and negative instances.

10. Concepts may also be acquired by learning rules that define the _____.

11. In practice, we frequently use prototypes (general _____ of the concept class) to identify concepts.

12. Concepts may be classified as conjunctive ("_____" concepts), disjunctive ("_____" concepts), or relational concepts.

13. The denotative meaning of a word or concept is its exact _____. Connotative meaning is _____ or emotional.

14. Connotative meaning can be measured with the semantic differential. Most connotative meaning involves the dimensions _____, strong-weak, and active-passive.

● What is the role of language in thinking?

Recite and Review: Pages 309-311

15. Language allows events to be encoded into _____ for easy mental manipulation.

16. Language is built out of phonemes (basic speech _____) and morphemes (speech sounds collected into _____ units).

17. Thinking in language is influenced by meaning. The study of _____ is called semantics.

18. Language carries meaning by combining a set of symbols or signs according to a set of _____ (grammar), which includes rules about word _____ (syntax).

19. Various sentences are created by applying transformation _____ to simple statements.

20. A true language is productive, and can be used to generate new ideas or possibilities. American Sign Language (ASL) and other _____ languages used by the deaf are true languages.

● Can animals be taught to use language?

Recite and Review: Pages 311-313

21. Animal communication is relatively limited because it lacks symbols that can be rearranged easily. As a result, it does not have the productive quality of _____ language.

22. Attempts to teach chimpanzees ASL and other non-verbal systems suggest to some that primates are capable of language use. However, others believe that the chimps are merely using _____ responses to get food and other reinforcers.

23. Studies that make use of lexigrams (_____ word-symbols) provide the best evidence yet of animal language use.

● What do we know about problem solving?

Recite and Review: Pages 313-317

24. The solution to a problem may be found mechanically (by trial and error or by _____ application of rules). However, mechanical solutions are frequently inefficient or ineffective, except where aided by _____.

25. Solutions by understanding usually begin with discovery of the _____ properties of an answer. Next comes proposal of a number of functional _____.

26. Problem solving is frequently aided by heuristics. These are strategies that typically _____ the search for solutions.

27. When understanding leads to a rapid _____, insight has occurred. Three elements of insight are _____ encoding, selective combination, and selective comparison.

28. Insights and other problem solving attempts can be blocked by fixation (a tendency to repeat _____ solutions).

29. Functional fixedness is a common _____, but emotional blocks, cultural values, learned conventions, and perceptual _____ are also problems.

● *What is artificial intelligence?*

Recite and Review: Pages 317-318

30. Artificial intelligence refers to computer _____ that can perform tasks that require _____ when done by people.

31. Two principal areas of artificial intelligence research are _____ simulations and expert systems.

32. Expert human problem solving is based on organized _____ and acquired strategies, rather than some general improvement in thinking ability.

● *How is human intelligence defined and measured?*

Recite and Review: Pages 319-321

33. Intelligence refers to one's general capacity to act purposefully, think _____, and deal effectively with the _____.

34. In practice, writing an intelligence test provides an operational _____ of intelligence.

35. The first practical _____ _____ was assembled in 1904, in Paris, by Alfred Binet.

36. A modern version of Binet's test is the *Stanford-Binet* _____ _____, Fourth Edition.

37. The Stanford-Binet measures _____ reasoning, quantitative reasoning, abstract/visual reasoning, and short-term _____.

38. A second major intelligence test is the *Wechsler* _____ *Intelligence Scale, Third Edition* (WAIS-III). The WAIS-III measures both verbal and performance (_____) intelligence.

39. Intelligence tests have also been produced for use with _____ of people. The *Scholastic Assessment Test* (SAT), measures a variety of _____ aptitudes and it can be used to estimate intelligence.

● *How do IQ scores relate to achievement and thinking ability?*

Recite and Review: Pages 321-328

40. Intelligence is expressed in terms of an intelligence _____ (IQ). IQ is defined as mental age (MA) divided by chronological age (CA) and then multiplied by _____.

41. An "average" IQ of _____ occurs when mental age _____ chronological age.

42. Modern IQ tests no longer calculate _____ directly. Instead, the final score reported by the test is a deviation IQ, which gives a person's _____ intellectual standing in his or her age group.

43. When graphed, the distribution (percentage of people receiving each score) of IQ scores approximates a normal (_____-shaped) _____.

44. People with IQs above 140 are considered to be in the _____ or "genius" range.

45. Studies done by Lewis Terman showed that the gifted tend to be _____ in many respects, such as achievement, physical appearance, and mental health.

46. The most successful gifted persons tend to be those who are persistent and _____ to learn and succeed.

47. By criteria other than _____, a large proportion of children might be considered gifted or talented in one way or another.

48. Howard Gardner believes that _____ IQ tests define intelligence too narrowly. According to Gardner, intelligence consists of abilities in language, logic and _____, _____ and spatial thinking, music, kinesthetic skills, intrapersonal skills, interpersonal skills, and naturalist skills.

49. The terms mentally _____ and developmentally disabled are applied to those whose IQ falls below _____ or who lack various adaptive behaviors.

50. Further classifications of retardation are: _____ (50-55 to 70), moderate (35-40 to 50-55), _____ (20-25 to 35-40), and profound (below 20-25).

51. About _____ percent of the cases of mental retardation are organic, being caused by _____ injuries, fetal damage, metabolic disorders, or genetic abnormalities. The remaining cases are of undetermined cause.

52. Many cases of subnormal intelligence are thought to be the result of familial retardation (a low level of _____ stimulation in the home, poverty, and poor nutrition).

53. Studies of family relationships in humans, especially comparisons between fraternal twins and identical twins (who have identical _____), also suggest that intelligence is partly _____.

54. However, environment is also important, as revealed by changes in tested intelligence induced by _____ environments and improved education.

55. _____ therefore reflects the combined effects of heredity and environment.

56. Differences in the average IQ scores for various racial groups are based on environmental differences, not _____.

● *What is the nature of creative thinking?*

Recite and Review: Pages 328-332

57. To be creative, a solution must be _____ and sensible as well as original.

58. _____ may be deductive or inductive, logical or illogical.

59. Creative thinking requires divergent thought, characterized by fluency, flexibility, and _____.

60. Tests of _____, such as the *Unusual Uses Test*, the *Consequences Test*, and the *Anagrams Test*, measure the capacity for divergent thinking.

61. Five stages often seen in creative problem solving are orientation, _____, incubation, illumination, and verification.

62. Studies suggest that creative persons share a number of identifiable general traits, _____ abilities, thinking _____, and personality characteristics. There is only a small correlation between IQ and creativity.

● *How accurate is intuition?*

Recite and Review: Pages 332-333

63. Intuitive thinking often leads to _____. Wrong conclusions may be drawn when an answer seems highly representative of what we already believe is _____. (That is, when people apply the representativeness heuristic.)
64. A second problem is ignoring the base rate (or underlying _____) of an event.
65. Clear thinking is usually aided by stating or framing a problem in _____ terms.

● *What can be done to improve thinking and to promote creativity?*

Recite and Review: PSYCHOLOGY IN ACTION

66. _____ sets can act as major barriers to creative _____.
67. Creativity can be enhanced by defining problems _____, by establishing a creative atmosphere, restating a problem in _____ ways, by allowing _____ for incubation, by seeking _____ input, by taking sensible risks, and by looking for analogies.
68. Brainstorming, in which the production and criticism of ideas is kept _____, also tends to enhance creative problem solving.

CONNECTIONS

1. _____	cognition	a.	3-D images
2. _____	language	b.	remembered perceptions
3. _____	social stereotypes	c.	images created by brain
4. _____	mental rotation	d.	mental class
5. _____	reverse vision	e.	implicit actions
6. _____	stored images	f.	thinking
7. _____	kinesthetic imagery	g.	ideal or model
8. _____	concept	h.	semantic differential
9. _____	prototype	i.	faulty, oversimplified concepts
10. _____	connotative meaning	j.	symbols and rules

11. _____	word meanings	a. meaningful unit
12. _____	morpheme	b. ASL
13. _____	phoneme	c. semantics
14. _____	"hidden" grammar	d. lexigrams
15. _____	Washoe	e. language sound
16. _____	if-then statement	f. mechanical solution
17. _____	Kanzi	g. thinking strategy
18. _____	trial-and-error	h. element of insight
19. _____	heuristic	i. conditional relationship
20. _____	selective comparison	j. transformation rules

21. _____	Binet	a. same genes
22. _____	identical twins	b. relative standing
23. _____	IQ	c. Wechsler test
24. _____	deviation IQ	d. first intelligence test
25. _____	verbal reasoning	e. block design
26. _____	memory test	f. *Army Alpha*
27. _____	WAIS	g. bell shape
28. _____	performance test	h. digit span
29. _____	group test	i. MA/CA * 100
30. _____	normal curve	j. absurdities

31. _____	fixation	a. knowledge plus rules
32. _____	expert system	b. many types of solutions
33. _____	fluency	c. one correct answer
34. _____	flexibility	d. moment of insight
35. _____	originality	e. underlying odds
36. _____	convergent thinking	f. analysis of logic
37. _____	Anagrams Test	g. many solutions
38. _____	illumination	h. blind to alternatives
39. _____	base rate	i. measures divergent thinking
40. _____	syllogism	j. novelty of solutions

CHECK YOUR MEMORY

Check Your Memory: Pages 304-305

1. Cognitive psychology is the study of sensation, memory, and learning. T or F?
2. Images, concepts, and language may be used to mentally represent problems. T or F?
3. Images are generalized ideas of a class of related objects or events. T or F?
4. Blindfolded chess players mainly use concepts to represent chess problems and solutions. T or F?

Check Your Memory: Pages 305-307

5. Images are used to make decisions, change feelings, and to improve memory. T or F?
6. Mental images may be used to improve memory and skilled actions. T or F?
7. The visual cortex is activated when a person has a mental image. T or F?
8. The more the image of a shape has to be rotated in space, the longer it takes to tell if it matches another view of the same shape. T or F?
9. People who have good imaging abilities tend to score high on tests of creativity. T or F?
10. The smaller a mental image is, the harder it is to identify its details. T or F?
11. People with good kinesthetic imagery tend to learn sports skills faster than average. T or F?

Check Your Memory: Pages 307-309

12. Concept formation is typically based on examples and rules. T or F?
13. Prototypes are very strong negative instances of a concept. T or F?
14. "Greater than" and "lopsided" are relational concepts. T or F?
15. The semantic differential is used to rate the objective meanings of words and concepts. T or F?

Check Your Memory: Pages 309-311

16. Encoding is the study of the meanings of language. T or F?
17. The Stroop interference test shows that thought is greatly influenced by language. T or F?
18. Morphemes are the basic speech sounds of a language. T or F?
19. Syntax is a part of grammar. T or F?
20. Noam Chomsky believes that a child who says, "I drinked my juice," has applied the semantic differential to a simple, core sentence. T or F?
21. ASL has 600,000 root signs. T or F?
22. True languages are productive, thus ASL is not a true language. T or F?

Check Your Memory: Pages 311-313

23. Animal communication can be described as productive. T or F?
24. Chimpanzees have never learned to speak even a single word. T or F?
25. One of Sarah chimpanzee's outstanding achievements was mastery of sentences involving transformational rules. T or F?
26. Some "language" use by chimpanzees appears to be no more than simple operant responses. T or F?
27. Only a minority of the things that language-trained chimps "say" have anything to do with food. T or F?
28. Language-trained chimps have been known to hold conversations when no humans were present. T or F?

29. Kanzi's use of grammar is on a par with that of a 2-year-old child. T or F?

Check Your Memory: Pages 313-317

30. Except for the simplest problems, mechanical solutions are typically best left to computers. T or F?
31. Karl Dunker's famous tumor problem could only be solved by trial-and-error. T or F?
32. In solutions by understanding, functional solutions are usually discovered by use of a random search strategy. T or F?
33. Working backward from the desired goal to the starting point can be a useful heuristic. T or F?
34. In problem solving, rapid insights are more likely to be correct than those that develop slowly. T or F?
35. Selective encoding refers to bringing together seemingly unrelated bits of useful information. T or F?
36. Functional fixedness is an inability to see new uses for familiar objects. T or F?

Check Your Memory: Pages 317-318

37. AI is frequently based on a set of rules applied to a body of information. T or F?
38. Computer simulations are used to test models of human cognition. T or F?
39. Much human expertise is based on acquired strategies for solving problems. T or F?
40. Chess experts have an exceptional ability to remember the positions of chess pieces placed at random on a chessboard. T or F?

Check Your Memory: Pages 319-321

41. Alfred Binet's first test was designed to measure mechanical aptitude. T or F?
42. Lewis Terman helped write the Stanford-Binet intelligence test. T or F?
43. Mental age refers to average mental ability for a person of a given age. T or F?
44. Mental age can't be higher than chronological age. T or F?
45. An IQ will be greater than 100 when CA is larger than MA. T or F?
46. Average intelligence is defined as an IQ from 90 to 109. T or F?
47. Modern IQ tests give scores as deviation IQs. T or F?
48. The WISC is designed to test adult performance intelligence. T or F?
49. The digit symbol task is considered a performance subtest of the WAIS. T or F?
50. The Stanford-Binet, Wechsler's, and the SAT are all group intelligence tests. T or F?

Check Your Memory: Pages 321-328

51. In a normal curve, a majority of scores are found near the average. T or F?
52. An IQ above 130 is described as "bright normal." T or F?
53. The correlation between IQ scores and school grades is .5. T or F?
54. Only 12 people out of 100 score above 130 on IQ tests. T or F?
55. Gifted children tend to get average IQ scores by the time they reach adulthood. T or F?
56. Gifted persons are more susceptible to mental illness. T or F?
57. Talking in complete sentences at age 2 is regarded as a sign of giftedness. T or F?
58. The moderately retarded can usually learn routine self-help skills. T or F?
59. The IQs of identical twins are more alike than those of fraternal twins. T or F?
60. Adult intelligence is approximately 50 percent hereditary. T or F?

Check Your Memory: Pages 328-332

61. In inductive thinking, a general rule is inferred from specific examples. T or F?

62. Fluency and flexibility are measures of convergent thinking. T or F?

63. Creative thinkers typically apply reasoning and critical thinking to novel ideas after they produce them. T or F?

64. Creative ideas combine originality with feasibility. T or F?

65. Creative problem solving temporarily stops during the incubation period. T or F?

66. Creative people have an openness to experience and they have a wide range of knowledge and interests. T or F?

Check Your Memory: Pages 332-333

67. Intuition is a quick, impulsive insight into the true nature of a problem and its solution. T or F?

68. The probability of two events occurring together is lower than the probability of either one occurring alone. T or F?

69. The representativeness heuristic is the strategy of stating problems in broad terms. T or F?

70. Framing refers to the way in which a problem is stated or structured. T or F?

Check Your Memory: PSYCHOLOGY IN ACTION

71. Creative problem solving involves defining problems as narrowly as possible. T or F?

72. It is wise to allow time for incubation if you are seeking a creative solution to a problem. T or F?

73. Edward de Bono suggests that digging deeper with logic is a good way to increase your creativity. T or F?

74. People seeking creative solutions should avoid taking risks; doing so just leads to dead-ends. T or F?

75. Delaying evaluation during the early stages of creative problem solving tends to lead to poor thinking. T or F?

76. The cross-stimulation effect is an important part of brainstorming in groups. T or F?

FINAL SURVEY AND REVIEW

● *What is the nature of thought?*

1. _____ psychology is the study of human information processing (thinking, _____, and problem solving).

2. Thinking is the manipulation of internal _____ of external problems or situations.

3. Three basic units of thought are _____, _____, and language or _____.

● *In what ways are images related to thinking?*

4. Most people have internal images of one kind or another. Images may be based on
_____ _____ in memory or they may be created.

5. The _____ of images used in problem solving may change. Images may be three-dimensional and they may be _____ in space to answer questions.

6. Many of the systems in the _____ that are involved in processing _____
images work in reverse to create _____ images.

7. Kinesthetic _____ are created from produced, remembered, or imagined muscular
sensations. Kinesthetic sensations and _____ seem to help structure thinking
for many people.

● *How are concepts learned?*

8. A concept is a _____ idea of a class of objects or events.

9. Forming concepts may be based on experiences with positive and _____
_____.

10. Concepts may also be acquired by learning _____ that define the concept.

11. In practice, we frequently use _____ (general models of the concept class) to
identify concepts.

12. Concepts may be classified as _____ ("and" concepts),
_____ ("either-or" concepts), or relational concepts.

13. The _____ meaning of a word or concept is its exact definition.
_____ meaning is personal or emotional.

14. Connotative meaning can be measured with the _____ differential. Most
connotative meaning involves the dimensions good-bad, _____, and
_____.

● *What is the role of language in thinking?*

15. Language allows events to be _____ into symbols for easy mental manipulation.

16. Language is built out of _____ (basic speech sounds) and
_____ (speech sounds collected into meaningful units).

17. Thinking in language is influenced by meaning. The study of meaning is called
_____.

18. Language carries meaning by combining a set of symbols or signs according to a set of rules
(_____), which includes rules about word order (_____).

19. Various sentences are created by applying _____ rules to simple
statements.

20. A true language is _____, and can be used to generate new ideas or possibilities. _____ _____ Language (ASL) and other gestural languages used by the deaf are true languages.

● *Can animals be taught to use language?*

21. _____ communication is relatively limited because it lacks symbols that can be rearranged easily. As a result, it does not have the _____ quality of human language.

22. Attempts to teach chimpanzees ASL and other non-verbal systems suggest to some that _____ are capable of language use. However, others believe that the chimps are merely using operant responses to get food and other _____.

23. Studies that make use of _____ (geometric word-symbols) provide the best evidence yet of animal language use.

● *What do we know about problem solving?*

24. The solution to a problem may be found _____ (by trial and error or by rote application of rules). However, _____ solutions are frequently inefficient or ineffective, except where aided by computer.

25. Solutions by _____ usually begin with discovery of the general properties of an answer. Next comes proposal of a number of _____ (workable) solutions.

26. Problem solving is frequently aided by _____. These are strategies that typically narrow the search for solutions.

27. When understanding leads to a rapid solution, _____ has occurred. Three elements of _____ are selective _____, selective combination and selective comparison.

28. Insights and other problem solving attempts can be blocked by _____ (a tendency to repeat wrong solutions).

29. _____ fixedness is a common fixation, but emotional _____, cultural _____, learned conventions, and perceptual habits are also problems.

● *What is artificial intelligence?*

30. Artificial intelligence refers to _____ _____ that can perform tasks that require intelligence when done by _____.

31. Two principal areas of artificial intelligence research are computer simulations and _____.

32. Expert human problem solving is based on _____ knowledge and acquired _____, rather than some general improvement in thinking ability.

● *How is human intelligence defined and measured?*

33. Intelligence refers to one's general capacity to act _____, _____ rationally, and deal effectively with the environment.

34. In practice, writing an intelligence test provides an _____ definition of intelligence.

35. The first practical intelligence test was assembled in 1904, in Paris, by _____ _____.

36. A modern version of that test is the _____ *Intelligence Scale, Fourth Edition.*

37. The scale measures verbal reasoning, _____ reasoning, _____/visual reasoning, and short-term memory.

38. A second major intelligence test is the _____ *Adult Intelligence Scale-III* (WAIS-III). The WAIS-III measures both _____ and _____ (non-verbal) intelligence.

39. Intelligence tests have also been produced for use with groups of people. The _____ _____ *Test* (SAT), measures a variety of mental _____ and it can be used to estimate intelligence.

● *How do IQ scores relate to achievement and thinking ability?*

40. Intelligence is expressed in terms of an intelligence quotient (IQ). IQ is defined as _____ _____ (MA) divided by _____ _____ (CA) and then multiplied by 100.

41. An "average" IQ of 100 occurs when _____ age equals _____ age.

42. Modern IQ tests no longer calculate IQ directly. Instead, the final score reported by the test is a _____ _____, which gives a person's relative intellectual standing in his or her age group.

43. When graphed, the _____ (percentage of people receiving each score) of IQ scores approximates a _____ (bell-shaped) curve.

44. People with IQs above _____ are considered to be in the gifted or "genius" range.

45. Studies done by Lewis _____ showed that the _____ tend to be superior in many respects, such as achievement, physical appearance, and mental health.

46. The most _____ gifted persons tend to be those who are _____ and motivated to learn and succeed.

47. By criteria other than IQ, a large proportion of children might be considered _____ or _____ in one way or another.

48. Howard _____ believes that traditional IQ tests define intelligence too narrowly. According to Gardner, intelligence consists of abilities in _____, logic and math, visual and spatial thinking, _____, kinesthetic skills, intrapersonal skills, interpersonal skills, and _____ skills.

49. The terms mentally retarded and _____ disabled are applied to those whose IQ falls below 70 or who lack various _____ behaviors.

50. Further classifications of retardation are: mild (50-55 to 70), _____ (35-40 to 50-55), severe (20-25 to 35-40), and _____ (below 20-25).

51. About 50 percent of the cases of mental retardation are _____, being caused by birth injuries, fetal damage, metabolic disorders, or _____ abnormalities. The remaining cases are of undetermined cause.

52. Many cases of subnormal intelligence are thought to be the result of _____ retardation (a low level of intellectual stimulation in the home, poverty, and poor nutrition).

53. Studies of family relationships in humans, especially comparisons between _____ twins and _____ twins, suggest that intelligence is partly hereditary.

54. However, _____ is also important, as revealed by changes in tested intelligence induced by stimulating _____ and improved education.

55. Intelligence therefore reflects the combined effects of _____ and _____.

56. Differences in the average IQ scores for various racial groups are based on _____ differences, not heredity.

● *What is the nature of creative thinking?*

57. To be creative, a solution must be practical and sensible as well as _____.

58. Thinking may be deductive or _____, _____ or illogical.

59. Creative thinking requires _____ thought, characterized by _____, flexibility, and originality.

60. Tests of creativity, such as the *Unusual _____ Test*, the *Consequences Test*, and the *Anagrams Test*, measure the capacity for _____ thinking.

61. Five stages often seen in creative problem solving are orientation, preparation, _____, _____, and verification.

62. Studies suggest that creative persons share a number of identifiable general traits, thinking abilities, thinking styles, and _____ characteristics. There is only a small _____ between IQ and creativity.

● *How accurate is intuition?*

63. Intuitive thinking often leads to errors. Wrong conclusions may be drawn when an answer seems highly _____ of what we already believe is true. (That is, when people apply the representativeness _____.)

64. A second problem is ignoring the _____ _____ (or underlying probability) of an event.

65. Clear thinking is usually aided by stating or _____ a problem in broad terms.

● *What can be done to improve thinking and to promote creativity?*

66. Mental _____ can act as major barriers to _____ thinking.

67. Creativity can be enhanced by defining problems broadly, by establishing a creative atmosphere, by allowing time for _____, by restating a problem in different ways, by seeking varied _____, by taking sensible _____, and by looking for analogies.

68. _____, in which the production and criticism of ideas is kept separate, also tends to enhance creative problem solving.

MASTERY TEST

1. The mark of a true language is that it must be
   a. spoken   b. productive   c. based on spatial grammar and syntax   d. capable of encoding conditional relationships

2. Computer simulations and expert systems are two major applications of
   a. AI   b. ASL   c. brainstorming   d. problem framing

3. Failure to wear automobile seat belts is an example of which intuitive thinking error?
   a. allowing too much time for incubation   b. framing a problem broadly   c. ignoring base rates
   d. recognition that two events occurring together are more likely than either one alone

4. One thing that images, concepts, and symbols all have in common is that they are
   a. morphemes   b. internal representations   c. based on reverse vision   d. translated into micromovements

5. To decide if a container is a cup, bowl, or vase, most people compare it to
   a. a prototype   b. its connotative meaning   c. a series of negative instances   d. a series of relevant phonemes

6. During problem solving, being "cold," "warm," or "very warm" is closely associated with
   a. insight   b. fixation   c. automatic processing   d. rote problem solving

7. The *Anagrams Test* measures
   a. mental sets   b. inductive thinking   c. logical reasoning   d. divergent thinking

8. "Either-or" concepts are
   a. conjunctive   b. disjunctive   c. relational   d. prototypical

9. Which term does not belong with the others?
   a. selective comparison   b. functional fixedness   c. learned conventions   d. emotional blocks

10. Separate collections of verbal and performance subtests are a feature of the
   a. WAIS   b. Gardner-8   c. CQT   d. Stanford-Binet

11. Mental retardation is formally defined by deficiencies in
    a. aptitudes and self-help skills   b. intelligence and scholastic aptitudes
    c. language and spatial thinking   d. IQ and adaptive behaviors

12. A 12-year-old child, with an IQ of 100, must have an MA of
    a. 100   b. 12   c. 10   d. 15

13. The difference between prime beef and dead cow is primarily a matter of
    a. syntax   b. conjunctive meaning   c. semantics   d. the productive nature of language

14. Culture-fair tests attempt to measure intelligence without being affected by a person's
    a. verbal skills   b. cultural background   c. educational level   d. all of the preceding

15. Which of the listed terms does NOT correctly complete this sentence: Insight involves selective
    _____.
    a. encoding   b. combination   c. comparison   d. fixation

16. Which of the following is LEAST likely to predict that a person is creative?
    a. high IQ   b. a preference for complexity   c. fluency in combining ideas   d. use of mental images

17. "Try working backward from the desired goal to the starting point or current state." This advice describes a
    a. syllogism   b. heuristic   c. prototype   d. dimension of the semantic differential

18. Language allows events to be _____ into _____.
    a. translated, concepts   b. fixated, codes   c. rearranged, lexigrams   d. encoded, symbols

19. "A triangle must be a closed shape with three sides made of straight lines." This statement is an example of a
    a. prototype   b. positive instance   c. conceptual rule   d. disjunctive concept

20. Fluency, flexibility, and originality are all measures of
    a. inductive thinking   b. selective comparison   c. intuitive framing   d. divergent thinking

21. The form of imagery that is especially important in music, sports, dance, and martial arts is
    a. kinesthetic imagery   b. semantic imagery   c. prototypical imagery   d. conjunctive imagery

22. Among animals trained to use language, Kanzi has been unusually accurate at
    a. using proper syntax   b. substituting gestures for lexigrams   c. expressing conditional relationships
    d. forming chains of operant responses

23. The largest number of people are found in which IQ range?
    a. 80-89   b. 90-109   c. 110-119   d. below 70

24. Looking for analogies and delaying evaluation are helpful strategies for increasing
    a. divergent thinking   b. convergent thinking   c. functional fixedness   d. concept formation

25. Comparing 2 three-dimensional shapes to see if they match is easiest if only a small amount of
    _____ is required.
    a. conceptual recoding   b. mental rotation   c. concept formation   d. kinesthetic transformation

26. The good-bad dimension on the semantic differential is closely related to a concept's
    a. disjunctive meaning   b. conjunctive meaning   c. connotative meaning   d. denotative meaning

27. Questions about vocabulary, comprehension, and absurdities would be found in which ability area of the Stanford-Binet?
    a. verbal reasoning   b. quantitative reasoning   c. abstract/visual reasoning   d. short-term memory

28. The directions "modify, magnify, rearrange, and suspend judgment" could be expected to aid a group engaged in
    a. a means-ends analysis   b. base rate framing   c. brainstorming
    d. solving delayed response problems

29. According to Noam Chomsky, surface sentences are created by applying _____ to simple sentences.
    a. encoding grammars   b. transformation rules   c. conditional prototypes   d. selective conjunctions

30. The occurrence of an insight corresponds to which stage of creative thinking?
    a. verification   b. incubation   c. illumination   d. fixation

ANSWERS

Recite and Review

1. information
2. internal
3. language
4. created
5. change, space
6. visual
7. muscular, Kinesthetic
8. class
9. positive
10. concept
11. models
12. and, either-or

13. definition, personal
14. good-bad
15. symbols
16. sounds, meaningful
17. meaning
18. rules, order
19. rules
20. gestural
21. human
22. operant
23. geometric
24. rote, computer
25. general, solutions
26. narrow

27. solution, selective
28. wrong
29. fixation, habits
30. programs, intelligence
31. computer
32. knowledge
33. rationally, environment
34. definition
35. intelligence test
36. *Intelligence Scale*
37. verbal, memory
38. *Adult,* non-verbal
39. groups, mental

40. quotient, 100
41. 100, equals
42. IQs, relative
43. bell, curve
44. gifted
45. superior
46. motivated
47. IQ
48. traditional, math, visual
49. retarded, 70
50. mild, severe
51. 50, birth
52. intellectual
53. genes, hereditary
54. stimulating
55. Intelligence
56. genetics (or heredity)
57. practical
58. Thinking
59. originality
60. creativity
61. preparation
62. thinking, styles
63. errors, true
64. probability
65. broad
66. Mental, thinking
67. broadly, different, time, varied
68. separate

Connections

1. f
2. j
3. i
4. a
5. c
6. b
7. e
8. d
9. g
10. h
11. c
12. a
13. e
14. j
15. b
16. i
17. d
18. f
19. g
20. h
21. d
22. a
23. i
24. b
25. j
26. h
27. c
28. e
29. f
30. g
31. h
32. a
33. g
34. b
35. j
36. c
37. i
38. d
39. e
40. f

Check Your Memory

1. F
2. T
3. F
4. F
5. T
6. T
7. T
8. T
9. T
10. T
11. T
12. T
13. F
14. T
15. F
16. F
17. T
18. F
19. T
20. F
21. F
22. F
23. F
24. F
25. F
26. T
27. T
28. T
29. T
30. T
31. F
32. F
33. T
34. T
35. F
36. T
37. T
38. T
39. T
40. F
41. F
42. T
43. T
44. F
45. F
46. T
47. T
48. F
49. T
50. F
51. T
52. F
53. T
54. F
55. F
56. F
57. T
58. F
59. T
60. T
61. T
62. F
63. T
64. T
65. F

66. T
67. F
68. T
69. F
70. T
71. F
72. T
73. F
74. F
75. F
76. T

Final Survey and Review

1. Cognitive, language
2. representations
3. images, concepts, symbols
4. information stored
5. size, rotated
6. brain, visual, mental
7. images, micromovements
8. generalized
9. negative instances
10. rules
11. prototypes
12. conjunctive, disjunctive
13. denotative, Connotative
14. semantic, strong-weak, active-passive
15. encoded
16. phonemes, morphemes
17. semantics
18. grammar, syntax
19. transformation
20. productive, American Sign
21. Animal, productive
22. primates, reinforcers
23. lexigrams
24. mechanically, mechanical
25. understanding, functional
26. heuristics
27. insight, insight, encoding
28. fixation
29. Functional, blocks, values
30. computer programs, people
31. expert systems
32. organized, strategies
33. purposefully, think
34. operational
35. Alfred Binet
36. *Stanford-Binet*
37. quantitative, abstract
38. *Wechsler,* verbal, performance
39. *Scholastic Assessment,* aptitudes
40. mental age, chronological age
41. mental, chronological
42. deviation IQ
43. distribution, normal
44. 140
45. Terman, gifted
46. successful, persistent
47. gifted, talented
48. Gardner, language, music, naturalist
49. developmentally, adaptive
50. moderate, profound
51. organic, genetic
52. familial
53. fraternal, identical
54. environment, environments
55. heredity, environment
56. environmental
57. original
58. inductive, logical
59. divergent, fluency
60. *Uses,* divergent
61. incubation, illumination
62. personality, correlation
63. representative, heuristic
64. base rate
65. framing
66. sets, creative
67. incubation, input, risks
68. Brainstorming

Mastery Test

1. b (p. 310)
2. a (p. 318)
3. c (p. 332)
4. b (p. 304)
5. a (p. 308)
6. a (p. 315)
7. d (p. 330)
8. b (p. 308)
9. a (p. 316)
10. a (p. 322)
11. d (p. 325)
12. b (p. 321)
13. c (p. 309)
14. d (p. 322)
15. d (p. 316)
16. a (p. 332)
17. b (p. 314)
18. d (p. 309)
19. c (p. 307)
20. d (p. 329)
21. a (p. 307)
22. a (p. 312)
23. b (p. 324)
24. a (p. 335-336)
25. b (p. 305)
26. c (p. 308)
27. a (p. 320)
28. c (p. 336)
29. b (p. 310)
30. c (p. 331)

Chapter 10
Motivation and Emotion

CHAPTER OVERVIEW

Motivation typically involves needs, drives, goals, and goal attainment. Three types of motives are primary motives, stimulus motives, and secondary motives. Most primary motives maintain homeostasis.

Hunger is influenced by the stomach, blood sugar levels, metabolism in the liver, fat stores in the body, activity in the hypothalamus, diet, and other factors. Eating disorders are serious and sometimes fatal problems. Behavioral dieting uses self-control techniques to change basic eating patterns and habits.

Thirst and other basic motives are affected by many factors, but they are primarily controlled by the hypothalamus. Pain avoidance is episodic and partially learned. The sex drive is non-homeostatic. To some extent, it is influenced by hormone levels in the body.

The stimulus motives include drives for information, exploration, manipulation, and sensory input. Drives for stimulation are partially explained by arousal theory. Optimal performance on a task usually occurs at moderate levels of arousal. Circadian rhythms are closely tied to sleep, activity, and energy cycles.

Social motives, which are learned, account for much of the diversity of human motivation. The need for achievement is a social motive correlated with success in many situations.

Maslow's hierarchy of motives categorizes needs as basic or growth oriented. Self-actualization, the highest and most fragile need, is reflected in meta-needs. In many situations, extrinsic motivation can lower intrinsic motivation, enjoyment, and creativity.

Emotions are linked to basic adaptive behaviors. Other major elements of emotion are bodily changes, emotional expressions, and emotional feelings. Physiological changes during emotion are caused by adrenaline and the autonomic nervous system (ANS). The sympathetic branch of the ANS arouses the body and the parasympathetic branch quiets it. Basic emotional expressions are unlearned. Facial expressions are central to emotion. Body gestures and movements (body language) also express feelings. A variety of theories have been proposed to explain emotion.

Emotional intelligence involves a combination of skills, such as self-awareness, empathy, self-control, and an understanding of how to use emotions. For success in many situations, emotional intelligence is as important as IQ.

LEARNING OBJECTIVES

To demonstrate mastery of this chapter, you should be able to:

1. Define *motivation.*

2. Describe a motivational sequence using the need reduction model.

3. Explain how the incentive value of a goal can affect motivation, and describe how incentive value is related to internal need.

4. List and describe the three types of motives and give an example of each.

5. Define *homeostasis.*

6. Discuss why hunger cannot be fully explained by the contractions of an empty stomach.

7. Describe the relationship of each of the following to hunger:
   a. blood sugar
   b. liver
   c. hypothalamus
       1. satiety system (ventromedial hypothalamus)
       2. blood sugar regulator (paraventricular nucleus)
       3. neuropeptide Y (NPY)
       4. glucagon-like peptide 1 (GLP-1)

8. Explain how a person's set point is related to obesity in childhood and adulthood.

9. Explain the relationship between how much a person overeats and the person's obesity.

10. Describe the relationship between emotionality and overeating.

11. Explain the paradox of "yo-yo" dieting.

12. Explain what is meant by behavioral dieting, and describe the techniques which can enable you to control your weight.

13. Describe the impact of cultural factors and taste on hunger.

14. Explain how a taste aversion is acquired, give a practical example of the process, and briefly explain why psychologists believe these aversions exist.

15. Describe the essential features of the eating disorders anorexia nervosa and bulimia nervosa. Explain what causes them and what treatment is available for them.

16. Name the brain structure that appears to control thirst (as well as hunger). Differentiate extracellular and intracellular thirst.

17. Explain how the drive to avoid pain and the sex drive differ from other primary drives.

18. Briefly describe the impact of hormones and alcohol on the sex drive.

19. Describe the evidence for the existence of stimulus drives for exploration, and manipulation, curiosity, and stimulation.

20. Explain the arousal theory of motivation including the inverted U function.

21. Relate arousal to the Yerkes-Dodson law and give an example of it.

22. Describe the two major components of test anxiety and describe four ways to reduce it.

23. Define *need for achievement* (nAch) and differentiate it from the need for power.
24. Describe people who are achievers, and relate nAch to risk taking.
25. Describe the research of Russell, Rowe, and Smouse concerning the effectiveness of subliminal perception.
26. Explain the influences of drive and determination in the development of success for high achievers.
27. List (in order) the needs found in Maslow's hierarchy of motives.
28. Explain why Maslow's lower (physiological) needs are considered prepotent.
29. Define *meta-need* and give an example of one.
30. Distinguish between intrinsic and extrinsic motivation, and explain how each type of motivation may affect a person's interest in work, leisure activities, and creativity.
31. Explain what is meant by the phrase, "emotions aid survival."
32. List and describe the three major elements of emotions.
33. List the eight primary emotions proposed by Plutchik and explain his concept of mixing them.
34. Explain how a person may experience two opposite emotions simultaneously.
35. Describe, in general, the effects of the sympathetic and the parasympathetic branches of the ANS during and after emotion.
36. Describe the relationship between pupil dilation and emotion. (See Highlight 10-4.)
37. Define *parasympathetic rebound* and discuss its possible involvement in cases of sudden death.
38. Describe the cost of suppressing emotions.

The following objectives are related to the material in the "Exploring Psychology" section of the text.
39. Explain how the polygraph detects "lies."
40. Discuss the limitations and/or accuracy of lie detector devices.

41. Discuss Darwin's view of human emotion.
42. Briefly describe cultural and gender differences in emotion.
43. Describe the evidence that supports the conclusion that most emotional expressions are universal.
44. Define *kinesics.*
45. List and describe the three emotional messages conveyed by facial expressions and body language.
46. Explain how overall posture can indicate one's emotional state.
47. Briefly describe the James-Lange theory of emotion.
48. Briefly describe the Cannon-Bard theory of emotion.
49. Briefly describe Schachter's cognitive theory of emotion and give experimental evidence to support his theory.
50. Describe and give an example of the effects of attribution on emotion.
51. Briefly describe the facial feedback hypothesis.
52. Discuss the role of appraisal in the contemporary model of emotion.

The following objectives are related to the material in the "Psychology in Action" section of the text.
53. Describe the concept of emotional intelligence and how it may enhance one's life.

54. List five emotional intelligence skills.

55. Briefly describe the benefits of positive emotion.

RECITE AND REVIEW

● *What is motivation? Are there different types of motives?*

Recite and Review: Pages 341-343

1. Motives _____ (begin), sustain (perpetuate), and direct _____.

2. Motivation typically involves the sequence _____, drive, _____, and goal attainment (need reduction).

3. Behavior can be activated either by needs (_____) or by goals (_____).

4. The attractiveness of a _____ and its ability to initiate action are related to its incentive value (its value above and beyond its capacity to fill a _____).

5. Three principal types of motives are primary motives, stimulus motives, and _____ motives.

6. Most _____ motives operate to maintain a _____ state of bodily equilibrium called homeostasis.

● *What causes hunger? Overeating? Eating disorders?*

Recite and Review: Pages 343-349

7. Hunger is influenced by a complex interplay between distention (fullness) of the _____, hypoglycemia (low _____ sugar), metabolism in the _____, and fat stores in the body.

8. The most direct control of eating is exerted by the hypothalamus, which has areas that act like feeding (_____) and satiety (_____) systems for hunger and eating.

9. The lateral hypothalamus acts as a _____ system; the ventromedial hypothalamus is part of a _____ system; the paraventricular nucleus influences both hunger and satiety.

10. Other factors influencing hunger are the set point for the proportion of _____ in the body, external eating cues, the attractiveness and variety of _____.

11. Hunger is also influenced by emotions, learned _____ preferences and _____ aversions (such as bait shyness in animals), and cultural values.

12. Anorexia nervosa (self-inflicted _____) and bulimia nervosa (_____ and purging) are two prominent eating disorders.

13. Both eating disorders tend to involve conflicts about self-image, self-control, and _____.

● *Is there more than one type of thirst? In what ways are pain avoidance and the sex drive unusual?*

Recite and Review: Pages 350-351

14. Like hunger, thirst and other basic motives are affected by a number of _____ factors, but are primarily under the central control of the hypothalamus in the _____.
15. Thirst may be either intracellular (when _____ is lost from inside _____) or extracellular (when _____ is lost from the spaces between _____).
16. Pain avoidance is unusual because it is episodic (associated with particular conditions) as opposed to cyclic (occurring in regular _____).
17. Pain avoidance and pain tolerance are partially _____ (influenced by training).
18. The sex drive in many lower animals is related to estrus (or "heat") in _____. The sex drive is unusual in that it is non-homeostatic (both its _____ and its reduction are sought).
19. Sex _____ in both males and females may be related to bodily levels of androgens.

● *How does arousal relate to motivation?*

Recite and Review: Pages 352-354

20. The stimulus drives reflect needs for information, exploration, manipulation, and _____ input.
21. Drives for stimulation are partially explained by arousal theory, which states that an ideal level of _____ _____ will be maintained if possible.
22. The desired level of _____ or stimulation varies from person to person, as measured by the *Sensation-Seeking Scale*.
23. Optimal performance on a task usually occurs at _____ levels of arousal. This relationship is described by an inverted U function.
24. The Yerkes-Dodson law further states that for _____ tasks the ideal arousal level is higher, and for _____ tasks it is lower.
25. Circadian _____ within the body are closely tied to sleep, activity levels, and energy cycles. Time zone travel and shift work can seriously disrupt _____ and bodily rhythms.
26. If you anticipate a _____ in body rhythms, you can gradually preadapt to your new _____ over a period of days.

● *What are social motives? Why are they important?*

Recite and Review: Pages 354-356

27. _____ motives are learned through socialization and cultural conditioning.
28. One of the most prominent social motives is the _____ for achievement (nAch).
29. High nAch is correlated with _____ in many situations, with occupational choice, and with moderate _____ taking.

30. Self-confidence affects _____ because it influences the challenges you will undertake, the _____ you will make, and how long you will _____ when things don't go well.

● *Are some motives more basic than others?*

Recite and Review: Pages 356-358

31. Maslow's hierarchy (rank ordering) of motives categorizes needs as _____ and growth oriented.

32. _____ needs in the hierarchy are assumed to be prepotent (dominant) over _____ needs.

33. _____-actualization, the highest and most fragile need, is reflected in meta-_____.

34. In many situations, extrinsic motivation (that which is induced by obvious _____ rewards) can reduce intrinsic motivation, enjoyment, and creativity.

● *What happens during emotion? Can "lie detectors" really detect lies?*

Recite and Review: Pages 359-364

35. Emotions are linked to many basic adaptive _____, such as attacking, retreating, feeding, and reproducing.

36. Other major elements of emotion are physiological changes in the body, emotional expressions, and emotional _____.

37. The following are considered to be primary emotions: fear, surprise, _____, disgust, _____, anticipation, joy, and trust (acceptance). Other emotions seem to represent mixtures of the primaries.

38. Physical changes associated with emotion are caused by the action of adrenaline, a _____ released into the bloodstream, and by activity in the autonomic _____ _____ (ANS).

39. The sympathetic _____ of the ANS is primarily responsible for arousing the body, the parasympathetic _____ for quieting it.

40. Sudden death due to prolonged and intense emotion is probably related to parasympathetic _____ (excess activity). Heart attacks caused by sudden intense emotion are more likely due to sympathetic _____.

41. The polygraph, or "lie detector," measures _____ _____ by monitoring heart rate, blood pressure, breathing rate, and the galvanic skin response (GSR).

42. Asking a series of _____ and irrelevant questions may allow the detection of _____, but overall, the accuracy of the lie detector has been challenged by many researchers.

Recite and Review: Pages 365-367

43. Basic emotional expressions, such as smiling or baring one's teeth when angry, appear to be
_____.

44. Facial expressions of _____, anger, disgust, _____, and happiness are recognized by people of all cultures.

45. Body gestures and movements (body language) also express _____, mainly by communicating emotional _____.

46. Three dimensions of _____ expressions are pleasantness-unpleasantness, attention-rejection, and activation.

47. The study of _____ _____ is known as kinesics.

Recite and Review: Pages 367-370

48. The James-Lange theory of emotion says that emotional experience _____ an awareness of the bodily reactions of emotion.

49. In contrast, the Cannon-Bard theory says that bodily reactions and emotional experience occur _____ _____ _____ and that emotions are organized in the brain.

50. Schachter's cognitive theory of emotion emphasizes the importance of _____, or interpretations, applied to feelings of bodily arousal.

51. Also important is the process of attribution, in which bodily _____ is attributed to a particular person, object, or situation.

52. The facial feedback hypothesis holds that sensations and information from emotional _____ help define what emotion a person is feeling.

53. Contemporary views of emotion place greater emphasis on how _____ are appraised. Also, all of the elements of emotion are seen as interrelated and interacting.

Recite and Review: PSYCHOLOGY IN ACTION

54. Emotional intelligence involves the following skills: _____-awareness, empathy, _____-control, and an understanding of how to use _____.

55. Emotionally intelligent people are good at reading facial expressions, tone of voice, and other signs of _____.

56. They also use their _____ to enhance thinking and decision making.

57. _____ emotions are not just a luxury. They tend to encourage personal growth and social connection

CONNECTIONS

1. _____ physiological needs
2. _____ safety and security
3. _____ self-actualization
4. _____ lateral hypothalamus
5. _____ basic needs
6. _____ esteem and self-esteem
7. _____ paraventricular nucleus
8. _____ growth needs
9. _____ love and belonging
10. _____ ventromedial hypothalamus

11. _____ need
12. _____ incentive value
13. _____ secondary motives
14. _____ homeostasis
15. _____ satiety system
16. _____ feeding system
17. _____ hunger and satiety
18. _____ weight cycling
19. _____ estrus
20. _____ circadian

a. steady state
b. lateral hypothalamus
c. internal deficiency
d. learned goals
e. estrogen levels
f. yo-yo dieting
g. about a day
h. paraventricular nucleus
i. ventromedial hypothalamus
j. goal desirability

21. _____ changes eating habits
22. _____ nAch
23. _____ meta-needs
24. _____ mood
25. _____ sympathetic branch
26. _____ control questions
27. _____ body language
28. _____ sadness
29. _____ anxiety
30. _____ SSS

a. standards of excellence
b. prolonged mild emotion
c. lie detection
d. behavioral dieting
e. sensation seekers
f. appraisal of loss
g. appraisal of threat
h. self-actualization
i. kinesics
j. fight or flight

CHECK YOUR MEMORY

Check Your Memory: Pages 341-343

1. The terms need and drive are used interchangeably to describe motivation. T or F?
2. Incentive value refers to the "pull" of valued goals. T or F?
3. Primary motives are based on needs that must be met for survival. T or F?
4. Much of the time, homeostasis is maintained by automatic reactions within the body. T or F?

Check Your Memory: Pages 343-349

5. Cutting the sensory nerves from the stomach abolishes hunger. T or F?
6. Lowered levels of glucose in the blood can cause hunger. T or F?
7. The body's hunger center is found in the thalamus. T or F?
8. The paraventricular nucleus is sensitive to neuropeptide Y. T or F?
9. Both glucagon-like peptide 1 (GLP-1) and leptin act as stop signals that inhibit eating. T or F?
10. Dieting speeds up the body's metabolic rate. T or F?
11. People who diet intensely every other day lose as much weight as those who diet moderately every day. T or F?
12. Exercise makes people hungry and tends to disrupt dieting and weight loss. T or F?
13. Behavioral dieting changes habits without reducing the number of calories consumed. T or F?
14. Charting daily progress is a basic behavioral dieting technique. T or F?
15. Taste aversions may be learned after longer time delays than in other forms of classical conditioning. T or F?
16. Many victims of anorexia nervosa overestimate their body size. T or F?

Check Your Memory: Pages 350-351

17. Bleeding, vomiting, or sweating can cause extracellular thirst. T or F?
18. Intracellular thirst is best satisfied by a slightly salty liquid. T or F?
19. Tolerance for pain is largely unaffected by learning. T or F?
20. Castration of a male animal typically abolishes the sex drive. T or F?
21. Getting drunk *decreases* sexual desire, arousal, pleasure, and performance. T or F?

Check Your Memory: Pages 352-354

22. It is uncomfortable to experience both very high and very low levels of arousal. T or F?
23. Disinhibition and boredom susceptibility are characteristics of sensation-seeking persons. T or F?
24. For nearly all activities, the best performance occurs at high levels of arousal. T or F?
25. Test anxiety is a combination of arousal and excessive worry. T or F?
26. Being overprepared is a common cause of test anxiety. T or F?
27. Changes in body temperature are closely related to circadian rhythms. T or F?
28. Adapting to rapid time zone changes is easiest when a person travels east, rather than west. T or F?

Check Your Memory: Pages 354-356

29. The need for achievement refers to a desire to have impact on other people. T or F?

30. People high in nAch generally prefer "long shots" or "sure things." T or F?
31. Subliminal motivational tapes are no more effective than placebo tapes that lack any "hidden messages." T or F?
32. Benjamin Bloom found that high achievement is based as much on hard work as it is on talent. T or F?
33. For many activities, self-confidence is one of the most important sources of motivation. T or F?

Check Your Memory: Pages 356-358

34. Maslow's hierarchy of needs places self-esteem at the top of the pyramid. T or F?
35. Maslow believed that needs for safety and security are more potent than needs for love and belonging. T or F?
36. Meta-needs are the most basic needs in Maslow's hierarchy. T or F?
37. Intrinsic motivation occurs when obvious external rewards are provided for engaging in an activity. T or F?
38. People are more likely to be creative when they are intrinsically motivated. T or F?

Check Your Memory: Pages 359-364

39. Most physiological changes during emotion are related to the release of adrenaline into the brain. T or F?
40. Robert Plutchik's theory lists contempt as a primary emotion. T or F?
41. For most students, elevated moods tend to occur on Saturdays and Tuesdays. T or F?
42. Positive emotions are processed mainly in the left hemisphere of the brain. T or F?
43. The sympathetic branch of the ANS is under voluntary control and the parasympathetic branch is involuntary. T or F?
44. The parasympathetic branch of the ANS slows the heart and lowers blood pressure. T or F?
45. Most sudden deaths due to strong emotion are associated with the traumatic disruption of a close relationship. T or F?

Check Your Memory: Pages 365-367

46. The polygraph measures the body's unique physical responses to lying. T or F?
47. Only a guilty person should react emotionally to irrelevant questions. T or F?
48. Control questions used in polygraph exams are designed to make almost everyone anxious. T or F?
49. The lie detector's most common error is to label innocent persons guilty. T or F?
50. Children born deaf and blind express emotions with their faces in about the same way as other people do. T or F?
51. The "A-okay" hand gesture means "everything is fine" around the world. T or F?
52. Facial blends mix two or more basic expressions. T or F?
53. Liking is expressed in body language by leaning back and relaxing the extremities. T or F?
54. Gestures such as rubbing hands, twisting hair, and biting lips are consistently related to lying. T or F?
55. People from Asian cultures are more likely to express anger in public than people from Western cultures. T or F?
56. In Western cultures, men tend to be more emotionally expressive than women. T or F?

Check Your Memory: Pages 367-370

57. The James-Lange theory of emotion says that we see a bear, feel fear, are aroused, and then run. T or F?

58. According to Schachter's cognitive theory, arousal must be labeled in order to become an emotion. T or F?

59. Making facial expressions can actually cause emotions to occur and alter physiological activities in the body. T or F?

60. Emotional appraisal refers to deciding if your own facial expressions are appropriate for the situation you are in. T or F?

61. Moving toward a desired goal is associated with the emotion of happiness. T or F?

62. Emotional intelligence refers to the ability to use primarily the right cerebral hemisphere to process emotional events. T of F?

Check Your Memory: PSYCHOLOGY IN ACTION

63. People who excel in life tend to be emotionally intelligent. T or F?

64. People who are empathetic are keenly tuned in to their own feelings. T or F?

65. People who are emotionally intelligent know what causes them to feel various emotions. T or F?

66. Negative emotions can be valuable because they impart useful information to us. T or F?

67. Positive emotions produce urges to be creative, to explore, and to seek new experiences. T or F?

68. A first step toward becoming emotionally intelligent is to pay attention to and value your feelings and emotional reactions. T or F?

FINAL SURVEY AND REVIEW

● *What is motivation? Are there different types of motives?*

1. Motives initiate (begin), _____ (perpetuate), and _____ activities.

2. Motivation typically involves the sequence need, _____, goal, and goal _____ (need reduction).

3. Behavior can be activated either by _____ (push) or by _____ (pull).

4. The attractiveness of a goal and its ability to initiate action are related to its _____ _____.

5. Three principal types of motives are _____ motives, _____ motives, and _____ motives.

6. Most primary motives operate to maintain a steady state of bodily equilibrium called _____.

● *What causes hunger? Overeating? Eating disorders?*

7. Hunger is influenced by a complex interplay between _____ (fullness) of the stomach, _____ (low blood sugar), metabolism in the liver, and fat stores in the body.

8. The most direct control of eating is exerted by the _____, which has areas that act like feeding (start) and _____ (stop) systems for hunger and eating.

9. The _____ hypothalamus acts as a feeding system; the _____ hypothalamus is part of a satiety system; the paraventricular _____ influences both hunger and satiety.

10. Other factors influencing hunger are the _____ _____ for the proportion of fat in the body, external eating _____, the attractiveness and variety of diet.

11. Hunger is also influenced by emotions, learned taste preferences and taste _____ . (such as _____ _____ in animals), and cultural values.

12. _____ nervosa (self-inflicted starvation) and _____ nervosa (gorging and purging) are two prominent eating disorders.

13. Both eating disorders tend to involve conflicts about _____, self-control, and anxiety.

● *Is there more than one type of thirst? In what ways are pain avoidance and the sex drive unusual?*

14. Like hunger, thirst and other basic motives are affected by a number of bodily factors, but are primarily under the central control of the _____ in the brain.

15. Thirst may be either _____ (when fluid is lost from inside cells) or _____ (when fluid is lost from the spaces between cells).

16. Pain avoidance is unusual because it is _____ (associated with particular conditions) as opposed to _____ (occurring in regular cycles).

17. Pain _____ and pain _____ are partially learned.

18. The sex drive in many lower animals is related to _____ (or "heat") in females. The sex drive is unusual in that it is non-_____ (both its arousal and its reduction are sought).

19. Sex drive in both males and females may be related to bodily levels of _____.

● *How does arousal relate to motivation?*

20. The _____ drives reflect needs for information, _____, manipulation, and sensory input.

21. Drives for stimulation are partially explained by _____ _____, which states that an ideal level of bodily arousal will be maintained if possible.

22. The desired level of arousal or stimulation varies from person to person, as measured by the _____ *Scale.*

23. Optimal performance on a task usually occurs at moderate levels of arousal. This relationship is described by an _____ _____ function.

24. The _____ law further states that for simple tasks the ideal arousal level is higher, and for complex tasks it is lower.

25. _____ rhythms within the body are closely tied to sleep, activity levels, and energy cycles. Travel across _____ _____ and shift work can seriously disrupt sleep and bodily rhythms.

26. If you anticipate a change in body rhythms, you can gradually _____ to your new schedule over a period of days.

● *What are social motives? Why are they important?*

27. Social motives are learned through _____ and cultural conditioning.
28. One of the most prominent social motives is the need for _____ (nAch).
29. _____ nAch is correlated with success in many situations, with occupational choice, and with _____ risk taking.
30. _____ affects motivation because it influences the challenges you will undertake, the effort you will make, and how long you will persist when things don't go well.

● *Are some motives more basic than others?*

31. Maslow's _____ (rank ordering) of motives categorizes needs as basic and _____ oriented.
32. Lower needs in the hierarchy are assumed to be _____ (dominant) over higher needs.
33. Self-_____, the highest and most fragile need, is reflected in _____-needs.
34. In many situations, _____ motivation (that which is induced by obvious external rewards) can reduce _____ motivation, enjoyment, and creativity.

● *What happens during emotion? Can "lie detectors" really detect lies?*

35. Emotions are linked to many basic _____ behaviors, such as attacking, retreating, feeding, and reproducing.
36. Other major elements of emotion are physiological changes in the body, emotional _____, and emotional feelings.
37. The following are considered to be _____ emotions: fear, surprise, sadness, disgust, anger, anticipation, joy, and trust (acceptance).
38. Physical changes associated with emotion are caused by the action of _____, a hormone released into the bloodstream, and by activity in the _____ nervous system (ANS).
39. The _____ branch of the ANS is primarily responsible for arousing the body, the _____ branch for quieting it.
40. Sudden death due to prolonged and intense emotion is probably related to _____ rebound (excess activity). Heart attacks caused by sudden intense emotion are more likely due to _____ arousal.
41. The _____, or "lie detector," measures emotional arousal by monitoring heart rate, blood pressure, breathing rate, and the _____ skin response (GSR).
42. Asking a series of _____ and _____ questions may allow the detection of lies, but overall, the accuracy of the lie detector has been challenged by many researchers.

● *How accurately are emotions expressed by "body language" and the face?*

43. Basic emotional _____, such as smiling or baring one's teeth when angry, appear to be unlearned.

44. _____ expressions of fear, anger, disgust, sadness, and happiness are recognized by people of all cultures.

45. Body _____ and movements (body language) also express feelings, mainly by communicating emotional tone.

46. Three dimensions of emotional expressions are pleasantness-unpleasantness, attention-rejection, and _____.

47. The study of body language is known as _____.

● *How do psychologists explain emotions?*

48. The _____-Lange theory of emotion says that emotional experience follows an awareness of the bodily reactions of emotion.

49. In contrast, the _____-Bard theory says that bodily reactions and emotional experience occur at the same time and that emotions are organized in the brain.

50. Schachter's _____ theory of emotion emphasizes the importance of labels, or interpretations, applied to feelings of bodily _____.

51. Also important is the process of _____, in which bodily arousal is attributed to a particular person, object, or situation.

52. The _____ _____ hypothesis holds that sensations and information from emotional expressions help define what emotion a person is feeling.

53. Contemporary views of emotion place greater emphasis on how situations are _____ (evaluated). Also, all of the elements of emotion are seen as interrelated and interacting.

● *What does it mean to have "emotional intelligence"?*

54. Emotional _____ involves the following skills: self-awareness, _____, self-control, and an understanding of how to use emotions.

55. Emotionally intelligent people are good at reading _____ expressions, tone of _____, and other signs of emotion.

56. They also use their feelings to enhance _____ and _____ making.

57. Positive emotions are not just a luxury. They tend to encourage personal _____ and _____ connection

MASTERY TEST

1. Which of the following is NOT one of the signs of emotional arousal recorded by a polygraph?
   a. heart rate   b. blood pressure   c. pupil dilation   d. breathing rate

2. Plain water is most satisfying when a person has _____ thirst.
   a. intracellular   b. hypothalamic   c. extracellular   d. homeostatic

3. We have a biological tendency to associate an upset stomach with foods eaten earlier. This is the basis for the development of
   a. taste aversions   b. yo-yo dieting   c. bulimia   d. frequent weight cycling

4. Strong external rewards tend to undermine
   a. extrinsic motivation   b. intrinsic motivation   c. prepotent motivation   d. stimulus motivation

5. Activity in the ANS is directly responsible for which element of emotion?
   a. emotional feelings   b. emotional expressions   c. physiological changes   d. misattributions

6. Empathy is a major element of
   a. nAch   b. intrinsic motivation   c. emotional intelligence   d. the sensation-seeking personality

7. Motivation refers to the ways in which activities are initiated, sustained, and
   a. acquired   b. valued   c. directed   d. aroused

8. The psychological state or feeling we call thirst corresponds to which element of motivation?
   a. need   b. drive   c. deprivation   d. incentive value

9. People who score high on the SSS generally prefer
   a. low levels of arousal   b. moderate levels of arousal   c. high levels of arousal   d. the middle of the V function

10. Which facial expression is NOT recognized by people of all cultures?
    a. anger   b. disgust   c. optimism   d. fear

11. Learning to weaken eating cues is useful in
    a. self-selection feeding   b. yo-yo dieting   c. rapid weight cycling   d. behavioral dieting

12. People who score high on tests of the need for achievement tend to be:
    a. motivated by power and prestige   b. attracted to longshots   c. sensation seekers
    d. moderate risk takers

13. Which theory holds that emotional feelings, arousal, and behavior are generated simultaneously in the brain?
    a. James-Lange   b. Cannon-Bard   c. cognitive   d. attribution

14. Compared with people in North America, people in Asian cultures are less likely to express which emotion?
a. anger b. jealousy c. curiosity d. fear

15. Binge eating is most associated with
a. bulimia nervosa b. bait shyness c. low levels of NPY d. anorexia nervosa

16. Goals that are desirable are high in
a. need reduction b. incentive value c. homeostatic valence d. motivational "push"

17. _____ is to pain avoidance as _____ is to the sex drive.
a. Non-homeostatic, episodic b. Episodic, non-homeostatic c. Non-homeostatic, cyclic
d. Cyclic, non-homeostatic

18. A specialist in kinesics could be expected to be most interested in
a. facial blends b. circadian rhythms c. sensation seeking d. primary motives

19. Coping statements are a way to directly correct which part of test anxiety?
a. overpreparation b. under-arousal c. excessive worry d. compulsive rehearsal

20. Drives for exploration and activity are categorized as
a. primary motives b. secondary motives c. stimulus motives d. extrinsic motives

21. Sudden death following a period of intense fear may occur when _____ slows the heart to a stop.
a. a sympathetic overload b. adrenaline poisoning c. opponent-process feedback
d. a parasympathetic rebound

22. People who enjoy skydiving and ski jumping are very likely high in
a. parasympathetic arousal b. extrinsic motivation c. their desires to meet meta-needs
d. the trait of sensation seeking

23. You could induce eating in a laboratory rat by activating the
a. lateral hypothalamus b. corpus callosum c. rat's set point d. ventromedial hypothalamus

24. People think cartoons are funnier if they see them while holding a pen crosswise in their teeth. This observation supports
a. the James-Lange theory b. the Cannon-Bard theory c. Schachter's cognitive theory
d. the facial feedback hypothesis

25. Basic biological motives are closely related to
a. nAch b. homeostasis c. activity in the thalamus d. levels of melatonin in the body

26. Self-actualization is to _____ needs as safety and security are to _____ needs.
    a. growth, basic   b. basic, meta-   c. prepotent, basic   d. meta-, extrinsic

27. Which of the following is NOT a core element of emotion?
    a. physiological changes   b. emotional expressions   c. emotional feelings   d. misattributions

28. The effects of a "supermarket diet" on eating are related to the effects of _____ on eating.
    a. anxiety   b. incentive value   c. metabolic rates   d. stomach distention

29. According to the Yerkes-Dodson law, optimum performance occurs at _____ levels of arousal for simple tasks and _____ levels of arousal for complex tasks.
    a. higher, lower   b. lower, higher   c. minimum, high   d. average, high

30. Contemporary models of emotion place greater emphasis on _____, or the way situations are evaluated.
    a. appraisal   b. attribution   c. feedback   d. emotional tone

ANSWERS

Recite and Review

1. initiate, activities
2. need, goal
3. push, pull
4. goal, need
5. secondary
6. primary, steady
7. stomach, blood, liver
8. start, stop
9. feeding, satiety
10. fat, diet
11. taste, taste
12. starvation, gorging
13. anxiety
14. bodily, brain
15. fluid, cells, fluid, cells
16. cycles
17. learned
18. females, arousal
19. drive

20. sensory
21. physical arousal
22. arousal
23. moderate
24. simple, complex
25. rhythms, sleep
26. change, schedule
27. Social
28. need
29. success, risk
30. motivation, effort, persist
31. basic
32. Lower, higher
33. Self, needs
34. external
35. behaviors
36. feelings
37. sadness, anger
38. hormone, nervous system
39. branch, branch
40. rebound, arousal

41. emotional arousal
42. relevant, lying
43. unlearned
44. fear, sadness
45. feelings, tone
46. facial
47. body language
48. follows
49. at the same time
50. labels
51. arousal
52. expressions
53. situations
54. self, self, emotions
55. emotion
56. feelings (or emotions)
57. Positive

Connections

1. h
2. g
3. d
4. a
5. j
6. e
7. c
8. i
9. f
10. b
11. c
12. j
13. d
14. a
15. i
16. b
17. h
18. f
19. e
20. g
21. d
22. a
23. h
24. b
25. j
26. c
27. i
28. f
29. g
30. e

Check Your Memory

1. F
2. T
3. T
4. T
5. F
6. T
7. F
8. T
9. T
10. F
11. T
12. F
13. F
14. T
15. T
16. T
17. T
18. F
19. F
20. T
21. T
22. T
23. T
24. F
25. T
26. F
27. T
28. F
29. F
30. F
31. T
32. T
33. T
34. F
35. T
36. F
37. F
38. T
39. F
40. F
41. F
42. T
43. F
44. T
45. T
46. F
47. F
48. T
49. T
50. T
51. F
52. T
53. F
54. F
55. F
56. F
57. F
58. T
59. T
60. F
61. T
62. F
63. T
64. F
65. T
66. T
67. T
68. T

Final Survey and Review

1. sustain, direct
2. drive, attainment
3. needs, goals
4. incentive value
5. primary, stimulus, secondary
6. homeostasis
7. distention, hypoglycemia
8. hypothalamus, satiety
9. lateral, ventromedial, nucleus
10. set point, cues
11. aversions, bait shyness
12. Anorexia, bulimia
13. self-image
14. hypothalamus
15. intracellular, extracellular
16. episodic, cyclic
17. avoidance, tolerance
18. estrus, homeostatic
19. androgens
20. stimulus, exploration
21. arousal theory
22. *Sensation-Seeking*
23. inverted U
24. Yerkes-Dodson
25. Circadian, time zones
26. preadapt
27. socialization
28. achievement
29. High, moderate
30. Self-confidence
31. hierarchy, growth
32. prepotent
33. actualization, meta
34. extrinsic, intrinsic
35. adaptive
36. expressions
37. primary

38. adrenaline, autonomic
39. sympathetic, parasympathetic
40. parasympathetic, sympathetic
41. polygraph, galvanic
42. relevant, irrelevant
43. expressions
44. Facial
45. gestures
46. activation
47. kinesics
48. James
49. Cannon
50. cognitive, arousal
51. attribution
52. facial feedback
53. appraised
54. intelligence, empathy
55. facial, voice
56. thinking, decision
57. personal, social

Mastery Test

1. c (p. 363)
2. a (p. 350)
3. a (p. 348)
4. b (p. 358)
5. c (p. 360)
6. c (p. 371)
7. c (p. 341)
8. b (p. 341)
9. c (p. 353)
10. c (p. 365)
11. d (p. 347)
12. b (p. 355)
13. b (p. 368)
14. a (p. 365)
15. a (p. 348)
16. b (p. 342)
17. b (p. 350-351)
18. a (p. 366)
19. c (p. 354)
20. c (p. 342)
21. d (p. 363)
22. d (p. 353)
23. a (p. 344)
24. d (p. 369)
25. b (p. 342)
26. a (p. 356)
27. d (p. 359-360)
28. b (p. 342, 346)
29. a (p. 354)
30. a (p. 370)

Chapter 11
Personality

CHAPTER OVERVIEW

Personality refers to unique and enduring behavior patterns. Character is personality evaluated. Temperament refers to the hereditary and physiological aspects of one's emotional nature. Personality traits are lasting personal qualities. Personality types are categories defined by groups of shared traits. Behavior is also influenced by self-concept. Personality theories combine various ideas and principles to explain personality.

Allport's trait theory classifies traits as common, individual, cardinal, central, or secondary. Cattell's trait theory attributes visible surface traits to the existence of 16 underlying source traits. The five-factor model reduces traits to 5 dimensions. Traits appear to interact with situations to determine behavior. Behavioral genetics suggests that heredity influences personality traits.

Like other psychodynamic approaches, Sigmund Freud's psychoanalytic theory emphasizes unconscious forces and conflicts within the personality. Behavioral theories of personality emphasize learning, conditioning, and the immediate effects of the environment. Social learning theory adds cognitive elements, such as perception, thinking, and understanding to the behavioral view. Many differences between males and females are based on social learning. Humanistic theory emphasizes subjective experiences and needs for self-actualization.

Techniques typically used for personality assessment are interviews, direct observation, questionnaires, and projective tests.

Shyness is a mixture of social inhibition and social anxiety. It is marked by heightened public self-consciousness and a tendency to regard one's shyness as a lasting trait. Shyness can be lessened by changing self-defeating beliefs and by improving social skills.

LEARNING OBJECTIVES

To demonstrate mastery of this chapter, you should be able to:

1. Define the term *personality* and explain how personality differs from character and temperament.
2. Discuss the stability of personality.
3. Define the term *trait.*
4. Describe the trait approach and the type approach to personality, and explain the shortcoming of the type approach.

5. Explain the concepts *self-concept* and *self-esteem* and how they affect behavior and personal adjustment.
6. Briefly describe cultural differences in self-esteem.
7. Define the term *personality theory*.
8. List and describe the five broad perspectives of personality included in this chapter.
9. Characterize the general approach to the study of personality taken by a trait theorist.
10. Distinguish common traits from individual traits.
11. Define and give examples of Allport's *cardinal traits, central traits,* and *secondary traits.*
12. Distinguish between surface traits and source traits, and state how Cattell measures source traits.
13. Explain how Cattell's approach to personality traits differed from Allport's approach.
14. Discuss the five-factor model of personality.
15. Explain what a trait-situation interaction is.

The following objectives are related to the material in the "Exploring Psychology" section of the text.
16. Explain how twin studies are used to assess the relative contributions of heredity and environment to personality.
17. Discuss how the similarities in the personalities of twins can be explained.
18. Assess the relative contributions of heredity and environment to the makeup of personality.

19. List and describe the three parts of the personality according to Freud.
20. Describe the dynamic conflict between the three parts of the personality, and relate neurotic and moral anxiety to the conflict.
21. Describe the relationships among the three parts of the personality and the three levels of awareness.
22. List and describe Freud's four psychosexual stages. In your answer include an explanation of fixation and the corresponding age range for each stage.
23. Discuss the positive and the negative aspects of Freud's developmental theory.
24. Explain how behaviorists view personality and traits. Include a definition of the term situational determinants.
25. Explain how learning theorists view the structure of personality. Include in your discussion the terms habit, drive, cue, response, and reward.
26. Explain how learning theory and social learning theory differ. Include in your discussion a description of the terms *psychological situation, expectancy, reinforcement value,* and *self-reinforcement.*
27. Explain how self-reinforcement is related to self-esteem and depression.
28. Using the behavioristic view of development, explain why feeding, toilet training, sex training, and learning to express anger or aggression may be particularly important to personality formation.
29. Describe the role of identification, imitation, and social reinforcement in the development of sex-appropriate behavior.
30. Briefly explain how the humanists set themselves apart from the Freudian and behaviorist viewpoint of personality.
31. Describe the development of Maslow's interest in self-actualization.

32. Using at least five of the characteristics of self-actualizers listed in your text, describe a self-actualizing person. From the original list of eleven, evaluate yourself and explain what may be helping or hindering your self-actualization.

33. List and briefly explain or describe (where applicable) eight steps to promote self-actualization.

34. Describe Rogers's view of the normal or fully functioning individual.

35. Describe Rogers's view of an incongruent person.

36. Explain how possible selves help translate our hopes, dreams, and fears and ultimately direct our future behavior.

37. Explain how conditions of worth, positive self regard, and organismic valuing may affect personality formation.

38. Discuss the following assessment techniques in terms of purpose, method, advantages, and limitations:
    a. unstructured and structured interviews (include halo effect)
    b. direct observation (include rating scales, behavioral assessment and situational testing)
    c. personality questionnaires (include validity, reliability, and a description of the MMPI-2)
    d. honesty tests
    e. projective tests (include descriptions of Rorschach, TAT)

39. Describe the personality characteristics of sudden murderers, and explain how their characteristics are related to the nature of their homicidal actions.

The following objectives are related to the material in the "Psychology in Action" section of the text.

40. List and describe the three elements of shyness.

41. State what situations usually cause shyness.

42. Compare the personality of the shy and the non-shy. Include the concepts labeling and self-esteem.

43. List and discuss the three major areas that can help reduce shyness.

RECITE AND REVIEW

● *How do psychologists use the term personality? What core concepts make up the psychology of personality?*

Recite and Review: Pages 376-380

1. Personality is made up of one's unique and relatively stable _____ patterns.

2. Character is personality that has been judged or _____. That is, it is the possession of desirable qualities.

3. Temperament refers to the _____ and physiological aspects of one's emotional nature.

4. Personality traits are lasting personal qualities that are inferred from _____.

5. A personality type is a style of personality defined by having a group of related _____ or similar characteristics.

6. Two widely recognized personality _____ are an introvert (shy, self-centered person) and an extrovert (bold, outgoing person).

7. Behavior is influenced by self-concept, which is a person's perception of his or her own _____ traits.

8. _____ theories combine interrelated assumptions, ideas, and principles to explain personality.

9. Four major types of personality theories are: _____, psychodynamic, behavioristic, and humanistic.

● *Are some personality traits more basic or important than others?*

Recite and Review: Pages 380-384

10. Trait _____ attempt to specify qualities of personality that are most lasting or characteristic of a person.

11. Gordon Allport made useful distinctions between common traits (which are shared by most members of a culture) and _____ traits (characteristics of a single person).

12. Allport also identified cardinal traits (a trait that influences nearly all of a person's activities), central traits (core traits of personality), and _____ traits (superficial traits).

13. The theory of Raymond Cattell attributes visible _____ traits to the existence of 16 underlying source traits (which he identified using factor _____).

14. Source traits are measured by the *Sixteen* _____ _____ *Questionnaire* (16 PF).

15. The outcome of the 16 PF and other personality tests may be graphically presented as a _____ profile.

16. The five-factor model of personality reduces traits to 5 _____ dimensions of personality.

17. The five factors are: extroversion, _____, conscientiousness, neuroticism, and openness to _____.

18. _____ interact with situations to determine behavior.

19. Heredity is responsible for 25 to 50 percent of the variation in personality _____.

20. Studies of separated _____ twins suggest that heredity contributes significantly to adult personality traits. Overall, however, personality is shaped as much, or more by differences in environment.

● *How do psychodynamic theories explain personality?*

Recite and Review: Pages 384-389

21. Psychodynamic theories focus on the inner workings of personality, especially hidden or _____ forces and internal conflicts.

22. According to Sigmund Freud's psychoanalytic theory, personality is made up of the id, _____, and superego.

23. The id operates on the pleasure _____. The ego is guided by the reality _____.

24. The _____ is made up of the conscience and the ego ideal.

25. Libido, derived from the _____ instincts, is the primary _____ running the personality.

26. Conflicts within the personality may cause neurotic _____ or moral _____ and motivate use of ego-defense mechanisms.

27. The personality operates on three levels, the _____, preconscious, and unconscious.

28. The id is completely _____; the ego and superego can operate at all three levels of awareness.

29. The Freudian view of personality development is based on a series of psychosexual _____: the _____, anal, phallic, and genital.

30. Fixations (unresolved emotional conflicts) at any stage can leave a lasting imprint on _____.

31. Freud's theory pioneered the idea that feeding, toilet training, and early sexual experiences leave an imprint on _____.

● *What do behaviorists emphasize in their approach to personality?*

Recite and Review: Pages 389-393

32. Behavioral theories of personality emphasize _____, conditioning, and immediate effects of the environment.

33. Learning theorists generally stress the effects of prior learning and _____ determinants of behavior.

34. Learning theorists John Dollard and Neal Miller consider _____ the basic core of personality. _____ express the combined effects of drive, cue, response, and _____.

35. _____ learning theory adds cognitive elements, such as perception, thinking, and understanding to the behavioral view of personality.

36. Examples of social learning concepts are the _____ situation (the situation as it is perceived), expectancies (expectations about what effects a response will have), and reinforcement _____ (the subjective value of a reinforcer or activity).

37. Some social learning theorists treat "conscience" as a case of _____-reinforcement.

38. The behavioristic view of personality development holds that social reinforcement in four situations is critical. The critical situations are _____, toilet or cleanliness training, sex training, and _____ or aggression training.

39. Identification (feeling emotionally connected to a person) and _____ (mimicking another person's behavior) are of particular importance in sex (or gender) training.

● *How do humanistic theories differ from other perspectives?*

Recite and Review: Pages 393-398

40. Humanistic theory views human nature as _____, and emphasizes subjective experience, _____ choice, and needs for self-actualization.

41. Abraham Maslow's study of self-actualizers identified characteristics they share, ranging from efficient perceptions of reality to frequent _____ _____ (temporary moments of self-actualization).

42. Carl Rogers's theory views the _____ as an entity that emerges when experiences that match the self-_____ are symbolized (admitted to consciousness), while those that are incongruent are excluded.

43. The incongruent person has a highly unrealistic _____ and/or a mismatch between the _____ and the ideal self.

44. The congruent or _____ functioning person is flexible and open to experiences and feelings.

45. In the development of personality, humanists are primarily interested in the emergence of a _____ and in self-evaluations.

46. As parents apply conditions of _____ (standards used to judge thoughts, feelings, and actions) to a child, the child begins to do the same.

47. Internalized conditions of worth contribute to incongruence, they damage _____ self-regard, and they disrupt the organismic _____ process.

● *How do psychologists measure personality?*

Recite and Review: Pages 398-405

48. Techniques typically used for personality assessment are _____, observation, questionnaires, and projective _____.

49. Structured and unstructured _____ provide much information, but they are subject to _____ bias and misperceptions. The halo effect may also _____ accuracy.

50. Direct observation, sometimes involving situational tests, behavioral assessment, or the use of _____ scales, allows evaluation of a person's actual _____.

51. Personality questionnaires, such as the _____ _____ *Personality Inventory-2* (MMPI-2), are objective and _____, but their validity is open to question.

52. Honesty tests, which are essentially personality _____, are widely used by businesses to make hiring decisions. Their validity is hotly debated.

53. Projective tests ask a subject to project thoughts or feelings onto an ambiguous _____ or unstructured situation.

54. The *Rorschach,* or _____ test, is a well-known projective technique. A second is the _____ *Apperception Test* (TAT).

55. The validity and objectivity of projective tests are quite _____. Nevertheless, projective techniques are considered useful by many clinicians, particularly as part of a _____ battery.

● *What causes shyness? What can be done about it?*

Recite and Review: PSYCHOLOGY IN ACTION

56. Shyness is a mixture of _____ inhibition and _____ anxiety.

57. Shy persons tend to lack social skills and they feel social anxiety (because they believe they are being _____ by others).

58. Shy persons also have a self-defeating bias in their _____ (they tend to blame _____ for social failures).

59. Shyness is marked by heightened _____ self-consciousness (awareness of oneself as a _____ object) and a tendency to regard shyness as a lasting trait.

60. Shyness can be lessened by changing self-defeating _____ and by improving _____ skills.

CONNECTIONS

1.	_____	character	a.	heart-attack risk
2.	_____	trait	b.	hot-tempered
3.	_____	Type A	c.	personality judged
4.	_____	melancholic	d.	cheerful
5.	_____	choleric	e.	source traits
6.	_____	phlegmatic	f.	culturally typical
7.	_____	sanguine	g.	sluggish
8.	_____	16 PF	h.	universal dimensions
9.	_____	common traits	i.	sad, gloomy
10.	_____	Big Five	j.	lasting personal quality

11.	_____	trait-situation	a.	mouth
12.	_____	Thanatos	b.	pride
13.	_____	Eros	c.	genitals
14.	_____	conscience	d.	female conflict
15.	_____	ego ideal	e.	interaction
16.	_____	oral stage	f.	male conflict
17.	_____	anal stage	g.	death instinct
18.	_____	phallic stage	h.	elimination
19.	_____	Oedipus	i.	life instinct
20.	_____	Electra	j.	guilt

21. _____	honesty test	a. interview problem
22. _____	behavior genetics	b. evaluation fears
23. _____	Maslow	c. shoot-don't-shoot
24. _____	Rogers	d. personality questionnaire
25. _____	social learning	e. faking good
26. _____	halo effect	f. fully functioning person
27. _____	MMPI	g. self-actualization
28. _____	validity scale	h. twin studies
29. _____	social anxiety	i. cognitive behaviorism
30. _____	situational test	j. integrity at work

CHECK YOUR MEMORY

Check Your Memory: Pages 376-380

1. The term *personality* refers to charisma or personal style. T or F?
2. Personality is a person's relatively stable pattern of attitudes. T or F?
3. Character refers to the inherited "raw material" from which personality is formed. T or F?
4. In Asian cultures, self-esteem is strongly tied to personal achievement, rather than group success. T or F?
5. Traits are stable or lasting qualities of personality, displayed in most situations. T or F?
6. Personality traits typically become quite stable by age 30. T or F?
7. Paranoid, dependent, and antisocial personalities are regarded as personality types. T or F?
8. Two major dimensions of Eysenck's personality theory are stable-unstable and calm-moody. T or F?
9. Trait theories of personality stress subjective experience and personal growth. T or F?

Check Your Memory: Pages 380-384

10. Extroverted students tend to study in noisy areas of the library. T or F?
11. Nearly all of a person's activities can be traced to one or two common traits. T or F?
12. Roughly 7 central traits are needed, on the average, to describe an individual's personality. T or F?
13. Allport used factor analysis to identify central traits. T or F?
14. The 16 PF is designed to measure surface traits. T or F?
15. Judging from scores on the 16 PF, airline pilots have traits that are similar to creative artists. T or F?
16. As one of the Big Five factors, neuroticism refers to having negative, upsetting emotions. T or F?
17. The expression of personality traits tends to be influenced by external situations. T or F?
18. Similarities between reunited identical twins show that personality is mostly shaped by genetics. T or F?
19. Studies of identical twins show that personality traits are approximately 70 percent hereditary. T or F?
20. Some of the coincidences shared by identical twins appear to be based on the fallacy of positive instances. T or F?

Check Your Memory: Pages 384-389

21. The id is totally unconscious. T or F?
22. The ego is guided by the pleasure principle. T or F?
23. The superego is the source of feelings of guilt and pride. T or F?
24. Threats of punishment from the Thanatos cause moral anxiety. T or F?
25. Oral-dependent persons are gullible. T or F?
26. Vanity and narcissism are traits of the anal-retentive personality. T or F?
27. The genital stage occurs between the ages of 3 and 6, just before latency. T or F?
28. Boys are more likely to develop a strong conscience if their fathers are affectionate and accepting. T or F?
29. Freud regarded latency as the most important stage of psychosexual development. T or F?
30. Erik Erikson's psychosocial stages were derived, in part, from Freud's psychosexual stages. T or F?

Check Your Memory: Pages 389-393

31. Behaviorists view personality as a collection of learned behavior patterns. T or F?
32. Behaviorists attribute our actions to prior learning and specific situations. T or F?
33. According to Dollard and Miller, habits are acquired through observational learning. T or F?
34. Cues are signals from the environment that guide responses. T or F?
35. An expectancy refers to the anticipation that making a response will lead to reinforcement. T or F?
36. People who are depressed tend to engage in high rate of self-reinforcement to make themselves feel better. T or F?
37. Social reinforcement is based on attention and approval from others. T or F?
38. In elementary school, misbehaving boys typically get more attention from teachers than girls do. T or F?

Check Your Memory: Pages 393-398

39. Humanists believe that humans are capable of free choice. T or F?
40. To investigate self-actualization, Maslow studied eminent men and women exclusively. T or F?
41. Self-actualizers usually try to avoid task centering. T or F?
42. Personal autonomy is a characteristic of the self-actualizing person. T or F?
43. Information inconsistent with one's self-image is described as incongruent. T or F?
44. Poor self-knowledge is associated with high self-esteem because people do not have to think about their own faults. T or F?
45. Congruence represents a close correspondence between self-image, the ideal self, and the true self. T or F?
46. Images of possible selves typically cause feelings of incongruence. T or F?
47. Rogers believed that organismic valuing is healthier than trying to meet someone else's conditions of worth. T or F?

Check Your Memory: Pages 398-405

48. Planned questions are used in a structured interview. T or F?
49. The halo effect may involve either a positive or a negative impression. T or F?
50. Personality questionnaires are used to do behavioral assessments. T or F?
51. Judgmental firearms training is a type of honesty test. T or F?

52. Items on the MMPI-2 were selected for their ability to identify persons with psychiatric problems. T or F?
53. The validity scale of the MMPI-2 is used to rate Type A behavior. T or F?
54. The psychasthenia scale of the MMPI-2 detects the presence of phobias and compulsive actions. T or F?
55. It is very easy to fake responses to a projective test. T or F?
56. The TAT is a situational test. T or F?
57. Habitually violent prison inmates are aggressive and overcontrolled. T or F?

Check Your Memory: PSYCHOLOGY IN ACTION

58. Shyness is closely related to private self-consciousness. T or F?
59. Non-shy persons believe that external situations cause their occasional feelings of shyness. T or F?
60. The odds of meeting someone interested in socializing are about the same wherever you are. T or F?
61. Open-ended questions help keep conversations going. T or F?

FINAL SURVEY AND REVIEW

● *How do psychologists use the term personality? What core concepts make up the psychology of personality?*

1. _____ is made up of one's unique and relatively stable behavior _____.

2. _____ is personality that has been judged or evaluated. That is, it is the possession of desirable qualities.

3. _____ refers to the hereditary and physiological aspects of one's emotional nature.

4. Personality _____ are lasting personal qualities that are inferred from behavior.

5. A personality _____ is a style of personality defined by having a group of related traits or similar characteristics.

6. Two widely recognized personality types are an _____ (shy, self-centered person) and an _____ (bold, outgoing person).

7. Behavior is influenced by _____, which is a person's perception of his or her own personality traits.

8. Personality _____ combine interrelated assumptions, ideas, and principles to explain personality.

9. Four major types of personality theories are: trait, _____, behavioristic, and _____.

● *Are some personality traits more basic or important than others?*

10. _____ theories attempt to specify qualities of personality that are most lasting or characteristic of a person.

11. Gordon _____ made useful distinctions between _____ traits (which are shared by most members of a culture) and individual traits (characteristics of a single person).

12. He also identified _____ traits (a trait that influences nearly all of a person's activities), _____ traits (core traits of personality), and secondary traits (superficial traits).

13. The theory of Raymond _____ attributes visible surface traits to the existence of 16 underlying _____ traits (which he identified using _____ analysis).

14. _____ _____ are measured by the *Sixteen Personality Factor Questionnaire* (16 PF).

15. The outcome of the 16 PF and other personality tests may be graphically presented as a trait _____.

16. The _____ model of personality reduces traits to 5 universal dimensions of personality.

17. They are: _____, agreeableness, conscientiousness, _____, and openness to experience.

18. Traits _____ with _____ to determine behavior.

19. Heredity is responsible for _____ to _____ percent of the variation in personality traits.

20. Studies of separated identical twins suggest that _____ contributes significantly to adult personality traits. Overall, however, personality is shaped as much, or more by differences in _____.

● *How do psychodynamic theories explain personality?*

21. Psychodynamic theories focus on the inner workings of _____, especially hidden or unconscious forces and internal _____.

22. According to Sigmund Freud's _____ theory, personality is made up of the _____, ego, and _____.

23. The id operates on the _____ principle. The ego is guided by the _____ principle.

24. The superego is made up of the _____ and the _____ ideal.

25. _____, derived from the life _____, is the primary energy running the personality.

26. Conflicts within the personality may cause _____ anxiety or _____ anxiety and motivate use of ego-defense mechanisms.

27. The personality operates on three levels, the conscious, _____, and _____.

28. The _____ is completely unconscious; the _____ and _____ can operate at all three levels of awareness.

29. The Freudian view of personality development is based on a series of _____ stages: the oral, anal, _____, and genital.

30. _____ (unresolved emotional conflicts) at any stage can leave a lasting imprint on personality.

31. Freud's theory pioneered the idea that _____, _____ training, and early sexual experiences leave an imprint on personality.

● *What do behaviorists emphasize in their approach to personality?*

32. _____ theories of personality emphasize learning, conditioning, and immediate effects of the environment.

33. Learning theorists generally stress the effects of prior learning and situational _____ of behavior.

34. Learning theorists John Dollard and Neal Miller consider habits the basic core of personality. Habits express the combined effects of _____, _____, response, and reward.

35. Social learning theory adds _____ elements, such as perception, thinking, and understanding to the behavioral view of personality.

36. Examples of social learning concepts are the psychological situation (the situation as it is perceived), _____ (expectations about what effects a response will have), and _____ value (the subjective value of a reinforcer or activity).

37. Some social learning theorists treat "conscience" as a case of self-_____.

38. The behavioristic view of personality development holds that social reinforcement in four situations is critical. The critical situations are feeding, _____ _____, sex training, and anger or _____ training.

39. _____ (feeling emotionally connected to a person) and imitation (mimicking another person's behavior) are of particular importance in sex (or gender) training.

● *How do humanistic theories differ from other perspectives?*

40. Humanistic theory views human nature as good, and emphasizes _____ experience, free choice, and needs for self-_____.

41. Abraham _____ study of _____ identified characteristics they share, ranging from efficient perceptions of reality to frequent peak experiences.

42. Carl Rogers's theory views the self as an entity that emerges when experiences that match the self-image are _____ (admitted to consciousness), while those that are _____ are excluded.

43. The _____ person has a highly unrealistic self-image and/or a mismatch between the self-image and the _____ self.

44. The _____ or fully functioning person is flexible and open to experiences and feelings.

45. In the development of personality, humanists are primarily interested in the emergence of a self-image and in _____.

46. As parents apply _____ of worth (standards used to judge thoughts, feelings, and actions) to a child, the child begins to do the same.

47. Internalized _____ _____ contribute to incongruence, they damage positive self-regard, and they disrupt the _____ valuing process.

● *How do psychologists measure personality?*

48. Techniques typically used for personality assessment are interviews, direct
_____, questionnaires, and _____ tests.

49. Structured and _____ interviews provide much information, but they are subject to interviewer _____ and misperceptions. The halo effect may also lower the accuracy of an interview.

50. Direct observation, sometimes involving _____ tests, _____ assessment, or the use of rating scales, allows evaluation of a person's actual behavior.

51. Personality questionnaires, such as the *Minnesota Multiphasic* _____ _____-2 (MMPI-2), are objective and reliable, but their _____ is open to question.

52. _____ tests, which are essentially personality questionnaires, are widely used by businesses to measure integrity and make hiring decisions.

53. _____ tests ask subjects to react to an ambiguous stimulus or unstructured situation.

54. The _____, or inkblot test, is a well-known projective technique. A second is the *Thematic* _____ *Test* (TAT).

55. The _____ and objectivity of projective tests are quite low. Nevertheless, projective techniques are considered useful by many clinicians, particularly as part of a test _____.

● *What causes shyness? What can be done about it?*

56. Shyness is a mixture of social _____ and social anxiety.

57. Shy persons tend to lack social _____ and they feel social anxiety (because they believe they are being evaluated by others).

58. Shy persons also have a _____ bias in their thinking (they tend to blame themselves for social failures).

59. Shyness is marked by heightened public self-_____ (awareness of oneself as a _____ object) and a tendency to regard shyness as a lasting _____.

60. Shyness can be lessened by changing _____ beliefs and by improving social _____.

MASTERY TEST

1. The hereditary aspects of a person's emotional nature define his or her
   a. character b. personality c. cardinal traits d. temperament

2. Two parts of the psyche that operate on all three levels of awareness are the
   a. id and ego b. ego and superego c. id and superego d. id and ego ideal

3. The four critical situations Miller and Dollard consider important in the development of personality are feeding, toilet training,
   a. sex, and aggression   b. cleanliness, and language   c. attachment, and imitation   d. social learning

4. Scales that rate a person's tendencies for depression, hysteria, paranoia, and mania are found on the
   a. MMPI-2   b. Rorschach   c. TAT   d. 16 PF

5. In the five-factor model, people who score high on openness to experience are
   a. intelligent   b. extroverted   c. choleric   d. a personality type

6. Maslow used the term _____ to describe the tendency to make full use of personal potentials.
   a. full functionality   b. self-potentiation   c. ego-idealization   d. self-actualization

7. Studies of reunited identical twins support the idea that
   a. personality traits are 70 percent hereditary   b. fixations influence the expression of personality traits
   c. personality traits are altered by selective mating and placement in families of comparable status
   d. personality is shaped as much or more by environment as by heredity

8. A person's perception of his or her own personality is the core of
   a. temperament   b. source traits   c. self-concept   d. trait-situation interactions

9. Which of the following concepts is NOT part of Dollard and Miller's behavioral model of personality?
   a. drive   b. expectancy   c. cue   d. reward

10. The terms *structured* and *unstructured* apply most to
    a. the halo effect   b. interviews   c. questionnaires   d. honesty tests

11. Behavioral theorists account for the existence of a conscience with the concept of
    a. traits of honesty and integrity   b. the superego   c. self-reinforcement   d. conditions of worth

12. Feelings of pride come from the _____, a part of the _____.
    a. libido, conscience   b. ego ideal, superego   c. reality principle, superego   d. superego, ego

13. Four types of temperament recognized by the early Greeks are: melancholic, choleric, phlegmatic and
    a. sanguine   b. sardonic   c. sagittarian   d. sagacious

14. Freud believed that boys identify with their fathers in order to resolve the _____ conflict.
    a. Animus   b. Electra   c. Oedipus   d. Persona

15. Maslow regarded peak experiences as temporary moments of
    a. task-centering   b. congruent selfhood   c. self-actualization   d. organismic valuing

16. Ambiguous stimuli are used primarily in the
    a. MMPI-2 b. Shoot-Don't-Shoot Test c. Rorschach d. 16 PF

17. A person who is generally extroverted is more outgoing in some situations than in others.
    This observation supports the concept of
    a. trait-situation interactions b. behavioral genetic determinants c. situational fixations
    d. possible selves

18. Allport's concept of central traits is most closely related to Cattell's
    a. surface traits b. source traits c. secondary traits d. cardinal traits

19. According to Freud, tendencies to be orderly, obstinate, and stingy are formed during
    the _____ stage.
    a. genital b. anal c. oral d. phallic

20. Which of the following is NOT part of Carl Rogers's view of personality?
    a. possible selves b. organismic valuing c. conditions of worth d. congruence

21. Rating scales are primarily used in which approach to personality assessment?
    a. projective testing b. direct observation c. questionnaires d. the TAT technique

22. Which theory of personality places the greatest emphasis on the effects of the environment?
    a. trait b. psychodynamic c. behavioristic d. humanistic

23. Freudian psychosexual stages occur in the order:
    a. oral, anal, genital, phallic b. oral, phallic, anal, genital c. genital, oral, anal, phallic
    d. oral, anal, phallic, genital

24. Rogers described mismatches between one's self-image and reality as a state of
    a. moral anxiety b. incongruence c. basic anxiety d. negative symbolization

25. All but one of the following are major elements of shyness; which does not apply?
    a. private self-consciousness b. social anxiety c. self-defeating thoughts d. belief that
    shyness is a lasting trait

26. People who all grew up in the same culture would be most likely to have the same _____ traits.
    a. cardinal b. common c. secondary d. source

27. A trait profile is used to report the results of
    a. the 16 PF b. situational tests c. the TAT d. the inkblot test

28. An emphasis on the situational determinants of actions is a key feature
    of _____ theories of personality.
    a. psychodynamic b. projective c. behaviorist d. humanist

29. Expectancies and the psychological situation are concepts important to
   a. the five-factor model   b. development of the superego   c. social learning theory   d. Maslow

30. In Asian cultures, _____ tends to be more strongly related to group membership and the success of the group.
   a. temperament   b. character   c. self-esteem   d. moral anxiety

ANSWERS

Recite and Review

1. behavior
2. evaluated
3. hereditary
4. behavior
5. traits
6. types
7. personality
8. Personality
9. trait
10. theories
11. individual
12. secondary
13. surface, analysis
14. *Personality Factor*
15. trait
16. universal
17. agreeableness, experience
18. Traits
19. traits
20. identical
21. unconscious
22. ego
23. principle, principle
24. superego
25. life, energy
26. anxiety, anxiety
27. conscious
28. unconscious
29. stages, oral
30. personality
31. personality

32. learning
33. situational
34. habits, Habits, reward
35. Social
36. psychological, value
37. self
38. feeding, anger
39. imitation
40. good, free
41. peak experiences
42. self, image
43. self-image, self-image
44. fully
45. self-image
46. worth
47. positive, valuing
48. interviews, tests
49. interviews, interviewer, lower
50. rating, behavior
51. *Minnesota, Multiphasic,* reliable
52. questionnaires
53. stimulus
54. inkblot, *Thematic*
55. low, test
56. social, social
57. evaluated
58. thinking, themselves
59. public, social
60. beliefs, social

Connections

1. c
2. j
3. a
4. i
5. b
6. g
7. d
8. e
9. f
10. h
11. e
12. g
13. i
14. j
15. b
16. a
17. h
18. c
19. f
20. d
21. j
22. h
23. g
24. f
25. i
26. a
27. d
28. e
29. b
30. c

Check Your Memory

1. F
2. F
3. F
4. F
5. T
6. T
7. T
8. F
9. F
10. T
11. F
12. T
13. F
14. F
15. F
16. T
17. T
18. F
19. F
20. T
21. T
22. F
23. T
24. F
25. T
26. F
27. F
28. T
29. F
30. T
31. T
32. T
33. F
34. T
35. T
36. F
37. T
38. T
39. T
40. F
41. F
42. T
43. T
44. F
45. T
46. F
47. T
48. T
49. T
50. F
51. F
52. T
53. F
54. T
55. F
56. F
57. F
58. F
59. T
60. F
61. T

Final Survey and Review

1. Personality, patterns
2. Character
3. Temperament
4. traits
5. type
6. introvert, extrovert
7. self-concept
8. theories
9. psychodynamic, humanistic
10. Trait
11. Allport, common
12. cardinal, central
13. Cattell, source, factor
14. Source traits
15. profile
16. five-factor
17. extroversion, neuroticism
18. interact, situations
19. 25, 50
20. heredity, environment
21. personality, conflicts
22. psychoanalytic, id, superego
23. pleasure, reality
24. conscience, ego
25. Libido, instincts
26. neurotic, moral
27. preconscious, unconscious
28. id, ego, superego
29. psychosexual, phallic
30. Fixations
31. feeding, toilet
32. Behavioral
33. determinants
34. drive, cue
35. cognitive
36. expectancies, reinforcement
37. reinforcement
38. toilet training, aggression
39. Identification
40. subjective, actualization
41. Maslow's, self-actualizers
42. symbolized, incongruent
43. incongruent, ideal
44. congruent
45. self-evaluations
46. conditions
47. conditions of worth, organismic
48. observation, projective
49. unstructured, bias
50. situational, behavioral
51. *Personality Inventory*, validity
52. Honesty
53. Projective
54. *Rorschach, Apperception*
55. validity, battery
56. inhibition
57. skills
58. self-defeating
59. consciousness, social, trait
60. self-defeating, skills

Mastery Test

1. d (p. 376)
2. b (p. 387)
3. a (p. 392)
4. a (p. 402)
5. a (p. 382)
6. d (p. 394)
7. d (p. 384)
8. c (p. 378)
9. b (p. 392)
10. b (p. 399)
11. c (p. 391)
12. b (p. 386)
13. a (p. 379)

14. c (p. 388)
15. c (p. 394)
16. c (p. 402)
17. a (p. 383)
18. b (p. 381)
19. b (p. 388)

20. a (p. 395-397)
21. b (p. 400)
22. c (p. 398)
23. d (p. 388)
24. b (p. 396)
25. a (p. 406)

26. b (p. 380)
27. a (p. 381)
28. c (p. 390)
29. c (p. 391)
30. c (p. 379)

Chapter 12
Health, Stress, and Coping

CHAPTER OVERVIEW

Health psychologists study behavioral risk factors and health-promoting behaviors. Various "lifestyle" diseases are directly related to unhealthy personal habits. Stress is also a major risk factor. At work, prolonged stress can lead to burnout. Emotional appraisals greatly affect our stress reactions and coping attempts. Traumatic stressors, such as violence, torture, or natural disasters, tend to produce severe stress reactions.
Frustration and conflict are common sources of stress. Major behavioral reactions to frustration include persistence, more vigorous responding, circumvention, direct aggression, displaced aggression and escape or withdrawal. Five major types of conflict are approach-approach, avoidance-avoidance, approach-avoidance, double approach-avoidance, and multiple approach-avoidance.

Anxiety, threat, or feelings of inadequacy frequently lead to the use of defense mechanisms. Common defense mechanisms include compensation, denial, fantasy, intellectualization, isolation, projection, rationalization, reaction formation, regression, repression, and sublimation. Learned helplessness explains some depression and some failures to cope with threat. Mastery training acts as an antidote to helplessness.

A large number of life changes can increase susceptibility to illness. However, immediate health is more closely related to the severity of daily hassles or microstressors. Intense or prolonged stress may cause psychosomatic problems. Biofeedback may be used to combat stress and psychosomatic illnesses. People with Type A personalities run a heightened risk of suffering a heart attack. People with hardy personality traits are resistant to stress. The body reacts to stress in a pattern called the general adaptation syndrome (G.A.S.). In addition, stress may lower the body's immunity to disease.

The College Life Stress Inventory, which is similar to the SRRS, can be used to rate the amount of stress an undergraduate student has experienced. A number of coping skills can be applied to manage stress. Most focus on bodily effects, ineffective behaviors, and upsetting thoughts.

LEARNING OBJECTIVES

To demonstrate mastery of this chapter, you should be able to:

1. Describe health psychology including its focus.
2. Define the terms *behavioral medicine* and *lifestyle diseases*.

3. List eleven behavioral risk factors that can adversely affect one's health.

4. Define the term *disease-prone personality*.

5. Briefly describe the research demonstrating the relationship of health-promoting behaviors and longevity.

6. Describe the impact of refusal-skills training, life skills training, and community health campaigns on illness prevention.

7. Define the term *wellness* by listing the characteristics of wellness.

8. Explain the similarity between your body's stress reaction and emotion.

9. List four aspects of stress that make it more intense and damaging.

10. Describe burnout. List and describe the three aspects of the problem.

11. Describe three things that can be done to help reduce burnout.

12. Give an example of how primary and secondary appraisal is used in coping with a threatening situation.

13. Explain how the perception of control of a stressor influences the amount of threat felt.

14. Differentiate problem-focused coping from emotion-focused coping and explain how they may help or hinder each other.

The following objectives are related to the material in the "Exploring Psychology" section of the text.

15. Describe the impact of traumatic stress, and list five ways to cope with reactions to traumatic stress.

16. Briefly describe what happens when traumatic stresses are severe or repeated.

17. List and describe the two different kinds of frustration.

18. List four factors that increase frustration.

19. List and describe five common reactions to frustration (see Figure 12.3).

20. Explain how scapegoating is a special form of displaced aggression.

21. Describe and give an example of each of the following four types of conflict:
    a. approach-approach
    b. avoidance-avoidance
    c. approach-avoidance (include the terms ambivalence and partial approach in your response)
    d. double approach-avoidance (include the term vacillate in your response)

22. Define the term *defense mechanism*. Discuss the positive value of defense mechanisms.

23. Describe the following defense mechanisms and give an example of each:

    a. denial   d. regression   g. compensation
    b. repression   e. projection   h. sublimation
    c. reaction formation   f. rationalization

24. Describe the development of learned helplessness and relate this concept to attribution and depression.

25. Explain how learned helplessness may be prevented from spreading.

26. List three similarities between learned helplessness and depression.

27. Discuss the concept of hope and its relationship to mastery training.

28. Describe the six problems that typically contribute to depression among college students.

29. List the five conditions of depression and describe how it can be combated.

30. Discuss the relationship between life changes and long-term health. Describe the SRRS. Explain how hassles are related to immediate health.
31. Distinguish between psychosomatic disorders and hypochondria.
32. Name several of the most common types of psychosomatic problems.
33. List the causes of psychosomatic disorders.
34. Discuss biofeedback in terms of the process involved and its possible applications.
35. Differentiate between Type A and Type B personalities. Note the twelve strategies for reducing hostility that apply to you.
36. Describe what a hardy personality is and list the three ways such people view the world.
37. Explain the concept of the General Adaptation Syndrome. List and describe its three stages.
38. Explain how stress affects the immune system.

The following objectives are related to the material in the "Psychology in Action" section of the text.
39. Define the term stress management. Briefly discuss the College Life Stress Inventory.
40. List the three responses that are triggered by stress and discuss the stress management techniques that can be used to diminish or break the cycle of each response.
41. Define *stereotyped response* and give an example of it.
42. Discuss three effective ways to avoid frustration.
43. List four things to remember when dealing with conflict or a difficult decision.

RECITE AND REVIEW

● *What is health psychology? How does behavior affect health?*

Recite and Review: Pages 411-415

1. Health psychologists are interested in _____ that helps maintain and promote health. The related field of behavioral medicine applies psychology to _____ treatment and problems.
2. Most people today die from lifestyle diseases caused by unhealthy personal _____.
3. Studies have identified a number of behavioral risk factors, which increase the chances of _____ or injury.
4. A general disease-prone personality pattern also raises the risk of _____.
5. Health-promoting _____ tend to maintain good health. They include practices such as getting regular exercise, controlling _____ and alcohol use, maintaining a balanced _____, getting good medical care, avoiding _____ deprivation, and managing stress.
6. Health psychologists attempt to promote wellness (a positive state of _____) through community health _____ that educate people about risk factors and healthful behaviors.

● *What is stress? What factors determine its severity?*

Recite and Review: Pages 415-419

7. Stress occurs when we are forced to _____ or adapt to external demands.

8. Stress is more damaging in situations involving pressure (responding at full capacity for long periods), a lack of _____, unpredictability of the stressor, and _____ or repeated emotional shocks.

9. _____ is intensified when a situation is perceived as a threat and when a person does not feel competent to cope with it.

10. In _____ settings, prolonged stress can lead to burnout, marked by emotional _____, depersonalization (detachment from others), and reduced personal accomplishment.

11. The _____ (initial) appraisal of a situation greatly affects our emotional response to it. Stress reactions, in particular, are related to an appraisal of _____.

12. During a _____ appraisal some means of coping with a situation is selected. Coping may be either problem-focused (managing the situation) or emotion-focused (managing one's emotional reactions) or both.

13. Traumatic _____, such as violence, torture, or natural disasters, tend to produce severe _____ reactions.

14. Traumatic _____ leave people feeling threatened, vulnerable, and with the sense that they are losing control over their _____.

15. Severe or _____ traumatic _____ can leave people with lasting emotional handicaps called stress disorders.

● *What causes frustration and what are typical reactions to it?*

Recite and Review: Pages 420-421

16. Frustration is the negative emotional state that occurs when progress toward a _____ is _____. Sources of frustration may be external or personal.

17. External frustrations are based on delay, failure, rejection, loss, and other direct blocking of motives. Personal frustration is related to _____ characteristics over which one has little control.

18. Frustrations of all types become more _____ as the strength, urgency, or importance of the blocked motive increases.

19. Major behavioral reactions to frustration include persistence, more _____ responding, and circumvention of barriers.

20. Other reactions to frustration are _____ aggression, displaced aggression (including scapegoating), and escape, or _____.

● *Are there different types of conflict? How do people react to conflict?*

Recite and Review: Pages 421-423

21. _____ occurs when we must choose between contradictory alternatives.

22. Three basic types of conflict are approach-approach (choice between two _____
alternatives), avoidance-avoidance (both alternatives are _____), and approach-avoidance
(a goal or activity has both positive and negative aspects).

23. More complex conflicts are: double approach-avoidance (both alternatives have
_____ and _____ qualities) and multiple approach-avoidance (several
alternatives each have good and bad qualities).

24. Approach-approach conflicts are usually the _____ to resolve.

25. Avoidance conflicts are _____ to resolve and are characterized by inaction,
indecision, freezing, and a desire to escape (called _____ the field).

26. People usually remain in approach-avoidance conflicts, but fail to fully resolve them. Approach-
avoidance conflicts are associated with ambivalence (_____ feelings) and _____
approach.

27. Vacillation (wavering between choices) is the most common reaction to double
_____ conflicts.

● *What are defense mechanisms?*

Recite and Review: Pages 424-426

28. Anxiety, threat, or feelings of _____ frequently lead to the use of psychological
defense mechanisms. These are habitual strategies used to avoid or reduce anxiety.

29. A number of defense mechanisms have been identified, including denial, fantasy, intellectualization,
isolation, projection, rationalization, _____ formation, regression, and
_____ (motivated forgetting).

30. Two defense mechanisms that have some _____ qualities are compensation and
sublimation.

● *What do we know about coping with feelings of helplessness and depression?*

Recite and Review: Pages 426-429

31. Learned helplessness is a learned inability to overcome obstacles or to _____ punishment.

32. Learned helplessness explains the failure to cope with some threatening situations. The symptoms of
learned helplessness and depression are nearly _____.

33. Mastery _____ and hope act as antidotes to helplessness.

34. Depression (a state of deep sadness or despondency) is a serious emotional problem. Actions and
thoughts that counter feelings of helplessness tend to _____ depression.

● *How is stress related to health and disease?*

Recite and Review: Pages 430-437

35. Work with the *Social Readjustment Rating Scale* (SRRS) indicates that a large number of life
_____ units (LCUs) can increase susceptibility to _____ or illness.

36. Immediate health is more closely related to the intensity and severity of daily annoyances, known as
_____ or microstressors.

37. Intense or prolonged stress may damage the body in the form of psychosomatic disorders (illnesses in which _____ factors play a part). T or F?

38. Psychosomatic (mind-body) disorders have no connection to hypochondria, the tendency to imagine that one has a _____.

39. During biofeedback training, bodily processes are _____ and converted to a signal that indicates what the body is doing.

40. Biofeedback allows alteration of many bodily activities. It shows promise for promoting _____, self-regulation, and for treating some psychosomatic illnesses.

41. People with Type A (_____ attack prone) personalities are competitive, striving, and frequently angry or hostile, and they have a chronic sense of _____ urgency.

42. _____ and hostility are especially likely to increase the chances of heart attack.

43. People who have traits of the hardy personality seem to be resistant to _____, even if they also have Type A traits.

44. The body reacts to stress in a series of stages called the _____ adaptation syndrome (G.A.S.).

45. The stages of the G.A.S. are alarm, resistance, and exhaustion. The G.A.S. contributes to the development of _____ disorders.

46. Stress weakens the immune system and lowers the body's resistance to _____.

● *What are the best strategies for managing stress?*

Recite and Review: PSYCHOLOGY IN ACTION

47. Most stress management skills focus on one of three areas: bodily effects, ineffective _____, and upsetting _____.

48. Bodily effects can be managed with exercise, meditation, progressive _____, and guided _____.

49. The impact of ineffective behavior can be remedied by slowing down, getting organized, striking a balance between "good stress" and _____, accepting your limits, and seeking social support.

50. A good way to control upsetting thoughts is to replace negative self-statements with _____ coping statements.

CONNECTIONS

1.	_____	risk factors	a. leading cause of death
2.	_____	tobacco	b. ANS arousal
3.	_____	refusal skills	c. blocked motive
4.	_____	stress reaction	d. lifestyle diseases
5.	_____	burnout	e. psychological escape
6.	_____	primary appraisal	f. scapegoat
7.	_____	frustration	g. approach-avoidance
8.	_____	displaced aggression	h. "Am I in trouble?"
9.	_____	apathy	i. job stress
10.	_____	ambivalence	j. smoking prevention

11. _____	compensation	a. Fulfilling unmet desires in imagined activities.
12. _____	denial	b. Separating contradictory thoughts into "logic-tight" mental compartments.
13. _____	fantasy	
14. _____	intellectualization	c. Preventing actions by exaggerating opposite behavior.
15. _____	isolation	d. Justifying your behavior by giving reasonable but false reasons for it.
16. _____	projection	
17. _____	rationalization	e. Unconsciously preventing painful thoughts from entering awareness.
18. _____	reaction formation	
19. _____	regression	f. Counteracting a real or imagined weakness by seeking to excel.
20. _____	repression	g. Retreating to an earlier level of development.
21. _____	sublimation	h. Attributing one's own shortcomings or unacceptable impulses to others.

i. Protecting oneself from an unpleasant reality by refusing to perceive it.

j. Working off unacceptable impulses in constructive activities.

k. Thinking about threatening situations in impersonal terms.

22. _____	learned helplessness	a. LCU
23. _____	mastery training	b. stress resistant
24. _____	SRRS	c. mind-body
25. _____	hassle	d. self-regulation
26. _____	hardy personality	e. cardiac personality
27. _____	psychosomatic	f. alarm reaction
28. _____	biofeedback	g. microstressor
29. _____	Type A	h. hope
30. _____	G.A.S.	i. shuttle box

CHECK YOUR MEMORY

Check Your Memory: Pages 411-415

1. Heart disease, lung cancer, and stroke are typical lifestyle diseases. T or F?

2. Illicit use of drugs is the second most common cause of death in the United States, after smoking. T or F?

3. People with disease-prone personalities are depressed, anxious, and hostile. T or F?

4. Unhealthy lifestyles typically involve multiple risks. T or F?

5. A major community study done in California found that eating breakfast and not eating between meals are two of the most important health-promoting behaviors. T or F?

6. Community health campaigns provide refusal skills training to large numbers of people. T or F?

7. Wellness can be described as an absence of disease. T or F?

Check Your Memory: Pages 415-419

  8. Unpleasant activities produce stress, whereas, pleasant activities do not. T or F?

  9. Initial reactions to stressors are similar to those that occur during strong emotion. T or F?

10. Short-term stresses rarely do any damage to the body. T or F?

11. Unpredictable demands increase stress. T or F?

12. Pressure occurs when we are faced with a stressor we can control. T or F?

13. Burnout is especially a problem in helping professions. T or F?

14. The opposite of burnout is positive job engagement. T or F?

15. Stress is often related to the meaning a person places on events. T or F?

16. The same situation can be a challenge or a threat, depending on how it is appraised. T or F?

17. In a secondary appraisal, we decide if a situation is relevant or irrelevant, positive or threatening. T or F?

18. When confronted by a stressor, it is best to choose one type of coping—problem focused or emotion focused. T or F?

19. Emotion-focused coping is best suited to managing stressors you cannot control. T or F?

20. Nightmares, grief, flashbacks, nervousness, and depression are common reactions to traumatic stress. T or F?

21. It is possible to have stress symptoms from merely witnessing traumatically stressful events on television. T or F?

22. An excellent way to cope with traumatic stress is to stop all of your daily routines and isolate yourself from others. T or F?

Check Your Memory: Pages 420-421

23. Delays, rejections, and losses are good examples of personal frustrations. T or F?

24. Varied responses and circumvention attempt to directly destroy or remove barriers that cause frustration. T or F?

25. Scapegoating is a good example of escape or withdrawal. T or F?

26. Abuse of drugs can be a way of psychologically escaping frustration. T or F?

Check Your Memory: Pages 421-423

27. Approach-approach conflicts are fairly easy to resolve. T or F?

28. Indecision, inaction, and freezing are typical reactions to approach-approach conflicts. T or F?

29. People find it difficult to escape approach-avoidance conflicts. T or F?

30. Wanting to eat, but not wanting to be overweight, creates an approach-approach conflict. T or F?

31. People are very likely to vacillate when faced with a double approach-avoidance conflict. T or F?

Check Your Memory: Pages 424-426

32. Defense mechanisms are used to avoid or distort sources of threat or anxiety. T or F?

33. Denial is a common reaction to bad news, such as learning that a friend has died. T or F?

34. In reaction formation, a person fulfills unmet desires in imagined achievements. T or F?

35. A child who becomes homesick while visiting relatives may be experiencing a mild regression. T or F?

36. Denial and repression are the two most positive of the defense mechanisms. T or F?

Check Your Memory: Pages 426-429

37. The deep depression experienced by prisoners of war appears to be related to learned helplessness. T or F?

38. Learned helplessness occurs when events appear to be uncontrollable. T or F?

39. Attributing failure to lasting, general factors, such as personal characteristics, tends to create the most damaging feelings of helplessness.

40. Mastery training restores feelings of control over the environment. T or F?

41. At any given time, 52 to 61 percent of all college students are experiencing the symptoms of depression. T or F?

42. Depression is more likely when students find it difficult to live up to idealized images of themselves. T or F?

43. Writing rational answers to self-critical thoughts can help counteract feelings of depression.

Check Your Memory: Pages 430-437

44. Scores on the SRRS are expressed as life control units. T or F?

45. A score of 300 LCUs on the SRRS is categorized as a major life crisis. T or F?

46. According to the SRRS, being fired at work involves more LCUs than divorce does. T or F?

47. Microstressors tend to predict changes in health 1 to 2 years after the stressful events took place. T or F?

48. Psychosomatic disorders involve actual damage to the body or damaging changes in bodily functioning. T or F?

49. A person undergoing biofeedback can sleep if he or she desires—the machine does all the work. T or F?

50. Type B personalities are more than twice as likely to suffer heart attacks as Type A personalities. T or F?

51. People with the hardy personality type tend to see life as a series of challenges. T or F?

52. In the stage of resistance of the G.A.S., people have symptoms of headache, fever, fatigue, upset stomach, and the like. T or F?

53. Serious health problems tend to occur when a person reaches the stage of exhaustion in the G.A.S. T or F?

54. Stress management training can actually boost immune system functioning. T or F?

Check Your Memory: PSYCHOLOGY IN ACTION

55. Concern about being pregnant is the most stressful item listed on the *College Life Stress Inventory*. T or F?

56. Exercising for stress management is most effective when it is done daily. T or F?

57. Guided imagery is used to reduce anxiety and promote relaxation. T or F?

58. Merely writing down thoughts and feelings about daily events can provide some of the benefits of social support. T or F?

59. To get the maximum benefits, coping statements should be practiced in actual stressful situations. T or F?

60. Persistence must be flexible before it is likely to aid a person trying to cope with frustration. T or F?

FINAL SURVEY AND REVIEW

● *What is health psychology? How does behavior affect health?*

1. Health psychologists are interested in behavior that helps maintain and promote health. The related field of _____ _____ applies psychology to medical treatment and problems.
2. Most people today die from _____ diseases caused by unhealthy personal habits.
3. Studies have identified a number of behavioral _____ _____, which increase the chances of disease or injury.
4. A general _____ personality pattern also raises the risk of illness.
5. Health-_____ behaviors tend to maintain good health. They include practices such as getting regular exercise, controlling smoking and alcohol use, maintaining a balanced diet, getting good medical care, avoiding sleep _____, and managing _____.
6. Health psychologists attempt to promote _____ (a positive state of health) through _____ _____ campaigns that educate people about risk factors and healthful behaviors.

● *What is stress? What factors determine its severity?*

7. Stress occurs when we are forced to adjust or _____ to external _____.
8. Stress is more damaging in situations involving _____ (responding at full capacity for long periods), a lack of control, unpredictability of the _____, and intense or repeated emotional shocks.
9. Stress is intensified when a situation is perceived as a _____ and when a person does not feel _____ to cope with it.
10. In work settings, prolonged stress can lead to _____, marked by emotional exhaustion, _____ (detachment from others), and reduced personal accomplishment.
11. The primary _____ of a situation greatly affects our emotional response to it. Stress reactions, in particular, are related to an _____ of threat.
12. During a secondary appraisal some means of coping with a situation is selected. Coping may be either _____-focused (managing the situation) or _____-focused (managing one's emotional reactions) or both.
13. _____ stressors, such as violence, torture, or natural disasters, tend to produce severe stress reactions.
14. Traumatic stresses leave people feeling threatened, vulnerable, and with the sense that they are losing _____ over their lives.
15. Severe or repeated traumatic stress can leave people with lasting emotional handicaps called _____ _____.

● *What causes frustration and what are typical reactions to it?*

16. _____ is the negative emotional state that occurs when progress toward a goal is blocked. Sources of frustration may be external or _____.

17. _____ frustrations are based on delay, failure, rejection, loss, and other direct blocking of motives. _____ frustration is related to personal characteristics over which one has little control.

18. Frustrations of all types become more intense as the strength, urgency, or importance of the _____ _____ increases.

19. Major behavioral reactions to frustration include _____, more vigorous responding, and _____ of barriers.

20. Other reactions to frustration are direct aggression, _____ aggression (including _____), and escape, or withdrawal.

● *Are there different types of conflict? How do people react to conflict?*

21. Conflict occurs when we must choose between _____ alternatives.

22. Three basic types of conflict are _____ (choice between two positive alternatives), _____ (both alternatives are negative), and approach-avoidance (a goal or activity has both positive and negative aspects).

23. More complex conflicts are: _____ approach-avoidance (both alternatives have positive and negative qualities) and _____ approach-avoidance (several alternatives each have good and bad qualities).

24. _____ conflicts are usually the easiest to resolve.

25. _____ conflicts are difficult to resolve and are characterized by inaction, indecision, freezing, and a desire to escape (called leaving the field).

26. People usually remain in approach-avoidance conflicts, but fail to fully resolve them. Approach-avoidance conflicts are associated with _____ (mixed feelings) and partial approach.

27. _____ (wavering between choices) is the most common reaction to double approach-avoidance conflicts.

● *What are defense mechanisms?*

28. Anxiety, threat, or feelings of inadequacy frequently lead to the use of psychological _____ _____. These are habitual strategies used to avoid or reduce _____.

29. A number of defense mechanisms have been identified, including _____ (refusing to perceive an unpleasant reality), fantasy, intellectualization, isolation, projection, _____ (justifying one's behavior), reaction formation, regression, and repression.

30. Two defense mechanisms that have some positive qualities are _____ and _____.

● *What do we know about coping with feelings of helplessness and depression?*

31. Learned _____ is a learned inability to overcome obstacles or to avoid _____.

32. The symptoms of learned helplessness and _____ are nearly identical.

33. _____ training and hope act as antidotes to helplessness.

34. _____ (a state of deep sadness or despondency) is a serious emotional problem. Actions and thoughts that counter feelings of _____ tend to reduce depression.

● *How is stress related to health and disease?*

35. Work with the _____ _____ _____ *Scale* (SRRS) indicates that a large number of life change units (LCUs) can increase susceptibility to accident or illness.

36. Immediate health is more closely related to the intensity and severity of daily annoyances, known as hassles or _____.

37. Intense or prolonged stress may damage the body in the form of _____ disorders (illnesses in which psychological factors play a part).

38. _____ (mind-body) disorders have no connection to _____, the tendency to imagine that one has a disease.

39. During _____ training, bodily processes are monitored and converted to a _____ that indicates what the body is doing.

40. Biofeedback allows alteration of many bodily activities. It shows promise for promoting relaxation, self-_____, and for treating some psychosomatic illnesses.

41. People with _____ _____ (heart attack prone) personalities are competitive, striving, and frequently _____ or hostile, and they have a chronic sense of time urgency.

42. Anger and hostility are especially likely to increase the chances of _____ _____.

43. People who have traits of the _____ personality seem to be resistant to stress, even if they also have Type A traits.

44. The body reacts to stress in a series of stages called the general _____ _____ (G.A.S.).

45. The stages of the G.A.S. are _____, resistance, and _____. The G.A.S. contributes to the development of psychosomatic disorders.

46. Stress weakens the _____ system and lowers the body's resistance to illness.

● *What are the best strategies for managing stress?*

47. Most stress management skills focus on one of three areas: bodily effects, _____ behavior, and _____ thoughts.

48. Bodily effects can be managed with exercise, meditation, _____ relaxation, and _____ imagery.

49. The impact of ineffective behavior can be remedied by slowing down, getting organized, striking a balance between "good stress" and relaxation, accepting your _____, and seeking _____ support.

50. A good way to control upsetting thoughts is to replace _____ self-statements with positive _____ statements.

MASTERY TEST

1. When stressful events appear to be uncontrollable, two common reactions are
   a. apathy and double-approach conflict   b. helplessness and depression
   c. assimilation and marginalization   d. psychosomatic disorders and hypochondria

2. The *College Life Stress Inventory* is most closely related to the
   a. SRRS   b. G.A.S.   c. K.I.S.   d. *Disease-Prone Personality Scale*

3. We answer the question "Am I okay or in trouble" when making
   a. negative self-statements   b. coping statements   c. a primary appraisal   d. a secondary appraisal

4. Which of the following is NOT a major symptom of burnout?
   a. emotional exhaustion   b. depersonalization   c. reduced accomplishment
   d. dependence on co-workers

5. A child who displays childish speech and infantile play after his parents bring home a new baby shows signs of
   a. compensation   b. reaction formation   c. regression   d. sublimation

6. Persistent but inflexible responses to frustration can become
   a. stereotyped behaviors   b. imagined barriers   c. negative self-statements
   d. sublimated and depersonalized

7. The leading cause of death in the United States is
   a. tobacco   b. diet/inactivity   c. alcohol   d. infection

8. Both mountain climbing and marital strife
   a. are behavioral risk factors   b. are appraised as secondary threats   c. cause stress reactions
   d. produce the condition known as pressure

9. LCUs are used to assess
   a. burnout   b. social readjustments   c. microstressors   d. what stage of the G.A.S. a person is in

10. Sujata is often ridiculed by her boss, who also frequently takes advantage of her. Deep inside, Sujata has come to hate her boss, yet on the surface she acts as if she likes him very much. It is likely that Sujata is using the defense mechanism called
    a. reaction formation   b. Type B appraisal   c. problem-focused coping   d. sublimation

11. Lifestyle diseases are of special interest to _____ psychologists.
    a. health b. community c. wellness d. psychosomatic

12. Which of the following is NOT characteristic of the hardy personality?
    a. commitment b. a sense of control c. accepting challenge d. repression

13. Unhealthy lifestyles are marked by the presence of a number of
    a. health refusal factors b. behavioral risk factors c. cultural stressors
    d. Type B personality traits

14. The most effective response to a controllable stressor is
    a. problem-focused coping b. emotion-focused coping c. leaving the field d. depersonalization

15. Delay, rejection, failure, and loss are all major causes of
    a. pressure b. frustration c. conflict d. helplessness

16. There is evidence that the core lethal factor of Type A behavior is
    a. time urgency b. anger and hostility c. competitiveness and ambition
    d. accepting too many responsibilities

17. What stress, smoking, and overeating all have in common is that they are behavioral
    a. hassles b. risk factors c. sources of burnout d. causes of depersonalization

18. A person is caught between "the frying pan and the fire" in an _____ conflict.
    a. approach-approach b. avoidance-avoidance c. approach-avoidance d. double appraisal

19. Which of the following is NOT one of the major health-promoting behaviors listed in the text?
    a. do not smoke b. get adequate sleep c. get regular exercise d. avoid eating between meals

20. Ambivalence and partial approach are very common reactions to what type of conflict?
    a. approach-approach b. avoidance-avoidance c. approach-avoidance d. multiple avoidance

21. Which of the following terms does not belong with the others?
    a. Type A personality b. stage of exhaustion c. displaced aggression d. psychosomatic disorder

22. Coping statements are a key element in
    a. stress inoculation b. the K.I.S. technique c. guided imagery d. refusal skills training

23. Which of the following factors typically minimizes the amount of stress experienced?
    a. predictable stressors b. repeated stressors c. uncontrollable stressors d. intense stressors

24. Scapegoating is closely related to which response to frustration?
    a. leaving the field b. displaced aggression c. circumvention d. reaction formation

25. The study of the ways in which stress and the immune system affect susceptibility to disease is called
    a. neuropsychosymptomology b. immunohypochondrology c. psychosomatoneurology
    d. psychoneuroimmunology

26. Refusal skills training is typically used to teach young people how to
    a. avoid drug use b. cope with burnout c. resist stressors at home and at school d. avoid forming habits that lead to heart disease

27. Which combination is most relevant to managing bodily reactions to stress?
    a. social support, self pacing b. exercise, social support c. exercise, negative self-statements
    d. progressive relaxation, guided imagery

28. Stress reactions are most likely to occur when a stressor is viewed as a _____ during the _____.
    a. pressure, primary appraisal b. pressure, secondary appraisal c. threat, primary appraisal
    d. threat, secondary appraisal

29. External symptoms of the body's adjustment to stress are least visible in which stage of the G.A.S?
    a. alarm b. regulation c. resistance d. exhaustion

30. A perceived lack of control creates a stressful sense of threat when combined with a perceived
    a. sense of time urgency b. state of sublimation c. need to change secondary risk factors
    d. lack of competence

ANSWERS

Recite and Review

1. behavior, medical
2. habits
3. disease (or illness)
4. illness (or disease)
5. behaviors, smoking, diet, sleep
6. health, campaigns
7. adjust
8. control, intense
9. Stress
10. work, exhaustion
11. primary, threat
12. secondary

13. stressors, stress
14. stresses, lives
15. repeated, stress
16. goal, blocked
17. personal
18. intense
19. vigorous
20. direct, withdrawal
21. Conflict
22. positive, negative
23. positive, negative
24. easiest
25. difficult, leaving
26. mixed, partial
27. approach-avoidance

28. inadequacy
29. reaction, repression
30. positive
31. avoid
32. identical
33. training
34. reduce
35. change, accident
36. hassles
37. psychological
38. disease
39. monitored
40. relaxation
41. heart, time
42. Anger

43. stress
44. general
45. psychosomatic
46. disease (or illness)
47. behavior, thoughts
48. relaxation, imagery
49. relaxation
50. positive

Connections

1. d
2. a
3. j
4. b
5. i
6. h
7. c
8. f
9. e
10. g
11. f
12. i
13. a
14. k
15. b
16. h
17. d
18. c
19. g
20. e
21. j
22. i
23. h
24. a
25. g
26. b
27. c
28. d
29. e
30. f

Check Your Memory

1. T
2. F
3. T

4. T
5. F
6. F
7. F
8. F
9. T
10. T
11. T
12. F
13. T
14. T
15. T
16. T
17. F
18. F
19. T
20. T
21. T
22. F
23. F
24. F
25. F
26. T
27. T
28. F
29. T
30. F
31. T
32. T
33. T
34. F
35. T
36. F
37. T
38. T
39. T
40. T
41. F
42. T
43. T
44. F
45. T
46. F
47. F
48. T
49. F
50. F
51. T
52. F

53. T
54. T
55. F
56. T
57. T
58. T
59. T
60. T

Final Survey and Review

1. behavioral medicine
2. lifestyle
3. risk factors
4. disease-prone
5. promoting, deprivation, stress
6. wellness, community health
7. adapt, demands
8. pressure, stressor
9. threat, competent
10. burnout, depersonalization
11. appraisal, appraisal
12. problem, emotion
13. Traumatic
14. control
15. stress disorders
16. Frustration, personal
17. External, Personal
18. blocked motive
19. persistence, circumvention
20. displaced, scapegoating
21. contradictory
22. approach-approach, avoidance-avoidance
23. double, multiple
24. Approach-approach
25. Avoidance
26. ambivalence
27. Vacillation
28. defense mechanisms, anxiety
29. denial, rationalization
30. compensation, sublimation
31. helplessness, punishment
32. depression
33. Mastery
34. Depression, helplessness

35. *Social Readjustment Rating*
36. microstressors
37. psychosomatic
38. Psychosomatic, hypochondria
39. biofeedback, signal
40. regulation
41. Type A, angry
42. heart attack
43. hardy
44. adaptation syndrome
45. alarm, exhaustion
46. immune
47. ineffective, upsetting
48. progressive, guided
49. limits, social
50. negative, coping

Mastery Test

1. b (p. 427)
2. a (p. 430)
3. c (p. 418)
4. d (p. 417)
5. c (p. 425)
6. a (p. 441)
7. a (p. 411)
8. c (p. 415)
9. b (p. 430)
10. a (p. 425)
11. a (p. 411)
12. d (p. 434-435)
13. b (p. 412)
14. a (p. 418)
15. b (p. 420)
16. b (p. 433)

17. b (p. 412)
18. b (p. 422)
19. d (p. 413)
20. c (p. 423)
21. c (p. 421, 432, 436)
22. a (p. 440)
23. a (p. 416)
24. b (p. 421)
25. d (p. 436)
26. a (p. 414)
27. d (p. 439-440)
28. c (p. 417-418)
29. c (p. 436)
30. d (p. 418)

Chapter 13
Psychological Disorders

CHAPTER OVERVIEW

Abnormal behavior is defined by subjective discomfort, deviation from statistical norms, social non-conformity, and cultural or situational contexts. Disordered behavior is also maladaptive. Major types of psychopathology are described by DSM-IV-TR. Insanity is a legal term, not a mental disorder.

Personality disorders are deeply ingrained maladaptive personality patterns, such as the antisocial personality. Anxiety disorders, dissociative disorders, and somatoform disorders are characterized by high levels of anxiety, rigid defense mechanisms, and self-defeating behavior patterns.

Anxiety disorders include generalized anxiety disorder, panic disorder (with or without agoraphobia), agoraphobia, specific phobia, social phobia, obsessive-compulsive disorders, and post-traumatic or acute stress disorders. Dissociative disorders may take the form of amnesia, fugue, or identity disorder (multiple personality). Somatoform disorders center on physical complaints that mimic disease or disability.

Psychodynamic explanations of anxiety disorders emphasize unconscious conflicts. The humanistic approach emphasizes faulty self-images. The behavioral approach emphasizes the effects of learning, particularly avoidance learning. The cognitive approach stresses maladaptive thinking patterns.

Psychosis is a break in contact with reality. Persons suffering from delusional disorders have delusions of grandeur, persecution, infidelity, romantic attraction, or physical disease. The most common delusional disorder is paranoid psychosis.

Schizophrenia is the most common psychosis. Four types of schizophrenia are: disorganized, catatonic, paranoid, and undifferentiated. Explanations of schizophrenia emphasize environmental stress, inherited susceptibility, and biochemical abnormalities.

Mood disorders involve disturbances of emotion. Two moderate mood disorders are dysthymic disorder and cyclothymic disorder. Major mood disorders include bipolar disorders and major depressive disorder. Seasonal affective disorder is another common form of depression. Biological, psychoanalytic, cognitive, and behavioral theories of depression have been proposed. Heredity is clearly a factor in susceptibility to mood disorders.

Two basic approaches to treating major disorders are psychotherapy and medical therapies.

Suicide is statistically related to such factors as age, sex, and marital status. However, in individual cases the potential for suicide is best identified by a desire to escape, unbearable psychological pain, frustrated psychological needs, and a constriction of options. Suicide can sometimes be prevented by the efforts of family, friends, and mental health professionals.

LEARNING OBJECTIVES

To demonstrate mastery of this chapter, you should be able to:

1. Present information to indicate the magnitude of mental health problems in this country.
2. Define *psychopathology*.
3. Describe the following ways of viewing normality including the shortcoming(s) of each:
   a. subjective discomfort
   b. statistical abnormality
   c. social nonconformity (include the concept of situational context)
   d. cultural relativity
4. Discuss gender bias in judging abnormality.
5. State conditions under which a person is usually judged to need help.
6. Explain the dangers of social stigma when using psychiatric labels.
7. Generally describe each of the following categories of mental disorders found in the DSM-IV-TR:
   a. psychotic disorders
   b. organic mental disorders
   c. substance related disorders
   d. mood disorders
   e. anxiety disorders
   f. somatoform disorders
   g. dissociative disorders
   h. personality disorders
   i. sexual and gender-identity disorders
8. List the four general risk factors that may contribute to mental disorders.
9. Distinguish the term *insanity* from true mental disorder.
10. List and briefly describe the ten different types of personality disorders. (See Table 13.3.)
11. Describe the distinctive characteristics, causes, and treatment of the antisocial personality.
12. Define *anxiety*.
13. Outline the four features of anxiety-related problems.
14. State what is usually meant when the term "nervous breakdown" is used.
15. Differentiate an adjustment disorder from an anxiety disorder.
16. Define the key element of most anxiety disorders.
17. Differentiate generalized anxiety disorders from the two types of panic disorders.
18. Describe the following conditions:
    a. agoraphobia
    b. specific phobia
    c. social phobia
    d. obsessive-compulsive disorder

     e. stress disorder
         i. acute stress disorder
         ii. post-traumatic stress disorder
     f. dissociative disorders
         i. dissociative amnesia
         ii. dissociative fugue
         iii. dissociative identity disorder
     g. somatoform disorders
         i. hypochondriasis
         ii. somatization disorder
         iii. pain disorder
         iv. conversion disorder

19. Discuss how each of the four major perspectives in psychology views anxiety disorders.
     a. psychodynamic
     b. humanistic-existential (include the concepts of self-image and existential anxiety)
     c. behavioral (include the terms self-defeating, paradox, avoidance learning, and anxiety reduction hypothesis)
     d. cognitive

20. Define what is meant by the term *psychosis*.
21. Define *delusion*.
22. Define *hallucination* and name the most common type.
23. Describe the emotion, communication, and personality changes that may occur in someone with a psychosis. Include an explanation of the frequency of occurrence for these changes.
24. Differentiate an organic from a functional psychosis.
25. Describe dementia.
26. Briefly describe Alzheimer's disease, including its incidence, symptoms, and neurological concomitants.
27. Describe the characteristics of delusional disorders, including each of the five delusional types.
28. Describe a paranoid psychosis. Explain why treatment of this condition is difficult.
29. Generally describe schizophrenia.
30. List and describe the four major types of schizophrenia.
31. Explain how paranoid delusional disorder and paranoid schizophrenia differ.

The following objective is related to the material in the "Exploring Psychology" section of the text.
32. Describe the general relationship between violence and mental illness.

33. Describe the roles of the following three areas as causes of schizophrenia:
     a. environment
         i. prenatal problems and birth complications
         ii. psychological trauma
         iii. disturbed family environment

iv. deviant communication patterns
b. heredity
c. brain Chemistry
   i. dopamine
   ii. CT, MRI, and PET scans

34. Discuss the stress-vulnerability model of psychosis.

35. Describe the characteristics of depressive disorders. Include a description of dysthymia and cyclothymia.

36. List and describe the three major mood disorders.

37. Explain the difference between major mood disorders and dysthymia and cyclothymia.

38. Generally describe the likely causes of mood disorders.

39. Define and briefly discuss the symptoms of maternity blues and postpartum depression.

40. Define *seasonal affective disorder* (SAD), list five major symptoms, and briefly describe the treatment of SAD.

41. List and describe the two basic kinds of treatment for psychosis.

The following objectives are related to the material in the "Psychology in Action" section of the text.

42. Discuss how each of the following factors affects suicide rates: season, sex, age, income, marital status.

43. List the eight major risk factors that typically precede suicide. Discuss why people try to kill themselves.

44. Name/identify the twelve warning signs of suicide.

45. List four common characteristics of suicidal thoughts and feelings.

46. Explain how you can help prevent suicide.

RECITE AND REVIEW

● *How is normality defined, and what are the major psychological disorders?*

Recite and Review: Pages 444-452

1. Psychopathology refers to mental _____ themselves or to psychologically _____ behavior.

2. Formal definitions of abnormality usually take into account subjective _____ (private feelings of suffering or unhappiness).

3. Statistical definitions define abnormality as an extremely _____ or _____ score on some dimension or measure.

4. Social non-conformity is a failure to follow societal _____ for acceptable conduct.

5. Frequently, the _____ or situational context that a behavior takes place in affects judgments of normality and abnormality.

6. _____ of the preceding definitions are relative standards.

7. A key element in judgments of disorder is that a person's _____ must be maladaptive (it makes it difficult for the person to _____ to the demands of daily life.

8. A _____ disorder is a significant impairment in psychological functioning.

9. Major disorders and categories of psychopathology are described in the *Diagnostic and Statistical* _____ *of* _____ *Disorders* (DSM-IV-TR).

10. Psychotic disorders are characterized by a retreat from _____, by hallucinations and delusions, and by _____ withdrawal.

11. Organic mental disorders are problems caused by _____ injuries and _____.

12. Substance related disorders are defined as abuse of or dependence on _____ - or behavior-altering _____.

13. Mood disorders involve disturbances in affect, or _____.

14. Anxiety disorders involve high levels of fear or _____ and distortions in behavior that are _____ related.

15. Somatoform disorders involve physical symptoms that mimic physical _____ or injury for which there is no identifiable _____.

16. Dissociative disorders include cases of sudden amnesia, multiple _____, or episodes of depersonalization.

17. Personality disorders are deeply ingrained, unhealthy _____ patterns.

18. Sexual and gender disorders include _____ identity disorders, paraphilias, and _____ dysfunctions.

19. In the past, the term *neurosis* was used to describe milder, _____ related disorders. However, the term is fading from use.

20. Insanity is a _____ term defining whether a person may be held responsible for his or her actions. Sanity is determined in _____ on the basis of testimony by expert witnesses.

● *What is a personality disorder?*

Recite and Review: Pages 452-453

21. Personality disorders are deeply ingrained _____ personality patterns.

22. The personality disorders are: antisocial, avoidant, _____, dependent, histrionic, narcissistic, obsessive-_____, paranoid, schizoid, and schizotypal.

23. Antisocial persons (sociopaths) seem to lack a _____. They are _____ shallow and manipulative.

● *What problems result when a person suffers high levels of anxiety?*

Recite and Review: Pages 454-460

24. Anxiety disorders, dissociative disorders, and somatoform disorders are involve high levels of _____, rigid _____ mechanisms, and self-defeating behavior patterns.

25. The term *nervous breakdown* has no formal meaning. However, "emotional breakdowns" do correspond somewhat to adjustment disorders, in which the person is overwhelmed by ongoing _____ _____.

26. Anxiety disorders include generalized anxiety disorder (chronic _____ and worry) and panic disorder (anxiety attacks, panic, free-_____ anxiety).

27. Panic disorder may occur with or without agoraphobia (fear of _____ places, unfamiliar situations, or leaving the _____).

28. Other anxiety disorders are agoraphobia and _____ phobia (irrational fears of specific objects or situations).

29. In the anxiety disorder called social phobia, the person fears being _____, evaluated, embarrassed, or humiliated by others in _____ situations.

30. Obsessive-compulsive disorders (obsessions and compulsions), and post-traumatic stress disorder or acute stress disorder (emotional disturbances triggered by severe _____) are also classified as _____ disorders.

31. Dissociative disorders may take the form of dissociative amnesia (loss of _____ and personal identity) or _____ fugue (flight from familiar surroundings).

32. A more dramatic problem is dissociative identity disorder, in which a person develops _____ personalities.

33. Somatoform disorders center on physical complaints that mimic _____ or disability.

34. In hypochondriasis, persons think that they have specific diseases, when they are, in fact _____.

35. In a somatization disorder, the person has numerous _____ complaints. The person repeatedly seeks medical _____ for these complaints, but no organic problems can be found.

36. Somatoform pain refers to discomfort for which there is no identifiable _____ cause.

37. In conversion disorders, actual symptoms of disease or disability develop but their causes are really _____.

● *How do psychologists explain anxiety-based disorders?*

Recite and Review: Pages 460-461

38. The psychodynamic approach emphasizes _____ conflicts within the personality as the cause of disabling anxiety.

39. The humanistic approach emphasizes the effects of a faulty _____.

40. The behavioral approach emphasizes the effects of previous _____, particularly avoidance _____.

41. Some patterns in anxiety disorders can be explained by the _____ reduction hypothesis, which states that immediate _____ from anxiety rewards self-defeating behaviors.

42. According to the cognitive view, distorted _____ patterns cause anxiety disorders.

● *What are the general characteristics of psychotic disorders?*

Recite and Review: Pages 462-464

43. Psychosis is a _____ in contact with reality.

44. Psychosis is marked by delusions, _____ (false sensations), and sensory changes.

45. Other symptoms of psychosis are disturbed emotions, disturbed communication, and _____ disintegration.

46. An organic psychosis is based on known injuries or _____ of the brain.

47. The most common _____ problem is dementia, a serious mental impairment in old age caused by deterioration of the _____ .

48. One of the common causes of _____ is Alzheimer's disease.

● *How do delusional disorders differ from other forms of psychosis?*

Recite and Review: Page 464-465

49. A diagnosis of delusional disorder is based primarily on the presence of _____ .

50. Delusions may concern grandeur, _____ (harassment or threat), infidelity, _____ attraction, or physical disease.

51. The most common delusional disorder is paranoid psychosis. Because they often have intense and irrational delusions of _____ , paranoids may be violent if they believe they are threatened.

● *What forms does schizophrenia take? What causes it?*

Recite and Review: Pages 465-471

52. Schizophrenia is distinguished by a _____ between _____ and emotion, and by delusions, hallucinations, and communication difficulties.

53. Disorganized schizophrenia is marked by extreme _____ disintegration and silly, bizarre, or obscene behavior. _____ impairment is usually extreme.

54. Catatonic schizophrenia is associated with stupor, _____ (inability to speak), _____ flexibility, and odd postures. Sometimes violent and agitated behavior also occurs.

55. In paranoid schizophrenia (the most common type), outlandish delusions of grandeur and _____ are coupled with psychotic symptoms and personality breakdown.

56. Undifferentiated schizophrenia is the term used to indicate a _____ of clear-cut patterns of disturbance.

57. Current explanations of schizophrenia emphasize a combination of environmental _____, inherited susceptibility, and biochemical _____ in the body or brain.

58. A number of environmental factors appear to increase the risk of developing schizophrenia. These include viral _____ during the mother's pregnancy and _____ complications.

59. Early psychological _____ (psychological injury or shock) and a disturbed _____ environment, especially one marked by deviant communication, also increase the risk of schizophrenia.

60. Studies of _____ and other close relatives strongly support heredity as a major factor in schizophrenia.

61. Recent biochemical studies have focused on abnormalities in brain _____ substances, especially dopamine and its receptor sites.

62. Additional abnormalities in brain structure or _____ have been detected in schizophrenic brains by the use of CT scans, MRI scans, and PET scans.

63. The dominant explanation of schizophrenia is the _____-vulnerability model.

● *What are mood disorders? What causes depression?*

Recite and Review: Pages 472-475

64. Mood disorders primarily involve disturbances of mood or _____.

65. Long-lasting, though relatively moderate, _____ is called a dysthymic disorder.

66. Chronic, though moderate, swings in mood between _____ and _____ are called a cyclothymic disorder.

67. In a bipolar I disorder the person alternates between extreme mania and _____.

68. In a bipolar II disorder the person is mostly _____, but has had at least one episode of hypomania (mild _____).

69. The problem known as major depressive disorder involves extreme sadness and despondency, but no evidence of _____.

70. Postpartum depression is a mild to moderate depressive disorder that affects many women after they give birth. Postpartum depression is more serious than the more common _____ _____.

71. Major mood disorders more often appear to be endogenous (produced from _____) rather than reactions to _____ events.

72. _____ affective disorder (SAD), which occurs during the _____ months is another common form of depression. SAD is typically treated with phototherapy.

73. Biological, psychoanalytic, cognitive, and _____ theories of depression have been proposed. Heredity is clearly a factor in susceptibility to mood disorders.

74. Psychotherapy is any psychological treatment for behavioral or emotional problems. _____ _____ disorders are more often treated medically, rather than with psychotherapy.

● *Why do people commit suicide? Can suicide be prevented?*

Recite and Review: PSYCHOLOGY IN ACTION

75. _____ is statistically related to such factors as age, sex, and marital status.

76. Major risk factors for suicide include _____ or _____ abuse, a prior attempt, depression, hopelessness, antisocial behavior, suicide by relatives, shame, failure, or rejection, and the availability of a _____.

77. In individual cases the potential for suicide is best identified by a desire to _____, unbearable psychological pain, frustrated psychological needs, and a constriction of _____.

78. Suicidal _____ usually precede suicide threats, which progress to suicide attempts.

79. Suicide can often be prevented by the efforts of family, friends, and mental health professionals to establish _____ and rapport with the person, and by gaining day-by-day commitments from her or him.

CONNECTIONS

1. _____ DSM-IV-TR
2. _____ drapetomania
3. _____ psychosis
4. _____ mood disorder
5. _____ somatoform disorder
6. _____ insanity
7. _____ organic disorder
8. _____ neurosis
9. _____ paraphilia
10. _____ amok

a. culturally recognized disorder
b. physical symptoms
c. legal problem
d. outdated term
e. sexual deviation
f. diagnostic manual
g. retreat from reality
h. fear of germs
i. brain pathology
j. mania or depression

11. _____ dependent personality
12. _____ histrionic personality
13. _____ narcissistic personality
14. _____ antisocial personality
15. _____ obsessive-compulsive
16. _____ schizoid personality
17. _____ avoidant personality
18. _____ borderline personality
19. _____ paranoid personality
20. _____ schizotypal personality

a. self-importance
b. rigid routines
c. submissiveness
d. little emotion
e. attention seeking
f. unstable self-image
g. odd, disturbed thinking
h. suspiciousness
i. fear of social situations
j. no conscience

21. _____ adjustment disorder
22. _____ generalized anxiety
23. _____ panic disorder
24. _____ agoraphobia
25. _____ specific phobia
26. _____ social phobia
27. _____ PTSD
28. _____ acute stress disorder
29. _____ glove anesthesia
30. _____ fugue

a. afraid to leave the house
b. fears being observed
c. conversion disorder
d. one month after extreme stress
e. dissociation
f. within weeks after extreme stress
g. sudden attacks of fear
h. normal life stress
i. chronic worry
j. fears objects or activities

31. _____	schizotypal	a.	incoherence, bizarre thinking
32. _____	catatonic type	b.	false belief
33. _____	paranoid type	c.	personality disorder
34. _____	disorganized type	d.	depression and hypomania
35. _____	psychological trauma	e.	stuporous or agitated
36. _____	twin studies	f.	severe mania and depression
37. _____	dopamine	g.	genetics of schizophrenia
38. _____	delusion	h.	grandeur or persecution
39. _____	bipolar I	i.	chemical messenger
40. _____	bipolar II	j.	risk factor for schizophrenia

CHECK YOUR MEMORY

Check Your Memory: Pages 444-452

1. Psychopathology refers to the study of mental disorders and to disorders themselves. T or F?
2. One out of every 10 persons will require mental hospitalization during his or her lifetime. T or F?
3. Statistical definitions do not automatically tell us where to draw the line between normality and abnormality. T or F?
4. All cultures classify people as abnormal if they fail to communicate with others. T or F?
5. Gender is a common source of bias in judging normality. T or F?
6. Being a persistent danger to oneself or others is regarded as a clear sign of disturbed psychological functioning. T or F?
7. Poverty, abusive parents, low intelligence, and head injuries are risk factors for mental disorder. T or F?
8. "Organic mental disorders" is one of the major categories in DSM-IV-TR. T or F?
9. Koro, locura, and zar are brain diseases that cause psychosis. T or F?
10. Multiple personality is a dissociative disorder. T or F?
11. Neurosis is a legal term, not a type of mental disorder. T or F?

Check Your Memory: Pages 452-453

12. Histrionic persons are preoccupied with their own self-importance. T or F?
13. Personality disorders usually appear suddenly in early adulthood. T or F?
14. The schizoid person shows little emotion and is uninterested in relationships with others. T or F?
15. "Psychopath" is another term for the borderline personality. T or F?
16. Sociopaths usually have a childhood history of emotional deprivation, neglect, and abuse. T or F?
17. Antisocial behavior typically declines somewhat after age 20. T or F?

Check Your Memory: Pages 454-460

18. Anxiety is an emotional response to an ambiguous threat. T or F?
19. Adjustment disorders occur when severe stresses outside the normal range of human experience push people to their breaking points. T or F?

20. Sudden, unexpected episodes of intense panic are a key feature of generalized anxiety disorder. T or F?

21. A person who fears he or she will have a panic attack in public places or unfamiliar situations suffers from acrophobia. T or F?

22. Arachnophobia, claustrophobia, and pathopobia are all specific phobias. T or F?

23. Many people who have an obsessive-compulsive disorder are checkers or cleaners. T or F?

24. PTSD is a psychological disturbance lasting more than one month after exposure to severe stress. T or F?

25. Multiple personality is the most common form of schizophrenia. T or F?

26. Depersonalization and fusion are the goals of therapy for dissociative identity disorders. T or F?

27. The word somatoform means "body form." T or F?

28. An unusual lack of concern about the appearance of a sudden disability is a sign of a conversion reaction. T or F?

Check Your Memory: Pages 460-461

29. Anxiety disorders appear to be partly hereditary. T or F?

30. The psychodynamic approach characterizes anxiety disorders as a product of id impulses that threaten a loss of control. T or F?

31. Carl Rogers interpreted emotional disorders as the result of a loss of meaning in one's life. T or F?

32. Disordered behavior is paradoxical, because it makes the person more anxious and unhappy in the long run. T or F?

33. The cognitive view attributes anxiety disorders to distorted thinking that leads to avoidance learning. T or F?

Check Your Memory: Pages 462-464

34. The most common psychotic delusion is hearing voices. T or F?

35. Even a person who displays flat affect may continue to privately feel strong emotion. T or F?

36. Extremely psychotic behavior tends to occur in brief episodes. T or F?

37. Severe brain injuries or diseases sometimes cause psychoses. T or F?

38. Children must eat leaded paint flakes before they are at risk for lead poisoning. T or F?

39. Roughly 80 percent of all cases of Alzheimer's disease are genetic. T or F?

Check Your Memory: Page 464-465

40. In delusional disorders, people have auditory hallucinations of grandeur or persecution. T or F?

41. Delusions of persecution are a key symptom of paranoid psychosis. T or F?

42. A person who believes that his body is diseased and rotting has a erotomanic type of delusional disorder. T or F?

Check Your Memory: Pages 465-471

43. One person out of 100 will become schizophrenic. T or F?

44. Schizophrenia is the most common dissociative psychosis. T or F?

45. Silliness, laughter, and bizarre behavior are common in disorganized schizophrenia. T or F?

46. Periods of immobility and odd posturing are characteristic of paranoid schizophrenia. T or F?
47. At various times, patients may shift from one type of schizophrenia to another. T or F?
48. Exposure to influenza during pregnancy produces children who are more likely to become schizophrenic later in life. T or F?
49. If one identical twin is schizophrenic, the other twin has a 46 percent chance of also becoming schizophrenic. T or F?
50. Excess amounts of the neurotransmitter substance PCP are suspected as a cause of schizophrenia. T or F?
51. The brains of schizophrenics tend to be more responsive to dopamine than the brains of normal persons. T or F?
52. PET scans show that activity in the frontal lobes of schizophrenics tends to be abnormally low. T or F?

Check Your Memory: Pages 472-475

53. The two most basic types of mood disorder are bipolar I and bipolar II. T or F?
54. In bipolar disorders, people experience both mania and depression. T or F?
55. If a person is moderately depressed for at least two weeks, a dysthymic disorder exists. T or F?
56. A cyclothymic disorder is characterized by moderate levels of depression and manic behavior. T or F?
57. Endogenous depression appears to be generated from within, with little connection to external events. T or F?
58. Behavioral theories of depression emphasize the concept of learned helplessness. T or F?
59. Overall, women are twice as likely as men are to become depressed. T or F?
60. SAD is most likely to occur during the winter, in countries lying near the equator. T or F?
61. Postpartum depression typically lasts from about two months to a year after giving birth. T or F?
62. At least three schizophrenic patients out of four are completely recovered 10 years after being diagnosed. T or F?

Check Your Memory: PSYCHOLOGY IN ACTION

63. The greatest number of suicides during a single day take place at New Year's. T or F?
64. More men than women complete suicide. T or F?
65. Suicide rates steadily decline after young adulthood. T or F?
66. Most suicides involve despair, anger, and guilt. T or F?
67. People who threaten suicide rarely actually attempt it—they're just crying wolf. T or F?
68. Only a minority of people who attempt suicide really want to die. T or F?
69. The risk of attempted suicide is high if a person has a concrete, workable plan for doing it. T or F?

FINAL SURVEY AND REVIEW

● *How is normality defined, and what are the major psychological disorders?*

1. _____ refers to mental disorders themselves or to psychologically unhealthy behavior.

2. Formal definitions of abnormality usually take into account _____ discomfort (private feelings of suffering or unhappiness).

3. _____ definitions define abnormality as an extremely high or low score on some dimension or measure.

4. _____ _____ is a failure to follow societal standards for acceptable conduct.

5. Frequently, the cultural or situational _____ that a behavior takes place in affects judgments of normality and abnormality.

6. All of the preceding definitions are _____ standards.

7. A key element in judgments of disorder is that a person's behavior must be _____ (it makes it difficult for the person to adapt to the environment).

8. A mental disorder is a significant impairment in _____ functioning.

9. Major disorders and categories of psychopathology are described in the _____ and _____ *Manual of Mental Disorders* (DSM-IV-TR).

10. _____ disorders are characterized by a retreat from reality, by _____ and delusions, and by social withdrawal.

11. _____ mental disorders are problems caused by brain injuries and diseases.

12. _____ _____ disorders are defined as abuse of or dependence on mood- or behavior-altering drugs.

13. _____ disorders involve disturbances in _____, or emotion.

14. _____ disorders involve high levels of fear or anxiety and distortions in behavior that are anxiety related.

15. _____ disorders involve physical symptoms that mimic physical disease or injury for which there is no identifiable cause.

16. _____ disorders include cases of sudden _____, multiple personality, or episodes of depersonalization.

17. _____ disorders are deeply ingrained, unhealthy personality patterns.

18. Sexual and gender disorders include gender _____ disorders, paraphilias, and sexual - _____ .

19. In the past, the term _____ was used to describe milder, anxiety related disorders. However, the term is fading from use.

20. _____ is a legal term defining whether a person may be held responsible for his or her actions. Sanity is determined in court on the basis of testimony by expert witnesses.

● *What is a personality disorder?*

21. Personality disorders are deeply _____ maladaptive personality patterns.

22. The personality disorders are: antisocial, avoidant, borderline, _____, histrionic, narcissistic, obsessive-compulsive, _____, schizoid, and _____ .

23. _____ persons (sociopaths) seem to lack a conscience. They are emotionally shallow and _____ .

● *What problems result when a person suffers high levels of anxiety?*

24. Anxiety disorders, _____ disorders, and _____ disorders are characterized by high levels of anxiety, rigid defense mechanisms, and self-defeating behavior patterns.

25. The term nervous _____ has no formal meaning. However, people do experience _____ disorders, in which the person is overwhelmed by ongoing life stresses.

26. Anxiety disorders include _____ anxiety disorder (chronic anxiety and worry) and _____ disorder (anxiety attacks, panic, free-floating anxiety).

27. Panic disorder may occur with or without _____ (fear of public places or leaving the home).

28. Other anxiety disorders are _____ (fear of public places, _____ situations, or leaving the home) and specific phobia (irrational fears of specific objects or situations).

29. In the anxiety disorder called _____ _____, the person fears being observed, _____, embarrassed, or humiliated by others in social situations.

30. _____-compulsive disorders, and _____ stress disorder (PTSD) or _____ stress disorder (emotional disturbances triggered by severe stress) are also classified as anxiety disorders.

31. Dissociative disorders may take the form of dissociative _____ (loss of memory and personal identity) or dissociative _____ (confused identity and flight from familiar surroundings).

32. A more dramatic problem is dissociative _____ _____, in which a person develops multiple personalities.

33. _____ disorders center on physical complaints that mimic disease or disability.

34. In _____, persons think that they have specific diseases, when they are, in fact healthy.

35. In a _____ disorder, the person has numerous physical complaints. The person repeatedly seeks medical treatment for these complaints, but no organic problems can be found.

36. _____ _____ refers to discomfort for which there is no identifiable physical cause.

37. In _____ disorders, actual symptoms of disease or disability develop but their causes are actually psychological.

● *How do psychologists explain anxiety-based disorders?*

38. The _____ approach emphasizes unconscious conflicts within the personality as the cause of disabling anxiety.

39. The _____ approach emphasizes the effects of a faulty self-image.

40. The _____ approach emphasizes the effects of previous learning, particularly _____ learning.

41. Some patterns in anxiety disorders can be explained by the anxiety _____ hypothesis, which states that immediate relief from anxiety rewards _____ behaviors.

42. According to the _____ view, distorted thinking patterns cause anxiety disorders.

● *What are the general characteristics of psychotic disorders?*

43. _____ is a break in contact with _____.

44. Psychosis is marked by _____ (false beliefs), hallucinations, and _____ changes.

45. Other symptoms of psychosis are disturbed emotions, disturbed _____, and personality _____ .

46. An _____ psychosis is based on known injuries or diseases of the brain.

47. The most common organic problem is _____, a serious mental impairment in old age caused by deterioration of the brain.

48. One of most common causes of dementia is _____ disease.

● *How do delusional disorders differ from other forms of psychosis?*

49. A _____ of _____ disorder is based primarily on the presence of delusions.

50. Delusions may concern _____ (personal importance), persecution, infidelity, romantic attraction, or physical _____ .

51. The most common delusional disorder is _____ psychosis. Because they often have intense and irrational delusions of persecution, afflicted persons may be _____ if they believe they are threatened.

● *What forms does schizophrenia take? What causes it?*

52. Schizophrenia is distinguished by a split between thought and _____, and by delusions, hallucinations, and _____ difficulties.

53. _____ schizophrenia is marked by extreme personality _____ and silly, bizarre, or obscene behavior. Social impairment is usually extreme.

54. _____ schizophrenia is associated with stupor, mutism, waxy _____, and odd postures. Sometimes violent and agitated behavior also occurs.

55. In _____ schizophrenia (the most common type), outlandish delusions of _____ and persecution are coupled with psychotic symptoms and personality breakdown.

56. _____ schizophrenia is the term used to indicate a lack of clear-cut patterns of disturbance.

57. Current explanations of schizophrenia emphasize a combination of _____ stress, inherited susceptibility, and _____ abnormalities in the body or brain.

58. A number of _____ factors appear to increase the risk of developing schizophrenia. These include viral infection during the mother's pregnancy and birth complications.

59. Early _____ trauma and a disturbed family environment, especially one marked by _____ communication, also increase the risk of schizophrenia.

60. Studies of twins and other close relatives strongly support _____ as a major factor in schizophrenia.

61. Recent biochemical studies have focused on abnormalities in brain transmitter substances, especially _____ and its _____ sites.

62. Additional abnormalities in brain structure or function have been detected in schizophrenic brains by the use of _____ scans, _____ scans, and _____ scans.

63. The dominant explanation of schizophrenia is the stress-_____ model.

● *What are mood disorders? What causes depression?*

64. Mood disorders primarily involve disturbances of _____ or emotion.

65. Long-lasting, though relatively moderate, depression is called a _____ disorder.

66. Chronic, though moderate, swings in mood between depression and elation are called a _____ disorder.

67. In a _____ _____ disorder the person alternates between extreme _____ and depression.

68. In a _____ _____ disorder the person is mostly depressed, but has had at least one episode of _____ (mild mania).

69. The problem known as _____ _____ disorder involves extreme sadness and despondency, but no evidence of mania.

70. _____ depression is a mild to moderate depressive disorder that affects many women after they give birth. It is more serious than the more common maternity blues.

71. Major mood disorders more often appear to be _____ (produced from within) rather than reactions to external events.

72. Seasonal _____ disorder (SAD), which occurs during the winter months is another common form of depression. SAD is typically treated with _____ (exposure to bright light).

73. _____, psychoanalytic, _____, and behavioral theories of depression have been proposed. Heredity is clearly a factor in susceptibility to mood disorders.

74. _____ is any psychological treatment for behavioral or emotional problems. Major mental disorders are more often treated medically.

● *Why do people commit suicide? Can suicide be prevented?*

75. Suicide is _____ related to such factors as age, sex, and marital status.

76. Major _____ _____ for suicide include drug or alcohol abuse, a prior attempt, depression, hopelessness, _____ behavior, suicide by relatives, shame, failure, or rejection, and the availability of a firearm.

77. In individual cases the potential for suicide is best identified by a desire to escape, unbearable psychological _____, _____ psychological needs, and a constriction of options.

78. Suicidal thoughts usually precede suicide _____, which progress to suicide _____.

79. Suicide can often be prevented by the efforts of family, friends, and mental health professionals to establish communication and _____ with the person, and by gaining day-by-day _____ from her or him.

MASTERY TEST

1. The difference between an acute stress disorder and PTSD is
   a. how long the disturbance lasts   b. the severity of the stress   c. whether the anxiety is free-floating
   d. whether dissociative behavior is observed

2. A person is at greatest risk of becoming schizophrenic if he or she has
   a. schizophrenic parents   b. a schizophrenic fraternal twin   c. a schizophrenic mother
   d. a schizophrenic sibling

3. A core feature of all abnormal behavior is that it is
   a. statistically extreme   b. associated with subjective discomfort   c. ultimately maladaptive
   d. marked by a loss of contact with reality

4. Excess amounts of dopamine in the brain, or high sensitivity to dopamine provides one major explantion for the problem known as
   a. PTSD   b. schizophrenia   c. major depression   d. SAD

5. The descriptions "acro," and "claustro," and "pyro" refer to
   a. common obsessions   b. specific phobias   c. free-floating anxieties   d. hypochondriasis

6. Glove anesthesia strongly implies the existence of a _____ disorder.
   a. organic   b. depersonalization   c. somatization   d. conversion

7. In the stress-vulnerability model of psychosis, vulnerability is primarily attributed to
   a. heredity   b. exposure to influenza   c. psychological trauma   d. disturbed family life

8. A patient believes that she has a mysterious disease that is causing her body to "rot away." What type of symptom is she suffering from?
   a. bipolar   b. delusion   c. neurosis   d. cyclothymic

9. Phototherapy is used primarily to treat
   a. postseasonal depression   b. SAD   c. catatonic depression   d. affective psychoses

10. Psychopathology is defined as an inability to behave in ways that
    a. foster personal growth and happiness   b. match social norms   c. lead to personal achievement
    d. do not cause anxiety

11. Which of the following is NOT characteristic of suicidal thinking?
    a. desires to escape   b. psychological pain   c. frustrated needs   d. too many options

12. Fear of using the rest room in public is
    a. a social phobia   b. an acute stress disorder   c. a panic disorder   d. an adjustment disorder

13. A person who displays personality disintegration, waxy flexibility, and delusions of persecution suffers
    from _____ schizophrenia.
    a. disorganized   b. catatonic   c. paranoid   d. undifferentiated

14. You find yourself in an unfamiliar town and you can't remember your name or address. It is likely that
    you are suffering from
    a. paraphilia   b. Alzherimer's disease   c. a borderline personality disorder   d. a dissociative disorder

15. A major problem with statistical definitions of abnormality is
    a. calculating the normal curve   b. choosing dividing lines   c. that they do not apply to groups of
    people   d. that they do not take norms into account

16. DSM-IV-TR primarily describes and classifies _____ disorders.
    a. mental   b. organic   c. psychotic   d. cognitive

17. A person who is a frequent "checker" may have which disorder?
    a. agoraphobia   b. somatization   c. free-floating fugue   d. obsessive-compulsive

18. The most direct explanation for the anxiety reducing properties of self-defeating behavior is found in
    a. an overwhelmed ego   b. avoidance learning   c. the loss of meaning in one's life   d. the concept of
    existential anxiety

19. A person with a(an) _____ personality disorder might be described as "charming" by
    people who don't know the person well.
    a. avoidant   b. schizoid   c. antisocial   d. dependent

20. One of the most powerful situational contexts for judging the normality of behavior is
    a. culture   b. gender   c. statistical norms   d. private discomfort

21. A person who is manic most likely suffers from a(an) _____ disorder.
    a. anxiety   b. somatoform   c. organic   d. mood

22. The principal problem in paranoid psychosis is
    a. delusions   b. hallucinations   c. disturbed emotions   d. personality disintegration

23. A problem that may occur with or without agoraphobia is
    a. dissociative disorder b. somatoform disorder c. panic disorder d. obsessive-compulsive disorder

24. Hearing voices that do not exist is an almost sure sign of a _____ disorder.
    a. psychotic b. dissociative c. personality d. delusional

25. A conversion reaction is a type of _____ disorder.
    a. somatoform b. dissociative c. obsessive-compulsive d. postpartum

26. The existence, in the past, of "disorders" such as "drapetomania" and "nymphomania" suggests that judging normality is greatly affected by
    a. gender b. cultural disapproval c. levels of functioning d. subjective discomfort

27. Which of the following terms does NOT belong with the others?
    a. neurosis b. somatoform disorder c. personality disorder d. dissociative disorder

28. Threats to one's self-image are a key element in the _____ approach to understanding anxiety and disordered functioning.
    a. Freudian b. humanistic c. existential d. behavioral

29. Which of the following is NOT classified as an anxiety disorder?
    a. adjustment disorder b. panic disorder c. agoraphobia d. obsessive-compulsive disorder

30. Cyclothymic disorder is most closely related to
    a. reactive depression b. major depressive disorder c. bipolar disorder d. SAD

ANSWERS

Recite and Review

1. disorders, unhealthy
2. discomfort
3. high, low
4. standards
5. cultural
6. All
7. behavior, adapt
8. mental
9. *Manual, Mental*
10. reality, social
11. brain, diseases
12. mood, drugs
13. emotion
14. anxiety, anxiety
15. disease, cause
16. personality
17. personality
18. gender, sexual
19. anxiety
20. legal, court
21. maladaptive
22. borderline, compulsive
23. conscience, emotionally
24. anxiety, defense
25. life stresses
26. anxiety, floating
27. public, home
28. specific
29. observed, social
30. stress, anxiety
31. memory, dissociative
32. multiple
33. disease
34. healthy
35. physical, treatment
36. physical
37. psychological
38. unconscious
39. self-image
40. learning, learning

41. anxiety, relief
42. thinking
43. break
44. hallucinations
45. personality
46. diseases
47. organic, brain
48. dementia
49. delusions
50. persecution, romantic
51. persecution
52. split, thought
53. personality, Social
54. mutism, waxy
55. persecution
56. lack
57. stress, abnormalities
58. infection, birth
59. trauma, family
60. twins
61. transmitter
62. activity
63. stress
64. emotion
65. depression
66. depression, elation
67. depression
68. depressed, mania
69. mania
70. maternity blues
71. within, external
72. Seasonal, winter
73. behavioral
74. Major mental
75. Suicide
76. alcohol, drug, firearm
77. escape, options
78. thoughts
79. communication

Connections

1. f
2. a
3. g
4. j
5. b
6. c

7. i
8. d
9. e
10. h
11. c
12. e
13. a
14. j
15. b
16. d
17. i
18. f
19. h
20. g
21. h
22. i
23. g
24. a
25. j
26. b
27. d
28. f
29. c
30. e
31. c
32. e
33. h
34. a
35. j
36. g
37. i
38. b
39. f
40. d

Check Your Memory

1. T
2. F
3. T
4. T
5. T
6. T
7. T
8. F
9. F
10. T
11. F

12. F
13. F
14. T
15. F
16. T
17. F
18. T
19. F
20. F
21. F
22. T
23. T
24. T
25. F
26. F
27. T
28. T
29. T
30. T
31. F
32. T
33. F
34. F
35. T
36. T
37. T
38. F
39. F
40. F
41. T
42. F
43. T
44. F
45. T
46. F
47. T
48. T
49. T
50. F
51. T
22. T
53. F
54. T
55. F
56. T
57. T
58. T
59. T
60. F

61. T
62. F
63. T
64. T
65. F
66. T
67. F
68. T
69. T

Final Survey and Review

1. Psychopathology
2. subjective
3. Statistical
4. Social non-conformity
5. context
6. relative
7. maladaptive
8. psychological
9. *Diagnostic, Statistical*
10. Psychotic, hallucinations
11. Organic
12. Substance related
13. Mood, affect
14. Anxiety
15. Somatoform
16. Dissociative, amnesia
17. Personality
18. identity, dysfunctions
19. neurosis
20. Insanity
21. ingrained
22. dependent, paranoid, schizotypal
23. Antisocial, manipulative
24. dissociative, somatoform
25. breakdown, adjustment
26. generalized, panic
27. agoraphobia
28. agoraphobia, unfamiliar
29. social phobia, evaluated

30. Obsessive, post-traumatic, acute
31. amnesia, fugue
32. identity disorder
33. Somatoform
34. hypochondriasis
35. somatization
36. Somatoform pain
37. conversion
38. psychodynamic
39. humanistic
40. behavioral, avoidance
41. reduction, self-defeating
42. cognitive
43. Psychosis, reality
44. delusions, sensory
45. communication, disintegration
46. organic
47. dementia
48. Alzheimer's
49. diagnosis, delusional
50. grandeur, disease
51. paranoid, violent
52. emotion, communication
53. Disorganized, disintegration
54. Catatonic, flexibility
55. paranoid, grandeur
56. Undifferentiated
57. environmental, biochemical
58. environmental
59. psychological, deviant
60. heredity
61. dopamine, receptor
62. CT, MRI, PET
63. vulnerability
64. mood
65. dysthymic
66. cyclothymic
67. bipolar I, mania
68. bipolar II, hypomania
69. major depressive
70. postpartum

71. endogenous
72. affective, phototherapy
73. Biological, cognitive
74. Psychotherapy
75. statistically
76. risk factors, antisocial
77. pain, frustrated
78. threats, attempts
79. rapport, commitments

Mastery Test

1. a (p. 457)
2. a (p. 468)
3. c (p. 446)
4. b (p. 469)
5. b (p. 456)
6. d (p. 459)
7. a (p. 470)
8. b (p. 462)
9. b (p. 475)
10. a (p. 445)
11. d (p. 478)
12. a (p. 456)
13. d (p. 465, 468)
14. d (p. 458)
15. b (p. 446)
16. a (p. 448)
17. d (p. 457)
18. b (p. 460)
19. c (p. 453)
20. a (p. 446)
21. d (p. 449)
22. a (p. 464)
23. c (p. 456)
24. a (p. 462)
25. a (p. 459)
26. b (p. 447)
27. a (p. 451)
28. b (p. 460)
29. a (p. 455)
30. c (p. 472-473)

Chapter 14
Therapies

CHAPTER OVERVIEW

Psychotherapies may be classified as individual, group, insight, action, directive, non-directive, or supportive, and combinations of these. Primitive and superstitious approaches to mental illness have included trepanning and demonology. More humane treatment began in 1793 with the work of Philippe Pinel in Paris.

Freudian psychoanalysis seeks to release repressed thoughts and emotions from the unconscious. Brief psychodynamic therapy has largely replaced traditional psychoanalysis.

Client-centered (or person-centered) therapy is a non-directive humanistic technique dedicated to creating an atmosphere of growth. Existential therapies focus on the meaning of life choices. Gestalt therapy attempts to rebuild thinking, feeling, and acting into connected wholes.

Behavior therapists use behavior modification techniques such as aversion therapy, systematic desensitization, operant shaping, extinction, and token economies.

Cognitive therapists attempt to change troublesome thought patterns. In rational-emotive behavior therapy, clients learn to recognize and challenge their own irrational beliefs.

Group therapies, such as psychodrama and family therapy, may be based on individual therapy methods or special group techniques. Sensitivity groups, encounter groups, and large-group awareness trainings also try to promote constructive changes.

All psychotherapies offer a caring relationship, emotional rapport, a protected setting, catharsis, explanations for one's problems, a new perspective, and a chance to practice new behaviors. Many basic counseling skills underlie the success of therapies. Successful therapists may also need to overcome cultural barriers to be effective with people from diverse backgrounds.

Three medical approaches to the treatment of psychological disorders are pharmacotherapy, electroconvulsive therapy, and psychosurgery.

Mental hospitalization can serve as a treatment for psychological disorders. Prolonged hospitalization has been discouraged by deinstitutionalization and by partial-hospitalization policies. Community mental health centers attempt to prevent mental health problems before they become serious.

Cognitive and behavioral techniques such as covert sensitization, thought stopping, covert reinforcement, and desensitization can aid self-management. In most communities, competent therapists can be located through public sources or by referrals.

LEARNING OBJECTIVES

To demonstrate mastery of this chapter, you should be able to:

1. Define *psychotherapy*.
2. Describe each of the following approaches to therapy:
   a. individual therapy
   b. group therapy
   c. insight therapy
   d. action therapy
   e. directive therapy
   f. non-directive therapy
   g. time-limited therapy
   h. supportive therapy
3. Evaluate what a person can expect as possible outcomes from psychotherapy.
4. Briefly describe the history of the treatment of psychological problems, including in your description trepanning, demonology, exorcism, ergotism, and Pinel.
5. Explain why the first formal psychotherapy was developed.
6. List the four basic techniques used in psychoanalysis and explain their purpose.
7. Name and describe the therapy that is frequently used today instead of psychoanalysis. Describe the criticism that helped prompt the switch, including the concept of spontaneous remission.
8. Contrast client-centered (humanistic) therapy and psychoanalysis.
9. Describe client-centered therapy including the four conditions that should be maintained for successful therapy.
10. Explain the approach of existential therapy and compare and contrast it with client-centered therapy. Name and describe one example of existential therapy.
11. Name a key aspect of existential therapy.
12. Briefly describe Gestalt therapy, including its main emphasis.

The following objectives are related to the material in the "Exploring Psychology" section of the text.
13. Discuss the limitations of media phone-in psychologists and describe what the APA recommends should be the extent of their activities.
14. Discuss the advantages and disadvantages of telephone therapy, cybertherapy, and videoconferencing therapy.

15. Contrast the goal of behavior therapy with the goal of insight therapies.
16. Define *behavior modification* and state its basic assumption.
17. Explain the relationship of aversion therapy to classical conditioning.
18. Describe aversion therapy and explain how it can be used to stop smoking and drinking.
19. Explain how relaxation, reciprocal inhibition, and use of a hierarchy are combined to produce desensitization.
20. State what desensitization is used for and give an example of desensitization therapy or vicarious desensitization therapy.
21. Explain how virtual reality exposure may be used to treat phobias.
22. Very briefly describe eye-movement desensitization and reprocessing.
23. List and briefly describe the seven operant principles most frequently used by behavior therapists.

24. Explain how nonreinforcement and time out can be used to bring about extinction of a maladaptive behavior.
25. Describe a token economy including its advantages and possible disadvantages. Include the terms *token* and *target behavior* in your description.
26. Describe what sets cognitive therapists apart from behavior therapists.
27. List and describe three thinking errors which underlie depression and explain what can be done to correct such thinking.
28. Describe the effectiveness of cognitive therapy for depression.
29. Describe rational-emotive behavior therapy.
30. List the three core ideas which serve as the basis of most irrational beliefs.
31. Describe the advantages of group therapy.
32. Briefly describe each of the following group therapies:
    a. psychodrama (include role-playing, role reversal, and mirror technique)
    b. family therapy
    c. group awareness training (include sensitivity groups, encounter groups, and large group awareness training)
33. Evaluate the effectiveness of encounter groups and sensitivity groups. Include the concept of the therapy placebo effect.
34. Discuss the effectiveness of psychotherapy.
35. Describe the rate at which doses of therapy help people improve.
36. List the eight goals of psychotherapy, and state the four means used to accomplish the goals.
37. List and briefly describe the nine points or tips which can help a person when counseling a friend.
38. List and explain the seven characteristics of culturally skilled counselors.
39. Define *pharmacotherapy*.
40. List and describe the three major classes of drugs used to treat psychopathology
41. Discuss the advantages and disadvantages of the use of pharmacotherapy in the treatment of psychosis.
42. Describe the risk-benefit controversy for drugs such as Clozaril and Risperdal.
43. Describe what is known about the uses and effectiveness of the following techniques in the treatment of psychosis:
    a. electroconvulsive therapy
    b. psychosurgery (include the term *deep lesioning*)
44. Describe the role of hospitalization and partial hospitalization in the treatment of psychological disorders.
45. Explain what deinstitutionalization is and how halfway houses have attempted to help in the treatment of mental health.
46. Discuss the role of community mental health centers in mental health.

The following objectives are related to the material in the "Psychology in Action" section of the text.
47. Describe how covert sensitization, thought-stopping, and covert reinforcement can be used to reduce unwanted behavior.
48. Give an example of how you can overcome a common fear or break a bad habit using the steps given for desensitization.
49. List and describe four indicators that may signal the need for professional psychological help.
50. List six methods a person can use for finding a therapist.
51. Describe how one can choose a psychotherapist.

52. Distinguish among paraprofessionals, peer counselors, and self-help groups.
53. Summarize what is known about the importance of the personal qualities of the therapist and the client for successful therapy.
54. List six psychotherapy danger signals.

RECITE AND REVIEW

● *How do psychotherapies differ? How did modern therapies originate?*

Recite and Review: Pages 483-485

1. Psychotherapy is any psychological technique used to facilitate _____ changes in a person's personality, _____, or adjustment.
2. _____ therapies seek to produce personal understanding. Action therapies try to directly change troublesome thoughts, feelings, or behaviors.
3. Directive therapists provide strong _____. Non-directive therapists assist, but do not _____ their clients.
4. Supportive therapies provide on-going support, rather than actively promoting personal _____.
5. Therapies may be conducted either individually or in groups, and they may be _____ limited (restricted to a set number of sessions).
6. Primitive approaches to mental illness were often based on _____.
7. Trepanning involved boring a hole in the _____.
8. Demonology attributed mental disturbance to supernatural forces and prescribed _____ as the cure.
9. In some instances, the actual cause of bizarre behavior may have been ergotism or _____ fungus _____.
10. More humane treatment began in 1793 with the work of Philippe Pinel who created the first _____ _____ in Paris.

● *Is Freudian psychoanalysis still used?*

Recite and Review: Pages 485-486

11. Sigmund Freud's psychoanalysis was the first formal _____.
12. Psychoanalysis was designed to treat cases of hysteria (physical symptoms without known _____ causes).
13. Psychoanalysis seeks to release repressed thoughts, memories, and emotions from the _____ and resolve _____ conflicts.
14. The psychoanalyst uses _____ association, _____ analysis, and analysis of resistance and transference to reveal health-producing insights.

15. Some critics have argued that traditional psychoanalysis may frequently receive credit for _____ remissions of symptoms. However, psychoanalysis has been shown to be better than no treatment at all.

16. _____ psychodynamic therapy (which relies on psychoanalytic theory but is brief and focused) is as effective as other major therapies.

● *What are the major humanistic therapies?*

Recite and Review: Pages 487-490

17. _____ therapies try to help people live up to their potentials and to give tendencies for mental health to emerge.

18. Carl Rogers's client-centered (or _____-centered) therapy is non-directive and is dedicated to creating an atmosphere of _____.

19. In client-centered therapy, unconditional _____ regard, _____ (feeling what another is feeling), authenticity, and reflection are combined to give the client a chance to solve his or her own problems.

20. Existential therapies focus on the end result of the _____ one makes in life.

21. Clients in existential therapy are encouraged through confrontation and encounter to exercise free _____, to take responsibility for their _____, and to find _____ in their lives.

22. Frederick Perls's Gestalt therapy emphasizes immediate _____ of thoughts and feelings.

23. The goal of Gestalt therapy is to rebuild thinking, feeling, and acting into connected _____ and to help clients break through emotional blocks.

24. Media psychologists, such as those found on the radio are supposed to restrict themselves to _____ listeners, rather than actually doing _____.

25. Telephone therapists and cybertherapists working on the _____ may or may not be competent. Even if they are, their effectiveness may be severely limited.

26. In an emerging approach called telehealth, _____ is being done at a distance, through the use of videoconferencing (two-way _____ links).

● *What is behavior therapy?*

Recite and Review: Pages 490-493

27. Behavior therapists use various behavior modification techniques that apply _____ principles to change human behavior.

28. Classical conditioning is a basic form of _____ in which existing reflex responses are _____ with new conditioned stimuli.

29. In aversion therapy, classical conditioning is used to associate maladaptive behavior with _____ or other aversive events in order to inhibit undesirable responses.

30. To be most effective, aversive _____ must be response-contingent (closely connected with responses).

● *How is behavior therapy used to treat phobias, fears, and anxieties?*

Recite and Review: Pages 493-495

31. Classical conditioning also underlies _____ desensitization, a technique used to reduce fears, phobias, and anxieties.

32. In desensitization, gradual _____ and reciprocal inhibition break the link between fear and particular situations.

33. Typical steps in desensitization are: Construct a fear hierarchy; learn to produce total _____; and perform items on the hierarchy (from least to most disturbing).

34. Desensitization may be carried out in real settings or it may be done by vividly _____ scenes from the fear hierarchy.

35. Desensitization is also effective when it is administered vicariously; that is, when clients watch _____ perform the feared responses.

36. In a newly developed technique, virtual _____ exposure is used to present _____ stimuli to patients undergoing desensitization.

37. Another new technique called eye-movement desensitization shows promise as a treatment for traumatic _____ and _____ disorders.

● *What role does reinforcement play in behavior therapy?*

Recite and Review: Pages 496-498

38. Behavior modification also makes use of operant principles, such as positive reinforcement, non-reinforcement, extinction, punishment, shaping, stimulus _____, and _____ out.

39. Non-reward can extinguish troublesome behaviors. Often this is done by simply identifying and eliminating _____.

40. Time out is an extinction technique in which attention and approval are withheld following undesirable _____.

41. Time out can also be done by _____ a person from the setting in which misbehavior occurs, so that it will not be reinforced.

42. To apply positive reinforcement and operant shaping, symbolic rewards known as tokens are often used. Tokens allow _____ reinforcement of selected target _____.

43. Full-scale use of _____ in an institutional setting produces a token economy.

44. Toward the end of a token economy program, patients are shifted to social rewards such as recognition and _____.

● *Can therapy change thoughts and emotions?*

Recite and Review: Pages 498-500

45. Cognitive therapy emphasizes changing _____ patterns that underlie emotional or behavioral problems.

46. The goals of cognitive therapy are to correct distorted thinking and/or teach improved coping _____.

47. Aron Beck's cognitive therapy for depression corrects major distortions in thinking, including _____ perception, overgeneralization, and all-or-nothing _____.

48. In a variation of cognitive therapy called rational-emotive behavior therapy (REBT), clients learn to recognize and challenge their own irrational _____ which lead to upsetting consequences.

● *Can psychotherapy be done with groups of people?*

Recite and Review: Pages 500-502

49. Group therapy may be a simple extension of _____ methods or it may be based on techniques developed specifically for groups.

50. In psychodrama, individuals use _____ playing, _____ reversals, and the mirror technique to gain insight into incidents resembling their real-life problems.

51. In family therapy, the family group is treated as a _____ so that the entire _____ system is changed for the better.

52. Although they are not literally _____, sensitivity groups and encounter groups attempt to encourage positive personality change.

53. In recent years, commercially offered large-group awareness _____ have become popular.

54. The therapeutic benefits of large-group techniques are questionable and may reflect nothing more than a _____ placebo effect.

● *What do various therapies have in common?*

Recite and Review: Pages 502-505

55. To alleviate personal problems, all psychotherapies offer a caring relationship and _____ rapport in a protected _____.

56. All therapies encourage catharsis and they provide explanations for the client's _____.

57. In addition, psychotherapy provides a new perspective and a chance to practice new _____.

58. Many basic _____ skills are used in therapy. These include listening actively and helping to clarify the problem.

59. Effective therapists also focus on feelings and avoid giving unwanted _____.

60. It helps to accept the person's perspective, to reflect thoughts and feelings, and to be patient during _____.

61. In counseling it is important to use _____ questions when possible and to maintain confidentiality.

62. Many _____ barriers to effective counseling and therapy exist.

63. Culturally skilled _____ have the knowledge and skills needed to intervene successfully in the lives of clients from diverse cultural backgrounds.

64. The culturally skilled counselor must be able to establish rapport with a person from a _____ cultural background and adapt traditional theories and techniques to meet the needs of clients from non-European ethnic or racial groups.

● *How do psychiatrists treat psychological disorders?*

Recite and Review: Pages 505-509

65. Three _____ (bodily) approaches to treatment of psychosis are pharmacotherapy (use of _____), electroconvulsive therapy (ECT) (brain shock for the treatment of depression), and psychosurgery (surgical alteration of the _____).

66. Pharmacotherapy is done with _____ tranquilizers (anti-anxiety drugs), antipsychotics (which reduce delusions and _____), and antidepressants (_____ elevators).

67. All psychiatric drugs involve a trade-off between _____ and benefits.

68. _____ hospitalization is considered a form of treatment for mental disorders.

69. Prolonged hospitalization has been discouraged by deinstitutionalization (reduced use of commitment to treat mental disorders) and by _____-hospitalization policies.

70. Half-way _____ within the community can help people make the transition from a hospital or institution to _____ living.

71. Community mental health centers were created to help avoid or minimize

_____.

72. Community mental health centers also have as their goal the prevention of mental health problems through education, consultation, and _____ intervention.

● *How are behavioral principles applied to everyday problems? How would a person go about finding professional help?*

Recite and Review: PSYCHOLOGY IN ACTION

73. In covert sensitization, aversive _____ are used to discourage unwanted behavior.

74. Thought stopping uses mild _____ to prevent upsetting thoughts.

75. Covert reinforcement is a way to encourage desired _____ by mental rehearsal.

76. Desensitization pairs _____ with a hierarchy of upsetting images in order to lessen fears.

77. In most communities, a competent and reputable therapist can usually be located through public sources of information or by a _____.

78. Practical considerations such as _____ and qualifications enter into choosing a therapist. However, the therapist's personal characteristics are of equal importance.

79. Self-help _____, made up of people who share similar problems, can sometimes add valuable support to professional treatment.

CONNECTIONS

1. _____ trepanning
2. _____ exorcism
3. _____ ergotism
4. _____ Pinel
5. _____ Freud
6. _____ dream analysis
7. _____ transference
8. _____ spontaneous remission
9. _____ Rogers
10. _____ rephrasing

a. tainted rye
b. old relationships
c. hysteria
d. reflection
e. waiting list control
f. client-centered
g. Bicêtre
h. latent content
i. possession
j. release of evil spirits

11. _____ authenticity
12. _____ existentialist
13. _____ distance therapy
14. _____ Gestalt therapy
15. _____ rapid smoking
16. _____ desensitization
17. _____ time out
18. _____ target behaviors
19. _____ overgeneralization
20. _____ REBT

a. telehealth
b. operant extinction
c. no facades
d. thinking error
e. being in the world
f. token economy
g. whole experiences
h. aversion therapy
i. irrational beliefs
j. fear hierarchy

21. _____ psychodrama
22. _____ family therapy
23. _____ sensitivity group
24. _____ encounter group
25. _____ media psychologist
26. _____ therapeutic alliance
27. _____ catharsis
28. _____ covert sensitization
29. _____ covert reinforcement
30. _____ self-help group

a. public education
b. enhanced self-awareness
c. emotional release
d. positive imagery
e. shared problems
f. systems approach
g. aversive imagery
h. role reversals
i. caring relationship
j. intense interactions

CHECK YOUR MEMORY

Check Your Memory: Pages 483-485

1. A particular psychotherapy could be both insight- and action-oriented. T or F?
2. With the help of psychotherapy, chances of improvement are fairly good for phobias and low self-esteem. T or F?
3. Psychotherapy is sometimes used to encourage personal growth for people who are already functioning well. T or F?
4. Personal autonomy, a sense of identity, and feelings of personal worth are elements of mental health. T or F?
5. Trepanning was really an excuse to kill people since none of the patients survived. T or F?
6. Exorcism sometimes took the form of physical torture. T or F?
7. Trepanning was the most common treatment for ergotism. T or F?
8. Pinel was the first person to successfully treat ergotism. T or F?
9. The problem Freud called hysteria is now called a somatoform disorder. T or F?

Check Your Memory: Pages 485-486

10. During free association, patients try to remember the earliest events in their lives. T or F?
11. Freud called transference the royal road to the unconscious. T or F?
12. The manifest content of a dream is its surface or visible meaning. T or F?
13. In an analysis of resistance, the psychoanalyst tries to understand a client's resistance to forming satisfying relationships. T or F?
14. Therapists use direct interviewing as part of brief psychodynamic therapy. T or F?
15. If members of a waiting list control group improve at the same rate as people in therapy, it demonstrates that the therapy is effective. T or F?

Check Your Memory: Pages 487-490

16. Through client-centered therapy, Carl Rogers sought to explore unconscious thoughts and feelings. T or F?
17. The client-centered therapist does not hesitate to react with shock, dismay, or disapproval to a client's inappropriate thoughts or feelings. T or F?
18. In a sense, the person-centered therapist acts as a psychological mirror for clients. T or F?
19. Existential therapy emphasizes our ability to freely make choices. T or F?
20. According to the existentialists, our choices must be courageous. T or F?
21. Existential therapy emphasizes the integration of fragmented experiences into connected wholes. T or F?
22. Fritz Perls was an originator of telehealth. T or F?
23. Gestalt therapy may be done individually or in a group. T or F?
24. Gestalt therapists urge clients to intellectualize their feelings. T or F?
25. The APA suggests that media psychologists should discuss only problems of a general nature. T or F?
26. The problem with doing therapy by videoconferencing is that facial expressions are not available to the therapist or the client. T or F?

Check Your Memory: Pages 490-493

27. Aversion therapy is based primarily on operant conditioning. T or F?

28. For many children, the sight of a hypodermic needle becomes a conditioned stimulus for fear because it is often followed by pain. T or F?

29. Rapid smoking creates an aversion because people must hyperventilate to smoke at the prescribed rate. T or F?

30. About one half of all people who quit smoking begin again. T or F?

31. In aversion therapy for alcohol abuse, the delivery of shock must appear to be response-contingent to be most effective. T or F?

32. Poor generalization of conditioned aversions to situations outside of therapy can be a problem. T or F?

Check Your Memory: Pages 493-495

33. During desensitization, the steps of a hierarchy are used to produce deep relaxation. T or F?

34. Relaxation is the key ingredient of reciprocal inhibition. T or F?

35. Clients typically begin with the most disturbing item in a desensitization hierarchy. T or F?

36. Desensitization is most effective when people are directly exposed to feared stimuli. T or F?

37. Live or filmed models are used in vicarious desensitization. T or F?

38. During eye-movement desensitization, clients concentrate on pleasant, calming images. T or F?

Check Your Memory: Pages 496-498

39. Operant punishment is basically the same thing as non-reinforcement. T or F?

40. Shaping involves reinforcing ever closer approximations to a desired response. T or F?

41. An undesirable response can be extinguished by reversing stimulus control. T or F?

42. Misbehavior tends to decrease when others ignore it. T or F?

43. To be effective, tokens must be tangible rewards, such as slips of paper or poker chips. T or F?

44. The value of tokens is based on the fact that they can be exchanged for other reinforcers. T or F?

45. A goal of token economies is to eventually switch patients to social reinforcers.

Check Your Memory: Pages 498-500

46. Cognitive therapy is especially successful in treating depression. T or F?

47. Depressed persons tend to magnify the importance of events. T or F?

48. Cognitive therapy is as effective as drugs for treating many cases of depression. T or F?

49. Stress inoculation is a form of rational-emotive behavior therapy. T or F?

50. The A in the ABC analysis of REBT stands for "anticipation." T or F?

51. The C in the ABC analysis of REBT stands for "consequence." T or F?

Check Your Memory: Pages 500-502

52. The mirror technique is the principal method used in family therapy. T or F?

53. Family therapists try to meet with the entire family unit during each session of therapy. T or F?

54. A "trust walk" is a typical sensitivity group exercise. T or F?

55. Sensitivity groups attempt to tear down defenses and false fronts. T or F?

56. Large-group awareness training has been known to create emotional crises where none existed before. T or F?

Check Your Memory: Pages 502-505

57. Half of all people who begin psychotherapy feel better after 8 sessions. T or F?

58. Emotional rapport is a key feature of the therapeutic alliance. T or F?

59. Therapy gives clients a chance to practice new behaviors. T or F?

60. Competent counselors do not hesitate to criticize clients, place blame when it is deserved, and probe painful topics. T or F?

61. "Why don't you . . . Yes, but . . ." is a common game used to avoid taking responsibility in therapy. T or F?

62. Closed questions tend to be most helpful in counseling another person. T or F?

63. Cultural barriers to effective counseling include differences in language, social class, and non-verbal communication. T or F?

64. A necessary step toward becoming a culturally skilled counselor is to adopt the culture of your clients as your own. T or F?

Check Your Memory: Pages 505-509

65. Major mental disorders are primarily treated with psychotherapy. T or F?

66. When used for long periods of time, major tranquilizers can cause a neurological disorder. T or F?

67. Two percent of all patients taking clozaril suffer from a serious blood disease. T or F?

68. ECT treatments are usually given in a series of 20 to 30 sessions, occurring once a day. T or F?

69. ECT is most effective when used to treat depression. T or F?

70. The prefrontal lobotomy is the most commonly performed type of psychosurgery today. T or F?

71. Psychosurgeries performed by deep lesioning can be reversed if necessary. T or F?

72. In the approach known as partial hospitalization, patients live at home. T or F?

73. Deinstitutionalization increased the number of homeless persons living in many communities. T or F?

74. Most half-way houses are located on the grounds of mental hospitals. T or F?

75. Crisis intervention is typically one of the services provided by community mental health centers. T or F?

Check Your Memory: PSYCHOLOGY IN ACTION

76. Disgusting images are used in thought stopping. T or F?

77. To do covert sensitization, you must first learn relaxation exercises. T or F?

78. Covert reinforcement should be visualized before performing steps in a fear hierarchy. T or F?

79. The tension-release method is used to produce deep relaxation. T or F?

80. Significant changes in your work, relationships, or use of drugs or alcohol can be signs that you should seek professional help. T or F?

81. Marital problems are the most common reason for seeing a mental health professional. T or F?

82. For some problems, paraprofessional counselors and self-help groups are as effective as professional psychotherapy. T or F?

83. All major types of psychotherapy are about equally successful. T or F?

FINAL SURVEY AND REVIEW

● *How do psychotherapies differ? How did modern therapies originate?*

1. _____ is any psychological technique used to facilitate positive changes in a person's _____, behavior, or adjustment.

2. Insight therapies seek to produce personal understanding. _____ therapies try to directly change troublesome thoughts, feelings, or behaviors.

3. _____ therapists provide strong guidance. _____ therapists assist, but do not guide their clients.

4. _____ therapies provide on-going assistance, rather than actively promoting personal change.

5. Therapies may be conducted either _____ or in _____, and they may be time _____ (restricted to a set number of sessions).

6. _____ approaches to mental illness were often based on superstition.

7. _____ involved boring a hole in the skull.

8. _____ attributed mental disturbance to supernatural forces and prescribed exorcism as the cure.

9. In some instances, the actual cause of bizarre behavior may have been _____, a type of _____ poisoning.

10. More humane treatment began in 1793 with the work of Philippe _____ who created the first mental hospital in _____.

● *Is Freudian psychoanalysis still used?*

11. Sigmund _____ _____ was the first formal psychotherapy.

12. Psychoanalysis was designed to treat cases of _____ (physical symptoms without known physical causes).

13. Psychoanalysis seeks to release _____ thoughts, memories, and emotions from the unconscious and resolve unconscious conflicts.

14. The psychoanalyst uses free _____, dream analysis, and analysis of _____ and transference to reveal health-producing insights.

15. Some critics have argued that traditional psychoanalysis may frequently receive credit for spontaneous _____ of symptoms. However, psychoanalysis has been shown to be better than no treatment at all.

16. Brief _____ therapy (which relies on _____ theory but is brief and focused) is as effective as other major therapies.

● *What are the major humanistic therapies?*

17. Humanistic therapies try to help people live up to their _____ and to give tendencies for mental health to emerge.

18. Carl _____ client-centered (or person-centered) therapy is non-_____ and is dedicated to creating an atmosphere of growth.

19. In client-centered therapy, _____ positive regard, empathy, authenticity, and _____ (restating thoughts and feelings) are combined to give the client a chance to solve his or her own problems.

20. _____ therapies focus on the end result of the choices one makes in life.

21. Clients in existential therapy are encouraged through _____ and _____ to exercise free will, to take responsibility for their choices, and to find meaning in their lives.

22. Frederick Perls's _____ therapy emphasizes immediate awareness of thoughts and feelings.

23. The goal of Perls's approach is to rebuild thinking, feeling, and acting into connected wholes and to help clients break through _____ _____.

24. _____ psychologists, such as those found on the radio are supposed to restrict themselves to educating listeners, rather than actually doing therapy.

25. Telephone therapists and _____ working on the Internet may or may not be competent. Even if they are, their effectiveness may be severely limited.

26. In an emerging approach called _____, therapy is being done at a distance, through the use of _____ (two-way audio-video links).

● *What is behavior therapy?*

27. _____ therapists use various behavior _____ techniques that apply learning principles to change human behavior.

28. _____ conditioning is a basic form of learning in which existing _____ responses are associated with new conditioned stimuli.

29. In _____ therapy, classical conditioning is used to associate maladaptive behavior with pain or other unpleasant events in order to inhibit undesirable responses.

30. To be most effective, aversive stimuli must be _____ (closely connected with responses).

● *How is behavior therapy used to treat phobias, fears, and anxieties?*

31. Classical conditioning also underlies systematic _____, a technique used to reduce fears, phobias, and anxieties.

32. In this approach, gradual adaptation and reciprocal _____ break the link between fear and particular situations.

33. Typical steps are: Construct a fear _____; learn to produce total relaxation; and perform items on the _____ (from least to most disturbing).

34. Desensitization may be carried out in real settings or it may be done by vividly imagining scenes from the _____ _____.

35. Desensitization is also effective when it is administered _____; that is, when clients watch models perform the feared responses.

36. In a newly developed technique, _____ reality _____ is used to present fear stimuli to patients undergoing desensitization.

37. Another new technique called _____ desensitization shows promise as a treatment for traumatic memories and stress disorders.

● *What role does reinforcement play in behavior therapy?*

38. Behavior modification also makes use of _____ principles, such as positive reinforcement, non-reinforcement, _____ (eliminating responses), punishment, _____ (molding responses), stimulus control, and time out.

39. _____ can extinguish troublesome behaviors. Often this is done by simply identifying and eliminating reinforcers.

40. Time out is an _____ technique in which attention and approval are withheld following undesirable responses.

41. Time out can also be done by removing a person from the _____ in which misbehavior occurs, so that it will not be _____.

42. To apply positive reinforcement and operant shaping, symbolic rewards known as _____ are often used. These allow immediate reinforcement of selected _____ behaviors.

43. Full-scale use of symbolic rewards in an institutional setting produces a _____ _____.

44. Toward the end of such programs, patients are shifted to _____ rewards such as recognition and approval.

● *Can therapy change thoughts and emotions?*

45. _____ therapy emphasizes changing thinking patterns that underlie emotional or behavioral problems.

46. Its goals are to correct distorted thinking and/or teach improved _____ skills.

47. Aron _____ therapy for depression corrects major distortions in thinking, including selective perception, _____ , and all-or-nothing thinking.

48. In a variation called _____ _____ therapy (REBT), clients learn to recognize and challenge their own irrational beliefs which lead to upsetting consequences.

● *Can psychotherapy be done with groups of people?*

49. _____ therapy may be a simple extension of individual methods or it may be based on techniques developed specifically for _____.

50. In _____, individuals use role playing, role _____, and the mirror technique to gain insight into incidents resembling real-life problems.

51. In _____ therapy, the _____ group is treated as a unit so that the entire family system is changed for the better.

52. Although they are not literally psychotherapies, sensitivity groups and _____ groups attempt to encourage positive personality change.

53. In recent years, commercially offered large-group _____ trainings have become popular.

54. The therapeutic benefits of large-group techniques are questionable and may reflect nothing more than a therapy _____ effect.

● *What do various therapies have in common?*

55. To alleviate personal problems, all psychotherapies offer a caring relationship and emotional _____ in a _____ setting.

56. All therapies encourage _____ (emotional release) and they provide explanations for the client's problems.

57. In addition, psychotherapy provides a new _____ and a chance to practice new behaviors.

58. Many basic counseling skills are used in therapy. These include listening _____ and helping to _____ the problem.

59. Effective therapists also focus on _____ and avoid giving unwanted advice.

60. It helps to accept the person's _____, to _____ thoughts and feelings, and to be patient during silences.

61. In counseling it is important to use open questions when possible and to maintain _____.

62. Many cultural _____ to effective counseling and therapy exist.

63. _____ _____ counselors have the knowledge and skills needed to intervene successfully in the lives of clients from diverse cultural backgrounds.

64. The aware counselor must be able to establish _____ with a person from a different cultural background and _____ traditional theories and techniques to meet the needs of clients from non-European ethnic or racial groups.

● *How do psychiatrists treat psychological disorders?*

65. Three somatic approaches to treatment of psychosis are _____ (use of drugs), _____ therapy (ECT), and psychosurgery.

66. Pharmacotherapy is done with minor tranquilizers (anti-anxiety drugs), _____ (which control delusions and hallucinations), and _____ (mood elevators).

67. All psychiatric drugs involve a trade-off between risks and _____.

68. Psychiatric _____ is considered a form of treatment for mental _____.

69. Prolonged hospitalization has been discouraged by _____ (reduced use of commitment to treat mental disorders) and by partial-hospitalization policies.

70. _____ houses within the community can help people make the transition from a hospital or institution to independent living.

71. _____ _____ health centers were created to help avoid or minimize hospitalization.

72. These centers also have as their goal the _____ of mental health problems through education, consultation, and crisis _____.

● *How are behavioral principles applied to everyday problems?*

73. In _____ sensitization, aversive images are used to discourage unwanted behavior.
74. _____ _____ uses mild punishment to prevent upsetting thoughts.
75. Covert _____ is a way to encourage desired responses by mental rehearsal.
76. _____ pairs relaxation with a hierarchy of upsetting images in order to lessen fears.

● *How would a person go about finding professional help?*

77. In most communities, a _____ and reputable therapist can usually be located through public sources of information or by a referral.
78. Practical considerations such as cost and qualifications enter into choosing a therapist. However, the therapist's _____ _____ are of equal importance.
79. _____ groups made up of people who share similar _____ can sometimes add valuable support to professional treatment.

MASTERY TEST

1. To demonstrate that spontaneous remissions are occurring, you could use a
   a. patient-defined hierarchy   b. waiting list control group   c. target behavior group
   d. short-term dynamic correlation

2. In desensitization, relaxation is induced to block fear, a process known as
   a. systematic adaptation   b. vicarious opposition   c. stimulus control   d. reciprocal inhibition

3. Role reversals and the mirror technique are methods of
   a. psychodrama   b. person-centered therapy   c. family therapy   d. brief psychodynamic therapy

4. One thing that both trepanning and exorcism have in common is that both were used
   a. to treat ergotism   b. by Pinel in the Bicêtre Asylum   c. to remove spirits
   d. to treat cases of hysteria

5. Unconditional positive regard is a concept particularly associated with
   a. Beck   b. Frankl   c. Perls   d. Rogers

6. Many of the claimed benefits of large-group awareness trainings appear to represent a therapy _____ effect.
   a. remission   b. education   c. placebo   d. transference

7. Personal change is LEAST likely to be the goal of
   a. supportive therapy   b. action therapy   c. desensitization   d. humanistic therapy

8. Inducing seizures is a standard part of using
   a. Gestalt therapy   b. antidepressants   c. ECT   d. cybertherapy

9. Which counseling behavior does not belong with the others listed here?
   a. paraphrasing   b. judging   c. reflecting   d. active listening

10. In psychoanalysis, the process most directly opposite to free association is
    a. resistance   b. transference   c. symbolization   d. remission

11. Identification of target behaviors is an important step in designing
    a. a desensitization hierarchy   b. activating stimuli   c. token economies   d. encounter groups

12. A person who wants to lose weight looks at a dessert and visualizes maggots crawling all over it. The person is obviously using
    a. systematic adaptation   b. covert sensitization   c. stress inoculation   d. systematic desensitization

13. Which of the following is NOT a humanistic therapy?
    a. client-centered   b. Gestalt   c. existential   d. cognitive

14. Not many emergency room doctors drive without using their seatbelts. This observation helps explain the effectiveness of
    a. systematic desensitization   b. aversion therapy   c. covert reinforcement   d. the mirror technique

15. Telephone counselors have little chance of using which element of effective psychotherapy?
    a. empathy   b. non-directive reflection   c. the therapeutic alliance   d. accepting the person's frame of reference

16. Which of the following is a self-management technique?
    a. thought stopping   b. vicarious reality exposure   c. REBT   d. EMDR

17. A good example of a non-directive insight therapy is _____ therapy.
    a. client-centered   b. Gestalt   c. psychoanalytic   d. brief psychodynamic

18. Which statement about psychotherapy is true?
    a. Most therapists are equally successful.   b. Most techniques are equally successful.
    c. Therapists and clients need not agree about the goals of therapy.   d. Effective therapists instruct their clients not to discuss their therapy with anyone else.

19. Analysis of resistances and transferences is a standard feature of
a. client-centered therapy b. Gestalt therapy c. REBT d. psychoanalysis

20. Both classical and operant conditioning are the basis for
a. desensitization b. token economies c. behavior therapy d. aversion therapy

21. Rational-emotive behavior therapy is best described as
a. insight, non-directive, individual b. insight, supportive, individual c. action, supportive, group
d. action, directive, individual

22. Deep lesioning is a form of
a. ECT b. psychosurgery c. pharmacotherapy d. PET

23. Identifying and removing rewards is a behavioral technique designed to bring about
a. operant shaping b. extinction c. respondent aversion d. token inhibition

24. Culturally skilled counselors must be aware of their own cultural backgrounds, as well as
a. the percentage of ethnic populations in the community b. that of their clients c. the importance
of maintaining confidentiality d. the life goals of minorities

25. A behavioral therapist would treat acrophobia with
a. desensitization b. aversion therapy c. covert sensitization d. cybertherapy

26. Which technique most closely relates to the idea of non-directive therapy?
a. confrontation b. dream analysis c. role reversal d. reflection

27. Fifty percent of psychotherapy patients say they feel better after the first _____ sessions.
a. 4   b. 8   c. 12   d. 20

28. Overgeneralization is a thinking error that contributes to
a. depression b. somatization c. phobias d. emotional reprocessing

29. Death, freedom, and meaning are special concerns of
a. REBT b. cognitive therapy c. existential therapy d. psychodrama

30. An intense awareness of present experience and breaking through emotional impasses is the heart of
a. action therapy b. Gestalt therapy c. time-limited therapy d. REBT

31. The ABCs of REBT stand for
a. anticipation, behavior, conduct b. action, behavior, conflict c. activating experience,
belief, consequence d. anticipation, belief, congruent experience

32. Which of the following in NOT a "distance therapy"?
a. REBT b. telephone therapy c. cybertherapy d. telehealth

33. Virtual reality exposure is a type of
    a. psychodrama   b. ECT therapy   c. cognitive therapy   d. desensitization

34. ECT is most often used to treat
    a. psychosis   b. anxiety   c. hysteria   d. depression

35. Which of the following is most often associated with community mental health programs?
    a. pharmacotherapy   b. covert reinforcement   c. crisis intervention   d. REBT

ANSWERS

Recite and Review

1. positive, behavior
2. Insight
3. guidance, guide
4. change
5. time
6. superstition
7. skull
8. exorcism
9. ergot, poisoning
10. mental hospital
11. psychotherapy
12. physical
13. unconscious, unconscious
14. free, dream
15. spontaneous
16. Brief
17. Humanistic
18. person, growth
19. positive, empathy
20. choices
21. will, choices, meaning
22. awareness
23. wholes
24. educating, therapy
25. Internet
26. therapy, audio-video
27. learning
28. learning, associated
29. pain
30. stimuli
31. systematic
32. adaptation
33. relaxation
34. imagining
35. models
36. reality, fear
37. memories, stress
38. control, time
39. reinforcers
40. responses
41. removing
42. immediate, behaviors
43. tokens
44. approval
45. thinking
46. skills
47. selective, thinking
48. beliefs
49. individual
50. role, role
51. unit, family
52. psychotherapies
53. trainings
54. therapy
55. emotional, setting
56. problems
57. behaviors
58. counseling
59. advice
60. silences
61. open
62. cultural
63. counselors
64. different
65. somatic, drugs, brain
66. minor, hallucinations, mood
67. risks
68. Mental or Psychiatric
69. partial
70. houses, independent
71. hospitalization
72. crisis
73. images
74. punishment
75. responses
76. relaxation
77. referral
78. cost (or fees)
79. groups

Connections

1. j
2. i
3. a
4. g
5. c
6. h
7. b

8. e
9. f
10. d
11. c
12. e
13. a
14. g
15. h
16. j
17. b
18. f
19. d
20. i
21. h
22. f
23. b
24. j
25. a
26. i
27. c
28. g
29. d
30. e

Check Your Memory

1. T
2. T
3. T
4. T
5. F
6. T
7. F
8. F
9. T
10. F
11. F
12. T
13. F
14. T
15. F
16. F
17. F
18. T
19. T
20. T
21. F
22. F

23. T
24. F
25. T
26. F
27. F
28. T
29. F
30. T
31. T
32. T
33. F
34. T
35. F
36. T
37. T
38. F
39. F
40. T
41. F
42. T
43. F
44. T
45. T
46. T
47. T
48. T
49. F
50. F
51. T
52. F
53. F
54. T
55. F
56. T
57. T
58. T
59. T
60. F
61. T
62. F
63. T
64. F
65. F
66. T
67. T
68. F
69. T
70. F
71. F

72. T
73. T
74. F
75. T
76. F
77. F
78. F
79. T
80. T
81. F
82. T
83. T

Final Survey and Review

1. Psychotherapy, personality
2. Action
3. Directive, Non-directive
4. Supportive
5. individually, groups, limited
6. Primitive
7. Trepanning
8. Demonology
9. ergotism, fungus
10. Pinel, Paris
11. Freud's, psychoanalysis
12. hysteria
13. repressed
14. association, resistance
15. remissions
16. psychodynamic, psychoanalytic
17. potentials
18. Rogers's, directive
19. unconditional, reflection
20. Existential
21. confrontation, encounter
22. Gestalt
23. emotional blocks
24. Media
25. cybertherapists
26. telehealth, videoconferencing
27. Behavior, modification
28. Classical, reflex
29. aversion
30. response-contingent

31. desensitization
32. inhibition
33. hierarchy, hierarchy
34. fear hierarchy
35. vicariously
36. virtual, exposure
37. eye-movement
38. operant, extinction, shaping
39. Non-reward (or non-reinforcement)
40. extinction
41. setting, reinforced
42. tokens, target
43. token economy
44. social
45. Cognitive
46. coping
47. Beck's, overgeneralization
48. rational-emotive behavior
49. Group, groups
50. psychodrama, reversals
51. family, family
52. encounter
53. awareness
54. placebo
55. rapport, protected
56. catharsis
57. perspective
58. actively, clarify
59. feelings
60. perspective, reflect

61. confidentiality
62. barriers
63. Culturally skilled
64. rapport, adapt
65. pharmacotherapy, electroconvulsive
66. antipsychotics, antidepressants
67. benefits
68. hospitalization, disorders
69. deinstitutionalization
70. Half-way
71. Community mental
72. prevention, intervention
73. covert
74. Thought stopping
75. reinforcement
76. Desensitization
77. competent
78. personal characteristics
79. Self-help, problems

Mastery Test

1. b (p. 486)
2. d (p. 493)
3. a (p. 501)
4. c (p. 484-485)
5. d (p. 488)
6. c (p. 502)

7. a (p. 483)
8. c (p. 506)
9. b (p. 504)
10. a (p. 486)
11. c (p. 497)
12. b (p. 510)
13. d (p. 498)
14. b (p. 492)
15. c (p. 503)
16. a (p. 510)
17. a (p. 483, 487)
18. b (p. 513)
19. d (p. 486)
20. c (p. 491)
21. d (p. 483, 499)
22. b (p. 507)
23. b (p. 496)
24. b (p. 505)
25. a (p. 493)
26. d (p. 488)
27. b (p. 502)
28. a (p. 498)
29. c (p. 488)
30. b (p. 488)
31. c (p. 499)
32. a (p. 489-490)
33. d (p. 494)
34. d (p. 506)
35. c (p. 508)

Chapter 15
Gender and Sexuality

CHAPTER OVERVIEW

A person's sex is determined by a combination of genetic sex, gonadal sex, hormonal sex, genital sex, and gender identity. The development of primary and secondary sexual characteristics is influenced by androgens and estrogens. Prenatal hormones may exert a biological biasing effect that combines with social factors to influence psychosexual development.

On most psychological dimensions, men and women are more alike than they are different. Social factors are especially apparent in learned gender identity and the effects of gender roles. Gender role socialization accounts for most observed male/female differences. Psychological androgyny is related to greater personal adaptability.

"Normal" sexual behavior is defined differently by various cultures. There is little difference in male and female sexual responsiveness. Sexual orientation refers to whether a person is heterosexual, homosexual, or bisexual. A combination of hereditary, biological, social, and psychological influences combine to produce one's sexual orientation.

Human sexual response can be divided into four phases: (1) excitement; (2) plateau; (3) orgasm; and (4) resolution, which apply to both males and females.

Atypical sexual behavior can produce troubling sexual disorders such as pedophilia and fetishism. Such disorders are called paraphilias.

Attitudes toward sexual behavior have grown more liberal, but actual changes in behavior have been more gradual. During the last 20 years there has been a steady increase in the incidence of sexually transmitted diseases, which has altered patterns of sexual behavior.

The principal problems in sexual adjustment are desire disorders, arousal disorders, orgasm disorders, and sexual pain disorders. Behavioral methods and counseling techniques can alleviate each problem. However, communication skills that foster and maintain intimacy are the real key to successful relationships.

LEARNING OBJECTIVES

To demonstrate mastery of this chapter, you should be able to:

1. Distinguish between the terms *sex* and *gender*. Differentiate primary from secondary sex characteristics and state (in general) what causes them.

2. Define or describe the following terms or concepts:
   a. menarche   b. ovulation   c. menopause   d. gonads
   e. estrogens   f. androgens   g. testosterone
3. List and describe the five dimensions of sex.
4. Explain how a person's sex develops. Include in your discussion a description of these conditions:
   a. androgen insensitivity   b. hermaphroditism
   c. androgenital syndrome   d. biological biasing effect
5. Describe the relationship between sex and intelligence.
6. Differentiate gender identity from gender role and explain how gender identity is formed.
7. Discuss whether there are universal psychological differences between males and females.
8. Define *gender role stereotypes*. Discuss how these stereotypes ignore the diversity of humanity.
9. Describe the effects of socialization on gender roles and include a discussion of instrumental and expressive behaviors.

The following objective is related to the material in the "Exploring Psychology" section of the text.
10. Explain the meaning of the term *androgyny* and its relationship to masculinity, femininity, and adaptability.

11. Describe the development of sexual behavior in humans and show how cultural norms influence that development. Define the term *erogenous zones*.
12. Explain the concept of a sexual script.
13. Discuss the differences between males and females in their degree of arousal to erotic stimuli.
14. Explain what causes differences in sex drives in males and females.
15. Describe the effects of alcohol, castration, and aging on the sex drive.
16. Discuss the frequency, importance, normality, and acceptability of masturbation.
17. Describe the factors that determine one's sexual orientation.
18. Describe the effect of heredity and hormones on one's sexual orientation.
19. Discuss homosexuality in terms of incidence, acceptability, psychological normality, and when homosexuals develop their sexual orientation.
20. Define the terms *homophobia* and *heterosexism*, and describe their significance to homosexuals.
21. List in order and briefly describe the four phases of sexual response in men and women.
22. Discuss the debate concerning possible differences between vaginal and clitoral orgasms and how the issue has been resolved.
23. Describe what is known concerning gender differences in sexual response styles in these two areas: rate of passage through the sexual phases and sexual responsiveness.
24. Explain the difference between public and private standards of sexual behavior.
25. Explain what sets true sexual deviations apart from other sexual activity.
26. Define paraphilia, and list and define eight paraphilias.
27. Describe exhibitionism, including who the offenders are, why they do it, and how one's reactions may encourage them.
29. Describe child molestation including who does it, what the offenders are like, and the factors that affect the seriousness of the molestation.
30. List seven ways to recognize molestation from a child's behavior.
31. List six tactics of molesters
32. Briefly discuss the damaging impact of child molestation on the victim.

33. List the two characteristics that emerge in the picture of sexual deviance.

34. List or describe four changes that have taken place in sexual attitudes or behavior that lead some people to label the differences a sexual revolution.

35. Summarize the current status of the sexual revolution. Explain how your answer reflects on the position of the double standard in our society.

36. Describe how the changing sexual attitudes and values of the society interact with one's personal freedom. Include the term *acquaintance rape*.

37. Describe the research demonstrating the relationship between gender role stereotyping and rape.

38. List and discuss five rape myths.

39. Explain why rape is not viewed by experts as primarily a sexual act.

40. Briefly describe what is currently known about the factors affecting the spread of AIDS. Include in your answer a discussion of "at-risk" groups, risky behaviors, and the impact that AIDS has on sexual practices.

The following objectives are related to the material in the "Psychology in Action" section of your text.

41. Describe the following sexual problems including the nature, cause, and treatment of each:
   a. desire disorders
       1. hypoactive sexual desire
       2. sexual aversion
   b. arousal disorders
       1. male erectile disorder
       2. female sexual arousal disorder
   c. orgasm disorders
       1. female orgasmic disorder
       2. male orgasmic disorder
       3. premature ejaculation
   d. sexual pain disorders
       1. dyspareunia
       2. vaginismus

42. Explain what is meant by referring to sex as a form of communication within a relationship.

43. List four elements of a healthy sexual relationship.

44. List seven techniques that can be followed to encourage effective communication in a relationship.

RECITE AND REVIEW

● *What are the basic dimensions of sex?*

Recite and Review: Pages 518-522

1. Physical differences between males and females can be divided into _____ and _____ sexual characteristics.

2. Primary sexual characteristics are the _____ and internal reproductive organs.

3. Secondary sexual characteristics are bodily features such as breast development, body _____, and facial hair.

4. Reproductive maturity in females is signaled by menarche (the onset of _____).
Soon after, ovulation (the release of _____, or eggs) begins.

5. The development of sexual characteristics is influenced by androgens (_____ sex hormones)
and estrogens (_____ sex hormones) secreted by the gonads (sex _____).

6. A person's sex can be broken down into genetic sex, gonadal sex, _____ sex, genital
sex, and _____ identity.

7. Sexual development begins with _____ sex (*XX* or *XY* chromosomes). Two *X*
chromosomes normally produce a _____; an *X* plus a *Y* produces a _____.

8. During prenatal sexual development, the presence of testosterone produces _____ genitals;
an absence of testosterone produces _____ genitals.

9. Androgen insensitivity, exposure to progestin, and the androgenital _____ result in
_____ ambiguities called hermaphroditism.

10. Many researchers believe that prenatal _____ can exert a biological biasing
_____ that combines with social factors present after birth to influence psychosexual development.

11. On most psychological dimensions, men and women are more _____ than they are
_____.

● *How does one's sense of maleness or femaleness develop?*

Recite and Review: Pages 522-524

12. Social factors are especially apparent in learned gender identity (a private sense of
_____ or _____) and the effect of gender roles (patterns of behavior
defined as male or female within a particular culture).

13. Gender identity, which is based to a large extent on labeling, usually becomes stable by age ____ or ____
years.

14. Gender roles contribute to the development of _____ _____ stereotypes (oversimplified
beliefs about the nature of men and women) that often distort perceptions about the kinds of occupations for
which men and women are suited.

15. _____ _____ socialization (learning gender roles) seems to account for most observed
male/female differences.

16. Parents tend to encourage _____ in instrumental behaviors and _____ in expressive
behaviors.

● *What is psychological androgyny (and is it contagious)?*

Recite and Review: Pages 524-526

17. Research conducted by Sandra Bem indicates that roughly one third of all persons are androgynous (they
possess both _____ and _____ traits).

18. Androgyny is measured with the *Bem* _____ _____ *Inventory* (BSRI).

19. Being _____ means that a person is independent and assertive.

20. Being _____ means that a person is nurturant and interpersonally oriented.

21. Psychological _____ appears related to greater adaptability or flexibility in behavior.

● *What are the most typical patterns of human sexual behavior?*

Recite and Review: Pages 527-532

22. Sexual behavior, including orgasm (sexual _____) is apparent soon after birth and expressed in various ways throughout life.

23. Sexual arousal is related to stimulation of the body's erogenous zones (areas that produce erotic _____), but cognitive elements such as _____ and images are equally important.

24. "Normal" sexual behavior is defined differently by various _____. Also, each person uses learned sexual scripts (plots or mental plans) to guide sexual behavior.

25. There is little difference in sexual _____ between males and females.

26. Evidence suggests that the sex drive peaks at a _____ age for females than it does for males, although this difference is diminishing.

27. Sex _____ in both males and females may be related to bodily levels of androgens.

28. Nocturnal _____ are a normal, but relatively minor, form of sexual release.

29. _____ (removal of the gonads) may or may not influence sex drive in humans, depending on how sexually experienced a person is. Sterilization (a vasectomy or tubal ligation) does not alter sex drive.

30. There is a gradual _____ in the frequency of sexual intercourse with increasing age.

31. Masturbation is a normal, harmless behavior practiced by a large percentage of the population. For many, masturbation is an important part of sexual self-_____.

32. Sexual orientation refers to one's degree of emotional and erotic attraction to members of the same _____, opposite _____, or both _____.

33. A person may be heterosexual, _____, or bisexual.

34. A combination of hereditary, biological, social, and psychological influences combine to produce one's _____ _____.

35. As a group, homosexual men and women do not differ psychologically from _____.

36. However, gay men and lesbians are frequently affected by homophobia (fear of _____) and heterosexism (the belief that heterosexuality is more natural than homosexuality).

● *To what extent do males and females differ in sexual response?*

Recite and Review: Pages 532-535

37. In a series of landmark studies, William _____ and Virginia Johnson directly observed sexual response in a large number of adults.

38. Human sexual response can be divided into four phases: (1) _____; (2) plateau; (3) _____; and (4) resolution.

39. Both males and females may go through all four stages in ____ or ____ minutes. But during lovemaking, most females typically take longer than this, averaging from 10 to 20 minutes.

40. Males experience a refractory period after _____ and ejaculation. Only 5 percent of men are _____-orgasmic.

41. Fifteen percent of women are consistently _____-orgasmic, and at least 48 percent are capable of _____ orgasm.

42. There do not appear to be any differences between "vaginal _____" and "clitoral _____" in the female.
43. Mutual _____ has been abandoned by most sex counselors as the ideal in lovemaking.

● *What are the most common sexual disorders?*

Recite and Review: Pages 535-536

44. Definitions of sexual deviance are highly _____. Many "sexually deviant" behaviors are acceptable in private or in some _____.
45. Sexual _____ that often cause difficulty are called paraphilias.
46. Some paraphilias include: pedophilia (sex with children), _____ (sexual arousal associated with inanimate objects), voyeurism (viewing the genitals of others without their permission), and _____ (displaying the genitals to unwilling viewers).
47. Other paraphilias are: transvestic fetishism (achieving sexual arousal by wearing clothing of the opposite sex), sexual _____ (deriving sexual pleasure from inflicting pain), sexual _____ (desiring pain as part of the sex act), and frotteurism (sexually touching or rubbing against a non-consenting person).
48. Exhibitionists are rarely dangerous and can best be characterized as sexually _____ and immature.
49. The effects of child molestation vary greatly, depending on the _____ of the molestation and the child's relationship to the molester.

● *Have recent changes in attitudes affected sexual behavior?*

Recite and Review: Pages 536-539

50. Attitudes toward sexual behavior, especially the behavior of others, have become more liberal, but actual changes in sexual _____ have been more gradual.
51. Another change has been _____ and more frequent sexual activity among adolescents and young adults, including larger percentages of people who have premarital _____.
52. Also evident are a greater acceptance of _____ sexuality and a narrowing of differences in male and female patterns of sexual _____. In other words, the double standard is fading.
53. Acquaintance (_____) rape and _____-supportive myths and attitudes remain major problems.
54. _____ is primarily a violent crime of aggression rather than a sex crime.

● *What impacts have sexually transmitted diseases had on sexual behavior?*

Recite and Review: Pages 539-542

55. During the last 20 years there has been a steady increase in the incidence of sexually transmitted _____ (STDs).
56. Part of this increase is due to the emergence of _____ _____ deficiency syndrome (AIDS) caused by the human immunodeficiency _____ (HIV).
57. STDs have had a sizable impact on patterns of sexual behavior, including increased awareness of high-_____ behaviors and some curtailment of _____ taking.

● *What are the most common sexual adjustment problems? How are they treated?*

Recite and Review: PSYCHOLOGY IN ACTION

58. The principal problems in sexual adjustment are _____ disorders, arousal disorders, orgasm disorders, and sexual _____ disorders.

59. Desire disorders include hypoactive _____ _____ (a loss of sexual desire) and _____ aversion (fear or disgust about engaging in sex).

60. Arousal disorders include _____ erectile disorder and _____ sexual arousal disorder.

61. Orgasm disorders are male orgasmic disorder (retarded _____), premature _____, and female orgasm disorder (an inability to reach orgasm during lovemaking).

62. Sexual pain disorders are dyspareunia (_____ intercourse) and vaginismus (_____ _____ of the vagina).

63. Behavioral methods such as sensate _____ and the squeeze technique have been developed to alleviate each problem. In addition, counseling can be quite helpful.

64. However, most sexual adjustment problems are closely linked to the general health of a couple's _____.

65. For this reason, communication skills that foster and maintain _____ are the key to successful relationships.

CONNECTIONS

1. _____	pelvic bone	
2. _____	urethra	
3. _____	labia minora	
4. _____	ovary	
5. _____	vagina	
6. _____	uterus	
7. _____	rectum	
8. _____	fallopian tube	
9. _____	clitoris	
10. _____	labia majora	
11. _____	urinary bladder	
12. _____	cervix	

a.
b.
c.
d.
e.
f.
g.

l.
k.
j.
i.
h.

13. _____	androgen	a. ovaries or testes
14. _____	estrogen	b. cultural pattern
15. _____	genetic sex	c. self-perception
16. _____	gonadal sex	d. AIDS
17. _____	hermaphroditism	e. female hormone
18. _____	gender identity	f. man-woman
19. _____	gender role	g. pain disorder
20. _____	androgyny	h. *XX* or *XY*
21. _____	STD	i. androgenital syndrome
22. _____	dyspareunia	j. testosterone

23. _____	Cowper's gland
24. _____	glans penis
25. _____	urethra
26. _____	seminal vesicle
27. _____	vas deferens
28. _____	pelvic bone
29. _____	urinary bladder
30. _____	testis
31. _____	rectum
32. _____	urethral orifice
33. _____	epididymis
34. _____	prostate

CHECK YOUR MEMORY

Check Your Memory: Pages 518-522

1. Primary sexual characteristics involve differences in the reproductive organs and the breasts. T or F?
2. The term menarche refers to the ending of regular monthly fertility cycles in females. T or F?
3. The female gonads are the ovaries. T or F?
4. Cowper's glands are female reproductive structures. T or F?
5. All individuals normally produce both androgens and testosterones. T or F?
6. Transsexuals are persons who have had their genetic sex altered medically. T or F?
7. Without testosterone, a human embryo will develop into a female. T or F?
8. Androgen insensitivity results in the development of female genitals. T or F?

9. Differences in male and female scores on the SAT have declined in recent years. T or F?

10. Observed differences in the abilities of males and females are based on averages, they tell nothing about a particular person. T or F?

Check Your Memory: Pages 522-524

11. Gender identity refers to all the behaviors that are defined as male or female by one's culture. T or F?

12. Babies are perceived differently and treated differently when they are labeled as males than when they are labeled as females. T or F?

13. Women continue to receive unequal pay for work comparable to that of men. T or F?

14. Even though their culture is quite different, the sex roles of Tchambuli men and women are almost identical to those in North America. T or F?

15. Boys are allowed to roam over wider areas than girls are. T or F?

16. Expressive behaviors are those that directly express a person's desire to attain a goal. T or F?

Check Your Memory: Pages 524-526

17. The BSRI consists of 20 masculine traits and 20 feminine traits. T or F?

18. About 50 percent of all people who take the BSRI are scored as androgynous. T or F?

19. Masculine men and feminine women consistently choose to engage in sex-appropriate activities. T or F?

20. Masculine men find it difficult to accept support from others. T or F?

21. Androgynous persons tend to be more satisfied with their lives than non-androgynous persons are. T or F?

Check Your Memory: Pages 527-532

22. Sexual scripts determine when, where, and with whom we are likely to express sexual feelings. T or F?

23. Women are less physically aroused by erotic stimuli than men are. T or F?

24. Women may engage in sexual activity at any time during their menstrual cycles. T or F?

25. More women than men have sexual dreams that result in orgasm. T or F?

26. Drunkenness lowers sexual arousal and performance. T or F?

27. Sterilization tends to abolish the sex drive in the sexually inexperienced. T or F?

28. Masturbation typically ends soon after people get married. T or F?

29. The average frequency of sexual intercourse declines dramatically between the ages of 30 and 39. T or F?

30. Your sexual orientation is revealed, in part, by who you have erotic fantasies about. T or F?

31. Gay males are converted to homosexuality during adolescence by other homosexuals. T or F?

32. Sexual orientation is a very stable personal characteristic. T or F?

33. Sexual orientation is influenced by heredity. T or F?

34. Hormone imbalances cause most instances of homosexuality and bisexuality. T or F?

35. Homosexual persons tend to discover their sexual orientation at a later age than heterosexual persons do. T or F?

Check Your Memory: Pages 532-535

36. Masters and Johnson's data on human sexuality was restricted to questionnaires and interviews. T or F?

37. During the excitement phase of sexual response, the nipples become erect in both males and females. T or F?

38. In males, orgasm is always accompanied by ejaculation. T or F?

39. Almost all women experience a short refractory period after ejaculation. T or F?

40. Both orgasm and resolution tend to last longer in females than they do in males. T or F?

41. Contemporary research has confirmed that clitoral orgasms are an inferior form of sexual response. T or F?

42. Women tend to go through the phases of sexual response more slowly than men do. T or F?

43. One woman in 3 does not experience orgasm during the first year of marriage. T or F?

Check Your Memory: Pages 535-536

44. Oral sex and masturbation are formally classified as paraphilias. T or F?

45. Frotteurism refers to sex with children. T or F?

46. Most exhibitionists are male and married. T or F?

47. An exhibitionist who approaches closer than arm's length may be dangerous. T or F?

48. In the majority of cases of child molesting, the offender is an acquaintance or relative of the child. T or F?

49. Child molesting is especially likely to be harmful if the molester is someone the child deeply trusts. T or F?

Check Your Memory: Pages 536-539

50. In recent decades the gap between sexual values and actual behavior has narrowed. T or F?

51. A majority of young adults continue to believe that premarital sex is unacceptable. T or F?

52. The incidence of extramarital sex has not changed much in the last 40 years. T or F?

53. The majority of men and women have sexual experiences before marriage. T or F?

54. About 12 percent of all adult Americans are sexually abstinent. T or F?

55. Women who are raped usually asked for trouble by wearing sexy clothes. T or F?

56. One woman in 70 will be raped in her lifetime. T or F?

57. The majority of rapists are friends or acquaintances of the victim. T or F?

58. Males high in sex role stereotyping are more aroused by stories about rape than males low in sex role stereotyping. T or F?

Check Your Memory: Pages 539-542

59. The first symptoms of AIDS may not appear for up to 7 years. T or F?

60. HIV infections are spread by direct contact with body fluids. T or F?

61. The AIDS epidemic has dramatically altered the sexual behavior of college students. T or F?

62. Most women who contract the HIV virus today do so through intravenous drug use. T or F?

63. It is unwise to count on a partner for protection from HIV infection. T or F?

64. Gonorrhea can be prevented by vaccination. T or F?

65. Hepatitis B can be prevented by vaccination. T or F?

66. Chlamydia is now the most common STD among men. T or F?

67. Many people suffering from STDs are asymptomatic. T or F?

Check Your Memory: PSYCHOLOGY IN ACTION

68. In a desire disorder the person desires sex, but does not become sexually aroused. T or F?

69. A person who is repelled by sex and seeks to avoid it suffers from a sexual aversion. T or F?

70. Men suffering from primary erectile dysfunction have never had an erection. T or F?

71. The squeeze technique is the most commonly recommended treatment for erectile disorders. T or F?

72. The majority of erectile dysfunctions are psychogenic. T or F?

73. Treatment for female sexual arousal disorder usually involves sensate focus. T or F?

74. Female orgasmic disorder is the female equivalent of premature ejaculation in the male. T or F?

75. Both males and females can experience dyspareunia. T or F?

76. Masters and Johnson regard all sexual problems as mutual, or shared by both parties. T or F?

77. Gunnysacking is an important communication skill that all couples should master. T or F?

78. Rather than telling your partner what he or she thinks, you should ask her or him. T or F?

FINAL SURVEY AND REVIEW

● *What are the basic dimensions of sex?*

1. Physical differences between males and females can be divided into primary and secondary
_____ _____.

2. _____ refers to the genitals and internal _____ organs.

3. _____ refers to bodily features such as _____ development in females, body shape, and facial _____.

4. Reproductive maturity in females is signaled by _____ (the onset of menstruation). Soon after, _____ (the release of eggs) begins.

5. The development of sexual characteristics is influenced by _____ (male sex hormones) and _____ (female sex hormones) secreted by the _____ (sex glands).

6. A person's sex can be broken down into _____ sex, _____ sex, hormonal sex, _____ sex, and gender identity.

7. Sexual development begins with genetic sex (*XX* or *XY* _____). Two ___s normally produce a female ___ plus a ___ produces a male.

8. During prenatal sexual development, the presence of _____ produces male _____; its absence produces female _____.

9. _____ insensitivity, exposure to progestin, and the androgenital syndrome result in sexual ambiguities called _____.

10. Many researchers believe that _____ hormones can exert a biological _____ effect that combines with social factors present after birth to influence psychosexual development.

11. On most _____ dimensions, men and women are more alike than they are different.

● *How does one's sense of maleness or femaleness develop?*

12. Social factors are especially apparent in learned _____ _____ (a private sense of maleness or femaleness) and the effect of _____ _____ (patterns of behavior defined as male or female within a particular culture).

13. Gender identity, which is based to a large extent on _____, usually becomes stable by age 3 or 4 years.

14. Gender roles contribute to the development of gender role _____ (oversimplified beliefs about the nature of men and women) that often distort perceptions about the kinds of occupations for which men and women are suited.

15. Gender role _____ (learning gender roles) seems to account for most observed male/female differences.

16. Parents tend to encourage boys in _____ behaviors (goal-directed actions) and girls in _____ (emotional) behaviors.

● *What is psychological androgyny (and is it contagious)?*

17. Research conducted by Sandra Bem indicates that roughly one _____ of all persons are _____ (they possess both masculine and feminine traits).

18. Androgyny is measured with the _____ *Sex Role* _____ (BSRI).

19. Being masculine means that a person is _____ and assertive.

20. Being feminine means that a person is _____ (helpful and comforting) and interpersonally oriented.

21. Psychological androgyny appears related to greater _____ or flexibility in behavior.

● *What are the most typical patterns of human sexual behavior?*

22. Sexual behavior, including _____ (sexual climax) is apparent soon after birth and expressed in various ways throughout life.

23. Sexual arousal is related to stimulation of the body's _____ zones (areas that produce erotic pleasure), but _____ elements such as thoughts and images are equally important.

24. "Normal" sexual behavior is defined differently by various cultures. Also, each person uses learned sexual _____ (plots or mental _____) to guide sexual behavior.

25. There is little _____ in sexual behavior between males and females.

26. Evidence suggests that the sex drive peaks at a later age for _____ than it does for _____, although this difference is diminishing.

27. Sex drive in both males and females may be related to bodily levels of _____.

28. _____ orgasms, which occur during sleep, are a normal form of sexual release.

29. Castration (removal of the gonads) may or may not influence sex drive in humans, depending on how sexually experienced a person is. _____ (a vasectomy or tubal ligation) does not alter sex drive.

30. There is a gradual decline in the _____ of sexual intercourse with increasing _____. However, many elderly persons remain sexually active and great variations exist at all ages.

31. _____ (sexual self-stimulation) is a normal, harmless behavior practiced by a large percentage of the population. For many, it is an important part of sexual self-discovery.

32. Sexual _____ refers to one's degree of emotional and erotic attraction to members of the same sex, opposite sex, or both sexes.

33. A person may be _____, homosexual, or _____.

34. A combination of _____, biological, _____, and psychological influences combine to produce one's sexual orientation.

35. As a group, _____ men and women do not differ psychologically from _____.

36. However, gay men and lesbians are frequently affected by _____ (fear of homosexuality) and _____ (the belief that heterosexuality is better than homosexuality).

● *To what extent do males and females differ in sexual response?*

37. In a series of landmark studies, William Masters and Virginia _____ directly observed sexual response in a large number of adults.

38. Human sexual response can be divided into four phases: (1) excitement; (2) _____; (3) orgasm; and (4) _____.

39. Both males and females may go through all four stages in 4 or 5 minutes. But during lovemaking, most _____ typically take longer than this, averaging from 10 to 20 minutes.

40. Males experience a _____ period after orgasm and ejaculation. Only 5 percent of men are multi-_____.

41. _____ percent of women are consistently _____, and at least 48 percent are capable of multiple orgasm.

42. There do not appear to be any differences between "_____ orgasms" and "_____ orgasms" in the female.

43. _____ orgasm has been abandoned by most sex counselors as the ideal in lovemaking.

● *What are the most common sexual disorders?*

44. Definitions of _____ _____ are highly subjective. Many publicly disapproved sexual behaviors are acceptable in private or in some cultures.

45. Sexual deviations that often cause difficulty are called _____ (destructive deviations in sexual preferences or behavior).

46. Some of these problems include: _____ (sex with children), fetishism (sexual arousal associated with inanimate objects), _____ (viewing the genitals of others without their permission), and exhibitionism (displaying the genitals to unwilling viewers).

47. Others are: _____ fetishism (achieving sexual arousal by wearing clothing of the opposite sex), sexual sadism (deriving sexual pleasure from inflicting pain), sexual masochism (desiring pain as part of the sex act), and _____ (sexually touching or rubbing against a non-consenting person).

48. _____ ("flashers") are rarely dangerous and can best be characterized as sexually inhibited and immature.

49. The effects of child molestation vary greatly, depending on the severity of the _____ and the child's _____ to the molester.

● *Have recent changes in attitudes affected sexual behavior?*

50. _____ toward sexual behavior, especially the behavior of others, have become more _____, but actual changes in sexual behavior have been more gradual.

51. Another change has been earlier and more frequent sexual activity among adolescents and young adults, including larger percentages of people who have _____ intercourse.

52. Also evident are a greater acceptance of female sexuality and a narrowing of differences in male and female patterns of sexual behavior. In other words, the _____ _____ is fading.

53. _____ (date) rape and rape-supportive _____ (false beliefs) and attitudes remain major problems.

54. Rape is primarily a violent crime of _____ rather than a sex crime.

● *What impacts have sexually transmitted diseases had on sexual behavior?*

55. During the last 20 years there has been a steady increase in the incidence of _____ _____ diseases (STDs).

56. Part of this increase is due to the emergence of acquired immune _____ syndrome (AIDS) caused by the human _____ virus (HIV).

57. _____ have had a sizable impact on patterns of sexual behavior, including increased awareness of high-risk behaviors and some curtailment of risk taking.

● *What are the most common sexual adjustment problems? How are they treated?*

58. The principal problems in sexual adjustment are desire disorders, _____ disorders, _____ disorders, and sexual pain disorders.

59. Desire disorders include _____ sexual desire (a loss of sexual desire) and sexual _____ (fear or disgust about engaging in sex).

60. Arousal disorders include male _____ disorder and female sexual _____ disorder.

61. Orgasm disorders are male orgasmic disorder (_____ ejaculation), _____ ejaculation, and female _____ disorder (an inability to reach orgasm during lovemaking).

62. Sexual pain disorders are _____ (painful intercourse) and _____ (muscle spasms of the vagina).

63. Behavioral methods such as _____ focus and the _____ technique for premature ejaculation have been developed to alleviate each problem. In addition, counseling can be quite helpful.

64. However, most sexual _____ problems are closely linked to the general health of a couple's relationship.

65. For this reason, _____ skills that foster and maintain intimacy are the key to successful relationships.

MASTERY TEST

1. The strength of the sex drive in both men and women increases when _____ levels are higher in the body.
   a. androgen b. progestin c. ovulin d. androgenin

2. Worldwide, the main source of HIV infection is
   a. heterosexual sex b. homosexual sex c. intravenous drug use d. blood transfusions

3. Boys are encouraged to be strong, aggressive, dominant, and achieving through the process of
   a. biological biasing   b. sexual orienting   c. gender adaptation   d. gender role socialization

4. Before birth, a genetic male will develop as a female if which condition exists?
   a. excessive progestin   b. an androgen insensitivity   c. the androgenital syndrome
   d. the testes produce testosterone

5. Concerning masturbation, it can be concluded that
   a. masturbation typically ceases after marriage   b. after age 30, women masturbate more than men do
   c. those who are most sexually active masturbate the most   d. masturbation slows psychosexual development

6. One of the greatest changes in attitudes toward sex in North America is a greater tolerance for
   a. teenage pregnancies   b. the sexual behavior of others   c. the double standard   d. STDs

7. The squeeze technique is typically used to treat
   a. dyspareunia   b. vaginismus   c. female sexual arousal disorder   d. premature ejaculation

8. In a female, gonadal sex is determined by the presence of
   a. estrogens   b. androgens   c. ovaries   d. a vagina and uterus

9. A policeman who accepts emotional support from others, especially from women, would most likely be scored as _____ on the BSRI.
   a. masculine   b. feminine   c. androgynous   d. expressive-nurturant

10. Which of the following is POOR advice for couples who want to communicate effectively and maintain intimacy?
    a. Avoid gunnysacking.   b. Avoid expressing anger.   c. Don't try to win.   d. Don't be a mind-reader.

11. The aspect of sex that is essentially formed by age 4 is
    a. gender identity   b. gender roles   c. sexual scripting   d. psychological androgyny

12. In a female, broadening of the hips and breast development are
    a. primary sexual characteristics   b. secondary sexual characteristics   c. caused by the release of androgens   d. associated with the presence of a *Y* chromosome

13. The first two phases of the sexual response cycle are
    a. excitement, arousal   b. arousal, orgasm   c. excitement, plateau   d. stimulation, arousal

14. A special danger in the transmission of STDs is that many people are _____ at first.
    a. non-infectious   b. androgynous   c. androgenital   d. asymptomatic

15. The presence of a *Y* chromosome is associated with
    a. hermaphroditism   b. prenatal testosterone   c. menarche   d. the presence of progestin

16. With respect to the behaviors parents encourage in their children, which is a correct match?
    a. controlling-female b. goal-oriented-female c. expressive-male d. instrumental-male

17. Which condition is LEAST likely to lower sexual performance?
    a. sterilization b. castration c. extreme alcohol intoxication d. sexual aversion

18. Prenatally masculinized females tend to be tomboys during childhood, and observation that supports the
    a. biological biasing effect b. estrogen paradox c. view that gender is genetically determined
    d. idea that gender role socialization is dominant

19. Which of the following increases the likelihood that a man will commit rape?
    a. drinking alcohol b. being high in gender role stereotyping c. belief in rape myths
    d. all of the preceding

20. Gender role _____ treat learned gender role differences as if they were real gender differences.
    a. labels b. behavior patterns c. stereotypes d. templates

21. Regarding sexual response it can be said that
    a. orgasm and resolution tend to last longer in women b. a short refractory period occurs just before orgasm in males c. some women skip the arousal phase of the cycle d. men are incapable of having second orgasms

22. The decline of the double standard refers to abandoning different standards for
    a. risky sex and "safe" sex b. heterosexual relationships and homosexual relationships c. sexuality before and after marriage d. male and female sexual behavior

23. Declines in the differences in male and female scores on the SAT call into question which concept?
    a. the androgenital syndrome b. the biological biasing effect c. gender role socialization
    d. gender identity

24. When expectations of a friendly first date clash with an attempted seduction the problem can be attributed to differences in
    a. gender roles b. erogenous confrontation c. gender myths d. sexual scripts

25. Which statement concerning sexual orientation is TRUE?
    a. Sexual orientation is partly hereditary. b. Homosexuality is caused by a hormone imbalance.
    c. Sexual orientation can be changed fairly easily. d. Heterosexual persons tend to discover their sexual orientation at a later date than homosexual persons do.

26. Which of the following is NOT one of the basic dimensions of sex?
    a. genetic sex b. gonadal sex c. hormonal sex d. androgenital sex

27. Pedophilia, fetishism, and sadism are classified as
    a. the three basic forms of child molestation b. STDs c. paraphilias d. hormonal disorders

28. All but one of the following is a rape myth. Which is NOT a myth?
a. Women who get raped ask for it in one way or another.   b. A majority of rapes are committed by a friend or acquaintance of the victim.   c. Women who are sexually active are usually lying if they say they were raped.   d. Many women who are raped secretly enjoy it.

29. Which of the following diseases is currently untreatable?
a. gonorrhea   b. chlamydia   c. syphilis   d. hepatitis B

30. The male sexual disorder that corresponds most closely to female sexual arousal disorder is
a. sexual aversion   b. erectile disorder   c. premature ejaculation   d. dyspareunia

ANSWERS

Recite and Review

1. primary, secondary
2. genitals
3. shape
4. menstruation, ova
5. male, female, glands
6. hormonal, gender
7. genetic, female, male
8. male, female
9. syndrome, sexual
10. hormones, effect
11. alike, different
12. maleness, femaleness
13. 3, 4
14. gender role
15. Gender role
16. boys, girls
17. masculine, feminine
18. *Sex Role*
19. masculine
20. feminine
21. androgyny
22. climax
23. pleasure, thoughts
24. cultures
25. responsiveness
26. later
27. drive
28. orgasms
29. Castration

30. decline (or decrease)
31. discovery
32. sex, sex, sex
33. homosexual
34. sexual orientation
35. heterosexuals
36. homosexuality
37. Masters
38. excitement, orgasm
39. 4, 5
40. orgasm, multi
41. multi, multiple
42. orgasms, orgasms
43. orgasm
44. subjective, cultures
45. deviations
46. fetishism, exhibitionism
47. sadism, masochism
48. inhibited
49. severity
50. behavior
51. earlier, intercourse
52. female, behavior
53. date, rape
54. Rape
55. diseases
56. acquired immune, virus
57. risk, risk
58. desire, pain
59. sexual desire, sexual
60. male, female

61. ejaculation, ejaculation
62. painful, muscle spasms
63. focus
64. relationship
65. intimacy

Connections

1. d
2. h
3. f
4. b
5. j
6. l
7. i
8. a
9. e
10. g
11. c
12. k
13. j
14. e
15. h
16. a
17. i
18. c
19. b
20. f
21. d
22. g

23. d
24. g
25. i
26. a
27. j
28. k
29. l
30. e
31. c
32. f
33. h
34. b

Check Your Memory

1. F
2. F
3. T
4. F
5. F
6. F
7. T
8. T
9. T
10. T
11. F
12. T
13. T
14. F
15. T
16. F
17. F
18. F
19. T
20. T
21. T
22. T
23. F
24. T
25. F
26. T
27. F
28. F
29. F
30. T
31. F
32. T
33. T
34. F
35. T

36. F
37. T
38. F
39. F
40. T
41. F
42. T
43. T
44. F
45. F
46. T
47. T
48. T
49. T
50. T
51. F
52. T
53. T
54. T
55. F
56. F
57. T
58. T
59. T
60. T
61. F
62. F
63. T
64. F
65. T
66. F
67. T
68. F
69. T
70. T
71. F
72. T
73. T
74. F
75. T
76. T
77. F
78. T

Final Survey and Review

1. sexual characteristics
2. Primary, reproductive
3. Secondary, breast, hair
4. menarche, ovulation
5. androgens, estrogens, gonads
6. genetic, gonadal, genital
7. chromosomes, *X, X, Y*
8. testosterone, genitals, genitals
9. Androgen, hermaphroditism
10. prenatal, biasing
11. psychological
12. gender identity, gender roles
13. labeling
14. stereotypes
15. socialization
16. instrumental, expressive
17. third, androgynous
18. *Bem, Inventory*
19. independent
20. nurturant
21. adaptability
22. orgasm
23. erogenous, cognitive
24. scripts, plans
25. difference
26. females, males
27. androgens
28. Nocturnal
29. Sterilization
30. frequency, age
31. Masturbation
32. orientation
33. heterosexual, bisexual
34. hereditary, social
35. homosexual, heterosexuals
36. homophobia, heterosexism
37. Johnson
38. plateau, resolution
39. females
40. refractory, orgasmic
41. Fifteen, multi-orgasmic
42. vaginal, clitoral
43. Mutual
44. sexual deviance
45. paraphilias
46. pedophilia, voyeurism
47. transvestic, frotteurism
48. Exhibitionists
49. molestation, relationship
50. Attitudes, liberal
51. premarital

52. double standard
53. Acquaintance, myths
54. aggression
55. sexually transmitted
56. deficiency, immunodeficiency
57. STDs
58. arousal, orgasm
59. hypoactive, aversion
60. erectile, arousal
61. retarded, premature, orgasm
62. dyspareunia, vaginismus
63. sensate, squeeze
64. adjustment
65. communication

Mastery Test

1. a (p. 528)
2. a (p. 540)
3. d (p. 522)
4. b (p. 519)
5. c (p. 529)
6. b (p. 537)
7. d (p. 546)
8. c (p. 519)
9. c (p. 525)
10. b (p. 548)
11. a (p. 522)
12. b (p. 518)
13. c (p. 533)
14. d (p. 539)
15. b (p. 519)

16. d (p. 524)
17. a (p. 529)
18. a (p. 520)
19. d (p. 538-539)
20. c (p. 523)
21. a (p. 533-535)
22. d (p. 538)
23. b (p. 522)
24. d (p. 527)
25. a (p. 531)
26. d (p. 519)
27. c (p. 535)
28. b (p. 539)
29. d (p. 540)
30. b (p. 544-545)

Chapter 16
Social Behavior

CHAPTER OVERVIEW

Social psychology is the study of behavior in social situations. Affiliating with others is related to needs for approval, support, friendship, information, and reassurance. Social comparison theory holds that we affiliate to evaluate our actions, feelings, and abilities.

Interpersonal attraction is increased by physical proximity, frequent contact, physical attractiveness, competence, similarity, and self-disclosure. Romantic love is marked by mutual absorption between lovers, who also like one another. Evolutionary psychology attributes human mating patterns to the reproductive challenges faced by men and women since the dawn of time.

Attribution theory summarizes how we make inferences about behavior. The fundamental attributional error is to think that the actions of others are the result of internal causes. Because of an actor-observer bias, we tend to attribute our own behavior to external causes.

Social influence refers to how our behavior is changed by the behavior of others. Examples are conformity, groupthink, obedience, and complying with direct requests. Self-assertion involves clearly stating your wants and needs to others. Learning to be assertive can be aided by role-playing.

Attitudes have belief, emotional, and action components. Attitudes are formed through direct contact, interacting with others, child-rearing, group pressures, peer-group influences, the mass media, and chance conditioning. Attitude change is related to reference group membership, to deliberate persuasion, and to personal experiences. Effective persuasion occurs when characteristics of the communicator, the message, and the audience are well matched. Cognitive dissonance theory explains how attitudes are maintained and changed. Brainwashing is forced attitude change. Some cults recruit new members with high-pressure techniques similar to brainwashing.

Prejudice is a negative attitude held toward out-group members. Prejudice can be attributed to scapegoating, personal prejudice, group norms, and authoritarian personality traits. Intergroup conflict leads to hostility and stereotyping. Status inequalities tend to build prejudices. Equal-status contact and superordinate goals tend to reduce these problems.

Ethologists blame aggression on instincts. Biological explanations emphasize brain mechanisms and physical factors. Aggression tends to follow frustration, especially when aggression cues are present. Social learning theory relates aggressive behavior to the influence of aggressive models.

Four decision points that must be passed before we give help to others are: noticing, defining an emergency, taking responsibility, and selecting a course of action. Helping is less likely at each point when other potential helpers are present. Giving help tends to encourage others to help too.

Multiculturalism is an attempt to give equal status to different ethnic, racial, and cultural groups. Cultural awareness is a key element in promoting greater social harmony.

LEARNING OBJECTIVES

To demonstrate mastery of this chapter, you should be able to:

1. Define *social psychology*.
2. Describe the research that indicates that humans have a need to affiliate.
3. Describe social comparison theory.
4. List and describe four factors that affect interpersonal attraction.
5. Describe the similarities and differences in what men and women look for in a mate.
6. Explain how self-disclosure is important in the process of getting to know someone. Explain how overdisclosure can affect the same process.
7. Describe Rubin's studies of romantic love.
8. Discuss the differences between loving and liking. Include the term *mutual absorption* in your discussion.
9. Define *evolutionary psychology*.
10. Discuss the possible evolution of male and female mate selection preferences.
11. Define the following terms:
    a. social role   b. ascribed role   c. achieved role   d. role conflict   e. status   f. norm
12. Explain what attribution theory is and the difference between internal and external causes of behavior.
13. Explain the fundamental attributional error.
14. Briefly discuss the research on the double standard in attribution of male and female success.
15. Define the term *social influence*.
16. Describe Asch's experiment on conformity and list any personal factors that can influence it.
17. Define *groupthink* and explain how it may contribute to poor decision-making. Describe six ways to prevent groupthink.
18. Explain how group sanctions and unanimity affect conformity.
19. Describe Milgram's study of obedience and identify the factors that affect the degree of obedience.
20. Describe the following methods of compliance.
    a. foot-in-the-door   b. door-in-the-face   c. low-ball technique
21. Define and discuss *passive compliance*.
22. Describe the process of assertiveness training, including the term *self-assertion*.
23. Describe how a person can learn to be more assertive using rehearsal, role-playing, overlearning, and the broken record technique.
24. Define *attitude*.
25. Describe the belief, emotional, and action components of an attitude.
26. List, describe, and give examples of six ways in which attitudes are acquired.
27. Explain why people may exhibit discrepancies between attitudes and behavior.
28. Differentiate between reference groups and membership groups.

29. Define *persuasion,* and list nine conditions of persuasion that can be applied to bring about attitude change.

30. Present an overview of cognitive dissonance theory, indicate its influence on attitude formation, and describe the effect of justification on dissonance.

The following objectives are related to the material in the "Exploring Psychology" section of the text.

31. List two types of forced attitude change.

32. Describe the three techniques used in brainwashing.

33. Explain how beliefs may unfreeze, change, and refreeze, and indicate how permanent the attitude changes brought about by brainwashing are.

34. Describe how cults are able to recruit, convert, and retain their members.

35. Define and differentiate prejudice and discrimination.

36. Explain how the following relate to the learning of prejudice:
    a. scapegoating
    b. direct experiences with members of the rejected group
    c. personal prejudice
    d. group prejudice
    e. personality characteristics—the authoritarian personality

37. Describe the characteristic beliefs (including ethnocentrism and dogmatism) and childhood experiences of the authoritarian personality.

38. Present the major characteristics of social stereotypes and indicate how they may lead to intergroup conflicts.

39. Describe symbolic prejudice.

40. Briefly describe the role of dehumanization in promoting violent conflicts.

41. Explain how status inequalities may lead to the development of stereotypes and how equal-status contact may reduce intergroup tension. Give an example of each situation.

42. Explain how superordinate goals can reduce conflict and hostility.

43. Explain how a "jigsaw" classroom utilizes superordinate goals and helps reduce prejudice.

44. Describe the relationship between aggression and each of the following:
    a. instincts
    b. biology
    c. frustration (include frustration-aggression hypothesis and aversive stimuli)
    d. aggression cues (include the weapons effect)
    e. social learning

45. With respect to the effects of violence on television:
    a. summarize the relationship between television violence and real life
    b. explain how television violence may teach antisocial actions, disinhibit dangerous impulses, and desensitize a person to violence

46. List six steps that parents can implement to buffer the impact of television on their children.

47. Define *prosocial behavior.*

48. Give an example of bystander apathy, and indicate the major factor that determines whether or not help will be given.

49. Trace the progress of an individual through the four decision points that must be passed before helping behavior is given.

50. Indicate how the presence of other people can influence apathy.

51. Define the term *empathic arousal.*

52. Briefly note how a person can "de-victimize" oneself.

The following objective is related to the material in the "Psychology in Action" section of the text.

53. Define *multiculturalism.*

54. List seven ways to "break the prejudice habit."

RECITE AND REVIEW

● *Why do people affiliate? What factors influence interpersonal attraction?*

Recite and Review: Pages 552-558

1. Social psychology studies how individuals behave, think, and feel in _____ situations.

2. The need to affiliate is tied to needs for _____, support, friendship, and _____.

3. Additionally, research indicates that we sometimes affiliate to _____ anxiety and uncertainty.

4. Social comparison theory holds that we affiliate to _____ our actions, feelings, and abilities.

5. Interpersonal attraction is increased by physical proximity (_____) and frequent _____.

6. Initial acquaintance and _____ are influenced by physical attractiveness (beauty), competence (high ability), and _____ (being alike).

7. A large degree of _____ on many dimensions is characteristic of _____ selection, a pattern called homogamy.

8. Self-disclosure (_____ oneself to others) occurs to a greater degree if two people like one another.

9. Self-disclosure follows a reciprocity _____: Low levels of self-disclosure are met with low levels in return, whereas moderate self-disclosure elicits more personal replies.

10. Overdisclosure tends to inhibit _____ by others.

11. Romantic love can be distinguished from liking by the use of attitude scales. Dating couples _____ and _____ their partners but only _____ their friends.

12. Romantic love is also associated with greater _____ absorption between people.

13. Evolutionary psychology attributes human _____ patterns to the differing reproductive challenges faced by men and women since the dawn of time.

● *How does group membership affect individual behavior?*

Recite and Review: Pages 558-560

14. One's position in _____ defines a variety of roles to be played.
15. _____ _____, which may be achieved or ascribed, are particular behavior patterns associated with social positions.
16. When two or more _____ roles are held, role conflict may occur.
17. Positions within _____ typically carry higher or lower levels of status. High status is associated with special privileges and respect.
18. Norms are _____ of conduct enforced (formally or informally) by _____.
19. Attribution theory is concerned with how we make inferences about the _____ of behavior.
20. Behavior can be attributed to internal _____ or external _____.
21. The fundamental attributional _____ is to ascribe the actions of others to _____ causes. This is part of the actor-observer bias, in which we ascribe the behavior of others to _____ causes, and our own behavior to _____ causes.

● *What have social psychologists learned about conformity, obedience, compliance and self-assertion?*

Recite and Review: Pages 560-568

22. Social influence refers to alterations in _____ brought about by the behavior of _____.
23. Conformity to group pressure is a familiar example of social influence. Virtually everyone _____ to a variety of broad social and cultural _____.
24. Conformity pressures also exist within small _____. The famous Asch experiments demonstrated that various _____ sanctions encourage conformity.
25. Groupthink refers to compulsive conformity in group _____ _____. Victims of groupthink seek to maintain each other's approval, even at the cost of critical thinking.
26. Obedience to _____ has been investigated in a variety of experiments, particularly those by Stanley Milgram.
27. _____ in Milgram's studies decreased when the victim was in the same room, when the victim and subject were face to face, when the authority figure was absent, and when others refused to obey.
28. Compliance with direct _____ by a person who has little or no social _____ is another means by which behavior is influenced.
29. Three strategies for inducing compliance are the _____-in-the-door technique, the door-in-the-_____ approach, and the low-ball technique.
30. Recent research suggests that in addition to excessive obedience to _____, many people show a surprising passive compliance to unreasonable _____.
31. Self-assertion involves clearly stating one's _____ and _____ to others.
32. Aggression expresses one's feelings and desires, but it _____ others.
33. Learning to be _____ is accomplished by role-playing and rehearsing assertive actions.

● *How are attitudes acquired and changed? Under what conditions is persuasion most effective?*

Recite and Review: Pages 568-570

34. Attitudes are learned tendencies to respond in a _____ or _____ way.
35. Attitudes are made up of a belief component, an emotional component, and an _____ component.
36. Attitudes may be formed by _____ contact, interaction with others, the effects of _____-rearing practices, and social pressures from group membership.
37. Peer group influences, the mass _____, and _____ conditioning (accidental learning) also appear to be important in attitude formation.
38. The _____ consequences of actions, how we think others will _____ our actions, and habits all influence whether attitudes are converted to actions.
39. Attitudes held with conviction are most likely to be _____ in behavior.
40. People tend to change their attitudes to match those of their reference group (a group the person _____ with and refers to for guidance).
41. Effective persuasion occurs when characteristics of the communicator, the _____, and the audience are well matched.
42. In general, a likable and believable communicator who repeats a credible message that arouses _____ in the audience and states clear-cut _____ will be persuasive.
43. Maintaining and changing attitudes is closely related to needs for _____ in thoughts and actions. Cognitive dissonance theory explains the dynamics of such needs.
44. Cognitive dissonance occurs when there is a _____ between thoughts or between thoughts and actions.
45. The amount of reward or justification (reasons) for one's actions influences whether _____ occurs.
46. We are motivated to _____ dissonance when it occurs, often by changing beliefs or attitudes.

● *Is brainwashing actually possible? How are people converted to cult membership?*

Recite and Review: Pages 574-575

47. Brainwashing is a form of _____ attitude change. It depends on control of the target person's total environment.
48. Three steps in brainwashing are unfreezing (loosening) old attitudes and beliefs, _____, and refreezing (rewarding and strengthening) new attitudes and beliefs.
49. Many cults recruit new members with high-pressure indoctrination techniques resembling _____.
50. Cults attempt to catch people when they are vulnerable. Then they combine isolation, displays of _____, discipline and rituals, intimidation, and escalating commitment to bring about _____.

● *What causes prejudice and intergroup conflict? What can be done about these problems?*

Recite and Review: Pages 576-581

51. Prejudice is a _____ attitude held toward members of various out-groups.
52. Racism, ageism, and sexism are specific types of prejudice based on race, age, and

_____.

53. One theory attributes prejudice to scapegoating, which is a type of displaced

_____.

54. A second account says that prejudices may be held for personal reasons such as direct threats to a person's well being (personal prejudice) or simply through adherence to group _____ (group prejudice).
55. Prejudiced individuals tend to have an authoritarian _____, characterized by rigidity, inhibition, intolerance, and _____-simplification.
56. Authoritarians tend to be very ethnocentric (they use their own _____ as a basis for judging all others).
57. Intergroup _____ gives rise to hostility and the formation of social stereotypes (over-simplified images of members of various groups).
58. Symbolic prejudice, or prejudice expressed in _____ ways, is common today.
59. _____ inequalities (differences in power, prestige, or privileges) tend to build prejudices.
60. Equal-status contact (social interaction on an equal footing) tends to _____ prejudice.
61. Superordinate _____ (those that rise above all others) usually reduce intergroup conflict.
62. On a small scale, jigsaw _____ (which encourage cooperation through _____ interdependence) have been shown to be an effective way of combating prejudice.

● *How do psychologists explain human aggression?*

Recite and Review: Pages 582-585

63. Ethologists explain aggression as a natural expression of inherited _____.
64. Biological explanations emphasize brain mechanisms and physical factors that _____ the threshold (trigger point) for aggression.
65. According to the frustration-_____ hypothesis, frustration and _____ are closely linked.
66. Frustration is only one of many aversive _____ that can arouse a person and make aggression more likely. Aggression is especially likely to occur when _____ cues (stimuli associated with aggression) are present.
67. Social learning theory has focused attention on the role of aggressive _____ in the development of aggressive behavior.
68. Aggressive _____ on television encourage aggression because they desensitize (lower the sensitivity of) _____ to violence and disinhibit (remove restraints against) aggressive impulses.

● *Why are bystanders so often unwilling to help in an emergency?*

Recite and Review: Pages 585-587

69. Prosocial behavior is _____, constructive, or altruistic toward others.

70. Bystander apathy is the unwillingness of bystanders to offer _____ to others during emergencies.

71. Four decision points that must be passed before a person gives help are: _____, defining an emergency, taking responsibility, and selecting a course of action.

72. Helping is _____ likely at each point when other potential helpers are present.

73. Helping is encouraged by general arousal, empathic _____, being in a good mood, low effort or _____, and perceived similarity between the victim and the helper.

● *What can be done to lower prejudice and promote social harmony?*

Recite and Review: PSYCHOLOGY IN ACTION

74. Multiculturalism is an attempt to give _____ status to different ethnic, racial, and cultural groups.

75. Greater tolerance can be encouraged by neutralizing stereotypes with individuating information (which helps see others as _____).

76. Tolerance comes from looking for commonalties with others and by avoiding the effects of just-world _____, self-fulfilling prophecies, and _____ competition.

77. _____ awareness is a key element in promoting greater social harmony.

CONNECTIONS

1. _____	superordinate	a. privilege and importance
2. _____	ascribed role	b. rule or standard
3. _____	achieved role	c. aggression target
4. _____	status	d. above all others
5. _____	broken record	e. over-simplified image
6. _____	norm	f. uncomfortable clash
7. _____	stereotype	g. group centered
8. _____	ethnocentric	h. unequal treatment
9. _____	scapegoat	i. assigned role
10. _____	discrimination	j. thought reform
11. _____	brainwashing	k. self-assertion technique
12. _____	dissonance	l. voluntary role

13. _____	attribution	a. relating self to others
14. _____	authoritarianism	b. honest expression
15. _____	need to affiliate	c. following authority
16. _____	social comparison	d. agression cue
17. _____	symbolic prejudice	e. yielding to requests
18. _____	weapons effect	f. rewards and punishments
19. _____	conformity	g. altruistic behavior
20. _____	group sanctions	h. desire to associate
21. _____	obedience	i. matching behavior
22. _____	compliance	j. F Scale
23. _____	assertiveness	k. modern bias
24. _____	prosocial	l. social inference

CHECK YOUR MEMORY

Check Your Memory: Pages 552-558

1. The Stanford prison experiment investigated the impact of the roles "prisoner" and "guard." T or F?
2. The need to affiliate is a basic human characteristic. T or F?
3. People who are frightened prefer to be with others who are in similar circumstances. T or F?
4. Social comparisons are used to confirm objective evaluations and measurements. T or F?
5. Useful social comparisons are usually made with persons similar to ourselves. T or F?
6. Nearness has a powerful impact on forming friendships. T or F?
7. Physical proximity leads us to think of people as competent, and therefore worth knowing. T or F?
8. The halo effect is the tendency to generalize a positive or negative first impression to other personal characteristics. T or F?
9. Physical attractiveness is closely associated with intelligence, talents, and abilities. T or F?
10. The risk of divorce is higher than average for couples who have large differences in age and education. T or F?
11. In choosing mates, women rank physical attractiveness as the most important feature. T or F?
12. Self-disclosure is a major step toward friendship. T or F?
13. Overdisclosure tends to elicit maximum self-disclosure from others. T or F?
14. The statement, "I find it easy to ignore _____'s faults" is an item on the Liking Scale. T or F?
15. Where their mates are concerned, men tend to be more jealous over a loss of emotional commitment than they are over sexual infidelities. T or F?

Check Your Memory: Pages 558-560

16. *Son, husband,* and *teacher* are achieved roles. T or F?

17. Persons of higher status tend to receive special treatment and privileges. T or F?

18. A group could have a high degree of structure but low cohesiveness. T or F?

19. The more trash that is visible in public places, the more likely people are to litter. T or F?

20. If someone always salts her food before eating, it implies that her behavior has an external cause. T or F?

21. Attributing the actions of others to external causes is the most common attributional error. T or F?

22. Good performances by women are more often attributed to luck than skill. T or F?

Check Your Memory: Pages 560-568

23. Conformity situations occur when a person becomes aware of differences between his or her own behavior and that of a group. T or F?

24. Most subjects in the Asch conformity experiments suspected that they were being deceived in some way. T or F?

25. Seventy-five percent of Asch's subjects yielded to the group at least once. T or F?

26. People who are anxious are more likely to conform to group pressure. T or F?

27. Groupthink is more likely to occur when people emphasize the task at hand, rather than the bonds between group members. T or F?

28. Rejection, ridicule, and disapproval are group norms that tend to enforce conformity. T or F?

29. A unanimous majority of 3 is more powerful than a majority of 8 with 1 person dissenting. T or F?

30. Milgram's famous shock experiment was done to study compliance and conformity. T or F?

31. Over half of Milgram's "teachers" went all the way to the maximum shock level. T or F?

32. Being face-to-face with the "learner" had no effect on the number of subjects who obeyed in the Milgram experiments. T or F?

33. People are less likely to obey an unjust authority if they have seen others disobey. T or F?

34. The foot-in-the-door effect is a way to gain compliance from another person. T or F?

35. The low-ball technique involves changing the terms that a person has agreed to, so that they are less desirable from the person's point of view. T or F?

36. Many people have difficulty asserting themselves because they have learned to be obedient and "good." T or F?

37. Self-assertion involves the rights to request, reject, and retaliate. T or F?

38. In order to be assertive, you should never admit that you were wrong. T or F?

Check Your Memory: Pages 568-570

39. Attitudes predict and direct future actions. T or F?

40. What you think about the object of an attitude makes up its belief component. T or F?

41. If both parents belong to the same political party, their child probably will too. T or F?

42. A person who deviates from the majority opinion in a group tends to be excluded from conversation. T or F?

43. Heavy TV viewers feel safer than average because they spend so much time in security at home. T or F?

44. An attitude held with conviction is more likely to be acted upon. T or F?

45. Our attitudes are more likely to match those held by members of our reference groups than our membership groups. T or F?
46. Persuasion refers to a deliberate attempt to change a person's reference groups. T or F?
47. Persuasion is less effective if the message appeals to the emotions. T or F?
48. For a poorly informed audience, persuasion is more effective if only one side of the argument is presented. T or F?
49. A persuasive message should not be repeated; doing so just weakens its impact. T or F?
50. Acting contrary to one's attitudes or self-image causes cognitive dissonance. T or F?
51. Public commitment to an attitude or belief makes it more difficult to change. T or F?
52. The greater the reward or justification for acting contrary to one's beliefs, the greater the cognitive dissonance felt. T or F?
53. Dissonance is especially likely to be felt when a person causes an undesired event to occur. T or F?

Check Your Memory: Pages 574-575

54. Roughly 16 percent of American POWs in the Korean war signed false confessions. T or F?
55. True brainwashing requires a captive audience. T or F?
56. In brainwashing, the target person is housed with other people who hold the same attitudes and beliefs that he or she does. T or F?
57. In most cases, the effects of brainwashing are very resistant to further change. T or F?
58. A cult is a group in which the belief system is more important than the leader who espouses it. T or F?
59. Cults play on emotions and discourage critical thinking. T or F?
60. Cult members are typically isolated from former reference groups. T or F?

Check Your Memory: Pages 576-581

61. Sexism is a type of prejudice. T or F?
62. The term *racial profiling* refers to giving preferential treatment to some students seeking admission to college. T or F?
63. Scapegoating is a prime example of discrimination. T or F?
64. A person who views members of another group as competitors for jobs displays group prejudice. T or F?
65. Authoritarian persons tend to be prejudiced against all out-groups. T or F?
66. The *F* in F scale stands for fanatic. T or F?
67. An authoritarian would agree that people can be divided into the weak and the strong. T or F?
68. Social stereotypes can be positive as well as negative. T or F?
69. Symbolic prejudice is the most obvious and socially unacceptable form of bigotry. T or F?
70. The key to creating prejudice in Jane Elliot's experiment was her use of scapegoating to cause group conflict. T or F?
71. Equal-status contact tends to reduce prejudice and stereotypes. T or F?
72. Superordinate groups help people of opposing groups to see themselves as members of a single larger group. T or F?

Check Your Memory: Pages 582-585

73. Ethologists argue that humans learn to be aggressive by observing aggressive behavior in lower animals. T or F?

74. Specific areas of the brain are capable of initiating or ending aggression. T or F?

75. Intoxication tends to raise the threshold for aggression, making it more likely. T or F?

76. Higher levels of the hormone testosterone are associated with more aggressive behavior by both men and women. T or F?

77. The frustration-aggression hypothesis says that being aggressive is frustrating. T or F?

78. People exposed to aversive stimuli tend to become less sensitive to aggression cues. T or F?

79. Murders are less likely to occur in homes where guns are kept. T or F?

80. Social learning theorists assume that instinctive patterns of human aggression are modified by learning. T or F?

81. Aggressive crimes in TV dramas occur at a much higher rate than they do in real life. T or F?

Check Your Memory: Pages 585-587

82. In the Kitty Genovese murder, no one called the police until after the attack was over. T or F?

83. In an emergency, the more potential helpers present, the more likely a person is to get help. T or F?

84. The first step in giving help is to define the situation as an emergency. T or F?

85. Emotional arousal, especially empathic arousal, lowers the likelihood that one person will help another. T or F?

86. You are more likely to help a person who seems similar to yourself. T or F?

87. In many emergency situations it can be more effective to shout "Fire!" rather than "Help!" T or F?

Check Your Memory: PSYCHOLOGY IN ACTION

88. Multiculturalism is an attempt to blend multiple ethnic backgrounds into one universal culture. T or F?

89. The emotional component of prejudicial attitudes may remain even after a person intellectually renounces prejudice. T or F?

90. Both prejudiced and non-prejudiced people are equally aware of social stereotypes. T or F?

91. Individuating information forces us to focus mainly on the labels attached to a person. T or F?

92. From a scientific point of view, "race" is a matter of social labeling, not a biological reality. T or F?

93. People who hold just-world beliefs assume that people generally get what they deserve. T or F?

94. Each ethnic group has strengths that members of other groups could benefit from emulating. T or F?

FINAL SURVEY AND REVIEW

● *Why do people affiliate? What factors influence interpersonal attraction?*

1. _____ _____ studies how individuals behave, think, and feel in social situations.

2. The _____ to _____ is tied to additional needs for approval, support, friendship, and information.

3. Additionally, research indicates that we sometimes affiliate to reduce _____ and uncertainty.

4. Social _____ theory holds that we affiliate to evaluate our actions, feelings, and abilities.

5. Interpersonal attraction is increased by physical _____ (nearness) and frequent contact.

6. Initial acquaintance and attraction are influenced by _____ attractiveness (beauty), _____ (high ability), and similarity.

7. A large degree of similarity on many dimensions is characteristic of mate selection, a pattern called _____.

8. _____ (revealing oneself to others) occurs to a greater degree if two people like one another.

9. Self-disclosure follows a _____ norm: Low levels of self-disclosure are met with low levels in return, whereas moderate self-disclosure elicits more personal replies.

10. _____ (excessive) tends to inhibit self-disclosure by others.

11. Romantic love can be distinguished from liking by the use of _____ _____. Dating couples love and like their partners but only like their friends.

12. Romantic love is also associated with greater mutual _____ between people.

13. _____ psychology attributes human mating patterns to the differing _____ challenges faced by men and women since the dawn of time.

● *How does group membership affect individual behavior?*

14. One's position in groups defines a variety of _____ to be played.

15. Social roles, which may be _____ or _____, are particular behavior patterns associated with social positions.

16. When two or more contradictory roles are held, role _____ may occur.

17. Positions within groups typically carry higher or lower levels of _____. _____ _____ is associated with special privileges and respect.

18. _____ are standards of conduct enforced (formally or informally) by groups.

19. _____ theory is concerned with how we make inferences about the causes of behavior.

20. Behavior can be attributed to _____ causes or _____ causes.

21. The _____ _____ error is to ascribe the actions of others to internal causes. This is part of an _____ bias, in which we ascribe the behavior of others to internal causes, and our own behavior to external causes.

● *What have social psychologists learned about conformity, obedience, compliance, and self-assertion?*

22. _____ _____ refers to alterations in behavior brought about by the behavior of others.

23. _____ to group pressure is a familiar example of social influence. Virtually everyone conforms to a variety of broad social and _____ norms.

24. Conformity pressures also exist within small groups. The famous _____ experiments demonstrated that various group _____ encourage conformity.

25. _____ refers to compulsive conformity in group decision making. Its victims seek to maintain each other's _____, even at the cost of critical thinking.

26. _____ to authority has been investigated in a variety of experiments, particularly those by Stanley _____.

27. Obedience in his studies _____ when the victim was in the same room, when the victim and subject were face to face, when the _____ figure was absent, and when others refused to obey.

28. _____ with direct requests by a person who has little or no social power is another means by which behavior is influenced.

29. Three strategies for getting people to comply are the foot-in-the-_____ technique, the _____-in-the-face approach, and the _____ technique.

30. Recent research suggests that in addition to excessive obedience to authority, many people show a surprising _____ compliance to unreasonable requests.

31. _____ involves clearly stating one's wants and needs to others.

32. _____ expresses one's feelings and desires, but it hurts others.

33. Learning to be assertive is accomplished by _____ and rehearsing assertive actions.

● *How are attitudes acquired and changed? Under what conditions is persuasion most effective?*

34. Attitudes are _____ _____ to respond in a positive or negative way.

35. Attitudes are made up of a _____ component, an _____ component, and an action component.

36. Attitudes may be formed by direct _____, interaction with others, the effects of child-rearing practices, and social pressures from _____ _____.

37. _____ group influences, the mass media, and chance _____ (accidental learning) also appear to be important in attitude formation.

38. The immediate _____ of actions, how we think others will evaluate our actions, and _____ all influence whether attitudes are converted to actions.

39. Attitudes held with _____ are most likely to be expressed in behavior.

40. People tend to change their attitudes to match those of their _____ group (a group the person identifies with and refers to for guidance).

41. Effective persuasion occurs when characteristics of the _____, the message, and the _____ are well matched.

42. In general, a likable and believable _____ who repeats a credible message that arouses emotion in the _____ and states clear-cut conclusions will be persuasive.

43. Maintaining and changing attitudes is closely related to needs for consistency in thoughts and actions. Cognitive _____ theory explains the dynamics of such needs.

44. Cognitive _____ occurs when there is a clash between _____ or between thoughts and actions.

45. The amount of _____ or _____ (reasons) for one's actions influences whether dissonance occurs.

46. We are motivated to reduce dissonance when it occurs, often by changing _____ or _____, rather than behavior.

● *Is brainwashing actually possible? How are people converted to cult membership?*

47. Brainwashing is a form of forced attitude change. It depends on _____ of the target person's total _____.
48. Three steps in brainwashing are _____ (loosening) old attitudes and beliefs, change, and _____ (rewarding and strengthening) new attitudes and beliefs.
49. Many cults recruit new members with high-pressure _____ techniques resembling brainwashing.
50. Cults attempt to catch people when they are vulnerable. Then they combine isolation, displays of affection, discipline and _____, intimidation, and escalating _____ to bring about conversion.

● *What causes prejudice and intergroup conflict? What can be done about these problems?*

51. Prejudice is a negative attitude held toward members of various _____.
52. _____, _____, and _____ are specific types of prejudice based on race, age, and gender.
53. One theory attributes prejudice to _____, which is a type of _____ aggression.
54. A second account says that prejudices may be held for personal reasons such as direct threats to a person's well being (_____ prejudice) or simply through adherence to group norms (_____ prejudice).
55. Prejudiced individuals tend to have an _____ personality, characterized by rigidity, inhibition, intolerance, and over-simplification.
56. Authoritarians tend to be very _____ (they use their own group as a basis for judging all others).
57. Intergroup conflict gives rise to hostility and the formation of _____ _____ (over-simplified images of members of various groups).
58. _____ prejudice, or prejudice expressed in disguised ways, is common today.
59. Status _____ (differences in power, prestige, or privileges) tend to build prejudices.
60. _____ contact (social interaction on an equal footing) tends to reduce prejudice.
61. _____ goals (those that rise above all others) usually reduce intergroup conflict.
62. On a small scale, _____ classrooms (which encourage cooperation through mutual _____) have been shown to be an effective way of combating prejudice.

● *How do psychologists explain human aggression?*

63. _____ explain aggression as a natural expression of inherited instincts.
64. Biological explanations emphasize brain mechanisms and physical factors that lower the _____ (trigger point) for aggression.
65. According to the _____-aggression hypothesis, _____ and aggression are closely linked.

66. Frustration is only one of many _____ stimuli that can arouse a person and make aggression more likely. Aggression is especially likely to occur when aggression _____ (stimuli associated with aggression) are present.

67. _____ _____ theory has focused attention on the role of aggressive models in the development of aggressive behavior.

68. Aggressive models on television encourage aggression because they _____ (lower the sensitivity of) viewers to violence and _____ (remove restraints against) aggressive impulses.

● *Why are bystanders so often unwilling to help in an emergency?*

69. Prosocial behavior is helpful, constructive, or _____ toward others.

70. Bystander _____ is the unwillingness of bystanders to offer help to others during emergencies.

71. Four decision points that must be passed before a person gives help are: noticing, defining an _____, taking _____, and selecting a course of action.

72. Helping is less likely at each point when other _____ _____ are present.

73. Helping is encouraged by general arousal, _____ arousal, being in a good mood, low effort or risk, and perceived _____ between the victim and the helper.

● *What can be done to lower prejudice and promote social harmony?*

74. _____ is an attempt to give equal status to different ethnic, racial, and cultural groups.

75. Greater tolerance can be encouraged by neutralizing stereotypes with _____ information (which helps see others as individuals).

76. Tolerance comes from looking for commonalties with others and by avoiding the effects of _____ beliefs, _____ prophecies, and social competition.

77. Cultural _____ is a key element in promoting greater social harmony.

MASTERY TEST

1. Homogamy is directly related to which element of interpersonal attraction?
   a. competence b. similarity c. beauty d. proximity

2. The weapons effect refers to the fact that weapons can serve as aggression
   a. thresholds b. cues c. models d. inhibitors

3. Suspicion and reduced attraction are associated with
   a. reciprocity b. self-disclosure c. competence and proximity d. overdisclosure

4. The Seekers's renewed conviction and interest in persuading others after the world failed to end can be explained by the
   a. social competition hypothesis b. frustration-persuasion hypothesis c. group's just-world beliefs
   d. theory of cognitive dissonance

5. One thing that *reduces* the chances that a bystander will give help in an emergency is
   a. heightened arousal b. empathic arousal c. others who could help d. similarity to the victim

6. One consequence of seeing aggression portrayed on TV is a loss of emotional response, called
   a. disinhibition b. disassociation c. deconditioning d. desensitization

7. If you are speaking to a well-informed audience, it is important to _____ if you want to persuade them.
   a. repeat your message b. give both sides of the argument c. be likable d. appeal to their emotions

8. "President of the United States" is
   a. an ascribed role b. an achieved role c. a structural norm d. a cohesive role

9. Where attribution is concerned, wants, needs, motives, or personal characteristics are perceived as
   a. external causes b. situational attributions c. discounted causes d. internal causes

10. Asch is to _____ experiments as Milgram is to _____ experiments.
   a. compliance, assertion b. conformity, obedience c. autokinetic, social power
   d. groupthink, authority

11. Social psychology is the scientific study of how people
   a. behave in the presence of others b. form into groups and organizations c. form and maintain interpersonal relationships d. make inferences about the behavior of others

12. "A person who first agrees with a small request is later more likely to comply with a larger demand." This statement summarizes the
   a. low-ball technique b. set-the-hook technique c. door-in-the-face effect d. foot-in-the-door effect

13. Which view of human aggression is most directly opposed to that of the ethologists?
   a. social learning b. brain mechanisms c. attributional d. innate releaser

14. Creating superordinate goals is an important way to
   a. reduce group conflict b. break the frustration-aggression link c. promote bystander intervention
   d. reverse self-fulfilling prophecies

15. A key element in the effectiveness of jigsaw classrooms is
   a. deindividuation b. the promotion of self-fulfilling prophecies c. mutual interdependence
   d. selecting competent student leaders

16. Which of the following factors tends to REDUCE prejudice and stereotyping?
    a. just-world beliefs b. social competition c. self-fulfilling prophecies d. individuating information

17. A "guard" in the Stanford prison experiment who discovers that one of the "prisoners" is a friend would very likely experience
    a. role conflict b. a change in status c. groupthink d. a shift to coercive power

18. Groupthink is a type of _____ that applies to decision making in groups.
    a. conformity b. social comparison c. social power d. obedience

19. A good antidote for social stereotyping is
    a. adopting just-world beliefs b. creating self-fulfilling prophecies c. accepting status inequalities
    d. seeking individuating information

20. An important difference between brainwashing and other types of persuasion is that brainwashing
    a. requires a captive audience b. is almost always permanent c. changes actions, not attitudes
    and beliefs d. is reversed during the refreezing phase

21. In Milgram's studies, the smallest percentage of subjects followed orders when
    a. the teacher and learner were in the same room b. the teacher received orders by phone
    c. the teacher and learner were face to face d. the experiment was conducted off campus

22. The most basic attributional error is to attribute the behavior of others to _____ causes, even when they are caused by _____ causes.
    a. inconsistent, consistent b. internal, external c. random, distinctive d. situational, personal

23. In an experiment, most women waiting to receive a shock preferred to wait with others who
    a. were about to be shocked b. did not share their fears c. were trained to calm them
    d. had been shocked the day before

24. Evolutionary theories attribute mate selection, in part, to the _____ of past generations.
    a. food-gathering habits b. tribal customs c. maternal instincts d. reproductive success

25. People tend to act like "what is beautiful is good." However, beauty has little connection to
    a. talents b. intelligence c. ability d. all of the preceding traits

26. Which of the following gives special privileges to a member of a group?
    a. convergent norms b. high cohesiveness c. actor-observer bias d. high status

27. Your actions are most likely to agree with one of your attitudes when
    a. the actions reverse an old habit b. the attitude is held with conviction c. you know that others
    disagree with your position d. you score high on an attitude scale

28. When we are subjected to conformity pressures, the _____ of a majority is more important the number of people in it.
a. unanimity b. cohesion c. proximity d. comparison level

29. If it is easier for Anglo Americans to get automobile insurance than it is for African Americans, then African Americans have experienced
a. discrimination b. scapegoating c. ethnocentrism d. personal prejudice

30. The Bennington College study showed that attitudes are not affected very much by
a. membership groups b. child-rearing c. reference groups d. chance conditioning

ANSWERS

Recite and Review

1. social
2. approval, information
3. reduce
4. evaluate
5. nearness, contact
6. attraction, similarity
7. similarity, mate
8. revealing
9. norm
10. self-disclosure
11. like, love, like
12. mutual
13. mating
14. groups
15. Social roles
16. contradictory
17. groups
18. standards, groups
19. causes
20. causes, causes
21. error, internal, internal, external
22. behavior, others
23. conforms, norms
24. groups, group
25. decision making
26. authority
27. Obedience

28. requests, power
29. foot, face
30. authority, requests
31. wants, needs
32. hurts
33. assertive
34. positive, negative
35. action
36. direct, child
37. media, chance
38. immediate, evaluate
39. expressed
40. identifies
41. message
42. emotion, conclusions
43. consistency
44. clash
45. dissonance
46. reduce
47. forced
48. changing
49. brainwashing
50. affection, conversion
51. negative
52. gender (or sex)
53. aggression
54. norms
55. personality, over
56. group
57. conflict

58. disguised
59. Status
60. reduce
61. goals
62. classrooms, mutual
63. instincts
64. lower
65. aggression, aggression
66. stimuli, aggression
67. models
68. models, viewers
69. helpful
70. help
71. noticing
72. less
73. arousal, risk
74. equal
75. individuals
76. beliefs, social
77. Cultural

Connections

1. d
2. i
3. l
4. a
5. k
6. b

7. e
8. g
9. c
10. h
11. j
12. f
13. l
14. j
15. h
16. a
17. k
18. d
19. i
20. f
21. c
22. e
23. b
24. g

Check Your Memory

1. T
2. T
3. T
4. F
5. T
6. T
7. F
8. T
9. F
10. T
11. F
12. T
13. F
14. F
15. F
16. F
17. T
18. T
19. T
20. F
21. F
22. T
23. T
24. F
25. T
26. T
27. F

28. F
29. T
30. F
31. T
32. F
33. T
34. T
35. T
36. T
37. F
38. F
39. T
40. T
41. T
42. T
43. F
44. T
45. T
46. F
47. F
48. T
49. F
50. T
51. T
52. F
53. T
54. T
55. T
56. F
57. F
58. F
59. T
60. T
61. T
62. F
63. F
64. F
65. T
66. F
67. T
68. T
69. F
70. F
71. T
72. T
73. F
74. T
75. F
76. T

77. F
78. F
79. F
80. F
81. T
82. T
83. F
84. F
85. F
86. T
87. T
88. F
89. T
90. T
91. F
92. T
93. T
94. T

Final Survey and Review

1. Social psychology
2. need, affiliate
3. anxiety
4. comparison
5. proximity
6. physical, competence
7. homogamy
8. Self-disclosure
9. reciprocity
10. Overdisclosure
11. attitude scales
12. absorption
13. Evolutionary, reproductive
14. roles
15. achieved, ascribed
16. conflict
17. status, High status
18. Norms
19. Attribution
20. internal, external
21. fundamental attributional, actor-observer
22. Social influence
23. Conformity, cultural
24. Asch, sanctions
25. Groupthink, approval
26. Obedience, Milgram

27. decreased, authority
28. Compliance
29. door, door, low-ball
30. passive
31. Self-assertion
32. Aggression
33. role-playing
34. learned tendencies
35. belief, emotional
36. contact, group membership
37. Peer, conditioning
38. consequences, habits
39. conviction
40. reference
41. communicator, audience
42. communicator, audience
43. dissonance
44. dissonance, thoughts
45. reward, justification
46. beliefs, attitudes
47. control, environment
48. unfreezing, refreezing
49. indoctrination
50. rituals, commitment
51. out-groups
52. Racism, ageism, sexism
53. scapegoating, displaced
54. personal, group
55. authoritarian

56. ethnocentric
57. social stereotypes
58. Symbolic
59. inequalities
60. Equal-status
61. Superordinate
62. jigsaw, interdependence
63. Ethologists
64. threshold
65. frustration, frustration
66. aversive, cues
67. Social learning
68. desensitize, disinhibit
69. altruistic
70. apathy
71. emergency, responsibility
72. potential helpers
73. empathic, similarity
74. Multiculturalism
75. individuating
76. just-world, self-fulfilling
77. awareness

Mastery Test

1. b (p. 554-555)
2. b (p. 583)
3. d (p. 556)

4. d (p. 572)
5. c (p. 586)
6. d (p. 584)
7. b (p. 571)
8. b (p. 559)
9. d (p. 559)
10. b (p. 561, 563)
11. a (p. 552)
12. d (p. 566)
13. a (p. 584)
14. a (p. 580)
15. c (p. 581)
16. d (p. 588)
17. a (p. 559)
18. a (p. 562)
19. d (p. 588)
20. a (p. 574)
21. b (p. 564)
22. b (p. 560)
23. a (p. 552)
24. d (p. 557)
25. d (p. 554)
26. d (p. 559)
27. b (p. 570)
28. a (p. 562)
29. a (p. 576)
30. c (p. 571)

Chapter 17
Applied Psychology

CHAPTER OVERVIEW

Applied psychologists attempt to solve practical problems. Some major applied specialties are: clinical and counseling, industrial/organizational, environmental, educational, legal, and sports psychology.

Industrial/organizational psychologists are interested in the problems people face at work. They specialize in personnel psychology and human relations at work. Personnel psychologists try to match people with jobs by combining job analysis with various tests and selection procedures. Two basic approaches to business and industrial management are scientific management and human relations approaches.

Communication at work can be improved by following a few simple guidelines for effective speaking and listening.

Environmental psychologists study the effects of behavioral settings, physical or social environments, and human territoriality, among many other major topics. Over-population is a major world problem, often reflected at an individual level in crowding. Environmental psychologists are solving many practical problems—from noise pollution to architectural design.

Educational psychologists seek to understand how people learn and teachers instruct. They are particularly interested in teaching styles and teaching strategies.

The psychology of law includes courtroom behavior and other topics that pertain to the legal system. Psychologists serve various consulting and counseling roles in legal, law enforcement, and criminal justice settings.

Sports psychologists seek to enhance sports performance and the benefits of sports participation. A careful task analysis of sports skills is a major tool for improving coaching and performance. The psychological dimension contributes greatly to peak performance.

Space psychologists study the behavioral challenges that accompany space flight, space habitats, and life in restricted environments.

LEARNING OBJECTIVES

To demonstrate mastery of this chapter, you should be able to:

1. Define the term *applied psychology.*
2. Describe the typical activities of an industrial/organizational psychologist.
3. Describe the activities of personnel psychologists by defining or describing the following areas:
    a. job analysis (include the term critical incidents)
    b. biodata

    c. personal interview (include the term halo effect)

    d. vocational interest text

    e. aptitude test

    f. multi-media computerized tests

    g. assessment center

    h. situational judgement tests

    i. in-basket test

    j. leaderless group discussion

4. Differentiate scientific management styles (Theory X) from human relations approaches (Theory Y) to management.

5. Contrast work efficiency *versus* psychological efficiency.

6. Define the terms *participative management, management by objectives, self-managed teams,* and *quality circles.*

7. List eight factors that seem to contribute the most to job satisfaction.

8. Explain the concept of *flextime.*

9. Discuss the four basic coping styles in making career decisions.

10. Explain how jobs may be enriched and what should be increased as a result.

11. Define *organizational culture* and *organizational citizenship.*

12. List and describe six ways to improve communication skills.

13. List and describe six ways to be a good listener.

14. Explain the main focus of environmental psychology, including three types of environments or settings of particular interest.

15. Define *personal space.*

16. Define *proxemics,* and describe the four basic spatial norms and the nature of the interactions that occur in each.

17. Define the term *territoriality.*

18. Discuss the results of animal experiments on the effects of overcrowding, and state the possible implications for humans.

19. Differentiate between crowding and density.

20. Define the term *attentional overload,* and describe the possible effects of noise pollution.

21. Explain how environmental assessment, architectural psychology, or even simple feedback can be used to solve environmental problems.

22. List eight strategies to promote recycling.

The following objective is related to the material in the "Exploring Psychology" section of the text.

23. Explain the concepts *social trap* and the *tragedy of the commons.* Explain how they can be avoided or escaped.

24. Discuss the psychology of law and identify topics of special interest.

25. Discuss the use of mock juries to examine the ways in which jurors reach decisions. Include four major problems in jury behavior discovered by jury research.

26. Define the term *scientific jury selection,* and describe four techniques commonly used to assess the potential usefulness of prospective jurors.

27. Describe what is meant by the term *death-qualified jury.*

28. Explain the ways in which a sports psychologist might contribute to peak performance by an athlete.

29. Define the term *task analysis.*

30. Define the terms *motor skill* and *motor program.*

31. List and explain six rules that can aid skill learning. Include the concept of *mental practice.* Discuss the concept of *peak performance.*

32. List six ways for athletes to mentally improve performance.

The following objectives are related to the material in the "Psychology in Action" section of your text.

33. Describe the main focus of a space psychologist.

34. Describe some of the human factors that space station design must take into account. Include a discussion of the difficulties involved in having astronauts from different cultures living and working together.

RECITE AND REVIEW

● *How is psychology applied in business and industry?*

Recite and Review: Pages 594-601

1. Applied psychology refers to the use of psychological principles and research methods to solve

_____ _____.

2. Major applied specialties include clinical and _____ psychology.

3. Other applied areas are related to business, such as _____/organizational psychology.

4. Psychology is also applied to problems that arise in the environment, in education, in law, and in

_____.

5. Industrial/organizational psychologists are interested in the problems people face at _____ and within organizations.

6. Typically they specialize in personnel psychology and human _____ at work.

7. Personnel psychologists try to match people with _____ by combining _____ analysis with a variety of selection procedures.

8. To effectively match people with jobs, it is important to identify critical incidents (situations with which _____ employees must be able to cope).

9. Personnel selection is often based on gathering biodata (detailed _____ information about an applicant).

10. The traditional _____ interview is still widely used to select people for jobs. However, interviewers must be aware of the halo effect and other sources of _____.

11. Standardized psychological _____, such as vocational interest tests, aptitude tests, and multi-media _____ tests, are mainstays of personnel selection.

12. In the assessment center approach, in-depth _____ of job candidates are done by observing them in simulated _____ situations.

13. Two popular assessment center techniques are the in-basket test, and leaderless _____ discussions.

14. Two basic approaches to business and industrial management are scientific management (Theory ___) and human relations approaches (Theory ___).

15. Theory ___ is most concerned with work efficiency (productivity), whereas, Theory ___ emphasizes psychological efficiency (good human relations).

16. Two common Theory ___ methods are participative management and _____ by objectives.

17. Recently, many companies have given employees more autonomy and responsibility by creating self-managed _____.

18. Below the management level, employees may be encouraged to become more involved in their work by participating in _____ circles.

19. Job satisfaction is related to _____, and it usually affects absenteeism, morale, employee turnover, and other factors that affect overall business efficiency.

20. Job satisfaction is usually enhanced by _____ ___ oriented job enrichment.

21. When they make career decisions, people tend to adopt a _____ that is _____ (effective and active), complacent (passive), defensive-avoidant (evasive and indecisive), or hypervigilant (frantic).

22. Businesses and other _____ tend to develop unique cultures. The most _____ members of an organization typically display good organizational citizenship.

● *What can be done to improve communication at work?*

Recite and Review: Pages 601-602

23. To improve communication at work you should state your message _____ and precisely.

24. Try to avoid overuse of obscure vocabulary, jargon, _____, and loaded words.

25. Learn and use people's _____. Be polite, but not servile.

26. Be expressive when you _____. Pay attention to non-verbal cues and the messages they send.

27. To be a good listener, you should _____ pay attention.

28. Try to identify the speaker's purpose and core _____.

29. Suspend evaluation while listening but check your _____ frequently and note non-verbal information.

● *What have psychologists learned about the effects of our physical and social environments?*

Recite and Review: Pages 603-613

30. Environmental psychologists are interested in the effects of behavioral _____, physical or _____ environments, and human territoriality, among many other major topics.

31. The study of _____ _____ is called proxemics.

32. Four basic spatial zones around each person's body are intimate distance (0-18 inches), _____ distance (1.5-4 feet), _____ distance (4-12 feet), and public distance (12 feet or more).

33. Norms for the use of personal space vary considerably in various _____.

34. Territorial behavior involves defining a space as one's own, frequently by placing _____ markers (signals of ownership) in it.

35. Over-population is a major world problem, often reflected at an individual level in _____.

36. Animal experiments indicate that excessive crowding can be unhealthy and lead to _____ and pathological behaviors.

37. However, human research shows that psychological feelings of _____ do not always correspond to density (the number of people in a given space).

38. One major consequence of _____ is attentional overload (stress caused when too many demands are placed on a person's attention).

39. Toxic or poisoned environments, pollution, excess consumption of natural resources, and other types of environmental _____ pose serious threats to future _____.

40. In many cases, solutions to environmental problems are the result of doing a careful _____ assessment (an analysis of the effects environments have on behavior).

41. Architectural psychology is the study of the effects _____ have on behavior and the design of _____ using _____ principles.

42. Recycling can be encouraged by monetary _____, removing barriers, persuasion, obtaining public commitment, _____ setting, and giving feedback.

43. A social trap is a social situation in which immediately rewarded actions have _____ effects in the long run.

44. One prominent social trap occurs when limited public _____ are overused, a problem called the tragedy of the commons.

● *What does psychology reveal about juries and court verdicts?*

Recite and Review: Pages 614-616

45. The psychology of law includes studies of courtroom behavior and other topics that pertain to the _____ system.

46. Studies of mock juries (_____ juries) show that jury decisions are often far from _____.

47. Psychologists are sometimes involved in jury _____. Demographic information, a community survey, non-verbal behavior, and looking for authoritarian _____ traits may be used to select jurors.

● *Can psychology enhance athletic performance?*

Recite and Review: Pages 616-618

48. Sports psychologists seek to enhance sports performance and the benefits of sports _____.

49. A careful task analysis breaks _____ _____ into their subparts.

50. Motor skills are the core of many sports performances. Motor skills are non-verbal _____ chains assembled into a smooth sequence.

51. Motor skills are guided by internal _____ plans or models called motor programs.

52. _____ performances are associated with the flow experience, an unusual mental state.

53. Top athletes typically _____ their arousal level so that it is appropriate for the task. They also focus _____ on the task and mentally rehearse it beforehand.

54. Most top athletes use various self-regulation strategies to _____ their performances and make necessary adjustments.

● *How is psychology being applied in space missions?*

Recite and Review: PSYCHOLOGY IN ACTION

55. Space psychologists study the many behavioral challenges that accompany space flight and life in restricted _____.

56. Space habitats (living areas) must be designed with special attention to environmental stressors, such as noise, control of the environment, _____ cycles, and _____ restriction.

57. Psychological issues, such as _____ isolation, _____ resolution, privacy, cultural differences, and maintaining mental health are equally important.

CONNECTIONS

1. _____	defensive-avoidant style	a.	simulated trial
2. _____	I/O psychology	b.	poor career decisions
3. _____	flexitime	c.	communication barrier
4. _____	biodata	d.	vocational interests
5. _____	mock jury	e.	essential work problem
6. _____	feedback	f.	variable schedule
7. _____	jargon	g.	work efficiency
8. _____	critical incident	h.	personal history
9. _____	Kuder	i.	information about effects
10. _____	in-basket test	j.	work and organizations
11. _____	Theory X	k.	psychological efficiency
12. _____	Theory Y	l.	typical work problems

13. _____	quality circle	a. persons in area
14. _____	territorial marker	b. better for thinking
15. _____	density	c. better for facts
16. _____	noise pollution	d. movement plan
17. _____	cognitive map	e. flow
18. _____	direct instruction	f. strong emotional meaning
19. _____	open teaching	g. ownership signal
20. _____	proxemics	h. discussion group
21. _____	loaded word	i. micro-society
22. _____	motor program	j. study of personal space norms
23. _____	peak performance	k. mental area plan
24. _____	space habitat	l. intrusive sounds

CHECK YOUR MEMORY

Check Your Memory: Pages 594-601

1. Applied psychology can be defined as the use of learning principles to change undesirable human behavior. T or F?

2. Psychological research has shown that the best fire alarm is a recorded voice. T or F?

3. During a fire in a high-rise building, you should use the elevators, rather than the stairwell, so that you can leave as quickly as possible. T or F?

4. Personnel psychology is a specialty of I/O psychologists. T or F?

5. The basic idea of flexitime is that employees can work as many or as few hours a week as they choose. T or F?

6. One way of doing a job analysis is to interview expert workers. T or F?

7. Critical incidents are serious employee mistakes identified by doing a job analysis. T or F?

8. Use of biodata is based on the idea that past behavior predicts future behavior. T or F?

9. Because of their many shortcomings, personal interviews are fading from use as a way of selecting job applicants. T or F?

10. The halo effect is a major problem in aptitude testing. T or F?

11. Excessive self-promotion tends to lower the ratings candidates receive in job interviews. T or F

12. "I would prefer to read a good book," is the kind of statement typically found on aptitude tests. T or F?

13. Multi-media computerized tests seek to present realistic work situations to job candidates. T or F?

14. Leaderless quality circles are a typical task applicants face in assessment centers. T or F?

15. Theory X assumes that workers enjoy autonomy and accept responsibility. T or F?

16. The main benefit of a Theory X management style is a high level of psychological efficiency among workers. T or F?

17. Participative management aims to make work a cooperative effort. T or F?

18. Quality circles are typically allowed to choose their own methods of achieving results as long as the group is effective. T or F?

19. Job satisfaction comes from a good fit between work and a person's interests, needs, and abilities. T or F?

20. Job enrichment involves assigning workers a large number of new tasks. T or F?

21. A hypervigilant style usually leads to the best career decsions. T or F?

22. People who display organizational citizenship tend to contribute in ways that are not part of their job description. T or F?

Check Your Memory: Pages 601-602

23. Effective communication addresses the who, what, when, where, how, and why of events. T or F?

24. Ambiguous messages are desirable because they leave others room to disagree. T or F?

25. Jargon is an acceptable means of communication as long as you are sure that listeners are familiar with it. T or F?

26. True politeness puts others at ease. T or F?

27. To add credibility to your message, you should learn to speak very slowly and deliberately. T or F?

28. Arriving late for meetings is a form of communication. T or F?

29. To be a good listener, learn to evaluate each sentence as it is completed. T or F?

30. Good listening improves communication as much as effective speaking does. T or F?

Check Your Memory: Pages 603-613

31. A study of the pace of life found that the three fastest cities in the U.S. are Boston, New York, and Los Angeles. T or F?

32. Environmental psychologists study physical environments rather than social environments. T or F?

33. A dance is a behavioral setting. T or F?

34. Most people show signs of discomfort when someone else enters their personal space without permission. T or F?

35. The Dutch sit closer together when talking than the English do. T or F?

36. Social distance basically keeps people within arm's reach. T or F?

37. Formal interactions tend to take place in the 4 to 12 foot range. T or F?

38. Saving a place at a theater is a type of territorial behavior. T or F?

39. Burglars tend to choose houses to break into that have visible territorial markers. T or F?

40. World population doubled between 1950 and 1987. T or F?

41. In Calhoun's study of overcrowding in a rat colony, food and water rapidly ran out as the population increased. T or F?

42. High densities invariably lead to subjective feelings of crowding. T or F?

43. Stress is most likely to result when crowding causes a loss of control over a person's immediate social environment. T or F?

44. People suffering from attentional overload tend to ignore non-essential events and their social contacts are superficial. T or F?

45. Exposure to toxic hazards increases the risk of mental disease, as well as physical problems. T or F?

46. Long-corridor dormitories reduce feelings of crowding and encourage friendships. T or F?

47. Providing feedback about energy consumption tends to promote conservation of resources. T or F?

48. Direct monetary rewards have little or no effect on whether or not people recycle. T or F?

Check Your Memory: Pages 614-616

49. In court, attractive defendants are less likely to be found guilty than unattractive persons. T or F?
50. Jurors are supposed to take into account the severity of the punishment that a defendant faces, but many don't. T or F?
51. Scientific jury selection is only used in laboratory studies—the practice isn't allowed in real jury trials. T or F?
52. Demographic information consists of the most prominent personality traits a person displays. T or F?
53. All members of a death-qualified jury must be opposed to the death penalty. T or F?

Check Your Memory: Pages 616-618

54. Peak performances in sports require both mental and physical training. T or F?
55. Distance running tends to reduce anxiety, tension, and depression. T or F?
56. The most accurate marksmen are those who learn to pull the trigger just as their heart beats. T or F?
57. Motor programs adapt complex movements to changing conditions. T or F?
58. Verbal rules add little to learning a sports skill; you should concentrate on lifelike practice. T or F?
59. To enhance motor skill learning, feedback should call attention to correct responses. T or F?
60. Mental practice refines motor programs. T or F?
61. The top athletes in most sports are the ones who have learned how to force the flow experience to occur. T or F?
62. Better athletes often use imagery, relaxation techniques, and fixed routines to control their arousal levels. T or F?

Check Your Memory: PSYCHOLOGY IN ACTION

63. Many of the social and psychological problems of space flight can be prevented by carefully selecting astronauts before they leave Earth. T or F?
64. In space, astronauts have no preference for rooms with an obvious top or bottom. T or F?
65. Sleep cycles are best allowed to run freely in space since there are no real light and dark cycles. T or F?
66. The need for privacy in space habitats can be met, in part, by defining private territories for each astronaut. T or F?
67. Most people in restricted environments prefer games and other interactive pastimes as a way to break the monotony. T or F?
68. In the specialized environment of a space station, differences in culture no longer seem important. T or F?
69. Fifteen percent of space inhabitants are expected to experience a serious psychological disturbance. T or F?
70. Most major problems facing the world day are behavioral. T or F?

FINAL SURVEY AND REVIEW

● *How is psychology applied in business and industry?*

1. Applied psychology refers to the use of psychological _____ and _____ methods to solve practical problems.

2. Major applied specialties include _____ and counseling psychology.

3. Other applied areas are related to business, such as industrial/_____ psychology.

4. Psychology is also applied to problems that arise in the natural and social _____, in _____, in law, and in sports.

5. _____ psychologists are interested in the problems people face at work and within organizations.

6. Typically they specialize in _____ psychology (testing, selecting, and promoting employees) and human relations at work.

7. _____ psychologists try to match people with jobs by combining job _____ with a variety of selection procedures.

8. To effectively match people with jobs, it is important to identify _____ incidents (situations with which competent employees must be able to cope).

9. Personnel selection is often based on gathering _____ (detailed biographical information about an applicant).

10. The traditional personal _____ is still widely used to select people for jobs. However, interviewers must be aware of the _____ effect and other sources of bias.

11. Standardized psychological tests, such as _____ interest tests, _____ tests, and multi-media computerized tests, are mainstays of personnel selection.

12. In the _____ _____ approach, in-depth evaluations of job candidates are done by observing them in simulated work situations.

13. Two popular assessment center techniques are the in-_____ test, and _____ group discussions.

14. Two basic approaches to business and industrial management are _____ management (Theory X) and _____ _____ approaches (Theory Y).

15. Theory X is most concerned with work _____ (productivity), whereas, Theory Y emphasizes _____ efficiency (good human relations).

16. Two common Theory Y methods are _____ management and management by _____.

17. Recently, many companies have given employees more autonomy and responsibility by creating _____ teams.

18. Below the management level, employees may be encouraged to become more involved in their work by participating in _____ _____.

19. Job _____ is related to productivity, and it usually affects absenteeism, _____, employee turnover, and other factors that affect overall business efficiency.

20. Comfort with one's work is usually enhanced by Theory Y-oriented job _____.

21. When they make career decisions, people tend to adopt a style that is vigilant (effective and active), _____ (passive), defensive-avoidant (evasive and indecisive), or _____ (frantic).

22. Businesses and other organizations tend to develop unique cultures. The most successful members of an organization typically display good _____ _____.

● *What can be done to improve communication at work?*

23. To improve communication at work you should state your _____ clearly and precisely.

24. Try to avoid overuse of obscure _____, _____ (inside lingo), slang, and loaded words.

25. Learn and use people's names. Be _____, but not servile.

26. Be _____ when you speak. Pay attention to _____ cues and the messages they send.

27. To be a good _____, you should actively _____ _____.

28. Try to identify the speaker's _____ and core message.

29. Suspend _____ while listening but check your understanding frequently and note non-verbal information.

● *What have psychologists learned about the effects of our physical and social environments?*

30. _____ psychologists are interested in the effects of _____ settings, physical or social environments, and human territoriality, among many other major topics.

31. The study of personal space is called _____.

32. Four basic spatial zones around each person's body are _____ distance (0-18 inches), personal distance (1.5-4 feet), social distance (4-12 feet), and _____ distance (12 feet or more).

33. _____ for the use of personal space vary considerably in various cultures.

34. Territorial behavior involves defining a space as one's own, frequently by placing territorial _____ (signals of ownership) in it.

35. _____ is a major world problem, often reflected at an individual level in crowding.

36. Animal experiments indicate that excessive _____ can be unhealthy and lead to abnormal and pathological behaviors.

37. However, human research shows that psychological feelings of crowding do not always correspond to _____ (the number of people in a given space).

38. One major consequence of crowding is _____ _____ (stress caused when too many demands are placed on a person's attention).

39. Toxic or poisoned environments, _____, excess consumption of natural _____, and other types of environmental damage pose serious threats to future generations.

40. In many cases, solutions to environmental problems are the result of doing a careful environmental _____ (an analysis of the effects environments have on behavior).

41. _____ psychology is the study of the effects buildings have on behavior and the design of buildings using psychological principles.

42. Recycling can be encouraged by _____ rewards, removing barriers, persuasion, obtaining public _____, goal setting, and giving feedback.

43. A social trap is a social situation in which _____ _____ actions have undesired effects in the long run.

44. One prominent social trap occurs when limited public resources are _____, a problem called the _____ of the _____.

● *What does psychology reveal about juries and court verdicts?*

45. The psychology of _____ includes studies of courtroom behavior and other topics that pertain to the legal system.

46. Studies of _____ juries (simulated juries) show that jury decisions are often far from objective.
47. Psychologists are sometimes involved in jury selection. _____ information (population data), a community survey, non-verbal behavior, and looking for _____ personality traits may be used to select jurors.

● Can psychology enhance athletic performance?

48. Sports psychologists seek to enhance sports _____ and the benefits of sports participation.
49. A careful _____ _____ breaks sports skills into their subparts.
50. _____ skills are the core of many sports performances. Such skills are non-_____ response _____ assembled into a smooth sequence.
51. Motor skills are guided by internal mental plans or models called _____ _____.
52. Peak performances are associated with the _____ experience, an unusual _____ state.
53. Top athletes typically adjust their _____ level so that it is appropriate for the task. They also focus attention on the task and mentally _____ it beforehand.
54. Most top athletes use various _____ strategies to evaluate their performances and make necessary adjustments.

● How is psychology being applied in space missions?

55. _____ psychologists study the many behavioral challenges that accompany space flight and life in _____ environments.
56. Space _____ (living areas) must be designed with special attention to environmental _____, such as noise, control of the environment, sleep cycles, and sensory restriction.
57. Psychological issues, such as social _____, conflict _____, privacy, cultural _____, and maintaining mental health are equally important.

MASTERY TEST

1. Procrastination, inaction, and indecision are most characteristic of the _____ style of career decision making.
   a. vigilant b. complacent c. defensive-avoidant d. hypervigilant

2. Which is POOR advice for learning motor skills?
   a. Observe a skilled model. b. Learn only non-verbal information. c. Get feedback.
   d. Avoid learning artificial parts of a task.

3. Which of the following would be a question for applied psychology?
   a. How does conditioning occur? b. How can eyewitness memory be improved? c. What are the most basic personality traits? d. Do athletes have unusual personality profiles?

4. Signs are placed on a recycling container each week showing how many aluminum cans were deposited during the previous week. This practice dramatically increases recycling, showing the benefits of using _____ to promote recycling.
   a. feedback   b. public commitment   c. consumer symbolization   d. persuasion

5. Psychological efficiency is promoted by
   a. scientific management   b. Theory Y   c. time-and-motion studies   d. progressive pay schedules

6. In court, being attractive does NOT help a defendant avoid being found guilty when
   a. a majority of jurors are also attractive   b. the defendant is a man   c. the defendant is over age 30
   d. being attractive helped the person commit a crime

7. The best antidote for social isolation on extended space missions is expected to be
   a. defining private social territories for crew members   b. coordinated sleep schedules   c. radio contact with Earth   d. making conflict resolution teams part of all missions

8. Which of the following is NOT a specialty of I/O psychologists?
   a. personnel psychology   b. theories of management   c. human relations   d. architectural psychology

9. Dividing long-corridor dormitories into two areas separated by a lounge
   a. makes residents feel more crowded, not less   b. decreases social contacts   c. increases energy consumption   d. decreases stress

10. You leave a book on a table in the library to save your place. The book is a territorial
    a. display   b. marker   c. strategy   d. control

11. When professional golfer Jack Nicklaus talks about "watching a movie" in his head before each shot, he is referring to the value of _____ for enhancing sports performance.
    a. mental practice   b. self-regulation   c. skilled modeling   d. task analysis

12. What cognitive maps, behavioral settings, and crowding have in common is that all
    a. are studied by community psychologists   b. produce attentional overload   c. are studied by environmental psychologists   d. are characteristics of Type A cities

13. Potentials for learning the skills used in various occupations are measured by
    a. interest tests   b. aptitude tests   c. in-basket tests   d. cognitive mapping

14. Looking at past behavior is a good way to predict future behavior. This is the principle behind using _____ to select people for employment.
    a. biodata   b. the halo effect   c. Theory Y   d. spaced interviewing

15. A good job analysis should identify
    a. critical incidents   b. compatible controls   c. motor programs   d. essential biodata

16. High _____ is experienced as crowding when it leads to a loss of _____ one's immediate environment.
    a. overload, attention to   b. density, control over   c. stimulation, interest in   d. arousal, contact with

17. Studies of flexitime would most likely be done by a _____ psychologist.
    a. community   b. environmental   c. I/O   d. consumer

18. The halo effect is a problem in
    a. collecting biodata   b. scoring interest inventories   c. conducting interviews   d. aptitude testing

19. Mental practice is one way to improve
    a. motor programs   b. the flow experience   c. the accuracy of cognitive maps   d. job satisfaction

20. Joan has been given a specific sales total to meet for the month, suggesting that she works for a company that uses
    a. quality circles   b. job enrichment   c. flexi-quotas   d. management by objectives

21. Which of the following is NOT recommended for people who want to be effective listeners in the workplace?
    a. Identify the speaker's purpose.   b. Evaluate as you listen.   c. Check your understanding.
    d. Attend to non-verbal messages.

22. Planning, control, and orderliness are typical of _____ management.
    a. Theory X   b. participative   c. Theory Y   d. enriched

23. A psychologist who checks demographic information, does a community survey, and looks for authoritarian traits is most likely
    a. a personnel psychologist   b. doing a community mental health assessment   c. a consumer welfare advocate   d. a legal consultant

24. A very important element of job enrichment is
    a. switching to indirect feedback   b. increasing worker knowledge   c. use of bonuses and pay incentives
    d. providing closer supervision and guidance

25. Large desks in business offices almost ensure that interactions with others take place at
    a. ascribed distance   b. social distance   c. personal distance   d. public distance

ANSWERS

Recite and Review

1. practical problems
2. counseling
3. industrial
4. sports
5. work
6. relations
7. jobs, job
8. competent
9. biographical
10. personal, bias
11. tests, computerized
12. evaluations, work
13. group
14. X, Y
15. X, Y
16. Y, management
17. teams
18. quality
19. productivity
20. Theory Y
21. style, vigilant
22. organizations, successful
23. clearly
24. slang
25. names
26. speak
27. actively
28. message
29. understanding
30. settings, social
31. personal space
32. personal, social
33. cultures
34. territorial
35. crowding
36. abnormal
37. crowding
38. crowding
39. damage, generations
40. environmental
41. buildings, buildings, behavioral
42. rewards, goal
43. undesired
44. resources
45. legal
46. simulated, objective
47. selection, personality
48. participation
49. sports skills
50. response
51. mental
52. Peak
53. adjust, attention
54. evaluate
55. environments
56. sleep, sensory
57. social, conflict

Connections

1. b
2. j
3. f
4. h
5. a
6. i
7. c
8. e
9. d
10. l
11. g
12. k
13. h
14. g
15. a
16. l
17. k
18. c
19. b
20. j
21. f
22. d
23. e
24. i

Check Your Memory

1. F
2. T
3. F
4. T
5. F
6. T
7. F
8. T
9. F
10. F
11. T
12. F
13. T
14. F
15. F
16. F
17. T
18. F
19. T
20. F
21. F
22. T
23. T
24. F
25. T
26. T
27. F
28. T
29. F
30. T
31. F
32. F
33. F
34. T
35. F
36. F
37. F
38. T
39. F
40. T
41. F
42. F
43. T
44. T

45. T
46. F
47. T
48. F
49. T
50. F
51. F
52. F
53. F
54. T
55. T
56. F
57. T
58. F
59. T
60. T
61. F
62. T
63. T
64. F
65. F
66. T
67. F
68. F
69. F
70. T

Final Survey and Review

1. principles, research
2. clinical, community
3. organizational
4. environment, education
5. Industrial/organizational
6. personnel
7. Personnel, analysis
8. critical
9. biodata
10. interview, halo

11. vocational, aptitude,
12. assessment center
13. basket, leaderless
14. scientific, human relations
15. efficiency, psychological
16. participative, objectives
17. self-managed
18. quality circles
19. satisfaction, morale
20. enrichment
21. complacent, hypervigilant
22. organizational citizenship
23. message
24. vocabulary, jargon
25. polite
26. expressive, non-verbal
27. listener, pay attention
28. purpose
29. evaluation
30. Environmental, behavioral
31. proxemics
32. intimate, public
33. Norms
34. markers
35. Over-population
36. crowding
37. density
38. attentional overload
39. pollution, resources
40. assessment
41. Architectural
42. monetary, commitment
43. immediately rewarded
44. overused, tragedy, commons
45. law
46. mock
47. Demographic, authoritarian

48. performance
49. task analysis
50. Motor, verbal, chains
51. motor programs
52. flow, mental
53. arousal, rehearse
54. self-regulation
55. Space, restricted
56. habitats, stressors
57. isolation, resolution, differences

Mastery Test

1. c (p. 600)
2. b (p. 617)
3. b (p. 593)
4. a (p. 610)
5. b (p. 598)
6. d (p. 614)
7. c (p. 620)
8. d (p. 594)
9. d (p. 609)
10. b (p. 606)
11. a (p. 617)
12. c (p. 604, 607, 609)
13. b (p. 596)
14. a (p. 595)
15. a (p. 594)
16. b (p. 607, 608)
17. c (p. 600)
18. c (p. 595)
19. a (p. 617)
20. d (p. 598)
21. b (p. 602)
22. a (p. 598)
23. d (p. 614-615)
24. b (p. 600)
25. b (p. 605)

Appendix
Statistics

OVERVIEW

Descriptive statistics are used to summarize data. Inferential statistics are used to make decisions and generalizations or to draw conclusions. Graphical statistics, such as histograms and frequency polygons, provide pictures (graphs) of groups of numbers. Measures of central tendency, such as the mean, median, and mode, supply a number describing an "average" or "typical" score in a group of scores. The range and standard deviation are measures of variability, or how spread out scores are. Standard scores (z-scores) combine the mean and standard deviation in a way that tells how far above or below the mean a particular score lies. The normal curve is a bell-shaped distribution of scores that has useful and well known properties.

While psychologists are ultimately interested in entire populations, they must usually observe only a representative sample. Nevertheless, it is possible to tell if the results of an experiment are statistically significant (unlikely to be due to chance alone).

When measurements, scores, or observations come in pairs, it is possible to determine if they are correlated. The correlation coefficient tells if the relationship between two measures is positive or negative and how strong it is. While correlations are quite useful, correlation does not demonstrate causation.

LEARNING OBJECTIVES

To demonstrate mastery of this chapter, you should be able to:

1. Define and distinguish between the two major types of statistics, *descriptive* and inferential statistics.

2. List the three types of descriptive statistics.

3. Describe graphical statistics, including the terms *frequency distribution, histogram,* and *frequency polygon.*

4. Define measures of central tendency, including the terms *mean, median,* and *mode.*

5. Define measures of variability, including the range, standard deviation, and standard scores (z-score).

6. Describe the normal curve. Include its relationship to the standard deviation and z-scores.

7. Define *inferential statistics.*

8. Distinguish between a population and a sample, and include the concepts of representative samples and random samples.

9. Explain the concept of statistical significance.

10. Describe the concept of correlation, including scatter diagrams.

11. Distinguish among positive relationships, negative relationships, and zero correlations.

12. Define the *coefficient of correlation,* including the value of a perfect positive or perfect negative correlation.

13. Briefly discuss the value of correlations for making predictions. Include the concept of percent of variance.

14. Discuss the relationship between correlation and cause-and-effect determination.

RECITE AND REVIEW

● *What are descriptive statistics?*

Recite and Review: Pages A2-A3

1. Descriptive statistics are used to _____ data. Inferential statistics are used to make decisions and generalizations or to draw _____.

2. Three basic types of _____ statistics are graphical statistics, measures of central tendency, and measures of variability.

3. A frequency distribution organizes data by breaking an entire range of scores into _____ of equal size. Then, the number of scores falling in each _____ is recorded.

4. Graphical statistics provide _____ (graphs) of collections of numbers.

5. A histogram is drawn by placing _____ intervals on the abscissa (_____ line) and frequencies on the ordinate (_____ line) of a graph.

6. Next, vertical bars are drawn for each class interval, with the _____ of the bars being determined by the number of scores in each class.

7. A frequency polygon (line graph) results when points are plotted at the _____ of each class interval and connected by lines.

● *How are statistics used to identify an average score?*

Recite and Review: Pages A3-A4

8. Measures of central tendency are numbers describing an "_____" or "typical" score in a group of scores.

9. The mean is calculated by _____ all the scores for a group and then dividing by the total number of scores.

10. The median is found by arranging scores from the highest to the lowest and then selecting the _____ score.

11. The mode is the _____ _____ occurring score in a group of scores.

● *What statistics do psychologists use to measure how much scores differ from one another?*

Recite and Review: Pages A4-A7

12. Measures of variability tell how varied or widely _____ scores are.

13. The range is the _____ score minus the _____ score.

14. The standard deviation is calculated by finding the difference between each score and the _____. These differences are then _____. Then the squared deviations are totaled and their mean is found.

15. Standard scores (___-scores) are found by subtracting the _____ from a score. The resulting number is then divided by the standard deviation.

16. Standard scores tell how far above or below the _____ a particular score lies.

17. When they are collected from large groups of people, many psychological measures form a normal _____.

18. In a normal curve, 68 percent of all scores fall between plus and minus 1 standard deviations from the _____.

19. Ninety-five percent of all cases fall between plus and minus ___ standard deviations from the mean.

20. Ninety-nine percent of all cases fall between plus and minus ___ standard deviations from the mean.

● *What are inferential statistics?*

Recite and Review: Page A7-A8

21. The _____ _____ of subjects, objects, or events of interest in a scientific investigation is called a population.

22. When an entire population cannot be observed, a sample (smaller cross section) of the _____ is selected.

23. Samples must be representative (they must truly reflect the characteristics of the _____).

24. _____ drawn from representative samples are assumed to apply to the entire population.

25. Tests of statistical significance tell how often the results of an experiment could have occurred by _____ alone.

26. An experimental result that could have occurred only 5 times out of 100 (or less) by chance alone is considered _____.

● *How are correlations used in psychology?*

Recite and Review: Pages A8-A10

27. When measurements, scores, variables, or observations come in pairs, it is possible to determine if they are correlated (varying together in an _____ fashion).
28. The coefficient of correlation tells if the relationship between two measures is _____ or _____ and how strong it is.
29. While correlations are quite useful, correlation does not _____ causation.

CONNECTIONS

1. _____	frequency distribution	a. z-score
2. _____	histogram	b. subset
3. _____	mean	c. model distribution
4. _____	range	d. graphed correlation
5. _____	standard deviation	e. randomly selected
6. _____	standard score	f. correlation coefficient
7. _____	normal curve	g. no relationship
8. _____	population	h. central tendency
9. _____	sample	i. grouped scores
10. _____	representative	j. entire set
11. _____	zero correlation	k. percent of variance
12. _____	scatter diagram	l. average squared difference
13. _____	Pearson *r*	m. picture of frequencies
14. _____	*r* squared	n. spread of scores

CHECK YOUR MEMORY

Check Your Memory: Pages A2-A3

1. Descriptive statistics extract and summarize information. T or F?
2. Inferential statistics are used to make pictures (graphs) out of data. T or F?
3. Measures of variability are descriptive statistics. T or F?
4. A frequency distribution is made by recording the most frequently occurring score. T or F?
5. A frequency polygon is a graphical representation of a frequency distribution. T or F?
6. On a graph, the ordinate is the line that shows the frequency of scores at the center of each class interval. T or F?

Check Your Memory: Pages A3-A4

7. The mean, median, and mode are all averages. T or F?
8. The median is the most frequently occurring score in a group of scores. T or F?
9. To find the mode, you would have to know how many people obtained each possible score. T or F?

Check Your Memory: Pages A4-A7

10. The standard deviations can be different in two groups of scores even if their means are the same. T or F?
11. To find the range, you would have to know what the highest and lowest scores are. T or F?
12. To find a z-score you must know the median and the standard deviation. T or F?
13. A z-score of 1 means that a person scored exactly at the mean. T or F?
14. The majority of scores are found near the middle of a normal curve. T or F?
15. Fifty percent of all scores are found below the mean in a normal curve. T or F?

Check Your Memory: Page A7-A8

16. Psychologists prefer to study entire populations whenever it is practical to do so. T or F?
17. Random selection of subjects usually makes a sample representative. T or F?
18. A result that could have occurred by chance alone 25 times out of 100 is considered statistically significant. T or F?
19. A probability of .05 or less is statistically significant. T or F?

Check Your Memory: Pages A8-A10

20. A scatter diagram is a plot of two sets of unrelated measurements on the same graph. T or F?
21. In a positive relationship, increases in measure X are matched by increases in measure Y. T or F?
22. A correlation coefficient of .100 indicates a perfect positive relationship. T or F?
23. The Pearson r ranges from −.100 to +.100. T or F?
24. Correlations allow psychologists to make predictions. T or F?
25. Two correlated measures may be related through the influence of a third variable. T or F?
26. Correlation proves that one variable causes another if the correlation coefficient is significant. T or F?

FINAL SURVEY AND REVIEW

● *What are descriptive statistics?*

1. _____ statistics are used to summarize data. _____
statistics are used to make decisions and generalizations or to draw conclusions.
2. Three basic types of descriptive statistics are graphical statistics, measures of _____
tendency, and measures of _____.

3. A _____ _____ organizes data by breaking an entire range of scores into classes of equal size. Then, the number of scores falling in each class is recorded.

4. _____ statistics provide pictures of collections of numbers.

5. A _____ is drawn by placing class intervals on the _____ (horizontal line) and frequencies on the _____ (vertical line) of a graph.

6. Next, vertical bars are drawn for each _____ _____, with the height of the bars being determined by the number of scores in each class.

7. A _____ _____ (line graph) results when points are plotted at the center of each class interval and connected by lines.

● *How are statistics used to identify an average score?*

8. Measures of _____ _____ are numbers describing an "average" or "typical" score in a group of scores.

9. The _____ is calculated by adding all the scores for a group and then _____ by the total number of scores.

10. The _____ is found by arranging scores from the highest to the lowest and then selecting the middle score.

11. The _____ is the most frequently occurring score in a group of scores.

● *What statistics do psychologists use to measure how much scores differ from one another?*

12. Measures of _____ tell how varied or widely spread scores are.

13. The _____ is the highest score minus the lowest score.

14. The _____ _____ is calculated by finding the difference between each score and the mean. These differences are then squared. Then the squared deviations are totaled and their mean is found.

15. _____ scores (z-scores) are found by subtracting the mean from a score. The resulting number is then divided by the _____ _____.

16. _____ tell how far above or below the mean a particular score lies.

17. When they are collected from large groups of people, many psychological measures form a _____ curve.

18. In such curves, _____ percent of all scores fall between plus and minus 1 standard deviations from the mean.

19. _____ percent of all cases fall between plus and minus 2 standard deviations from the mean.

20. _____ percent of all cases fall between plus and minus 3 standard deviations from the mean.

● *What are inferential statistics?*

21. The entire set of subjects, objects, or events of interest in a scientific investigation is called a
_____.

22. When an entire set cannot be observed, a _____ (smaller cross section) is selected.

23. Samples must be _____ (they must truly reflect the characteristics of the population).

24. Conclusions drawn from _____ _____ are assumed to apply to the entire population.

25. Tests of statistical _____ tell how often the results of an experiment could have occurred by chance alone.

26. An experimental result that could have occurred only ___ times out of _____ (or less) by chance alone is considered significant.

● *How are correlations used in psychology?*

27. When measurements, scores, variables, or observations come in pairs, it is possible to determine if they are _____ (varying together in an orderly fashion).

28. The _____ of correlation tells if the relationship between two measures is positive or negative and how _____ it is.

29. While correlations are quite useful, correlation does not demonstrate _____.

MASTERY TEST

1. _____ statistics are especially valuable for decision making and drawing conclusions.
   a. Graphical b. Descriptive c. Inferential d. Significant

2. Measures of central tendency are _____ statistics.
   a. graphical b. descriptive c. inferential d. significant

3. Sorting scores into classes is a necessary step in creating a
   a. frequency distribution b. correlation c. scatter diagram d. variability plot

4. Vertical bars are used to indicate frequencies in a
   a. frequency polygon b. scatter diagram c. normal distribution d. histogram

5. Which is NOT a measure of central tendency?
   a. mean b. midst c. mode d. median

6. A group of scores must be arranged from the lowest to the highest in order to find the
   a. mean   b. midst   c. mode   d. median

7. The _____ is sensitive to extremely high or low scores in a distribution.
   a. mean   b. midst   c. mode   d. median

8. Which is a measure of variability?
   a. Pearson r   b. z-score   c. midst   d. range

9. What two statistics are needed to calculate a standard score?
   a. range and midst   b. mean and standard deviation   c. range and mode
   d. standard deviation and z-score

10. If the mean on a test is 90, and the standard deviation is 10, a person with a z-score of –1 scored _____
    on the test.
    a. 70   b. 80   c. 100   d. 110

11. The largest percentage of scores fall between _____ SD in a normal curve.
    a. 0 and +1   b. +1 and –1   c. +2 and +3   d. –3 and –2

12. What percent of all cases are found between +3 SD and –3 SD in a normal curve?
    a. 50   b. 86   c. 95   d. 99

13. An effective way to make sure that a sample is representative is to
    a. use random selection   b. calculate the correlation coefficient   c. make sure that the standard
    deviation is low   d. use a scatter diagram

14. Results of an experiment that have a chance probability of _____ are usually regarded as statistically
    significant.
    a. .5   b. .05   c. 1.5   d. 1.05

15. A good way to visualize a correlation is to plot a
    a. frequency histogram   b. polygon coefficient   c. scatter diagram   d. normal ordinate

16. When measure X gets larger, measure Y gets smaller in a
    a. zero correlation   b. positive relationship   c. variable relationship   d. negative relationship

17. When plotted as a graph, a zero correlation forms a cluster of points in the shape of a
    a. diagonal oval to the right   b. diagonal oval to the left   c. horizontal line   d. circle

18. The largest possible correlation coefficient is
    a. 1   b. .001   c. 100   d. 10

19. To find the percent of variance in one measure accounted for by knowing another measure you should square the
   a. mean   b. z-score   c. Pearson *r*   d. standard deviation

20. Correlations do not demonstrate whether
   a. a relationship is positive or negative   b. a cause-and-effect connection exists
   c. knowing one measure allows prediction of another   d. two events are really co-relating

ANSWERS

Recite and Review

1. summarize, conclusions
2. descriptive
3. classes, class
4. pictures
5. class, horizontal, vertical
6. height
7. center
8. average
9. adding
10. middle
11. most frequently
12. spread
13. highest, lowest
14. mean, squared
15. z, mean
16. mean
17. curve
18. mean
19. 2
20. 3
21. entire set
22. population
23. population
24. Conclusions
25. chance
26. significant
27. orderly
28. positive, negative
29. demonstrate

Connections

1. i
2. m
3. h
4. n
5. l
6. a
7. c
8. j
9. b
10. e
11. g
12. d
13. f
14. k

Check Your Memory

1. T
2. F
3. T
4. F
5. T
6. F
7. T
8. F
9. T
10. T
11. T
12. F
13. F
14. T
15. T
16. T
17. T
18. F
19. T
20. F
21. T
22. F
23. F
24. T
25. T
26. F

Final Survey and Review

1. Descriptive, Inferential
2. central, variability
3. frequency distribution
4. Graphical
5. histogram, abscissa, ordinate
6. class interval
7. frequency polygon
8. central tendency
9. mean, dividing
10. median
11. mode
12. variability
13. range
14. standard deviation
15. Standard, standard deviation
16. Z-scores (or standard scores)
17. normal
18. 68
19. Ninety-five
20. Ninety-nine
21. population
22. sample
23. representative
24. representative samples
25. significance
26. 5, 100
27. correlated
28. coefficient, strong
29. causation

Mastery Test

1. c (p. A-1, A-7)
2. b (p. A-3)
3. a (p. A-2)
4. d (p. A-3)
5. b (p. A-3, A-4)
6. d (p. A-4)
7. a (p. A-3)
8. d (p. A-4)
9. b (p. A-4)
10. b (p. A-5)
11. b (p. A-6)
12. d (p. A-6)

13. a (p. A-8)   **17.** d (p. A-9)
14. b (p. A-8)   **18.** a (p. A-8)
15. c (p. A-8)   **19.** c (p. A-9)
16. d (p. A-8)   **20.** b (p. A-10)